Henry Thoreau: *A Life of the Mind*

Henry Thoreau

A Life of the Mind

Robert D. Richardson Jr.

*Designed and Illustrated
by Barry Moser*

University of California Press

Berkeley   Los Angeles   London

University of California Press
Berkeley and Los Angeles, California

University of California Press, Ltd.
London, England

Copyright © 1986 by
The Regents of the University of California

LIBRARY OF CONGRESS CATALOGING-IN-PUBLICATION DATA

Richardson, Robert D. Jr. 1934–
Henry Thoreau: A Life of the Mind.

Includes index.
1. Thoreau, Henry David, 1817–1862.   2. Authors, American—
19th century—Biography.   I. Title.
PS3053.R53   1986   818'.309 [B]   82-28845
ISBN 0-520-05495-4 (alk. paper)
ISBN 0-520-06346-5 (paper)

Printed in the United States of America
2 3 4 5 6 7 8 9

This book is dedicated to

W. J. BATE

*who teaches that "in and through the personal
rediscovery of the great, we find that we need not be
the passive victims of what we deterministically call
'circumstances.'. . . . But that by linking ourselves
. . . with the great we can become freer—freer to be
ourselves, to be what we most want and value."*

The Burden of the Past

Contents

Preface

This is an intellectual biography of Henry Thoreau from 1837, when he was twenty and finishing college, to his death in 1862. My main purpose has been to give an account of the development of Thoreau as a writer, a naturalist, and a reader. This has necessitated treating his life as a whole, and setting it in those public contexts which exist for every life, no matter how private. It is always remembered of Thoreau that he required a daily walk of at least four hours "sauntering through the woods and over the hills and fields, absolutely free from all worldly engagements." It is not always recalled that he spent at least that much time every day at his desk, reading and writing. Emerson said it best when he summed up Thoreau's education, and, thinking of the usual academic degree, conferred instead on his best friend that of "the bachelor of thought and nature."

There is a long-standing tradition of generosity and helpfulness among modern Thoreauvians that makes it a pleasure to acknowledge here a few of the many obligations I have incurred during the preparation of this volume. Anne McGrath, Malcolm Ferguson, Tom Blanding, and the others at the Thoreau Lyceum in Concord have helped with questions and materials, especially those relating to Ellen Sewall. Marcia Moss of the Concord Free Public Library has always been enthusiastic and helpful with all kinds of archival matters. Martin Ridge and the exemplary research staff of the Henry E. Huntington Library in San Marino made the research for the last part of this book go very quickly and pleasantly. I have also benefitted from the helpful cooperation of librarians at the Pierpont Morgan Library, the Berg Collection at the New York Public Library, the Boston Public Library, the Houghton Library at Harvard, and the Special Collections library at the University of Denver.

Evelyn Barish, Raymond Borst, John W. Clarkson Jr., Bradley Dean, Dana McLean Greeley, Robert Gross, Michael Meyer, Rosemary Mitten, Joseph J. Moldenhauer, Donald Mortland, Joel Myerson, Margaret Neussendorfer, Joel Porte, Barton L. St. Armand,

Richard Schnieder, Gayle L. Smith, and Kevin P. Van Anglen all provided information, assistance, or inspiration, and sometimes all three. Robert Sattelmeyer made available to me the invaluable results of his study of Thoreau's reading. Stuart James read an early draft and showed me many ways to make it better. Victor Castellani helped with Latin, John Livingston with ideas of history. Judy Parham created a vast card index to Thoreau's reading that was indispensable. Carolyn Martin and Bradford Morgan gave me new insights into *A Week* and *The Maine Woods*. Beth Witherell and her staff at the Thoreau Edition in Santa Barbara went far out of their way to provide endless copies of materials that are gradually being published in the handsome new Princeton volumes.

Walter Harding, dean of Thoreau scholars, has been wonderfully generous with information and encouragement to me, as to so many others who share his faithfulness to the Man of Concord. This book could not have been written without his leading the way. Philip Gura has helped in many ways. He first suggested that the book should extend all the way to Thoreau's death. I have traveled widely in Denver for many years now with Burton Feldman as co-adventurer in ideas, and it was he who persuaded me that one should reach for the general reader as well as the specialist. Allen Mandelbaum has encouraged and aided me, and improved the manuscript itself, in many and varied ways, and from start to finish. He believed in the project all along, and he communicated his enthusiasm to Stanley Holwitz and to the splendid editorial and production people at the University of California Press. I am delighted—and very flattered—that this book will have a place in the distinguished and compelling *oeuvre* of Barry Moser. A very great, long-standing, and ultimately unpayable debt is feebly acknowledged in the dedication.

This book is also for my daughters and my wife. It is for Lissa, whose cheerful and enterprising individualism confirmed for me that St. Henry can be the patron of women as well as men; for Anne, whose passion for commitment and relationship pushed me to attend to Thoreau's social and personal sides (she also gave the manuscript a searching and helpful reading); and for Elizabeth, who has been, through thick and thin, the toughest critic, the closest companion, and the most important colleague of all.

To live within limits, to want one thing, or a very few things, very much and love them dearly, cling to them, survey them from every angle, become one with them—that is what makes the poet, the artist, the human being.

Goethe

Henry Thoreau: *A Life of the Mind*

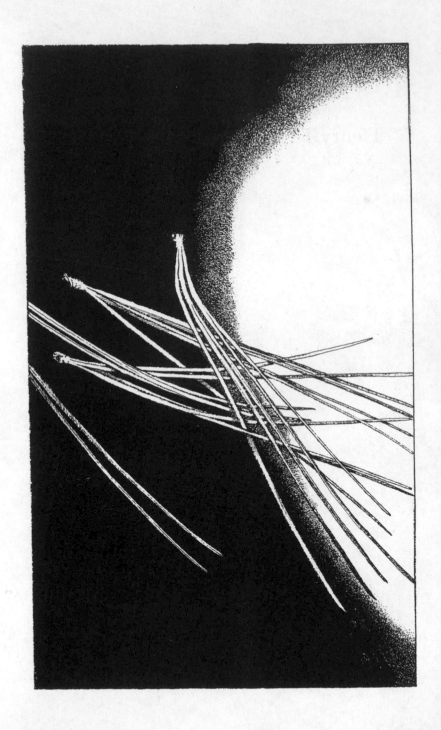

I. 1837

Return to Concord

1. Fall 1837: Commencement

R ETURNING TO CONCORD from Harvard College in the early fall of 1837, David H. Thoreau had just turned twenty. Of medium height, or a little below, with sloping shoulders and an out-of-doors complexion, he had about him the suggestion of a seafaring race. He walked with unusual energy and people remembered his open face and pleasant flexible mouth, and the strong Roman nose which some thought made him look like Caesar, while others were reminded of Emerson. He had fine light brown hair. He was not, on the whole, a striking or compelling figure except for one feature, his eyes, which were strong, serious, large, and deep set; bright blue in some lights, gray in others. As he walked around Concord people noticed that his eyes rarely left the ground. When he did look up, however, he swept in everything at a glance. His eyes had a startling earnestness, and they were alight with intelligence and humor.[1]

Harvard commencement had been held on the last day of August, following rather than preceding the summer vacation as was common in those days. Within two weeks, Thoreau was not only back in Concord, living with his family in the Parkman house facing Main Street (on the site of the present Public Library) but he had a job teaching in the Concord Public Schools. Eighteen thirty-seven was a year of financial crisis for the United States and the start of a serious depression that lasted into the 1840s. Bank after bank had suspended payment, and Thoreau was lucky to have any job at all, let alone a good one. But before he had held the job for two full weeks, he had thrown up the position rather than administer the expected daily canings. A famous anecdote tells how one of the Concord school board members, Nehemiah Ball, went one day to observe Thoreau's teaching, called him into the hall, and reprimanded him for not using the cane. Stung and angered past self-possession, the impulsive twenty-year-old teacher went back into the classroom, picked out six students at random—rather as one deals with mass mutiny in the army—and proceeded to beat them. He then quit the job. It was all terribly sudden. His entire career in the public schools was auspiciously launched and catastrophically concluded before a month had passed since commencement.[2]

But the fall was not all disappointment. A few days before his run-in with Ball, about the middle of September, he was out walking and searching for Indian relics with his brother John on a Sunday evening, "with our heads full of the past and its remains." Coming to the Sudbury River bank at the mouth of Swamp Bridge Brook, a spot overlooking Clamshell Hill with Nashawtuc Hill off to the right, Thoreau launched into "an extravagant eulogy on those savage times" when the Indians roamed the Concord woods before the white man came. Throwing himself into the part, he asked, "How often have they stood on this very spot, at this very hour? Here," he went on, "stood Tahatawan and there," pointing at random toward the ground, "is Tahatawan's arrowhead." It was a mere rhetorical flourish, the gesture of a boy playing Indians, but when he impulsively stooped—to complete the scene—and picked up the nearest bit of rock, it turned out to be "a most perfect arrowhead, as sharp as if just from the hands of the Indian fabricator." It was one of those small, lucky chances that happen to everyone, but to some more frequently than others. In later years, one visitor after another was to tell how Thoreau could find arrowheads almost at will. Partly, of course, he was looking for them and expecting to find them. But this one must have seemed like an omen, a sign that the young schoolteacher's imaginative sympathies, however extravagant and romantic, were at bottom neither foolish nor misplaced. He always insisted that his whole life had been one of extraordinary luck, and he could have said, as Picasso did of a similar life, "I do not seek, I find."[3]

This particular autumn was of good omen for Thoreau in other ways. For this was the time when he first became really close to Emerson, making a deep impression that the older man came back to again and again in later years. Emerson remembered Thoreau as a "strong healthy youth, fresh from college" that fall. Thoreau on his side had just read Emerson's *Nature* that spring. By the end of the third week in October, during that New England season which, Thoreau once remarked, would by itself "make the reputation of any climate,"

Emerson had persuaded Thoreau to start a journal and was encouraging him to think of writing as a career. Who could worry about being rejected by Nehemiah Ball when he had been accepted as a friend by Ralph Waldo Emerson?[4]

It was a busy, eventful fall. There were walks and river outings, there was the active family life at home with his mother, father, and brother, not to mention aunts and boarders. He also worked for his father, making pencils. After the first teaching fiasco, there was the anxious search for another job, and there was the tonic, life-changing friendship with Emerson. He was also doing a great deal of reading, writing, and thinking during this fall. As his habits became settled in later years, he found a daily walk of several hours' length a necessity. But he was from the start as much a writer as a walker, and a daily stint at his desk was always just as much a necessity to him. "I seek a garret," he wrote in the inaugural entry in his new journal. He traveled Concord in his walks and river outings. He traveled everywhere else via books in the garret, and in between trips, he wrote out his accounts of both kinds of excursion.[5]

Until this fall of 1837 Thoreau is an indistinct figure. There are some facts, some letters, various recollections of him as a boy or student, but everything is external, so to speak. We see him only as others saw him. Even his own letters and college themes seem written exclusively for others and almost all of this early material is curiously unrevealing. But when he begins, in October of 1837, to keep a journal, the quarry and substance of much of his best work, we begin to see the whole man as we follow the crowded, highly charged, and rapidly evolving inner life that accompanies the busy outer life and reveals the thoughts behind the eyes of the familiar photographs.

It is simply astonishing how many of his major themes appear in the record of this one autumn. He already takes a green interest in woods and fields. He was attracted to the river and its possibilities for travel and for metaphor. There is already in the midst of an increasingly busy life an unembarrassed interest in preserving some solitude for himself. There is a great deal this fall about poetry and poets—quotations from English poets, from Goethe and Virgil, and some of his best poems date from this year. Already he was preoccupied with the idea of a primitive, heroic life, distantly but attractively reflected in the early literature of northern Europe as well as in the ways of the

North American Indians. He is already interested in self-culture, what the Germans called *Bildung*, and already his jottings show that deepest, most constant characteristic of his encounter with the natural world, indeed with life: a passionate, ecstatic sense of joy.

All this fall Thoreau was reading Goethe and Virgil with an eagerness inspired by natural affinity. He divided his time between reading and translating Goethe's *Italian Journey* (*Italienische Reise*) from the German and walking about Concord. Just as Goethe recounts in that book his own discovery that the leaf is the law of plant morphology, so Thoreau began to perceive nature as infinite variations on certain underlying laws.

In Virgil he recognized something more important yet. Among his mid-November notes this sentence stands out: "I would read Virgil if only to be reminded of the identity of human nature in all ages." Plain, unoriginal, even flat-footed as this sounds, it is, together with its complementary idea of the identity of nature itself in all ages, the cornerstone of Thoreau's mature thought, the basis and starting point for his most deeply held, most characteristic convictions about history, nature, society, and the individual.

From the point of view of the newspapers, the great events of 1837 were the accession of Queen Victoria, the protest in Canada against English rule—a rebellion that broke into open warfare—and a serious financial panic in America which came right on the heels of the messy, unpopular, bitter, and inconclusive Seminole Indian War in Georgia and Florida. The chief events in young Thoreau's life that fall were his encounters with Emerson, Goethe, and Virgil. The fall itself had been his true commencement, and sometime before the year was out, as though to mark the new start, he changed the order of his given names so that he now first became Henry David.

2. Harvard under Quincy

From 1833 to 1837 Thoreau had been a student at Harvard College, and though he deprecated the college and the education it gave him, Harvard must be considered a major formative influence on his life. When he left Concord for Cambridge, he was only another country hopeful. Solitary, penniless, vaguely promising but overly head-strong, he was a marginal student with marginal prospects. When he returned from college, Harvard, with all its shortcomings, had taught him how to pass judgment on Harvard, and had in fact prepared him for a life of the mind. Acknowledgment would come later.

Harvard in 1833 was a small school, drawing most of its students from the nearby area and operating on a scale difficult to imagine today. In 1839–40, there were enrolled in all schools at Harvard just 432 students who, with a faculty of 25, occupied a handful of buildings in Cambridge, most of which had been built with public funds. With unpaved streets and pigs in sties behind University Hall, the place had a distinctly rural atmosphere, and Boston, across the river and eastward toward the bay, was still a city of only seventy-five thousand people.[1]

The college had a president, 11 professors, 7 instructors, 9 proctors (residential supervisor and teaching assistant combined), a bursar, a steward, and a librarian for its forty-one thousand books. There were no other administrators. Not even a dean was appointed until 1870. The president himself wrote letters of recommendation, computed grades, attended to breaches of discipline, and awarded scholarships. The college budget for 1840 came to just over $45,000 of which just over $28,000 was in salaries. The average professorial salary was $1,500 a year, which was three times as much as the highest paid schoolteacher in Concord. A village schoolteacher might start as low as $100 a year: a day laborer on the Erie canal made $.88 a day, and a carpenter made $1.25 a day.[2]

A year's tuition at the college was $55, and total costs for a student in the late 1830s ran to $188 a year. Textbooks were a major item, as was board, but fuel was larger than either. The average college room was heated only by an open fireplace and six cords of wood a year were required to heat it, at a total cost of $22.50, or more than 10 percent of the entire cost of going to college.

Harvard was a modest place in those days, and it was intensely local, drawing fewer students from Connecticut, for example, than Yale drew from Massachusetts. Harvard's graduating class of 39 students in 1836 falls well below Yale, Union, and Dartmouth with 81, 71, and 44 respectively. No college in the country had a graduating class over 100; college was still something reserved for only a very few. In the 1840s there was, in New England, one college student for every 1,294 people in the general population. The figure for 1985 was one college student for every 19.

Academically, Thoreau's Harvard was in a period of stagnation. Josiah Quincy was one of Harvard's poorer presidents, and the faculty, with a few shining exceptions, was not distinguished. The point of a college education was not liberal learning, but in President Quincy's words, a "thorough drilling." Even if professors wished to teach rather than drill, the teaching load was heavy, anywhere from twenty-five to nearly forty hours of classes a week, keeping Professor Felton in Greek, Professor Channing in rhetoric, and the other better-than-average instructors overburdened with mere schoolmastering. The curriculum was largely fixed and generally detested, consisting of three years of Greek, three of Latin, two of math, one of history, three of English, and two years of one modern language. Although a few electives had been allowed beginning in 1825, the college took care to discourage them by allowing them half the usual credit. Perhaps the worst aspect of the college was the hated marking system also begun in 1825, and refined to burdensome folly by Quincy. Under this system, every aspect of college life was graded and marked. Every student received a mark on a scale of eight every day for every recitation. Themes and other assignments counted for so many points each. The totals, which were used to determine class rank, upon which in turn rested the scholarship awards, were subject to all sorts of deductions, including disciplinary ones such as absence from chapel or class or curfew violation. A contemporaneous account tells how "at daily prayers a professor kept watch over the congregation from a sort of raised sentry box and noted down the names of any one guilty of a misdemeanor." All instructors and monitors sent up their marks weekly to "old Quin" who, more a headmaster than a college president, added up the scores himself. In Thoreau's case he made numerous undetected errors, which was probably inevitable in a scheme so complex that an average student would accumulate over fourteen thousand points before graduation. According to Quincy, young Thoreau had "imbibed some notions concerning emulation and college rank," which was his way of saying that Thoreau had expressed an unconcealed distaste for the system. He was not alone, and with a grading system that makes the modern grade point average calculated to three decimal places seem simplicity and fairness itself, it is no wonder that Thoreau lost his respect for it and perhaps for the college that permitted it, or that the school was restive under Quincy.[3]

The three Rs at Harvard during Thoreau's time were rote learning, regimentation, and rowdyism. Boys commonly entered college at fifteen, sometimes younger. Dress, hours, and attendance were all prescribed. Meals were in commons, and the food was said—as all college food is always said—to have been dreadful. Breakfast consisted of hot coffee, hot rolls, and butter. Supper was tea, cold rolls "of the consistency of wool," and no butter. The midday meal was the only one that was plentiful, and students sometimes affixed a piece of the noon meat to the underside of the table, with a fork, in order to have meat for supper. The boys rose half an hour before sunrise in winter, crowding into a bitterly cold, unheated chapel for services before breakfast. They rose, did their lessons, and went to bed by the bell, and the general atmosphere was more that of a boarding school than what we now think of as a college. The habits of the students were rough; throwing food at meals was nothing compared with the habitual destruction of property, which was not confined to breaking up furniture. Public rooms in inhabited buildings were blown up with gunpowder "every year," according to some accounts.[4]

In the spring of 1834, toward the end of Thoreau's freshman year, occurred the most violent rebellion of Harvard's history. Unable to find who was responsible for rioting that had begun with a student being insolent to a teacher and ended with hundreds of dollars' worth of damage in smashed furniture and broken windows, Quincy expelled the entire sophomore class. He further outraged student opinion by turning to the civil authorities to press charges in the public courts, then sitting in Concord. Student grievances were so well articulated that the board of overseers found it useful to issue a forty-seven-page pamphlet in response.

3. Thoreau at Harvard

When Thoreau came to college in the fall of 1833, he had just turned sixteen. He shared room number 20 in Hollis Hall with a boy from nearby Lincoln, Charles Stearns Wheeler. They lived in a plain room without carpets, with pine bedsteads, a washstand, desks, and chairs. Matches being unknown, they banked the fire carefully every night so it would start in the morning. Many rooms had a cannonball, useful when hot as a foot warmer, when cold to roll down the stairs in the middle of the night.

In his first year, Thoreau mostly took required courses, with what grace we do not know. He took mathematics, Greek, Latin, and history, to which he added Italian the second term. He did not take part in the Great Rebellion, and he ended the year high enough in his class to be awarded twenty-five dollars of what was called "exhibition money," which was the equivalent of a half-tuition scholarship. His sophomore year he took math, Greek, Latin, English, French, and again Italian. Junior year was more Greek, more Latin, more English, and more French, with short, one-term courses in theology, mental philosophy, and math. During the second term, he took a teaching leave to go tend school in Canton, Massachusetts, where he stayed with a fiery young intellectual, Orestes Brownson. A Unitarian minister whose association with the church would be short lived, Brownson's moral energy and reformist ideas strongly impressed young Thoreau. The two also studied German together. Thoreau's junior year was further broken up by absence and illness. Though he returned to college in March of 1836, he became ill and withdrew in May, before the end of the term.[1]

Back again in the fall of 1836, Thoreau took a three-term sequence in intellectual philosophy which examined Locke's *Essay on Human Understanding*, Say's *Political Economy*, and Story's *Commentaries on the Constitution of the United States*. He also took more English, some natural history and natural philosophy, and he kept up his modern languages. He did not cut a commanding figure among his classmates, who remembered him later, if at all, as quiet, serious, and a bit countrified. He seems to have stayed out of major trouble. He did get crosswise with Quincy over the marking system, though he ended up high enough in his class to have a commencement part and to take some of the prize money.

For years after his graduation, Thoreau had little good to say about his college education. When Emerson once remarked in company that, after all, Harvard did teach all the branches of learning, Thoreau replied, "yes, indeed, all the branches and none of the roots." *Walden* speaks tartly of Harvard's curriculum and argues that a more practical, less bookish approach would have been preferable. But his own reading at college was important, perhaps crucial, though his extracurricular reading rather than his required courses and themes best reflect what was actually on his mind. He belonged to one club, called the Institute of 1770, and he read a good deal from the club's library as well as the college library. As early as his first term in college he was reading Hall's *Travels in Canada*, Cox's *Adventures on the Columbia River*, and McKenney's *Sketches of a Tour to the Lakes*, already showing a predilection for travel literature he was never to lose. Before his freshman year was out he had read Irving's *Columbus* and *The Conquest of Granada*, Cochrane's *Travels in Columbia*, Bullock's *Travels in Mexico*, Mill's *History of the Crusades*, and Barrow's *A Voyage to Cochinchina* (now called Vietnam). He seems to have traveled widely in Cambridge.[2]

One thing Thoreau did acknowledge about his Harvard education was that three years of English with Professor Channing (brother of the famous Boston minister William Ellery Channing) had in fact taught him to express himself in writing. His college themes survive and they show him mastering a graceful, conventional, reasonably spare style. It is doubtful that Channing lit any literary fire in Thoreau, though some of Channing's students recalled wonderful evenings spent reading Chaucer in Channing's apartment. Channing was no Francis James Child, whose presence would first be felt at Harvard in the late forties and fifties, and the live literary center of the college was not, in Thoreau's day, in the English department, but in the Department of Modern Languages. This had been built up and championed by George Ticknor, who tried to bring to the little college in Cambridge some of the liveliness and reach of the great German universities. Ticknor emphasized a living knowledge of the language, laid great stress on modern literatures and cultures, and hired a group of native-speaking instructors from Europe. Thus it is not entirely unexpected that the most remarkable single thing about Thoreau's course work at Harvard is the amount of language study he did, especially in modern languages. In addition to eight terms of Greek and eight of Latin, Thoreau took five terms of Italian, four of French, four of German, and two of Spanish. Thoreau is always thought of as well educated and well read in the classics—and no one has ever written a better defense of them—but it is not always recalled that he could read French, German, and Italian with ease, and, more important, that he was both inclined and prepared to think of literature in a broad, multicultural sense.

Thoreau's interest in modern literature, especially his interest in modern poetry, seems to have begun during the spring of his sophomore year. From April through June he went from Johnson's "Preface to Shakespeare" to modern, indeed contemporaneous writings, such as Longfellow's *Outre-Mer*, Cooper's *The Headsman*, and Irving's *Crayon Miscellany*. It is conceivable that the impetus came from Channing, and barely possible that it came from Emerson, by whom Thoreau had been examined on Whately's *Rhetoric* in late February 1835, but the most likely person to have sparked such an interest would have been Longfellow. For it was during the spring of 1835 that Longfellow, then twenty-eight, agreed to come to Harvard to succeed Ticknor as head of the Department of Modern Languages. His first book, *Outre-Mer*, subtitled *A Pilgrimage Beyond the Sea*, came out in late May. Harvard's appointment of the young American writer must have stirred excitement among those who found Cambridge dusty and rule ridden.

Thoreau's interest in poetry seems to have begun the spring of Longfellow's appointment, and to have grown steadily during Thoreau's last two years at college. When Longfellow finally appeared in Cambridge during the spring of 1837 to take up his professorial duties after a two-year preparation of travel and study in Europe, he was just thirty years old. He wore wine-colored waistcoats and light gloves. He was a living poet still at the start of what was already regarded as a remarkable career. His life was touched with romance, travel, and tragedy. The young man from Concord went to hear the new professor's lectures on Northern language and literature; they were not at all what his classical training had prepared him for. They had the excitement of discovery and the fascination of novelty.[3]

4. Concord

The Concord to which Henry Thoreau returned in 1837 has been called a village, but it was really a good-sized town of two thousand inhabitants lying sixteen miles, or four hours by stage, west of Boston. Concord had been the first permanent European settlement above tidewater in Massachusetts, and it originally comprised an area of 36 square miles when Boston had occupied a mere 783 acres or just over one square mile. Bedford, Acton, Lincoln, and Carlisle were largely carved out of the original area of Concord. Thoreau's Concord still had 9 miles of river, the Concord, joined by the Assabet, flowing north first to a point in North Billerica where it provided the water for the Middlesex Canal between Lowell and Boston, then on to join the Merrimack, which in turn flowed to the sea up by Ipswich and Plum Island. Though boats loaded with wood and other cargoes from Maine frequently came to Concord from Boston via the canal and the river, the importance of the town was due not to its waterways but to its being a major crossroads. One road to Boston, the Lexington road, went past Emerson's house; the other, the Watertown road, went out past Walden Pond. Other roads spoked out to Sudbury and Southern New England, west to the Berkshire up-country, and north to New Hampshire. Concordians were proud of their town's past. Their grandparents had been conspicuous in the American Revolution, an event that lay just sixty years behind them, and the town was beginning to think about putting up monuments.[1]

Farming was still the principal occupation of Concord, but manufacturing was on the increase. In 1820, there were 262 men engaged in agriculture, 140 in manufacturing, 16 in commerce, and the balance was swinging toward the latter two. Concord had by 1837 been having its share of the booming national growth of the twenties and thirties. A lead pipe manufactory was set up in 1819, a shoe factory (actually just an ell tucked onto a house but employing between 10 and 20 people) was built in 1821. A group of entrepreneurs had set up the Milldam company in 1829, developing thereby a new commercial district in the center of town, and two new banks had been established, one in 1832 and the second in 1835. Concord had had a steam-driven smithy since 1832, and the town was also a center for the manufacture of pencils, clocks, hats, bellows, guns, bricks, barrels, and soap, all for the wholesale trade and all sold out of town. Wagons rumbled through town continually on roads that were both dusty and noisy. Concord was a busy transport hub and its numerous taverns were full of teamsters. It had six warehouses, a bindery, two saw mills, two grist mills and, over on the west side of town, a large five-story cotton mill, whose work force included nine men, three boys and thirty girls. Far from being a quiet, conservative, backward-looking rural village, Concord was a budding mill town, hoping to improve its river link to the canal, waiting impatiently for the railroad, and only prevented by its lack of major water power from rivaling nearby Lowell or South Hadley in the decades just ahead.[2]

Around the town was open countryside. At this time, some two-thirds of New England (excluding Maine) was cleared land, and in Concord township woodland accounted by 1830 for only one-sixth of the land, the rest being either in meadow, pasture, or tillage. The return of the forests, still going on today, but already marked even by 1900 when only a quarter of New England was still open, had not yet begun. Concord's fields and meadows lay open to the sun; it was a neat green landscape of tilled fields, mown meadows, and pasture land kept cropped by sheep. Hundreds of cows, oxen, and horses were pastured in the township, keeping underbrush down. One could see great distances from any sort of rise in the ground, and the impression generally was of rolling open farmland, broken here and there by woodlots, small stands of trees of six to ten acres each.[3]

In addition to the active agricultural life of the town, there was another reason why there was so little woodland. This was the last era before the widespread use of coal for home heating and everyone burned wood. A thrifty farmer needed six cords for the winter stove, an average household twenty cords a year, and Concord's minister, Ezra Ripley, had thirty cords a year as part of his salary. Boston needed six hundred thousand cords annually, and it was already coming from as far away as Maine. Thoreau noted in his journal that it was impossible to go walking in the Concord woods in any season during daylight hours without hearing the sound of axes.[4]

Farmers grew winter rye, corn, and potatoes. Some raised garden seeds, others were experimenting with teasel and with silkworm culture. Recently there had been a tendency to plant more fruit trees and grape vines. Field work was done by draft animals. Concord in 1831 had 177 horses and 418 oxen. Oxen were favored by New England farmers and could pull astounding loads. It is said that a single team pulled a lumber raft a mile long and weighing 800 tons along part of the Middlesex Canal at the rate of a mile an hour.

Concord had been an Indian fishing village before the white man came, but by Thoreau's time the salmon, shad, and alewives were gone, leaving mainly pike, perch, the common eel, the ugly parasitic lamprey eel, and some pout in the slow-moving rivers. Then, as now, the water's surface was half-covered in summer with duckweed, looking like green confetti.

Early settlers had found Concord damp, poor, low, and mean; it was, they complained, unusually subject to storms and full of swamps and impenetrable undergrowth. All that had changed by 1837. There were still extensive lowlands and swamps, but Concord on the whole was a healthy place. Surrounded by open land, it was drier than it is now, and it seems to have been relatively free of insects. Life expectancy was around forty, but almost one person in four lived until seventy. One out of every five died from fevers of various sorts, while one out of every seven deaths was from "consumption." The disease was endemic in many families, including Thoreau's.[5]

That fall of 1837, there were a number of unusually rapid changes taking place in the country, the state, and the town itself. Massachusetts was growing rapidly; its population increased by 20 percent during the thirties, and it would expand almost 35 percent during the forties, most of the growth being centered in the cities and in the lowlying valleys, while the higher counties such as Berkshire County actually were losing population. The city of Boston was expanding by 50 percent every ten years throughout the period. It would reach its peak as a port in 1840, when the Cunard White Star line would choose it for its American terminus. But the railroads were already threatening canal and coastal shipping traffic, and while Massachusetts would continue to build railways, it did not do so quickly enough. By 1850 Boston would be in steep decline as a port, having already lost the race to develop rail communications to the West.

Of the most immediate concern this fall, however, was the economic crisis the panic of 1837, as it was called. The boom years of economic expansion from 1825 on had created a large expansion of credit. From 1830 to 1837, for example, the supply of paper money had tripled, going from $51 million to $149 million. Then in 1836 the wheat crop failed, the price of cotton dropped by half, and overseas creditors, largely English, began demanding payment in gold. In May of 1837, most of the banks in the country stopped paying out specie.

A literal panic ensued. There were $100 million worth of mercantile failures in a single fortnight in New York City. Herman Melville's older brother Gansevoort was just one of those who went under that April. The magnitude of the $100 million collapse comes into focus when it is realized that the entire United States federal government expenditure for 1837 was just $37 million, Seminole Indian War and all.

The panic hit everywhere. Emerson's letters for this period show persistent, anxious, almost daily financial maneuvering designed to help his brother in New York meet his mounting obligations. The Thoreau family, never well off, watched as Henry got and then lost a solid well-paid teaching job. That was bad enough by itself, and none of them knew that they were only on the edge of what was to be a long depression reaching down into the mid-1840s. Little wonder that economics would be on everyone's mind, including Thoreau's.

5. Emerson

Until this fall, Thoreau's life can be seen as the unsurprising result of familiar and conventional shaping forces such as Concord, Harvard, and his immediate family. But through the extraordinary, catalytic, almost providential friendship of Emerson, Thoreau's life changed from the passive to the active mood. Emerson taught Thoreau that he could—indeed he must—shape his own life and pursue his own ends.

Emerson had ancestral roots and relations in Concord, but he himself had been born, brought up, and educated in the larger world of Boston. Indeed, Emerson had moved to Concord only quite recently, in 1834, when Thoreau was starting his sophomore year at college. Emerson was just thirty-one when he came to Concord. Behind him already was the tragic death of his young wife, Ellen, his resignation from the pulpit of his Boston church, and the nine-month European trip that had followed. He had met Wordsworth and Landor, and, best of all, at Craigenputtock in Scotland, the young Thomas Carlyle.[1]

Home from Europe in early October 1833, Emerson turned decisively from the religious, churchmanlike preoccupations in which he had been raised to a new concern with the problems posed by science and natural history. He also turned to a new career in public lecturing. As he moved to Concord in the fall of 1834 he was working on a book he had been thinking about for some time, to be called simply *Nature*.

In February of 1835, Thoreau was among the college boys Emerson was asked to examine on rhetoric. Nothing in the letters or journals of either suggests that any spark was then struck, that either saw anything remarkable in the other. Emerson was always on the lookout for gifted young people, but that spring and summer his life was full with other things. In July he bought the Coolidge house, half a mile east of Concord Village on the Lexington road, and in September he married Lydia Jackson and they moved in. The house became at once an intellectual gathering place, and Concord began to attract the young and the gifted. Emerson himself was young, active, sought after, hospitable, and brilliantly articulate. He possessed, to a remarkable degree, the gift of being able to hearten and encourage others, particularly the young and untried. More by sheer energy and this ability to excite, than by his substantive achievements, Emerson was already at the center of most that was new, exciting, and disturbing in ideas and literature in America at the time.

During the winter of 1836, for example, he was coming to grips with Bronson Alcott. A peddler turned teacher, Alcott was a talker of shattering, almost apostolic brilliance, but he could never get those rare qualities satisfactorily set down on paper. He wrote inspired, ecstatic gospels announcing childhood as the Word made Flesh, Coleridgean in intent, Alexandrian in language. Alcott's writing is strange only by rigid Addisonian standards. Neoplatonism and both German and French Romanticism afford numerous parallels to the orphic speech of Bronson Alcott. Emerson agonized over the syntactically sprung prose of the manuscript of *Psyche*, and sent it back to Alcott with criticism so gentle and so honest that Alcott completely rewrote it, without any improvement at all, and they went through the whole cycle again, and even again a third time.

At this same time, the magazine publication of Carlyle's *Sartor Resartus* was, through Emerson and others, making so great a stir in New England that it became possible to publish it in book form in Boston when no London publisher could yet be found. In April of 1836,

Emerson mailed Carlyle a copy of the first edition of *Sartor*. When America could recognize and support English genius before England itself, America's long day of dependence might indeed seem, finally, to be over. And despite the sudden and premature death of Emerson's brother Charles in May (another brother, Edward, had also died recently), Emerson was increasingly surrounded by people and their ideas and books and articles in a rush of intellectual life and activity that had the social cohesiveness of a club and the intellectual coherence of a movement.

That summer Margaret Fuller, then just twenty-six, made the first of her extended visits to Emerson's home. Bright and well read, she was yet another talker of transfixing brilliance. She also had ambitions as a writer, and since she had the whole Fuller family to support, she was determined to make a paying career out of her writing. She and Emerson talked about many things, including self-reliance, but most concentratedly about German literature. She, as well as Carlyle, was now absorbed in Goethe's writings and was working on a translation of Eckermann's great *Conversations with Goethe*. Emerson was working on his German, increasingly convinced, as were other friends such as Hedge from Bangor, and Parker and Ripley from Boston, that the most interesting intellectual and artistic currents, the really vital ideas seemed recently to have been coming out of Germany. No one, they thought, would be able to understand the nineteenth century without taking Kant, Herder, Hegel, and Goethe into account. Until one had read them, one's basic education was not complete.

During the fall of 1836, Emerson's first book, *Nature*, was published in September, and his first son, Waldo, was born in October. Buoyed up, particularly by the latter event, Emerson plunged energetically ahead, working up a series of lectures on "The Philosophy of History" to be given in Boston starting in December. They were successful, well attended, and as soon as he was finished, Emerson gave them all over again. Thoreau, nearing the end of his senior year across the river in Cambridge, must have heard something about them. In early April of 1837, Thoreau took Emerson's *Nature* out of the college library.

There is no record of what Thoreau saw in the book, but he took it out again the third week in June. Perhaps this second look was partly motivated by gratitude, since Emerson was, at that moment, writing to President Quincy to argue (successfully, as it would turn out) that Thoreau, despite lamentable irregularities, should be awarded a piece of the college prize money that June. However he got to the book, it had a profound impact on the young man about to graduate. Influence is an easy relation to claim. It makes writing easier to talk about, but it is also easy to claim too much for it. E. M. Forster has said sensibly that "the only books that influence us are those for which we are ready, and which have gone a little further down our particular path than we have yet gone ourselves." Thoreau was ready for Emerson's *Nature* for just that reason. Emerson was, at the moment, just a few steps farther along the path Thoreau himself had already taken.[2]

Emerson's *Nature* was no modest little exercise in nature writing. In ambition as well as title it rivals Lucretius's *De Rerum Natura*. Though written in language that has not fully shaken off the pulpit and that can therefore mislead one into thinking Emerson a spokesman for Christian values and a Christian worldview, Emerson's real purpose in *Nature* is radicalism itself, and his argument, resting on a rejection of historical Christianity, is not far from that of Thomas Paine when the latter wrote "that which is now called natural philosophy, embracing the whole circle of science . . . is the true theology." *Nature* showed Emerson's remarkable openness to science. He and his friends recognized no "two culture" split between literature and science; they believed that to study nature and to know oneself came at last to the same thing, which it was the purpose of literature to express.[3]

Nature is also a manifesto of transcendentalism, the American version of German philosophical idealism which had as a pair of cornerstones the belief that ideas lay behind and corresponded to material objects and the belief that intuition was a valid mode of knowing and was necessary as a counterbalance to experience. Most interesting of all for Thoreau is Emerson's insistence in *Nature* on a line of thought as old as classical Stoicism: that the individual, in searching for a reliable ethical standpoint, for an answer to the question of how one should live one's life, had to turn not to God, not to the *polis* or state, and not to society, but to nature for a usable answer. Stoicism taught, and Emerson was teaching, that the laws of nature were the same as the laws of human nature and that man could base a good life, a just life, on nature.

This was more than theory with Emerson. During the summer of 1837, for example, he felt closer to nature than he had in a long time. All that summer he took walks, visited Walden Pond, and worked in his garden, feeling contentedly close to nature as he weeded and watched the ripening corn and strawberries, while the Maryland Yellowthroat seemed, he said, to chant "Extacy, Extacy" to him all day long.[4]

At the end of August, Emerson gave the Phi Beta Kappa address at Thoreau's commencement. Thoreau may not have been there to hear Emerson say, in so many words, that the business of the American scholar would be to study nature and to know himself and that the two would be the same thing, but he would have read it even if he didn't hear it. Emerson, uncharacteristically, was pleased with the talk. It was printed, Carlyle praised it without reserve, and it quickly had a wide circulation.

As the fall wore on, Emerson was immersed in his forthcoming lecture series on "Human Culture" which was to carry further the ideas in the "Philosophy of History" series of the year before. Thus the ideas that were most engaging Emerson just at the time he really got to know Thoreau were his ideas about history. Carlyle had just sent over a copy of his new history of the French Revolution. Emerson read and admired it, and found that for him as for Carlyle, all his efforts to come to terms with his own times seemed to depend on how he viewed the past. He had already reached one major conclusion, and it seemed to hold. As he wrote in his journal toward the end of September 1837, "I get no further than my old doctrine that the Whole is in each man, and that a man may if he will as truly and fully illustrate the laws of Nature in his own experience as in the History of Rome or Palestine or England."[5]

Emerson's leading idea about history is that there is one mind, of which history is the record. Another way to put it is to say that human nature—the human mind—is and has been *essentially* the same in all ages and places. There are variations, of course, sometimes important and even blinding differences. But the similarities between people, even those of widely different times and places, far outweigh, *in importance*, the differences. If the human mind has always been essentially the same, then it has neither progressed nor declined from age to age. Chronology, therefore, is not what is important in history. All ages are equal; the world exists for the writer today just as much as it did for Homer. This way of looking at history, which sets the present as high as any past era, is a direct response to what W. J. Bate has so brilliantly described as the burden of the past, it is the basis for most of Emerson's best work from 1835 to 1850, and it quickly became a deep and permanent conviction—and a liberating, enabling conviction for Henry Thoreau. In October of 1837, evidently at Emerson's urging, he began to keep the journal that would be his own history, and by the third week in November he was telling himself to read Virgil to be reminded of the essential uniformity of human nature, past and present, Roman and American.

Emerson recalled later that his close association with Thoreau had begun sometime after Henry's return from college that fall of 1837. Emerson was then thirty-four, fourteen years Thoreau's senior, enough older to be hero and model, a sort of intellectual older brother, yet still close enough by age, energetic youthfulness, and choice of friends for Thoreau to feel that they belonged to the same generation. The age difference makes it easy to think of them as father and son, or mentor and student, but both of them insisted from the outset that the real relationship between them was that of friendship, taking the word in its most serious meaning, with everything it implies about loyalty, companionship, and presumptive equality.

Fall turned into winter. Emerson's journals show him thinking about Greece, Germany, the French Revolution. Thoreau's journals run a parallel course. By February, Thoreau was being invited to "teachers' meetings" at Emerson's and they were taking long walks together. What Thoreau admired in Emerson was the way in which his ideas took on the tangibleness of natural objects. Emerson, on his side, was delighted with his young friend's mind, all keenness and edge. He noted how "everything that boy says makes merry with society," and he urged him to write out an account of his college life.[6]

6. The Classics

Writing about the life of a student could be done two ways. One could concentrate on the schooling; in Thoreau's case that would probably have produced satire. Or one could focus on learning; that would be compelling and exciting, and that was what Thoreau did during the fall of 1837. He did not produce the essay Emerson was looking for, but from his encounters with the classics and with modern Germany we can get some idea of what Thoreau was able to carry away from college.

From the time he was twenty Thoreau treated the Greek and Roman classics in a personal, familiar, often playful way, referring to them as though he himself had just written them. The new Herderian or Emersonian view of history allowed, indeed, virtually compelled Thoreau to regard the classics as the still-vital expression of the real world in a living language. The world of the *Iliad* was as much his as Homer's.

During his schoolboy years at Concord Academy, he had studied Virgil (along with Caesar, Sallust, Cicero, and Horace) with Phineas Allen, and in later years he would read Virgil less for discovery than recovery. At college, during his first year he read Xenophon and Demosthenes and Aeschines with the generally despised Christopher Dunkin, and Livy and Horace with Henry McKean and Charles Beck. During his sophomore and junior years, he read Sophocles, Euripedes, and Homer with Professor Felton, and Cicero, Seneca, and Juvenal with Beck. This sounds impressive, but it was, of course, required of all students and was taught in a less than promising atmosphere. Recitations were merely sessions in which a master heard the day's lessons of a dozen or so students, "without comment or collateral instruction," as a contemporary grimly noted. James Freeman Clarke, graduating a few years before Thoreau entered, observed that "the faculty were not there to teach, but to see that boys got their lessons; to explain difficulties or elucidate a text would have seemed improper." Thoreau's interest in classics thus grew almost in defiance of his formal schooling. But grow it did. By the time Thoreau left college, he had an easy command of Greek and Latin, a wide acquaintance in classical literature, and some interest in the classical past as such. He had, for example, read several philosophical and historical romances about Greece and Rome, such as Thomas Gray's *The Vestal*, *A Tale of Pompeii* (1830) and Lydia Child's *Philothea* (1836) set in Plato's Greece. He was above all increasingly interested in classical thought, and he had already learned to think of the classics as having an unaging, perennial vitality. What he would later write in *Walden* he already felt to be true. "The heroic books, even if printed in the character of our mother tongue, will always be in a language dead to degenerate times." The real classics were heroic books, always alive to those who were themselves alive.[1]

This sense of the vitality of the classical past could only have been increased by Thoreau's reading during the fall of 1837 in Goethe's *Italian Journey*. The book records Goethe's unsuppressible excitement as he approaches Rome, heartland of the ancient world, its ability to touch him unweakened, its achievement undiminished by time.

Thoreau's sense of the nature of the classical achievement had, that fall, two main emphases. The first is the assertion of the importance and permanence of nature. In November, reading Virgil—characteristically it was the *Georgics*, not the *Aeneid*—Thoreau was struck by passages about the buds swelling on the vines and fruit scattered about under the trees. The point, he told himself, was that "it was the same world." His second observation followed naturally enough. If Virgil's was the same world as ours, then "the same men inhabited it." Neither nature nor human nature had changed, in essence, from Virgil's time to ours. Zeno and the Stoics taught the same thing. In early February 1838, Thoreau noted that "Zeno the stoic stood in precisely the same relation to the world that I do now." And reading Homer brought home the same point once more. In early March, Thoreau wrote in his journal, "Three thousand years and the world so little changed!—The *Iliad* seems like a natural sound which has reverberated to our days."[2]

Thoreau's conception of history, like Emerson's, would not concede any superiority to the Greeks and Romans. If nature was the same and if men were the same—two constants in a world of social change— then the modern writer stood in relation to his world in just the same way Homer stood in relation to his, and modern achievements could indeed rival the ancients. As Thoreau put it later, in "Walking," "I walk out into a nature such as the old prophets and poets, Menu, Moses, Homer, Chaucer, walked in."[3]

Because he saw history as he did, the classics were not a burden, not the never-to-be equaled achievement of others, but a promise of what he might also achieve. Here too Emerson showed the way. "They who made England, Italy or Greece venerable in the imagination," he insisted in "Self-Reliance," did so not by traveling, but "by sticking fast where they were, like an axis of the Earth." One might write *Iliad*s in Concord, then.

In enunciating this belief in the permanence of nature and of human nature, and the equivalence of all eras—that any age is a heroic age to the heroic individual—we come to what is perhaps the single most important set of convictions for the young Thoreau. It was not a creed or a theoretical construct, but the core of his practical, daily, actual belief. In William James's phrase, it was the "habitual center of his personal energies." Since we are the same men and women as those Greeks and Romans we so much admire, we may achieve as well as they did if we only will. Nostalgic adulation of the past is misplaced sentiment. "This lament for a golden age," Thoreau once said, "is simply a lament for golden men." Once he grasped it, once he had seen it squarely in concrete relation to his own personal life, Thoreau never gave up this belief. In his most eloquent and moving tribute to the classics, the chapter on "Reading" in *Walden*, he tried again to explain:

> The oldest Egyptian or Hindoo philosopher raised a corner of the veil from the statue of the divinity; and still the trembling robe remains raised, and I gaze upon as fresh a glory as he did, since it was I in him that was then so bold, and it is he in me that now reviews the vision.

If we can see as much and as well as they saw, we can also hope to write as well as they wrote. If, as Thoreau notes in his journal in mid-February of 1838, each of the sons of Greece "created a new heaven and a new earth for Greece," there was no compelling reason why each of the sons and daughters of Concord should not be able to do the same.[4]

7. Germany

New England's interest in modern Germany begins around 1812 with Joseph Buckminster's appointment to Harvard and Harvard's subsequent efforts to get some of its young men trained in modern German biblical scholarship. Bancroft, Ticknor, Cogswell, and Everett each brought back something, though each shrank from the full implications of the new learning. But with Emerson and his contemporaries —especially Ripley, Parker, Hedge, and Fuller—German thought and literature finally reached a wide audience in New England, contributing heavily to shaping the new temper of mind that came to be called transcendentalism. The very name, coming from German transcendental idealism, is itself a telling acknowledgment of the affinity the New Englanders felt for Germany. For Emerson and the circle of liberal intellectuals around him, Kant and Fichte were simply more important than Locke or Hume or the Scottish Common Sense school in philosophy; Goethe and Novalis were more important than Wordsworth or Keats in literature, and the work of Herder, Coleridge (himself strongly influenced by German thought), and Schleiermacher was more important in theology than Jonathan Edwards and the American Puritan tradition. One simply could not expect, in 1837, to understand the advanced intellectual atmosphere of the times without taking up Germany.[1]

Almost unavoidably then, Thoreau took four terms of German at college, beginning his junior year. Even when he took time off from college to do practice teaching in Canton, Massachusetts, he kept up with his German, sitting up late to study in the stimulating company of Orestes Brownson. The excitement Thoreau associated with the acquisition of German and the sense of new doors opening for him are attractively caught in his acknowledgment to Brownson that the stay in Canton had marked an era in his life, "the morning of a new Lebenstag," as he extravagantly put it. Back in college he was soon reading and quoting from Friedrich Schlegel's *Lectures on the History of Literature*. His interest in things German grew visibly during his senior year. German studies were flourishing all around him. Andrews Norton was preparing his massive refutation of German biblical criticism; Theodore Parker was translating the equally massive masterwork of De Wette, one of the best of those German critics; Elizabeth Peabody was deep in German historiography and mythography; Margaret Fuller was translating Goethe's *Eckermann's Conversations with Goethe*; and Emerson was lecturing that winter and spring of 1837 on the "Philosophy of History," his title and many of his ideas coming out of J. G. Herder.[2]

On the same day in early April 1837 that he first took Emerson's *Nature* out of the library, Thoreau also took out Carlyle's translation of Goethe's *Wilhelm Meister*, the long *Bildungsroman* that records the gradual growth of the hero away from his bourgeois world into the world of real ideas, true culture, and honest emotions. Beginning in late May, Thoreau also went to hear the inaugural lectures on German and Northern literature given by the newly arrived Professor Longfellow. Longfellow urged the importance of the Northern languages; he devoted one lecture to the then little-known subject of Anglo-Saxon literature, and two to Swedish literature. One lecture was a sketch of German literature and no fewer than three were on the life and writings of Goethe.[3]

Partly because of his own Northern French and Scottish ancestry, Thoreau felt kinship from the start, a family link, so to speak, with the Germanic or Northern languages, mythologies, and literatures. They were not, to him, essentially foreign; they were a part of his admittedly complex birthright. In later years his own name always seemed to him an only half-playful extension of the name Thor. As his college career drew to a close, his German studies were among the most vital of his interests; he became aware of his native language as one of the Northern family of languages. His ambition to be a poet was articulated by German as well as English ideas and examples, and from Brownson to Longfellow to Emerson, the interesting people around him were all working seriously on German texts. That fall, as he began to keep a proper journal, the first book to appear in Thoreau's pages was Goethe's *Torquato Tasso*; the second was Goethe's *Italian Journey*. No English translation then existed, and over the long winter months, Thoreau worked his way carefully through the volume.

The *Italian Journey*, still a most attractive introduction to Goethe, is a loose collection of journal notes and letters detailing with tremendous zest the eventful, watershed trip to Rome and Sicily from 1786 to 1788, undertaken when Goethe was thirty-seven, though one would hardly guess it from the almost boyish ebullience of the writing. The trip was not only a long-deferred quest for the classical heartland of his imagination but a psychological liberation from his celebrity (he was already a famous poet in Germany) and from his all-too-public position in Weimar. The book was the record of a pilgrimage of self-discovery—of the same genre but vastly better than Longfellow's *Outre-Mer*—in the guise of a travelogue, and Thoreau noted the sense of freedom, the thirsting urgency and above all the profound note of joy with which Goethe set out.

He admired Goethe's ability to combine the romantic view of the artist with a strong social sense, and he was impressed by Goethe's descriptive abilities, by how Goethe did not simply record his feelings about what he saw, but described what he saw objectively, as though he were "an unconcerned spectator." It was a major hint for his own descriptive efforts; no strings of colorful metaphors, no subjective emotionalism, just the thing itself, a kind of sketching with words.[4]

It is not quite accurate to say flatly that Goethe influenced Thoreau; no one more resisted influence in the usual sense. But, like Emerson, Goethe showed Thoreau the path to his own work. Reading Goethe's account of his Italian trip made Thoreau all the more eager to start on his own travels and to be about his own work. Standing in Rome, looking at paintings by Poussin, Claude Lorrain, and Salvator Rosa, Goethe had written, "I shall never rest until I know that all my ideas are derived, not from hearsay or tradition, but from my real living contact with the things themselves." The same was to be true for Thoreau. He might read things in the books of others, but his important ideas, however parallel to his reading they might seem, would have to be rooted in personal experience.[5]

An important example of how this process worked, one of the ideas which stayed with Thoreau for years, has its beginnings this fall of 1837 in Thoreau's reading of Goethe. One of the major unifying threads of the *Italian Journey* is Goethe's search for the primitive plant, the "original" plant form that would "explain" all subsequent botanical change. Goethe had brooded on this subject for years. Finally, he wrote, "while walking in the Public Garden of Palermo, it came to me in a flash that in the organ of the plant which we are accustomed to call the *leaf* lies the true Proteus who can hide or reveal himself in all vegetal forms. From first to last, the plant is nothing but leaf."[6]

This is the leading idea of Goethe's concept of the metamorphosis of plants, but more than that, it was for Goethe and it became for Emerson and Thoreau a key to understanding the innermost process of nature itself. What Emerson so often called "the metamorphosis" and symbolized by "the Proteus" was more than a natural process; it became for him the master symbol for *all* natural process. Before the ideas of evolution and natural selection became our catchall explanation of natural change—and our all-but-universal and therefore invisible metaphor for social change—the Romantic generation, from Goethe to Whitman, expressed its conception of the role of change in nature, quite detached from any notion of progress, in the idea of metamorphosis.

Emerson recognized that Goethe had "suggested the leading idea of modern botany" which he lucidly summarized as the proposition "that a leaf or the eye of a leaf is the unit of botany, and that every part of a plant is only a transformed leaf to meet a new condition; and by varying the conditions, a leaf may be converted into any other organ, and any other organ into a leaf." What Goethe had been doing was to look for the law or general principle that would explain a whole field of phenomena. A sharp frost late in November gave Thoreau his chance to do something similar. Trees, branches, grasses, everything was suddenly covered with fine ice crystals, a "wonderful ice foliage" which, Thoreau observed, answered "leaf for leaf to their summer dress." The ice crystals were not on the leaves but were themselves freestanding, leaflike formations of ice. Excitedly, Thoreau records how "it struck me that these ghost leaves and the green ones whose forms they assume, were the creatures of the same law."[7]

All through December and January he was on the lookout for similar formations, and he made numerous entries in his journal about the link between vegetation and crystallization. It was an exciting connection, this analogy, but more important, it shows Thoreau, like Goethe, intent on finding the general principles behind particular occurrences. Goethe, like Emerson—like Virgil, Homer, and the

Stoics—was valuable for Thoreau because he showed him his own way and was an actual example of how it could be done.

There is a quality of excitement and expectation, a kind of intellectual eagerness and generosity that mark much of Thoreau's inner life this fall of 1837 and the following winter. By March he was reading— or at least recalling—Mme de Stael's *Germany* (1812), that widely read introduction to German thought and culture. Mme de Stael ends her book with three strong chapters on "enthusiasm" which, she said, was the leading, all-important characteristic of the Germans. It was, in her view, the one indispensable key to the subject. What the Germans had taught her, they also taught Thoreau: "Thought is nothing without enthusiasm."[8]

8. *"Society"*

In mid-February of 1838, when Emerson suggested to Thoreau that he write out the history of his college life, he responded by writing a lecture, not on college life exactly, but on "Society." Written in March, and delivered in April, it was his first public lecture and it struck a characteristic note. Starting with the good Aristotelian position that "man was made for society," Thoreau wondered if the time-honored words had not "come to stand for another thing," almost the opposite of the original intent, making it necessary "in order to preserve its significance, to write it anew." Perhaps, he argued, it should be put "Society was made for Man." His trick of reversing common sayings and opinions could be annoying at times, but his point here was not a fractious denial of the importance of social organizations but simply a reminder to his listeners that society was only the means to the end of the individual self-fulfillment, and not the other way around.[1]

This sort of defense of the individual was not new. It was in the most approved Protestant and Jeffersonian traditions, and it was a stock subject for class exercises when Thoreau was an undergraduate. In his sophomore year Thoreau had written essays on "We are apt to become what others think us to be," and "On what grounds may the forms, ceremonies and restraints of polite society be objected to?" During his senior year he had written a short essay about the "duties, inconvenience, and dangers of conformity" which went well beyond the usual lip-service defense of the individual against social pressure. "The fear of displeasing the world ought not, in the least, to influence my actions," he had written, and his final reason had the brevity and simplicity of conviction. If we do not listen to our conscience, he said, "the principal avenue to reform would be closed."[2]

In writing about the dangers of finding one's personal identity threatened by social groups, Thoreau was reflecting nothing unusual for a twenty-year-old. College life unavoidably raised the issue of one's relation to groups, while life at home also involved groups of people. Returning to Concord, he found his father's household had no fewer than nine people in it. Schoolteaching in Concord's one-room schools was anything but solitary, and even the evenings at Emerson's were apt to be crowded. What is really remarkable about Thoreau's ideas on society at this point in his life is that he isn't more insistent in his self-assertion. His journal comments and his lecture both contain a surprisingly strong streak in praise of society and social impulses. He quotes Goethe approvingly on the need for getting beyond one's private circle and in touch with one's country and the larger world. "Heroes," he noted in December, "are famous or infamous because the progress of events has chosen to make them its stepping stones." Reflecting in March on what a man should do, he commented that, at the least, "he may not impose on his fellows."[3]

Indeed, however much the circle around Emerson was in favor of individual effort, it was not in fact antisociety. Emerson himself only attacked conformity when it was a question of "conforming to usages which are dead to you," and his only reason for objecting at all even to such conformity was that "it scatters your force." Neither he nor the others objected to one's conforming to usages he or she believed in. In fact, transcendentalism itself had a submerged vein of collectivism. It was characteristic of these Americans to urge individualism as the best means of social reform, and not just as self-aggrandizement or a narrow self-culture. In this they differed from the Germans, whose *Bildung* was a self-justifying concept of self-culture which Thomas Mann has complained led Germans who espoused it away from, rather than toward, political or social action. It is remarkable that most of the best known American transcendentalists became social or political activists: Theodore Parker in the antislavery movement, Margaret Fuller in feminism and in the Roman Revolution of 1848, George Ripley in the Brook Farm communitarian experiment, Bronson Alcott in teaching reform and organic farming, and Elizabeth Peabody in a host of causes including the establishment of kindergartens in the United States and the defense of the American Indians. Thoreau himself became an active and early supporter of John Brown, and even Emerson was far warmer and more active in the antislavery movement than most of those who mocked transcendentalists for having their heads in the clouds. If indeed they did, the clouds were more apt to be storm clouds of revolt than wisps of antisocial daydreaming.[4]

From the scraps that remain of Thoreau's April lecture, it is plain that he was talking not so much against society, but in favor of a finer and rarely realized kind of society or association. His tart jokes show more disappointment than disillusion as he describes a young man entering society. "With a beating heart he fares him forth, by the light of the stars, to this meeting of gods. But the illusion speedily vanishes; what at first seemed to him nectar and ambrosia, is discovered to be plain bohea [cheapest of the common China teas] and short ginger bread." Here, as so often, Thoreau is so quick to see through society, it almost seems as if he expected to. But while he could make wry comments on how society falls below our expectations of it, he could also make jokes about the self-pitying outsider. When it is a man's own look that "curdles all hearts," he said, "let him not complain of a sour reception."[5]

He pointed out that it was "in obedience to an instinct of their nature" that men had built and planted close to one another, but the trouble was that "they have not associated, they have only assembled." "Association" was a loaded word, soon to be very much in vogue as dozens of reform communities sprang up around the country. Thoreau invokes the word to show that what he really wants is not less society but a truer association of people, not just people in crowds, but groups of individuals who are friends. Indeed, Thoreau talked about truly valuable social relations in the same charged and emotional language he used for the subjects of love and friendship. Society was even important to his intellectual life. "In society," he wrote, "all the inspiration of my lonely hours seems to flow back on me, and then first have expression."[6]

As both journal and lecture make clear, Thoreau's main point about society this spring of 1838 is not a rejection of human society, not a repudiation of one's place in society, not even a denial of the importance of society. He was, of course, disappointed that society was no more satisfying than it was. But beyond that, his clever barbs and funny remarks are aimed not against society itself but against what may be called "social determinism." The danger in setting society at a higher value than the individual, the trouble with encouraging people to identify themselves primarily with some group, was that it then became easy to transfer the blame for one's own shortcomings to that group. If one looked to society for one's identity and one's satisfactions, then surely society should be held accountable for one's dissatisfactions, lack of identity, alienation. Emerson had already set himself against this view, and Thoreau was now thinking along the same line. "Man is the artificer of his own happiness," he bluntly declared to his journal in January. "Let him beware how he complains of the disposition of circumstances, for it is his own disposition he blames." This is not a defiant antisocial outburst nor a budding misanthropy. It is simply a refusal to blame others, or conditions, or society, for one's own failures. And if society can't be blamed for the bad, why should it be given credit for the good? Thoreau told his April audience at the Lyceum that if enough people only felt that they were in actual fact responsible for their own happiness, and would work to improve their own selves, then "society" would inevitably improve.

Concord itself might even improve.[7]

9. Concord Schoolmaster

Lecturing before an adult audience was a new undertaking for Thoreau. His usual relationship to his town was, in this period right out of college, that of a schoolteacher. It was, after all, what he had prepared for at college. He had done a short teaching stint in Canton his junior year, and it had gone well enough so that he was able to ask Brownson for further help later on. Upon graduation, his classmates had dispersed according to the still familiar pattern: some to law school, some to divinity school, one to a position as "graduate resident" at Harvard, and several into schoolteaching.

Thoreau's first real job was a piece of amazing good fortune. He was offered one of the two principal positions in the Concord Public School system, the position at the large Center Grammar School, at a salary of $500 a year. This was better than the $340 salary of the new assistant minister, the Reverend Mr. Frost at the First Parish, and not far below that of the eminent and venerable Dr. Ripley, the aging minister of the First Church, whose salary was $600 a year plus a house and $150 worth of cordwood.[1]

Concord's school system was made up at this time of seven districts, with eight schools for boys and eight for girls. The school budget for 1837–38 was $2,132.55, easily the major town expense. (Support of the poor came next at $800 a year, followed by roads and bridges.) There were male and female teachers in each of the seven districts, the man usually making $100 or so, the woman usually making about $40. The Center district—Thoreau's—had two male teachers, two female teachers, and over three hundred students. Thoreau himself was solely responsible for a hundred pupils. Of the twenty or so teachers employed by Concord, then, Thoreau had one of the two best paid positions. The pay was high because the responsibilities were heavy.[2]

Conditions in the schools were poor at best. Though the schools weighed heavily in the town budget, Concord's support was behind that of towns such as Brookline. The assortment of one-room schools had mostly been built in the very early years of the nineteenth century, and they had evolved into rough places. Students came home black and blue from fighting among themselves and from the physical discipline of the teachers. As a result, a private academy had been set up in Concord in 1822 so that serious, college-bound students could get a decent education. Thoreau and his brother, John, both attended Concord Academy rather than the public schools. But after college, it was to the public system that Thoreau returned, and in a very public, very exposed position.[3]

The schools themselves had "not a particle of paint on the interior

35

of one except the Centre," according to a school report of a few years later. "There is not," the report goes on, "a foot of playground or a tree around one. They all stand on and open directly to the street. When the school is out, there is no other place for the scholars but the middle of the street." The schools had next to no equipment. One or two had a few large maps. "As to apparatus, there is nothing worthy of the name in any schoolroom." The schools were heated by stoves, which were a constant problem. The rooms were sometimes near freezing, sometimes heated to 120 degrees, and often full of smoke. Ventilation was primitive. The school board once seriously entertained the idea that the general stuffiness and lack of oxygen were accountable for the slow wits of the students, and one report declares, with touching fervor, that "the first and most sacred duty of every teacher is to atttend to the temperature and ventilation of the school-room."[4]

Attendance was another major headache. Better in the winter term than the summer, it averaged two-thirds of the enrolled students, which meant that most students stayed away one day out of three. In the face of all this, the school board was not unreasonably convinced that strict discipline was essential. It may have been only the disciplinary problem that led the twenty-year-old Thoreau to quit his position, or it may be that he found the whole enterprise of trying to handle a stuffy roomful of between fifty and a hundred young boys more than he had bargained for. Writing to Orestes Brownson in December, some months after the incident, Thoreau stressed that he was now seeking a position "as teacher of a small school, or assistant in a large one." His position as chief teacher in Concord's largest school— more than half the size of Harvard College itself—may simply have been more than he could manage.[5]

At any rate, Thoreau left the job less than two weeks into the term. He still thought of himself as a teacher, however, and he went right to work to look for another position. And, however fond he was of Concord, he was perfectly willing to leave it for almost anywhere he could get a job. He had good recommendations. Emerson, President Quincy, and Brownson were willing to write on his behalf, and despite the public school incident, he had backers among Concord's most respected citizens. Thoreau inquired after jobs in Taunton, Massachusetts, in upstate New York, and in Alexandria, Virginia. In March he got wind of a large number of openings in the West—meaning Kentucky and thereabouts—and he was writing to his brother, then teaching in Taunton, about joining him in a job-seeking trip. Thoreau was full of enthusiasm and verve and evidently eager to get on with his calling and have a little adventure while doing it. "I wish you would write soon about this," he told John. "It is high season to start. The canals are now open, and travelling comparatively cheap. I think I can borrow the cash in this town. There's nothing like trying."[6]

Nothing came of these ventures, but he kept at it. In early May he set out to look for teaching jobs in Maine. He started by steamer from Boston, passing Gloucester's Eastern Point and Cape Ann. It was his first real trip on the ocean, and he stayed up late, seasick, but determined to see everything. He watched the lights and the land slip by under a bright moon. The water route was still the most practical way to get to Maine in a hurry. The steamer left him at Portland, and in the next few days he went through Brunswick, Bath, Gardiner, Hallowell, Augusta, China, Bangor, Oldtown, Belfast, Castine, and thence back via Belfast, Thomaston, and Bath to Portland. There were no teaching jobs, but he had glimpsed some grand country, including Penobscot Bay, which he had crossed and recrossed, by sail and by steam, and while coastal Maine was mostly cleared farmland in those days, there were great dark woods up in the interior, stretching hundreds of miles to Canada, with huge trees still bearing the king's seal (selected back before the revolution to be used for masts) up beyond Katahdin. Thoreau met an Indian at Oldtown, the most communicative man he met on this visit to taciturn Maine. Pointing up the Penobscot River, the Indian observed, "Two or three miles up the river one beautiful country."[7]

Up there was what had long since disappeared from Massachusetts—the real wilderness of uncut forests, lakes without cabins, and undammed streams. Up past the logging camps, where the rivers got smaller, there was country few white men had ever seen. The lure of Maine's backcountry, once felt, was not easily let go. Thoreau had had a sniff. He would come back again. But for now, there were no jobs, and he was a teacher, not a backwoodsman, so home he went to Concord, and he did what might have been predicted. Finding no jobs in the public schools, he opened a small private academy of his own.

Instead of a hundred he now had four students, with some prospect of a fifth. He taught from eight to twelve and from two to four. After that, he wrote John, "I read a little Greek or English, or for variety, take a stroll in the fields." It was a pleasant life, the summer fields were fuller than usual of berries that year, and his brother would soon be joining him in his attempt to run a school the right way. He was at last doing something about making a living, albeit a very small one. He was respectably employed, but even now, his mind was very much on other things.[8]

10. Poetry

Schoolteaching was all very well for the moment. It was, at least, a practical response to the nagging question of vocation ("What may a man do and not be ashamed of it? He may not do nothing, surely."). He was determined to make his own way, he refused to "impose on his fellows," but teaching only took care of feeding and clothing the outer man. Thoreau never thought of it as his life's work. What he really wanted to do was write. Lecturing was indeed a form of writing and there was a good deal of useful discipline involved in writing for a specific audience. There was also the example of Emerson, a practiced, fluent, effective speaker, much in demand and able to make $500 a year from lecturing. Lecturing was writing that might *eventually* pay well, but, at age twenty, what Thoreau really wanted to write was poetry.[1]

Back in his sophomore year, he had read Longfellow's *Outre-Mer*, and from that rambling travelogue Thoreau carefully extracted the interesting things Longfellow had to say about poetry. What Thoreau selected is a virtual "Defense of Poetry" by Longfellow. Longfellow's interest in medieval European poetry, heroic sagas, romances, and ballads was the chief, indeed the only thing of interest to Thoreau in the book. By the fall of his senior year, he was filling sheet after sheet of paper with long lists, phrases culled from Shakespeare, Dryden, Waller, and most of all, Milton. The lists, clearly not intended for college exercises, are the worksheets of a journeyman poet. He was learning most from Milton's adjectival practices, his ever-fresh ways to qualify things, "Fuming rill," "towering eagle," "rushing sound of onset," "Barbarous dissonance."[2]

Also in the spring and summer of his senior year came Longfellow's lectures on Northern literature, on Anglo-Saxon poetry, on English medieval poetry, and on Goethe. Here, as always, Longfellow concentrated on poetry, giving special emphasis to the early, the primitive, and the heroic.[3]

Thoreau's earliest poems reflect the very different kinds of verse he admired at the time. In some early efforts he worked to make phrases about Musketaquid, the Indian name for Concord River. But the native strain, if one may call it that, was quite absent from such a poem as "Godfrey of Boulogne," a Tasso-derived romantic crusader ballad that recalls both Longfellow and Mrs. Hemans: "The moon hung low o'er Provence vales, / 'Twas night upon the sea." Another early effort is one which Thoreau as a college senior wrote out, wrapped round a bunch of flowers, and tossed through the window of Lucy Brown, a Concord lady—older than Thoreau—and sister of Emerson's wife. There is some doubt as to which of Thoreau's poems was thus delivered. If, as seems likely, it was the one originally called "Sic Vita," but later retitled "Life is a Summer's Day," the gesture was more interesting than the verse.[4]

Yet another early poem, the "Speech of a Saxon Ealderman," which came directly out of an Anglo-Saxon original Thoreau had found in Joseph Bosworth's *The Elements of Anglo Saxon Grammar* (London, 1823), shows Thoreau's interest in the rough textures, the thew and sinew of the old English, and his Coleridgean skill at recreating the simplicity and directness of the old short line: "The hall is swept, / The table set, / And anxious guests are there."[5]

He also experimented with a smoother, more conventional, more latinate kind of romantic ballad. He was capable at this point of such atrocious rhymes as "streamlet" and "beamlet," but he also showed a genuine flair for the short-lined ballad measure.

Like torrents of the mountain
We've coursed along the lea,
From many a crystal fountain
Toward the far-distant sea.

Thoreau was at his best at oral forms, and his early notebooks are filled with medieval and Renaissance ballads and songs. His early poems suggest performance; they invariably sound better read aloud than they look on the page.[6]

Thoreau's first poems show an emerging romantic—not a transcendentalist—poet with an ear for Old English and for Milton, and with a strong leaning toward the stark strength and lyric brevity of early medieval verse. The summer of his senior year and that first fall back in Concord after college, Thoreau was reading Sidney's *Defense of Poesie*, excerpting Goethe's *Tasso* on the nature of the poet, and translating—rather flatly, it must be said—some of Goethe's own verse. By the following spring, however, he was back working on his own poetry again.

He produced now one remarkable poem about love and friendship. Called simply "Friendship," it is a moving, outspoken expression of obviously strong feelings: "I think awhile of Love, and while I think, / Love is to me a world." Emerson remarked later that Thoreau's biography was in his verses, and indeed his feelings are more often exposed in his poetry than anywhere else. The poem may be about his feelings for his brother John or it may be about his new relationship with Emerson. In either case, the depth of his intense admiring friendship comes clearly through the Herbertian simplicity of line, the Renaissance clarity of diction:

Two sturdy oaks I mean, which side by side,
        Withstand the winter's storm,
            And spite of wind and tide,
            Grow up the meadow's pride,
                For both are strong.[7]

Perhaps in response to some of Emerson's new ideas about its being "not metres but a metre-making argument that makes a poem," Thoreau began experimenting with a more modern diction reminding one now of Gray, now of Bryant. "The cliffs and springs" is an account of how a bird's song entices him out of the actual world so that he no longer feels the pull of "time or place, nor faintest trace / Of earth." Now, "the landscape's shimmer is my only space, / Sole remnant of a world." Reminiscent of Keats's great "Ode to a Nightingale," Thoreau's poem can be read as a first reaching for the transcendental dialectic of the real and the ideal, or the real and the imagined. Typically for Thoreau, the real is what endures at the end of the poem: "And I walk once more confounded a denizen of earth."[8]

The poetry of the spring of 1838 shows Thoreau trying, with some success, to adapt elements of the English tradition to Concord settings and personal themes. "The Bluebirds" fits the ballad form to Concord, and it has some perfect lyrical lines of an almost Goethean simplicity. "They seemed to come from the distant south, / Just over the Walden wood." There is also a Walden poem in Thoreau's Bryant-voice this spring, the beginnings of a poem, later published, on "Inspiration," and an interesting effort to fit the heroic couplet to a homely Concord theme in a poem called "May Morning." The last of these is revealing testimony to Thoreau's sense of the conflict between life in the school-room and the splendid, open-air, poetry-breeding experiences of nature and springtime. The poem begins "The school boy loitered on his way to school, / Scorning to live so rare a day by rule." The work-aday world of school and village life is like a sleep, but the poem ends with a joyous rush of "consciousness returning fast," an awakening to the full daylight sky:

My eyelids opened on a field of blue,

For close above a nodding violet grew,

A part of heaven it seemed, which one could scent,

Its blue commingling with the firmament.[9]

In 1839, Emerson praised with generous effusiveness some of Thoreau's early poetry as "the purest strain, and the loftiest, I think, that has yet pealed from this unpoetic American forest." What Emerson was recognizing in Thoreau was a strain not to be found in Bryant or Longfellow, a strain he himself sometimes tried for. There are, among Emerson's own poems, some short quatrains with compressed, ener-getic, surprising lines that make Emily Dickinson's expressed debt to him plausible. Emerson's:

To clothe the fiery thought

In simple words succeeds,

For still the craft of genius is

To mask a king in weeds.

or his "The sea is the road of the bold / Frontier of the wheat-sown plain" are very close, not only to Emily Dickinson but to the best of

Thoreau's early work. In addition to lines already cited, Thoreau could write such things as the following snatch, combining a sense of romantic longing and descriptive concreteness, and its terrific, cold, last line:

I am bound, I am bound, for a distant shore,
By a lonely isle, by a far Azore,
There it is, there it is, the treasure I seek,
On the barren sands of a desolate creek.

There is here a bleached-bone simplicity, a wavelike rhythm and a clean narrative tone the total effect of which is not to be matched until much later in the poems of John Masefield. The lines have the unmistakable tone of experienced emotion, and it seems, in Thoreau's phrase, that "the poem is drawn out from under the feet of the poet—his whole weight has rested on this ground." With this sort of start, and with his willingness to work hard at it, surely Thoreau was justified in thinking of himself as a poet. Emerson may have overpraised the early work, but his encouraging judgment was more challenge than charity. And who, in 1838, save Poe and Emerson himself, was writing better poetry in America?[10]

II. 1838-1840

The Ethical Imperatives
of Transcendentalism

11. Summer and Fall 1838

Through the summer and fall of 1838, Thoreau taught in his modest school and wrote letters about teaching to his brother, John, and his sister, Helen, both of whom were also teaching at the time. In October, although he was still applying for better-paying teaching positions elsewhere, he was beginning to be a part of Concord life, being elected secretary of the Concord Lyceum, the organization responsible for setting up the town's annual lecture series.

His efforts at formal writing this fall are mostly failures, partly because he was experimenting. Trying to make poetry out of the commonest stuff, and trying also to inject a little humor into it, he succeeded only in producing some awkwardly humorous verses about his unwaterproofed boots ("Anon with gaping fearlessness they quaff / The dewy nectar with a natural thirst"). Toward the end of December he began to hit a more promising vein in translations and imitations of Anacreon. "Along the leaves, along the branches, / The fruit, bending them down, flourishes." Again the classics showed him the way to his own local material.[1]

Also in December he was writing an essay on "Sound and Silence." His journal, from the earliest entries, records his unusual attentiveness to sounds of all kinds, the sound of a storm, a piano playing "The Battle of Prague," noises made by ice, church bells, crickets, evening revelry, cocks crowing. Whether of harmony or discord, Concord and its countryside were full of noises. Thoreau speaks continually—and longingly—of the desirability of a quiet life. But his essay scraps for "Sound and Silence" lack the personal and homely touch of the journal entries, running instead to ornate Elizabethan rhythm and euphuistic paradox ("as the truest Society approaches always nearer to Solitude, so the most excellent Speech finally falls into Silence"). Despite—or

perhaps because of—familiar echoes from Shakespeare ("Silence is
. . . balm to our every chagrin"), Thoreau's prose here is simply not
very good; it is mannered, "literary" in the worst sense, and dogged
by a persistent, mechanical perversity of paradox. "The orator . . . is
then most eloquent when most silent. He listens while he speaks—
and is a hearer along with his audience." There is, of course, a point
here, that silence is necessary to a real appreciation of sound and that
we sometimes have too little silence in our lives. The simple fact is
that Thoreau has now abandoned the conventional Addisonian prose
he was taught at school, but has not yet found his own voice. The
language then of the "Sound and Silence" fragments is weak and soft,
but it shows Thoreau's growing interest in the subjective side of literature, in the reader's response to the text. Thoreau is already fascinated by the way readers respond to direct narration, to what the
French call *recit*, the told story, to what we hear in the narrator's own
authenticating voice.[2]

"In all epics," writes Thoreau, "when after breathless attention, we
come to the significant words, 'he said,' then especially our inmost
man is addressed. We not unfrequently refer the interest which belongs to our own unwritten sequel—to the written and comparatively
lifeless page." Emerson once noted that the reason the young Thoreau
put every statement in a paradox was "the habit of a realist to find
things the reverse of their appearance." Here, however, mere stylistic
paradox gives way to fresh insight, seeing things in new combinations. Thoreau emphasizes the effect of reading on action and on what
happens when we allow the process to be reversed, and we allow a text
to usurp and redirect energies that should go into living.[3]

All through this summer and fall, Thoreau's journal style is more
expressive—more relaxed and concrete—than his formal writing,
whether of prose or verse. Over and over, his journal succeeds in catching and registering vivid moments of strong inner excitement, his
fundamental and all-important openness to experience. His "May
Morning" poem had spoken of a literal awakening, of "consciousness
returning fast," to a world in which the blue of a flower merged with
the blue of the sky. A poem of July, "Cliffs," is about one of those
hushed, still moments of summer and the accompanying sense of ec-

static enjoyment that lies deeper than the simple rapture of the senses. Reading Homer and applying it to his own life, he was looking for a present-day nineteenth-century equivalent of the old Homeric bravery, and noted in his journal on the day after his twenty-first birthday, "there are in each the seeds of a heroic ardor, which need only to be stirred in with the *soil where they lie*." And instead of doubting whether truth could be known or deprecating his own point of view, he boldly embraced the subjectivity that enabled him to affirm both. "Whatever of past or present wisdom has published itself to the world, is palpable falsehood till it come and utter itself by my side."[4]

Thoreau would not quite be able to settle for this as a philosophical principle—things would soon seem much more complicated—but he never lost the self-confidence, the almost visceral sureness of tone which came from his initial ability to simply *accept* himself and his own life as his only possible starting point. By August he was finding, and more important, could express his discovery—like that of Kant and Emerson—that the mere fact of consciousness was itself the best beginning one could want. In a passage recalling the famous "transparent eyeball" experience Emerson describes in *Nature*, Thoreau writes:

If with closed ears and eyes I consult consciousness for a moment—immediately are all walls and barriers dissipated—earth rolls from under me, and I float, by the impetus derived from the earth and the system—a subjective—heavily laden thought, in the midst of an unknown and infinite sea.[5]

During this summer and fall, he was more awake, more conscious of his own powers, more aware of himself and his surroundings. He saw things with new clarity and new intensity. "For the first time," he writes on September 5, "it occurred to me this afternoon what a piece of wonder a river is—A huge volume of matter ceaselessly rolling through the fields and meadows of this substantial earth." He knew too that it was, often, a matter of sheer physical exhilaration. "How unaccountable," he mused, eleven days later, "the flow of spirits in youth."[6]

Thoreau's heightened self-awareness went hand in hand with a heightened awareness of nature. The former led to a new awareness of the power that comes from unfettered self-acceptance; the latter began to demand expression in religious terms. Thoreau's recorded comments this year show a certain disdainful impatience with institutional religion, particularly Christianity. He finds divine service in the Academy Hall mere "weeping and wailing," church bells "wonderfully condescending," and his list of the "oldest books" (Homer, the Zendavesta, Confucius) pointedly excludes the Bible. But his running quarrel with Christianity should not be read as the mark of an irreligious or scoffing nature, and his feelings toward the natural world frequently compelled him to use sacred terminology. What is remarkable, and was to become characteristic, is that from now on, he almost always preferred to seek in Greek and Roman religion rather than in Christianity for his religious ideas, terms, and emotions. Commenting on a glorious, warm, quiet September afternoon, and trying to express his sense of profound contentment and the protective, nurturing, warming quality of the day, he borrowed the Latin word for nourishing, fair, gracious, and kind, a word often applied to Ceres, and gave it a new application. "Day and night seem henceforth but accidents—and the time is always a still even tide, and as the close of a happy day. . . . I know of no word so fit to express this disposition of Nature as *Alma Natura*."[7]

12. The Eye of Henry Thoreau

From the beginning, Thoreau's writing was marked by an intense interest in the wonders, not of the invisible, but of the visible world. "How much virtue there is in simply seeing," he once wrote. Like Emerson he used the language of vision deliberately and habitually, and like Emerson he believed that the poet's function was to "pierce this rotten diction" of stale phrase and dead metaphor, "and fasten words again to visible things." A good part of Thoreau's enterprise as a writer was finding ways to translate what he saw into words.[1]

Given this interest, it may at first seem odd that Thoreau, unlike, say, Hawthorne, took so little interest in photography, the new art which was being invented while he was in college, and which spread very rapidly in the next few years. We tend now to associate Thoreau with a certain kind of nature photography, due in large part to the loving labor of conservationist-photographers from Herbert Gleason to Eliot Porter, but Thoreau's own vision of nature did not lead him either to photography or even to the language of photography. We find instead a continuing interest in painting, a knowledgeable use of the terminology of painting and a way of seeing nature that has much in common with the great schools of mid-nineteenth-century American landscape painting, the Hudson River school and the Luminist school.[2]

There was a surprising availability of good painting in Boston during the years when Thoreau was a young man, even if it was a recent development. The Boston Athenaeum, then on Pearl Street, had been mounting annual exhibitions since 1827. Between 1833 and 1837—Thoreau's college years—one could have seen paintings in the Athenaeum by Turner, Poussin, Rembrandt, Guido Reni, Salvator Rosa, Titian, and Velázquez, to name only the best known of the hundreds of artists whose work was shown. And while many of these European pictures were copies, there was also, and more important, a profusion of original canvases by American painters. During the same four-year period, one could have seen numerous works by Cole, Copley, Allston, Durand, Inman, Mount, Quidor, Stuart, Sully, and West. (In later years all the great Luminist painters—Lane, Heade, Kensett, Gifford, and Church—exhibited at the Athenaeum, and there were special shows for Cole's *Course of Empire* in 1854 and Church's *Andes of Ecuador* in 1855.)[3]

In 1834 a second, rival gallery opened in Boston, and by 1838 the Athenaeum was responding to competition by putting on such special shows as a lithographic collection of masterpieces from Dresden and the first exhibition of John James Audubon's *Birds of America*. Art was very popular in Boston, in Cambridge, and even in Concord. Washington Allston had moved to Cambridge in 1830, where he labored on his vast, stalled *Feast of Belshazzar*. Courses in drawing were introduced at many schools in the 1840s. Every family had someone with a "gift" for drawing. One of the Alcott girls sketched, as did Thoreau's sister, Sophia. Prudence Ward, who boarded with the Thoreaus for years, did watercolors, while Sophia Peabody Hawthorne actually had a picture in the Athenaeum exhibition in 1834. Hawthorne himself took a keen interest in art, writing about it in numerous tales and sketches as well as in *The Marble Faun*; Hawthorne's workroom had the *Apollo Belvedere* on one side and Raphael's *Transfiguration* on the other side. Emerson had brought back from Italy a rich appreciation of its art, some copies of Michelangelo's work, and a taste for drawings.[4]

Thoreau's firsthand acquaintance with art, as with music, was no doubt limited, but his interest is evident. He was familiar with Burke's "A Philosophical Inquiry into the Origin of Our Ideas of the Sublime and Beautiful" from 1837 on, and he comments in 1839 on having seen some "illuminated" pictures. In 1840 he is referring in familiar terms to Guido Reni and Titian. His interest in Goethe extended to Goethe's own interest in art. Goethe himself sketched; the *Italian Journey* is full of talk about art, and he is very articulate about the problem of verbal descriptions of visual phenomena. Thoreau carefully noted Goethe's exactness, his detachment, his knack of keeping his own reflections out of the way. Longfellow's lectures on Goethe at Harvard had called attention to Goethe's visual quality. "Every thing makes a picture in his mind," Longfellow said. "He begins to sketch from nature, all that strikes his imagination. In this way he acquired a habit of close observation of external objects, looking at them not singly and in detail, but grouping them together, so as to form pictures."[5]

Thoreau was also alert to the visual qualities of Homer and Virgil. Often it is literally the visual appeal of the images, as in "iam laeto turgent in palmite gemmae" (already the buds are swelling on the happy vine sprouts). Also, from early on, he used terms from painting, being particularly open to "picturesque" elements in the landscape. His own early efforts at scenic description are, however, remarkably inept. Abstract and wordy, they are loaded with scene-killing comparisons that cannot be visualized. "First we have the grey twilight of the poets, with dark and barry clouds diverging to the zenith." But even in such botches, it can, I think, be seen that Thoreau wanted qualities beyond the simply pictorial in his landscapes. Hawthorne's son, Julian, commented in his *Memoirs* that he didn't think Thoreau

> cared much for what is called the beauties of nature; it was her way of working, her mystery, her economy in extravagance; he delighted to trace her footsteps toward their source, and to watch her growths and developments. . . . But of color or form as valued by artists I doubt whether he took heed.[6]

It is true that Thoreau always saw nature more as force, process, or energy than as mere picture, but he did not neglect the language of art as much as Julian Hawthorne suggests. If he rarely was interested in the kind of tame representations conveyed by the term *photographic* used in a pejorative sense, he was always alert both to art and to the language of art, to the terms that described effects, and to verbal equivalents of visual scenes. He delighted in the unplanned symmetries of inkblot drawings. He was interested in the art of seeing. At the start of "Sunday" in a *Week on the Concord and Merrimack Rivers* he would talk about objects that required "a separate intention of the eye." Later he would eagerly read such writers as Ruskin and Gilpin, whose work starts from the often ignored fact that the uneducated eye simply does not notice most of what is in front of it. Until our attention is called to this detail or that feature, we rarely scrutinize our surroundings, "in the full, clear sense of the word, we do not see."[7]

Thoreau's most interesting visual writing comes not when he is being most pictorial, most representational, most "photographic," but when he can use the visual scene to convey his awareness of the energy behind nature, creating and animating the scene we see, or when he describes a scene in such a way as to draw out or articulate the feelings of the observer. At the end of the great essay on "Walking," he describes a sunset with such skill that the writer's sense of wonder is kindled anew in the reader.

> We had a remarkable sunset one day last November. I was walking in a meadow, the source of a small brook, when the sun at last, just before setting, after a cold gray day, reached a clear stratum in the horizon, and the softest, brightest morning sunlight fell on the dry grass and on the stems of the trees in the opposite horizon, and on the leaves of the shrub-oaks on the hill-side, while our shadows stretched long over the meadow eastward, as if we were the only motes in its beams. It was such a light as

53

we could not have imagined a moment before, and the air was so warm
and serene that nothing was wanting to make a paradise of that meadow.
The light and the warmth here surround the reader-walker. By concentrating on process as well as scene Thoreau makes
us feel nature as well as see it.[8]

13. Self-Culture

Concord in the 1830s and 1840s—Emerson's Concord—was to
America what Goethe's Weimar had been to Germany. In each case,
a small if not humble society came to have enormous moral and intellectual importance for a country, coming eventually to symbolize the
best of the national culture. And both Concord and Weimar owed that
central and symbolic importance to their productive interest in what
John Stuart Mill called "the culture of the inward man." Concord was
acutely aware that it was following Weimar in this interest; nothing
Emerson and his friends took from Goethe's Germany was more important than the concept of *Bildung*.

Bildung, or personal culture, is, in Thomas Mann's fine account, "a
specifically German Idea. It comes from Goethe, it got from him the
connection with the plastic arts, the sense of freedom, civilized outlook and worship of life . . . and through Goethe this idea was elevated into an educational principle as in no other nation." The idea of
personal culture is quite different both from Matthew Arnold's nor-
mative public concept of culture as "the best that has been thought
and said," and from the anthropological use of the word *culture* to mean
the habits and customs of any distinct social or ethnic group. The
essentially individualistic inwardness of personal culture may owe
something to the eighteenth-century revival of Stoic thought. As a
recent commentator notes, "The notion of stoical self-respect, of inner
freedom, the 'No man need say "I must"' of Lessing, was of course
one of the central ideas of the German Enlightenment."[1]

With Goethe and with Wilhelm von Humboldt these ideas developed into a coherent and persuasive concept of the proper cultivation
and development of the self.

The inwardness, the culture [*Bildung*] of a German implies introspectiveness; an individualistic cultural conscience; consideration for the careful tending, the shaping, deepening, and perfecting of one's own personality . . . subjectiveness in the things of the mind . . . given to autobiographical confession and deeply personal.[2]

Professor Longfellow's lectures at Harvard had emphasized Goethe's pursuit of personal culture, using the term that would become standard in America: self-culture. "Self-culture . . . was Goethe's great study from youth to age," Longfellow said, and the result of this pursuit was that eventually he "became like the athlete of ancient story, drawing all his strength from earth. His model was the perfect man, as man; living, moving, laboring upon earth in the sweat of his brow. . . . He beheld beauty in everything and God in everything. This was his religion, to busy himself with the present; fulfilling his destiny, Like a star / without haste / but without rest."[3]

An interest in self-culture also marks Margaret Fuller's writing on Goethe, and the idea and the phrase came to have wide currency in America during the 1830s and 1840s. Frederic Hedge wrote an essay on self-culture. Horace Greeley had a talk he called "Self-culture"; so did William Ellery Channing. The latter, given in 1838, argues that self-culture is possible because we have the power of "acting on, determining, and forming ourselves," and he stresses the fact behind the metaphor. "To cultivate any thing, be it a plant, an animal, a mind, is to make grow. Growth, expression, is the end."[4]

But it is principally in Emerson's writings that the German concept of self-culture was taken over and reworked into the still-familiar American emphasis on self-reliance and self-improvement. Emerson had, in fact, been writing on the subject since at least 1828, long before his serious encounter with Goethe, and in the titles of some of his early sermons we can see how deeply he was interested in the problem of self-development. In October of 1828 he first preached on "Self Direction and Self Command," in November on "Self Knowledge and Self-Mastery." In May of 1829 he spoke on "Cultivating the Mind," in August on "Self-Command." In September of 1830 his topic was "Self-Culture," in December "Trust Yourself." In July of 1831 he talked on "Limits of Self-Reliance," and in the following February on "Self-Improvement," a favorite sermon he was to repeat fourteen times over the next four years.[5]

Although not so much influenced, he said, by the German concept of *Kultur* (public, "official" culture: plays, operas, cultural institutions and events), the idea of individual culture struck a deeply responsive chord in Emerson, and his study of Goethean and Herderian ideas of self-culture led Emerson to his 1837–38 lecture series called "Human Culture." Testimony to the importance he gave the subject is his catechistic note to himself in 1837: "What is culture? the chief end of man."[6]

Out of this long foreground of sermon and lecture came "The American Scholar" address and the essays on "History" and "Self-Reliance," with their emphasis on self-trust, self-development, and self-education. It is a misreading of Emerson's intent to think of his central theme of individualism as one rooted in "the attempt to deny the reality and importance of human interdependence," of his individualist as one "who subjects others to himself through his shrewdness in gauging their appetites or anticipating their needs." Emersonian individualism is neither antisocial nor imperial; it does not advocate withdrawal from society, nor does it seek to rule others. It is overwhelmingly concerned with the self-education and development of the individual, and convinced that there can be neither love nor society unless one first has a group of autonomous individuals. Emersonian self-reliance is, like the Stoic's self-respect, the necessary means to self-culture, to the development of the self. Insofar as it is a means to power it is only power over the self, not over others.[7]

Thoreau's own understanding of self-culture was characteristically personal. He was reading Goethe's *Wilhelm Meister*, pattern of all *Bildungsromans*, or novels of education, as a college student, and he was listening to Professor Longfellow's guarded endorsement of Goethe's lifelong interest in self-culture. He was also in constant contact with Emerson's urgent and attractive cultural individualism. But Thoreau's earliest journal entries show also a tough Stoic strain, as though self-culture required of him a tremendous effort of self-control. "Passion and appetite," he notes in August 1838, "are always an Unholy land in which one may wage most holy war." He followed up his military metaphor. "Let him steadfastly follow the banner of his faith till it is planted in the enemy's citadel." Nine months later, the same strain, only a little less harsh now, appears under the explicit heading "Self-Culture." "Who knows how incessant a surveillance a strong man may maintain over himself—how far subject passion and appetite to reason, and lead the life his imagination paints?"[8]

As time went on Thoreau dwelt less on the difficulties of self-control and (with more and more humor) increasingly on the life his imagination painted. Self-culture became a major concern, perhaps the major concern of his life, and increasingly he tried to reach behind the metaphor of cultivation to the reality. He came to value the Roman agricultural writers Varro, Columella, and Cato as much or more than Homer, as he came to believe that the cultivation of one's self has a good deal in common with the cultivation of the soil. He made his Walden Pond bean field a major metaphor for his particular idea of self-cultivation, which was to avoid the extremes of over-refinement on one side and savagery on the other. Cultivating two and a half acres, planting late, using no manure, and hoeing by hand, Thoreau harvested twelve bushels of beans, besides, as he said, some gains to his character. He took pride that his field was "the connecting link between wild and cultivated fields; as some states are civilized, and others half-civilized, and others savage or barbarous, so my field was, though not in a bad sense, a half-cultivated field."[9]

14. Ellen

During the latter half of July 1839, not long after Thoreau's twenty-second birthday, Ellen Sewall, then a girl of seventeen, came to Concord for a two-week visit. Although the Sewalls lived in Scituate, on the coast south of Boston, they had Concord connections. Ellen's eleven-year-old brother, Edmund, was recently enrolled as a student in Thoreau's school and her aunt, Prudence Ward, boarded with the Thoreaus. There was nothing unusual in the visit except that Thoreau fell utterly in love with her as soon as she arrived.

Ellen Sewall was remarkably beautiful. Slender, with well-proportioned features, she had the high cheekbones, straight nose, and clean profile of classical good looks and her vivacity survived daguerreotyping. Even the five-minute exposure common at the time, and responsible for the set expressions of most early portraits, has not concealed the pleasant mouth and its graceful amused curve, or the calm but interested expression of the eyes. She looks warm, intelligent, lively, and quite natural. Daguerreotyping brings out whatever hardness there is in a person; it found none in Ellen Sewall. When she arrived in Concord, there was a flurry of activity. She went walking and boating with both Henry and John, and within a week or so a vacationing Harvard student, John Shepard Keyes, was also squiring Ellen about. Half the young men in Concord, it seemed, were running after Ellen Sewall.[1]

Thoreau was, this summer of 1839, in an unusually open mood emotionally. Just a month before Ellen's arrival, her younger brother, Edmund, had come to Concord for a visit and Thoreau had been immediately attracted to the boy, taking him for walks, praising him as a "pure uncompromising spirit," and writing a poem to him in which the conventions of Elizabethan love poetry are used to articulate rather than repress the strong surge of affection Thoreau felt for this "gentle boy."

So was I taken unawares by this,
I quite forgot my homage to confess;
Yet now am forced to know, though hard it is
I might have loved him had I loved him less.[2]

Modern readers have been more squeamish about this poem and the relationship it celebrates than the Thoreaus or the Sewalls were at the time. Since it never crossed their minds that there might have been a physical attraction or longing behind all this, there was no reason for writer or reader to repress or conceal the emotional attraction. It is ironic that here, as in the case of Whitman, a strongly affectionate nature was in some ways freer to express itself (when it chose) before Freud made us so complexly self-aware of all the possible implications of our feelings.

At any rate, Thoreau had already been deeply impressed and moved by Edmund in June, and now in July his lovely sister, some six years older than Edmund, arrived. This time Thoreau was smitten beyond words. Neither letters nor poems—certainly no Elizabethan sonnet conventions—were adequate to express his feelings for Ellen Sewall. This single line occurs in his journal five days later: "There is no remedy for love but to love more."[3]

While in Concord, Ellen wrote home to her father about the numerous walks to Emerson Cliffs ("admiring the prospect which is indeed beautiful"), to Fairhaven Pond ("a sweet little pond"), to Walden Pond, to Annursnack Hill, up the Assabet River ("the pleasantest part of the excursion"), and she shaded the party's gaiety a bit for parental eyes. "We enjoyed this walk exceedingly (perhaps I should speak for myself) and were not at all fatigued by it." By the time Ellen's visit was over both John and Henry had fallen in love with her. Saying goodbye and leaving Concord, Ellen cried a little and we catch a glimpse of her as a bit sentimental, a dutiful daughter, a pretty young girl with somewhat predictable enthusiasms who has had a wonderful carefree two weeks away from home in the company of interesting, attentive, active young men.[4]

On August 31, less than a month after Ellen's departure, the Thoreau brothers set out for a week's boating trip down the Concord and up the Merrimack rivers, a trip which later became the framework for Thoreau's first book. Immediately upon their return to Concord, almost as soon as the boat was tied up, John went off to Scituate to see Ellen. All the indications are that it was John who had the inside track with Ellen at this time. John figures more prominently in her letters than Henry, and the references to Henry almost all have a tinge of mockery. What "real work" is Henry busy at? Does "Dr. Thoreau" still give advice gratis? Such a tone implies both a certain cousinly closeness and an amused recognition of Henry's evident stiffness. But the next sentence is full of Ellen's usual gaiety, with a little spice of affection. "I do not clean my brasses half as quick without the accompaniment of his flute." But it was John who came to visit, John who first sent presents, John who is treated without irony in Ellen's letters. However he put it to himself, Henry was unwilling or unable to assert his own interest in Ellen over John's. As if in compensation, Henry spent much of that fall in the grip, as he put it, of the "writing-demon." He worked on a translation of *Prometheus Bound*, on an essay on bravery, on an essay on the Roman Stoic and satirist Persius, on an essay on friendship. If he couldn't express his feelings about Ellen for fear of injuring his brother, Thoreau found ways to express his struggles with himself in literary form. Constrained as he was, he wanted to be brave and Stoical, but he was much interested in the relation of friendship to love. "Friendship," he wrote, "is a community of love," and he observed that "all romance is founded on friendship."[5]

Ellen came back to Concord for another visit the following summer. She went for a row with Thoreau, and his description in his journal is an implicit contrast between the outward simplicity and the inner complexity of the relations between them.

The other day I rowed in my boat a free—even lovely young lady—and as I plied the oars, she sat in the stern—and there was nothing but she between me and the sky. So might all our lives be picturesque if they were free enough—but mean relations and prejudices intervene to shut out the sky, and we never see a man as simple and distinct as the man-weathercock on a steeple.

The simpler truth was that neither Ellen nor Thoreau was really free. Ellen was understood to be John's girl, and Thoreau didn't feel free to pursue Ellen for himself. In July 1840, just as the newly founded *Dial* was coming out with Thoreau's first important literary contribution, his debut in print, John went again to Scituate and this time proposed to Ellen as they were walking on the beach. Ellen at first accepted, then either because of family pressure or because she suddenly realized she cared more for Henry than for John, she refused him. Thoreau couldn't openly exult over John's failure, but his journal clearly records his eternity of suspenseful waiting and his unconcealable joy at the outcome. "These two days . . . have been really an aeon in which a Syrian empire might rise and fall—How many Persias have been lost and won in the interim—Night is spangled with fresh stars." With John out of the way it was a new era, a new heaven, and a new hope.[6]

But Ellen was now sent off to Watertown, New York, to be out of the way of the transcendental Thoreau brothers, both of whom were deeply mistrusted by Ellen's father. Early in November 1840, despite the fresh obstacles, Thoreau himself finally proposed to Ellen in a lyrical and very intense letter. This time Ellen consulted her father *before* answering, and after her father had said no she wrote a short refusal to Henry. She was so mortified over the confused acceptance / rejection of John that she felt, as she later explained to her curious children, she could only follow her father's advice this time. Two years later she became safely engaged to a young minister named Joseph Osgood, whom she married in 1844.[7]

What kind of person was Ellen Sewall when Thoreau knew her?

Her own letters and journals show a rather conventional seventeen-year-old, impressionable and full of gaiety, changing very rapidly into an interesting young woman of quick sympathies and active feelings that ran up close to the surface much of the time. She loved company, and the hum of things going on. She always speaks of being lonely whenever anyone has just left. Her life in Scituate was not all smiles. During that fall of 1839, her father was going through the painful and public process of being dismissed from his duties. This not only made it harder for Ellen to go against his wishes but made home bleak. The Sewalls didn't celebrate Christmas (neither did the Thoreaus at this time; Thoreau's journal for these years makes almost no mention of festivals, holidays, or even birthdays), and Ellen wrote to her aunt, "Father wishes the old times back when Christmas day was such a happy day to him, at his father's house. I wish we were in the habit of celebrating Christmas."[8]

Ellen was sensitive to nature, which she describes easily and well. Her letters are full of the ocean; she notes everything from the spring tides to the terrible shipwrecks so frequent on the coast. She writes about the "moaning of the sea" and the "clouds promise of rain tomorrow." Like Thoreau she loved being out on moonlit evenings. She read Bulwer's *Last Days of Pompeii* ("very interesting") and, no doubt at the urging of the Thoreaus, Carlyle's *Sartor Resartus* ("what a queer book, but I like it much") and she read Longfellow's *Voices of the Night* and set herself to pick out the best poems.[9]

The difficulties of that first fall back at home after meeting the Thoreau brothers only brought out more clearly the side of Ellen that was cheerful, bright-eyed, interested in everything, and determined to make the best of things she couldn't change. She was sorry that Thoreau's sister Helen was always "so unwell when she comes home," because "she can enjoy so much less than if she were well." And in the same letter, to her Aunt Prudence, in which she briefly and painfully alludes to her letter of refusal to Thoreau, she tells about a Canadian couple she had met on a train to Albany, who "seemed so inclined to make the best of everything, that I liked them very much." It was a trait she admired in others because she hoped it was true of her.[10]

Clearly her trip to Concord and the attentions of the Thoreau boys, particularly Henry, were a special part of Ellen's young life. Her first thank-you letter, written immediately after her first trip to Concord, is surprising by its excess. "I shall always think of my visit to Concord as one of the happiest moments of my life." The event was just barely over, but already it is treated as a distant and treasured past. Over a year later, after John's proposal but before Henry's, she wrote again to her aunt about Concord in elegiac fashion, as though reconciled to losses eons ago. "What delightful walks we had together in Concord last summer. . . . Oh those were happy times." And in her diary for 1841, after the affair with Thoreau was all past, she wrote, "I wonder if his thoughts ever wander back to those times when the hours sped so pleasantly and we were so happy. I think they do. I little thought then that he cared for me so much as subsequent events have proved."[11]

Ellen may have sighed as a lover, but she obeyed as a daughter. She was prepared all along to renounce, but she would not forget. What she did, right from the start, was to enclose the wonderful summer romance in a cocoon of protective nostalgia. Thus the whole attractive but difficult episode ceased, almost as it was happening, to be a present experience and became instead a memory, seeming to lie far back in time, a romance on a Grecian urn.

As for Thoreau, he saw Ellen socially at fitful intervals after marriage; he took an emotional interest in other women who were mostly older or safely married or both; he was pursued with grim matrimonial design by one Miss Foord, but he never again let himself fall in love with an eligible woman. Ellen was the one real love of his life, and whatever crusty remarks of his about women and marriage may have got copied down, he told his sister, when he was dying and the subject of Ellen Sewall came up, "I have always loved her."[12]

15. The Rivers

On the last day of August 1839, just a month after Ellen's first trip to Concord, Henry and his brother John set out on a trip of their own. They planned to go north from Concord, Massachusetts, to Concord, New Hampshire, by river, canal, and river again, thence overland to the White Mountains, then return. Years later Henry came back to this, his first real excursion, for a framework for his first book, *A Week on the Concord and Merrimack Rivers*. Although the goal of the expedition was to climb Agiocochook (Mount Washington), which they did, and although Thoreau was and remained greatly interested in mountains, this trip was, from the beginning, more a river expedition than a hiking or climbing one. Thoreau was as much a man of the rivers as a man of the woods.[1]

John, then twenty-four, was two years older than Henry. Quiet, genial, and neat, he stood in strong contrast to the sharp-eyed, long-haired, unkempt Henry. John was like his father, and was considered the more promising of the boys, an opinion Henry probably shared without ever having put it that way to himself. John had never been in good health. Frail and terribly thin at 117 pounds, he had had "nosebleeds so violent that he fainted" by the time he was eighteen. He stood badly the strain of teaching, he was often down with "colic," but the underlying problem was tuberculosis, undiagnosed but sleeping, a deadly and in those days quite common family curse. The brothers were close in many ways; the entire family was a close unit. John was the older and admired brother, leading the way as a teacher in what Henry thought was his profession, too. Add to that the solicitude provoked by John's awful health, and now, as they got their boat ready to go, the fact that they had both just fallen in love with the same girl. As the two young men set out, the memory of Ellen Sewall was between them, creating in the weeks to come a new tension and a new bond between them.[2]

The mild Concord River flows north emptying into the south-running Merrimack just as it turns at Lowell to go east to the ocean, coming in at Newburyport behind Samuel Sewall's beloved Plum Island, north of Gloucester and Cape Ann. Although the Concord River runs right through the town of Concord, one is not really aware of it in the town itself. A contemporary noted that "there were no masts to offend the eye," and Emerson, when he went boating with Thoreau, was always amazed at how quickly, by crossing just one field to the boat and the river's edge, they were transported into a world utterly removed from that of the village, leaving behind "all time, all science, all history," entering "into Nature with one stroke of a paddle." Energetic newcomers to Concord such as Lemuel Shattuck could hope that the Concord would soon become a substantial inland waterway, and the Middlesex Canal, connecting the Concord and Merrimack rivers to Boston Harbor, made this a distinct possibility. But in 1839 the Concord was, as it still is, a quiet noncommercial river, almost entirely undeveloped along its banks, good for dreaming, drowsing, and dawdling if not for commerce.[3]

It rained all the day appointed for setting out; the brothers delayed for a bit, then decided to start anyway and pushed their heavy, wheeled boat, loaded with potatoes and melons, into the stream. They had built the boat themselves in a week and it was serviceable, though it was not quite the graceful working boat Thoreau makes us see when he likens it to a fisherman's dory. Waving goodbye to the little group of friends assembled on the bank, they set off down river. It was in most senses a tame enough undertaking as is comically emphasized by Thoreau's subsequent epical glamorizing. Billerica, the next town downriver after neighboring Bedford and Carlisle, becomes *"terra incognita,"* the Concord is likened to the Nile and the Scamander, the voyage itself a fit parallel to polar expeditions and heroic explorations. And, in fact, the trip *was* something of an adventure. Thoreau had been to Maine and elsewhere, but always by public transportation, rail or steam, or commercial sailing ship. And he had taken innumerable day hikes and afternoon paddles, but he had never before gone on a long trip under his own power, nor had he ever so much as spent the night out in a tent. Thus, as they slipped along the quiet river, unspoiled and uninhabited for long stretches on either side, the brothers really felt they were *out*, beyond the towns, not just between them. When they camped along shore the first night at Billerica, the boat's mast and the tent (a one-pole, teepee-like affair) intruded the lone note of geometry—human art—into an otherwise completely natural landscape. After supper they turned in, but Thoreau lay long awake, listening to the night sounds. They were not, after all, very far from the towns and they heard alarm bells, church bells, dogs barking in the distance, as well as fox and muskrat noises nearer the tent. The noises were surely both welcome and expected, but like all noises one's first night out, they sounded strangely distinct, and emphasized by their trivial prominence the depth of the country silence.[4]

The next day they turned into the Middlesex Canal, an eighteenth-century commercial waterway completed in 1803, which ran southeast from just above the Lowell Falls on the Merrimack down to Boston Harbor. The source of the canal's water supply was the Concord River itself, so that the brothers had only to turn into the canal, row a short six miles and drop, by locks, into the Merrimack. Full of traffic on weekdays, though already losing freight to the energetic young railroads, the canal was quiet on the Sunday morning the Thoreau brothers went through. The completely man-made canal ran between regular banks in utter geometrical contrast to the unspoiled river; the Thoreaus went through as quickly as they could, breaking a good many of the canal rules as they went. Their boat was smaller than the required minimum, it did not have a name or number visible, it was not drawn by an ox or a horse, they should not have been traveling on a Sunday unless bound for home, and they exceeded the four-miles-per-hour speed limit. Some townsfolk were offended at their breaking the Sabbath, but none of it bothered Sam Hadley, the Lowell lockkeeper, who dropped them twenty-seven feet down the grand three-step stone lock system into the Merrimack.[5]

During the next twelve days they worked their way upriver, past Nashua and Manchester, left the boat below the Hookset Falls, walked to Concord, took the stage to Franconia, spent three days in the mountains, and "did" Mount Washington in the most laconically reported excursion of Thoreau's career. The full account reads "Sept. 10th ascended the mountain and rode to Conway." Returning to Concord, New Hampshire, they proceeded to Hookset and their boat, and headed down the river for home.[6]

Thoreau later worked and reworked his river book, and in all its versions what stands out is not the goal or the getting there, but the setting out and the return. The element of quest is the least prominent aspect of the book, as it seems to have been of the trip itself. The tone of the outset is calm and tranquil, like the first two panels of Thomas Cole's *Voyage of Life* or some of the early raft scenes in *Huckleberry Finn*. This calm is impressed on the reader with vivid, visual details. Late the first afternoon Thoreau writes, "we passed a man on the shore fishing with a long birch pole, its silvery bark left on, and a dog at his side, rowing so near as to agitate his cork with our oars." Next morning the river was covered with fog, "but before we had rowed many rods, the sun arose and the fog rapidly dispersed, leaving a slight steam only to curl along the surface of the water." A bit farther along they watched, from the comfortable vantage of the boat, two men, evidently unfamiliar with the region, trying to cross the river. Everything is seen from a great distance over the water. "They seemed," Thoreau remarked, "to be learning much in a little time. They ran about like ants on a burning brand, and once more they tried the river here, and once more there, to see if water still indeed was not to be walked on." This tone of mild comedy continues as the Thoreaus pursue a huge "sturgeon," its "dark and monstrous back alternately rising and sinking in mid-stream." Creeping up on the huge fish, while it swam in place against the swift current, they tried to catch it. "But the halibut skinned monster, in one of those swift-gliding pregnant moments, without ever ceasing his bobbing up and down, saw fit, without a chuckle or another prelude, to proclaim himself a huge imprisoned spar, placed there as a buoy, to warn sailors of sunken rocks." At night the brothers lay in the tent, listening to the river "sucking and eddying away all night down toward the marts and the seaboard."[7]

The setting out had many moments of calm, the brothers had time for reflection on the river's loveliness, but the return was anything but calm. On the night before their last day, the weather suddenly changed. "That night was the turning point in the season. We had gone to bed in summer, and we awoke in autumn." The wind came up, fresh and cold, out of the north. The Thoreaus were up and on the river by five in the morning. It became a glorious day, clear, cool, brisk, blue with a bright mid-September northerly wind that freshened as the morning went on. They were bound downriver, they had the wind at their backs, they had had the wit to bring a sail, and now they fairly flew down the river starting at Bedford, New Hampshire (near Manchester), retracing in one exhilarating day the fifty miles it had taken them four days to accomplish coming up.[8]

The water gurgled under the stern, and the steering paddle had to be thrust deep into the water as they surged down the river. Scenery that had seemed fixed now changed and unrolled behind them. Bundled in their cloaks, they sat in the boat and watched as the miles unraveled at a speed that astonished passing scow boatmen. By Tyngsboro the river "opened into a broad and straight reach of great length, which we bounded merrily over before a smacking breeze. . . . The wind in the horizon rolled like a flood over valley and plain. . . . They were great and current motions, the flowing sail, the running stream, the waving tree, the roving wind."[9]

Later in the afternoon, as they turned into the canal, the wind dropped, and they pulled the boat through the canal and rowed home, arriving at dark "far in the evening" not at "fresh pastures . . ." but back where they had started. The boat nuzzled into its old spot on the shore, amid rushes still flattened from their setting out, "and we leaped gladly on shore, drawing it up, and fastening it to the wild apple tree, whose stem still bore the mark which its chain had worn in the chafing of the spring freshets."[10]

What great luck to have had such a splendid sailing day their last day out. Though written many years later, the Friday section of *A Week* rushes and sparkles with the sheer exhilaration of it. Though he often went sailing in later years, even going on the ocean down near Marshfield and Plymouth, this was the best, most stirring day's sail Thoreau ever had. It came back to him sometimes in dreams, he said. When, years later, he was near death, he asked his sister Sophia to read to him from *A Week*, and he smiled as she reached the last pages of "Friday." Among the last words Thoreau spoke were "Now comes good sailing." The trip was associated right from the start with strong feelings and vivid experiences. No sooner were the Thoreaus back in Concord than John went off to Scituate to see Ellen Sewall.[11]

16. Aeschylus, Bravery

The fall of 1839 was marked by "most serene autumn weather" and in one of his few nature notes for this season Thoreau noted that "the chirp of crickets may be heard at noon all over the land." Indoors, Emerson and his friends were preparing to launch their new quarterly magazine, Thoreau was reelected secretary and curator of the Concord Lyceum, and John pressed the courting of Ellen Sewall. Perhaps to avoid excessive brooding on the latter, Henry threw himself into his writing. By early November he was deep in a translation of Aeschylus' *Prometheus Bound*.[1]

Thoreau was interested in Aeschylus not as a playwright, but as a "seer," a poet, whose work spoke not of the high unattainable exploits of unapproachable heroes, but of a "common humanity." The praise of Aeschylus, like the praise of Homer, was that in his work one confronted nature itself. "Such naked speech," Thoreau commented approvingly, "is the standing aside of words to make room for thoughts." The passage of time gave Aeschylus no advantage in Thoreau's eyes. His humanity, or his common sense, could be no different from ours. Far from idolizing Aeschylus, Thoreau demanded that the author of *Prometheus Bound* demonstrate his present applicability: "All the past is here present to be tried, let it approve itself if it can." One of the things that did approve itself, in Thoreau's eyes, was an impression of Aeschylus as being, "like every genius," essentially solitary in his life and work. One more than half suspects Thoreau was describing himself when he commented that "Aeschylus was undoubtedly alone and without sympathy in his simple reverence for the mystery of the universe."[2]

Thoreau's interest in Prometheus was not so much the usual romantic admiration for the hero's rebellion against the rational, imperial authority of Zeus, as it was in Prometheus as an Orpheus figure, a bringer of light, law, and civilization. These, at any rate, are the sorts of passages he entered in his journal as he began the work of translating. He also saw in Prometheus—as he saw in Aeschylus and no doubt felt in himself as John continued to carry the day with Ellen—a man unjustly condemned to suffer in solitude. Stiffish as he could appear, he was anything but collected inside. As November advanced, he was beginning, at the advanced age of twenty-two, to feel a bit old: "I was not aware till to-day of a rising and risen generation," he noted. As he worked on Aeschylus he tried to deal with feelings of regret by embracing them—"make the most of your regrets . . . to regret deeply is to live afresh"—and he tried in his journal to talk down a despondency he could not deny. Most typically, instead of simply feeling sorry for himself, he began to work out an essay on "bravery."[3]

What he meant by "bravery" was not so much physical, as moral, courage. He admired "the great bravery" of Linnaeus calmly seeing to his "spare shirt" and "leather breeches" amid the excitement of setting out for Lapland. The general subject was very much in the air, of course. Carlyle in his *On Heroes, Hero-Worship, and the Heroic in History* (1840) was interested in moral courage, as was Emerson. "But who announces to us in journal, in pulpit, or in the street the secret of heroism?" Emerson asked in "The Young American." Margaret Fuller was also interested in the Prometheus figure, and her book *Woman in the Nineteenth Century* (1845) could have been called On Heroines, Heroism and the Heroic in the History of Women. Indeed, for this entire generation the problem of how to live a heroic life in the un-heroic modern world was a major concern. Thoreau first became interested in the problem this fall.[4]

To most people, then or now, bravery means physical courage first, and Thoreau used this expectation to begin what he called "A chapter on Bravery" with dashes of characteristic and characteristically unsatisfying paradox. "Bravery deals not so much in resolute action, as in healthy and assured rest. Its palmy state is staying at home. . . . One moment of serene and confident life is more glorious than a whole campaign of daring." He retold such anecdotes as the one in which "Samuel Johnson and his friend Savage, compelled by poverty to pass the night in the street, resolve that they will stand by their country," making it clear that what he admires here is the unwillingness to retreat into self-pity, even at three o'clock in the morning.[5]

This is clearly as valuable a trait for the poet or scientist as for the soldier, but, as this and the previous examples suggest, the leading metaphor and the dominant figure in Thoreau's essay on bravery is in fact the figure of the soldier. "No pains are spared to do honor to the brave soldier," he notes. "All guilds and corporations are taxed to provide him with fit harness and equipment. . . . The skill of a city enchaces and tempers his sword blade. . . . Wherever he goes, music precedes and prepares the way for him. His life is a holiday and the contagion of his example unhinges the universe. . . . He is the one only man." As usual, Thoreau exploits the figure of the soldier for paradox. "The brave man never heareth the din of war," he claims, for example. But behind, and giving point to the paradoxes, Thoreau reveals a genuine and deep sympathy with the soldier. There is irony but no paradox when he writes, "Men have made war from a deeper instinct than peace." We may well suspect a sense of fun that revels in the mischievous when he says, "the soldier is the practical idealist—he has no sympathy with matter, he revels in the annihilation of it," but he seems quite serious when he writes, "I have a deep sympathy with war it so apes the gait and bearing of the soul."[6]

All this must at first seem utterly out of character in a man who has become symbolic of conscientious objection, passive resistance, opposition to the Mexican War. Thoreau as the peaceful saunterer, the bachelor of nature and of books comes down to us as the living antithesis of the military mind. But he did in fact admire the figure of the soldier, and we miss an important side of Thoreau if we miss this.

Of course, the very word *soldier* still conveyed in 1839 the courage and self-reliance of the American militiaman of the Revolutionary era—the grandfathers of Thoreau's generation, rather than the uniformed unit who has lost his individuality in the modern war machine. In addition, Thoreau had been reading Aeschylus, and had not missed the fact that the greatest of Greek dramatists was prouder of having fought at Marathon than of having written the *Prometheus Bound*. Even Baudelaire—rebel and introvert as we think of him—would say that "there were no great men save the poet, the priest and the soldier. The man who sings, the man who offers sacrifice, and the man who sacrifices himself. The rest are born for the whip."[7]

Supplementing and encouraging this not-yet-debased admiration for the soldier is a very bold philosophical position, the Roman Stoic's conception of life as a battle in which every man is a soldier. As Albert Salomon's brilliant short essay on Epictetus points out, "the Roman Stoics coined the formula vivere militare! (life is being a soldier). . . . For this reason all Roman Stoics apply military metaphors and images." Thoreau was, like Emerson, importantly indebted to Stoicism. The *Enchiridion* of Epictetus appeared on Thoreau's 1838–39 list of classical reading. And very much in the spirit of Epictetus is Thoreau's saying "we do all stand in the front rank of the battle every moment of our lives," and "Waterloo is not the only battle ground—as many and fatal guns are pointed at my breast now as are contained in the English arsenals," or, "Every man is a warrior when he aspires."[8]

The figure of the soldier is central in Thoreau, not incidental.

Along with his gentleness, his shyness, his emotionalism, his calm, and his wit, there was steel in Thoreau. Emerson said he thought Thoreau required some opposition, some challenge in order to feel himself. He could be stubborn and combative. No man has ever been less inclined than Thoreau to mollify listeners or readers with a mush of concession. And however much we may suspect that the figure of the soldier was mainly important to Thoreau as metaphor, we should not lose sight of the real sympathy with the actual qualities that make the soldier a valuable metaphor. There may have been just a touch of the Old Norse battle spirit in Thoreau. His defense of John Brown, his refusal to shrink from advocating violence upon occasion, his more than theoretical interest in the wild qualities in nature and human nature—these are all important and real aspects of his character. He was not a yielding man; there was an inner hardness in him. He once advised a close friend, Harrison Blake, "if he could not do hard tasks, to take the soft ones, and when he liked anything, if only it was a picture or tune, to stay by it, and find out what he liked, and draw that sense or meaning out of it, and do *that*: harden it, somehow, and make it his own."[9]

This effort to grasp something, harden it, and make it thereby one's own is one way to describe the kind of soldierly quality Thoreau admired, the courage to live deeply and suck the marrow out of life. And so natural is the figure of the soldier as an expression of this that Thoreau has made it acceptable to us without our being aware of it. His single best remembered saying is, "If a man does not keep pace with his companions, perhaps it is because he hears a different drummer." In our interest to determine which drummer we ourselves are marching to, we forget that only soldiers march to drums at all.[10]

17. Transcendentalism

In 1833 Frederic Henry Hedge had published an article on Coleridge in the March issue of *The Christian Examiner*. Sharply critical of "the doings and not doings" of Coleridge himself, the essay was the first clear, unambiguous defense of modern German thought in America, and it delighted Emerson, who called the essay "a living, leaping logos." Hedge's father was a professor at Harvard, Hedge himself was very much involved in the new ideas of Kant and Schelling, and when, in 1835, he brought himself to accept a distant pulpit in Bangor, Maine, his desire to stay in touch with Boston and Cambridge led him to organize little get-togethers with like-minded people whenever he got up to Boston. Beginning in September 1836 with George Putnam, George Ripley, Hedge, and Emerson, the little group, known initially as "Hedge's Club," quickly expanded. A second meeting followed after an interval of only eleven days. Included were Orestes Brownson, James Freeman Clarke, Convers Francis, and Bronson Alcott; others, such as Theodore Parker, Margaret Fuller, Elizabeth Peabody, and Henry Thoreau came to be included later.[1]

Although they did not always agree on all issues—what group of reformers does?—they had a great deal in common. They were all young; at forty-one, Convers Francis was the oldest. There was a marked reform cast to their talk; they wanted a vehicle, a journal, for their views and they agreed on the importance—if not the details—of the new movement in German thought, thus ensuring that before long they would find themselves labeled transcendentalists. Because of the popular connotations of the word *transcendental*, it might have been better for the group to have called themselves American idealists. But the term is not inaccurate, nor was there widespread disagreement in educated circles as to what it meant. A writer in *The Dial* defined transcendentalism as "the recognition in man of the capacity of knowing truth intuitively." It was widely accepted that while the transcendental philosophy corroborated and infused new vitality into many other forms of thought—Platonism, Neoplatonism, mysticism, Eastern thought, French eclecticism, Goethean classicism, Stoicism, and the ideas of Gale, More, Pordage, Cudworth, and Berkeley—the immediate source of the present ferment of reappraisal was to be sought in one place above all others. The first history of the movement, written by the son of one of those involved, roundly declares that "The Transcendental Philosophy, so called, had a distinct origin in Immanuel Kant, whose *Critique of Pure Reason* was published in 1781, and opened a new epoch in metaphysical thought." Emerson himself gave the most lucid account in an 1842 address:

It is well known to most of my audience that the Idealism of the present day acquired the name of transcendental, from the use of that term by Immanuel Kant of Konigsburg, who replied to the skeptical philosophy of Locke which insisted that there was nothing in the intellect which was not previously in the experience of the senses, by showing that there was a very important class of ideas, or imperative forms, which did not come by experience, but through which experience was acquired: that these were intuitions of the mind itself; and he denominated them *Transcendental* forms. The extraordinary profoundness and precision of that man's thinking have given vogue to his nomenclature, in Europe and America, to that extent, that whatever belongs to the class of intuitive thought is popularly called at the present day *Transcendental*.[2]

The American idealists did not, singly or in a group, make a perceptible contribution to the development of German idealism. They pioneered no advance in metaphysics or epistemology. Insofar as the technical problem of knowledge concerned them, it was as it affected language and the communication of knowledge, and the New England group was a fertile one in ideas about the symbolic aspects of language. But their overriding interest was in the ethical implications of the new subjectivism. In ways that prefigure William James and pragmatism, they asked what the practical implications of the new ideas were for life and writing. Thus the great—and to a large extent still unrecognized—achievement of the transcendentalists as a group, and Parker and Ripley, Fuller and Peabody, Emerson and Thoreau in particular, was in working out the ethical implications of transcendentalism and making them widely accessible and, above all, liveable.[3]

It is therefore ironic that as a group they were thought—then as now—to have their heads in the clouds, to be impractical and otherworldly, vague, dreamy, and concerned with things that were neither real nor tangible. This was the indictment brought by State Street and Harvard College then, and the charges have never been completely withdrawn. But their ideas threatened institutions such as State Street, Harvard College, and the Unitarian Establishment, and the transcendentalists were, singly and as a group, more radical and more socially and politically activist than such writers as Poe, Hawthorne, or Melville, who held older, darker views of man and nature. Most of the transcendentalists found that the ethical consequences of transcendental idealism impelled them into social, political, and intellectual reform.

New England transcendentalists stressed individual autonomy and freedom rather than individual isolation or solipsism. They believed too that human nature in general is revealed to each person through his own nature in particular. So, while it was of course always possible for one to become lost or alienated, wandering in the "splendid labyrinth of [his] perceptions," it was neither desired nor approved. Instead, the strong ethical imperatives of New England transcendentalism led its members more often into the world than away from it.[4]

As the group was first forming, its members discussed eagerly the need for a journal, a practical vehicle for their views, and in the fall of 1838 they took active steps to make the journal a reality. Margaret Fuller would be the editor, and Emerson would also take a major hand, undertaking negotiations with publishers, promising to write for every issue, and engaging Fuller in endless correspondence as he canvassed friends and extorted manuscripts from Thoreau, Channing, Cranch, Alcott, and others. Emerson was looking for steady contributors, and he had his eye on Thoreau. Emerson and Thoreau were reading each other's poetry this fall and winter. Emerson obtained Thoreau's "Elegy" (probably the poem later printed as "Sympathy") for the new journal, and in March of 1840 he wrote Margaret Fuller that he would "now seriously ask [Thoreau] to give his aid" to the new enterprise. Alcott, another potential contributor, moved to Concord this month and in the literary excitement that bubbled up with the spring runoff Thoreau showed Emerson his essay on Persius. Emerson thought it very fresh and original, and though Thoreau had "too mean an opinion" of it to want to revise it, Emerson thought it well worth "the pains of a little blotting and sandpaper." Thoreau came around when he saw Emerson was serious, working on revisions while Emerson pressed Margaret Fuller to accept it for *The Dial*. She did not particularly like the essay, and she resisted accepting it by saying nothing. Emerson took every occasion to push the Persius piece, bringing up Thoreau's name with stubborn frequency. Though he conceded there was too much manner and too little method in the piece, he insisted it had "so much brilliancy and life in it that in our bold bible for The Young America, I think it ought to find a place."[5]

Still no softening, no concession, no word even, from the editor. Emerson kept pushing; he was nothing if not loyal. Finally, exasperated, he broke out in terms that forced the issue. "I want you to print Persius in the first number," he wrote Margaret. "Can you not, will you not, if it is good?" Bowing to the inevitable, she wrote back a long letter, one small sentence of which indicated, without enthusiasm, that Thoreau's Persius would go in the first issue of *The Dial*. There was no resisting Waldo Emerson when he had his mind made up.[6]

Emerson prized the satiric streak in Thoreau's talk and it was no accident that out of the 1840 list of possible subjects (love, sound and silence, Horace, Greek Poetry, The Brave Man, Memoirs of a Tour— a Chit-chat with Nature, Music) the essay Thoreau relinquished to *The Dial* under the vigorous prodding of his friend was one of two contemplated essays on Roman satire. Persius (A.D. 34–62), a contemporary of Nero, had died at twenty-eight after writing the six short satires by which he is remembered. Praised and translated by Dryden, Persius was, with Juvenal, a standard figure in the classical curriculum, a poet famous for obscurity, harsh attacks, and a passionate and consistent Stoicism that moved Dryden to a long salute to "the most noble, most generous, most beneficial . . . amongst all the sects." Thoreau's opening estimate of Persius is close to Dryden's. Persius is to be considered well below Horace, he and Juvenal are "measured fault-finders," his poems are "unmusical bickering with the follies of men." Where Dryden praised "the harsh cadence of a rugged line," Thoreau pointedly distinguishes Persius's kind of satire from that poetry or music which "remoulds language." Persius's is the kind of "satire [that] will not be sung." The trouble, Thoreau says, is that Persius is too negative, dwells too much on what is bad. This is far from a rejection of satire: Thoreau carefully praises Horace, saying he "would not have written satire so well, if he had not been inspired by it, as by a passion, and fondly cherished his vein." There is, he thought, more love than hate in Horace's odes. The same would in time be true of Thoreau's own satiric efforts.[7]

In the second section of the essay Thoreau switches abruptly from a consideration of written satire to what he calls a life of satire. "The divinest poem, or the life of a great man, is the severest satire, as impersonal as nature herself." Emerson had said the best use of the past was to regard our own life as the text, with books as the commentary. Not content simply to compare Persius with Horace, Thoreau was trying to ask what Persius has to say to those of the current generation who are trying to live their beliefs as well as write about them. With the cool effrontery of an Ezra Pound, Thoreau declares that there are perhaps twenty good lines in Persius of permanent as opposed to historical interest. Ignoring the elegant shipwreck trope Dryden so admired in the sixth satire, Thoreau gives the main weight of his essay to a careful reading of seven of those lines. Two lines, "It is not easy for every one to take murmurs and low / Whispers out of the temple—*et aperto vivere voto*—and live with open vow," permit Thoreau to insist on the distinction between the "man of true religion" who finds his open temple in the whole universe, and the "jealous privacy" of those who try to "carry on a secret commerce with the gods" whose hiding place is in some building. The distinction is between the open religion of the fields and woods, and the secret, closed religion of the churches.

Thoreau's best point takes a rebuke from the third satire against the casual life, against living *ex tempore*, and neatly converts it into a Thoreauvian paradox. Taking *ex tempore* literally, Thoreau discards its sense of offhand improvisation and takes it as a summons to live outside time, to live more fully than our ordinary consciousness of chronological time permits. "The life of a wise man," says Thoreau, "is most of all extemporaneous, for he lives out of an eternity which includes all time." Interpreting Persius through the lens of Emerson's "History," Thoreau contends that "all questions rely on the present for their solution. Time measures nothing but itself." Thoreau's Persius has gone beyond Stoicism to transcendentalism, insisting on open religious feelings as opposed to closed institutional dogmatic creeds, and on a passionate articulation of the absolute value of the present moment.[8]

18. Summer 1840

Even as Ellen had figured in the boat trip on the Merrimack the year before, so her next visit to Concord, in June of 1840, set Thoreau thinking of the trip and sent him back to his notes as he began to work up his account of the excursion. He wrote some descriptive passages, including some good ones on sounds. He remembered the sounds of a country drummer beating through the darkness as if "to wake the whole world to march to its melody." Even more than sights and sounds, he was exploring ideas this summer, and his notebooks now show, for the first time, some of the characteristic ideas of the volume he would eventually publish as *A Week on the Concord and Merrimack Rivers*. He explores religion as social ligature, something constricting and limiting, and he now first looks to the earliest history, to prehistory, as expressed in myth and in primitive poetry, for a better, earlier, more satisfying account of the world. Besides these themes, others equally fundamental to the finished *Week* were coming together as Thoreau struggled to make something of the meager events of the actual trip. As if to counterbalance his currently strong philosophical interests, he reminded himself that "our life is not all moral. Surely its actual phenomena deserve to be studied impartially."[1]

Between the ideas and the observations, the fundamental, shaping idea for what would become the book was now emerging. Thoreau's journal for March 21 celebrates the vernal equinox with an exuberant outburst on travel:

> By another spring I may be a mail carrier in Peru—or a South American planter—or a Siberian exile—or a Greenland whaler, or a settler on the Columbia River—or a Canton merchant—or a soldier in Florida—or a mackerel fisher of Cape Sable—or a Robinson Crusoe in the Pacific—or a silent navigator of any sea—So wide is the choice of parts.

There was, to be sure, little enough likelihood to most of these— Thoreau is not declaring an intent to travel or to seek his fortune abroad. The point, he was realizing, was that he was free to choose where or whether to go. He was not obliged to stay put. "Thank fortune we are not rooted to the soil and here is not all the world," he went on. "Shall we not compete with the buffalo who keeps pace with the seasons—cropping the pastures of the Colorado till a greener and sweeter grass awaits him by the Yellowstone." And if he was free to travel and free to choose, he now saw clearly and for the first time the desired direction of his travels. "Our limbs indeed have room enough but it is our souls that rust in a corner. Let us migrate interiorly without intermission, and pitch our tent each day nearer the western horizon."[2]

Self-discovery, self-conquest, interior migration; this was the structuring principle not only for *A Week on the Concord and Merrimack Rivers*, but for much of the rest of Thoreau's life. By the middle of August this perspective had deepened and was finding expression in well-turned phrases closer now to his mature style. "To travel and 'descry new lands' is to think new thoughts, and have new imaginings. In the spaces of thought are the reaches of land and water over which men go and come. The landscape lies fair within." And in November he wrote, hopefully, "the biography of a man who has spent his days in a library, may be as interesting as the Peninsular campaigns."[3]

Much of his own time this spring and summer was spent indoors reading, if not exactly in a library. His journal is full of references to Aristotle, Euripedes, Xenophon, Thales, and Plotinus. He was working his way slowly through Cudworth's *True Intellectual System of the Universe*. He had become interested in philosophy, and he was beginning to read for system, starting with Cudworth during the spring and early summer, and going on to Fénelon's *Vies des Philosophes* in July, and Degerando's *Histoire comparée* in the fall.[4]

Cudworth had been a leading figure among the seventeenth-century Cambridge Platonists. He had been friendly to the Commonwealth, he was not mystically inclined, and his great work, with its irresistible title, had several points of appeal for Thoreau. Cudworth's overriding aim had been, in the words of a nineteenth-century account contemporary with Thoreau, "to establish the liberty of human actions against the fatalists." The long and famous fourth chapter endeavors to refute Hobbes by showing that a primitive monotheism was implicit in ancient paganism. Among other bits of evidence, Thoreau's attention was caught by the orphic fragments from Proclus's commentary on Plato's *Timaeus*, in which the religious awe and devotionalism one usually associates with hymns to the Christian God are instead directed to Zeus:

Zeus was first, Zeus last—the thunderer;
Zeus the head, Zeus the middle; and all things were made from Zeus;
Zeus was a male, Zeus was an immortal maid;
Zeus the basis of the earth and of the starry heaven.

Thoreau was fascinated with the lines and the idea: he sought out a better text (in Eusebius's *Praeparationis Evangelicae*), translating and retranslating Proclus's praise of "the ruler of all" in whom were centered "Fire, and water, and earth, and ether, and night, and day / And Intelligence, progenitor, and Love causing much delight."[5]

Attributed to Orpheus, the lines reveal as few other surviving classical passages do (the description of the appearance of Isis in Apuleius cited by Margaret Fuller in *Woman in the Nineteenth Century* [1845] is another) how Greek myth expressed the religious attitudes of the Greeks. Proclus's Orphic lines may sound strongly analogous to Christian praise of God, and doubtless Thoreau responded to its appeal to the all-powerful father of all by whatever name, but he would also note in *A Week* that Zeus was in some ways preferable to Jehovah, being less exclusively male and much more nearly identified with nature. Thoreau may have had residual or environmental impulses toward Christianity. Certainly no one in his time and place could altogether avoid Christian acculturation, but consciously he was by now seeking a wider, older, specifically Greek basis for his own religious response to the world.[6]

The summer of 1840 was busy and exciting for the Concord circle around Emerson. The much-discussed journal became the reality of *The Dial*; everyone was buoyed up with a sense of purpose and enterprise. Emerson and Margaret Fuller wrote letters back and forth on editorial matters. Emerson was working on his essay on "Circles," and he was editing Channing's poetry. Though he spoke of being solitary, and indeed of his need for solitude, his letters at this time have unusual warmth and show a remarkable emotional expressiveness. Margaret Fuller had a way of emphasizing—indeed of insisting—that those around her be open, honest, and committed emotionally. She was not only unafraid of strong emotions, she liked them, made them a central subject of hers, and drew others to talk about them as well. Emerson's tone with her could be tender, praising, grateful, or confessional, but it was usually warm. One wonders what his wife Lydia (Lidian) thought of those letters.

Thanks my dear Margaret, for your good letter of Wednesday, and thanks evermore to you and to our friends and to the Framer and inspirer of all beauty and love, for the joy I have drawn and do still draw from these flying days—I shall never go quite back to my old arctic habits—I shall believe that nobleness is love, and delights in showing itself.[7]

The Dial appeared early in July. In dull brown wrappers, it looked like *The Christian Examiner* or any other current journal. Emerson thought its design cautious, its typography cramped—the poetry was set too small—and he confessed that after all the brave talk about a bold new journal, it was a bit too tame; not daring enough, he thought, "to scare the tenderest bantling of Conformity." Nevertheless it was a reality, and the group responsible for it was in its heyday. The transcendental club was going strong; the circle was expanding, more women were being included. George Ripley, tired of talking about reform in the pulpit, resigned from his church in late May in order to pursue his ideas in a more practical and effectual way. Among other possibilities, Ripley, Alcott, and Emerson were considering starting a new college. The hour for social reform seemed to have struck. Anything was possible. In a few months, the idea of Brook Farm would begin to materialize. The air was full of new beginnings.[8]

With the appearance of *The Dial*, Thoreau was a published writer. His work was in demand, at least by Emerson, and he was busy working on a variety of new subjects. He was twenty-three this month. As John went off to Scituate to propose and be turned down by Ellen Sewall, Thoreau was being carried along on the crest of the literary wave around him and within him. His journal is rich and varied and alive. He writes on heroism, on crusades, on enthusiasm, on the divine in man, on music, on art, on the glorious tonic of morning. With John's rejection by Ellen, Thoreau might now have a chance with her. Added to that, his literary career now seemed a possibility. He was filled with hope, and now for the first time he notes in his journal the phrase that became one of his most characteristic refrains,

"surely joy is the condition of life."[9]

19. Fall 1840

Much of Thoreau's reading during the summer and fall of 1840 was in surveys, histories, and collections of philosophy, as though he was trying to get an overview of the subject. From Cudworth's synoptic and sweeping *True Intellectual System of the Universe*, Thoreau went in July to Fénelon's *Vies des Philosophes*. Cudworth led him to Proclus and the Orphic, Fénelon to Solon, Pittacus, and Bias. Later, in September, he was working on Degerando's *Histoire comparée des systèmes de philosophie*, a book and a writer much in favor with many of the transcendentalists. In this work, too, Thoreau's interest centered in Greek thought, especially that of Thales. Clearly Thoreau was out to acquaint himself not only with Greek philosophy but with a variety of modern attempts to outline and systematize it.[1]

One of the reasons for the popularity of Degerando at this time was that in the second, 1822 edition of this book he had gone to great length to rewrite his earlier 1804 version so as to take account of the new interest in oriental thought so evident in such famous books as Creuzer's *Symbolik und Mythologie den alten Volker*. . . . This may not have been Thoreau's immediate reason for picking up Degerando, but this summer does mark his first serious engagement in Eastern thought and writing.

Thoreau had had a trickle of interest in the Orient—which meant, for the most part, in this era the Middle East. In 1834 he had read al-Asma'i's *Antar, a Bedoueen romance* and in 1837 he read Hammer-Purgstall's version of an ancient Persian romance, "Wamik and Asra." During the summer of 1838 he refers casually to Confucius and to the *Zendavesta*, the ancient sacred books of the Zoroastrians of Persia. But now in August of 1840, his curiosity shifted from Persia to India, and he began to read up on Hindustan with the thoroughness that was becoming habitual with him. He read Hugh Murray's *History and Descriptive Account of British India*, Ockley's *History of the Saracens* and Camoëns's *Lusiads*, the great sixteenth-century Portuguese epic about Vasco da Gama's discovery of India.

The book that really moved Thoreau this summer, however, was not one of these Western accounts of India, but one of India's own great texts, *The Laws of Menu*, with the gloss of Colucca, translated and published by Sir William Jones. From this volume Thoreau got firsthand (or as close to firsthand as anyone could then get in an America that did not teach Sanscrit in any of its universities) his earliest convincing demonstration that there had existed in ancient India a philosophical and religious culture as high and worthy as the Judeo-Christian, a culture of which the West had been almost completely unaware until the closing decades of the eighteenth century. By now Thoreau had also become aware of the claim—articulated by Friedrich Schlegel, and very much in the air at the time, but also available from Creuzer via Degerando—that the human race and all human culture had originated in the Orient. In the August heat of 1840, he began to record the thoughts stirred in him by *The Laws of Menu*: "In Imagination I seem to see there the grey temples and hoary brow of the earth. The great plain of India lies like a cup between the Himmaleh and the ocean, on the north and south—and the Indus and the Brahmapoutra, on the east and west, wherein the primeval race was received—as if it were the cradle of the human race."[2]

Thoreau's notebook entries this August were full of crucial insights, to be worked and reworked later. As usual, his interest in great philosophical truths or historical insight was kept down to earth, literally grounded, in his love of common natural facts. "I like to read of the 'pine, larch, spruce, and silver fir' which cover the southern face of the Himmaleh range," he wrote. Also, as usual, he strove to understand ancient India as no different, in essentials, from modern New England. Rather than regard Menu's book as "the whims of an Asiatic brain," he preferred to "imagine that this fair modern creation is only a reprint of the Laws of Menu."[3]

All his reading for this summer and fall of 1840 has a common thread, and that is the demonstration that the Bible-centered Judeo-Christian worldview was neither the only nor even necessarily the best account of things. As he found the ethical idealism of Greek philosophy still as applicable as Christian ethics, so he found the laws of Menu fully comparable with the laws of Moses as a culture-founding document. During the fall he also read Gibbon's *Autobiography* and Lyell's *Principles of Geology*, noting grimly of the latter that it is hard "to convince a man of an error. . . . It took 100 years to prove that fossils are organic, and 150 more, to prove that they are not to be referred to the Noachian deluge." Perhaps one reason why Darwin's *Origin of Species* made the impact it did on Thoreau and others in Concord when they read it shortly after publication in 1859 was that Thoreau had for many years understood the implications for biblical authority of the developmental or evolutionary argument. He had been keenly aware of the limitations and drawbacks of taking an exclusively Christian worldview since at least 1840.[4]

If his reading this summer and fall involved the exploration and mapping of large new worlds of ideas, his own writing was also seeking new forms and materials. He was encouraged by the publication of the Persius piece and the poem "Sympathy" in *The Dial*, he was cheered by Emerson's support, but still very uncertain of what direction to take. He read little poetry this year and the few poems he wrote are not, with one exception, among his best. They show a rather conventional romantic youth, somewhat understandably inclined to complain. The lamenting verses are in naked, almost comic contrast to the prose, which keeps hammering on the themes of bravery and action. A poem written in March begins "Two years and twenty now have flown / I only still am poor within; / The birds have sung their summer out, / But still my spring does not begin." And in August he was still feeling idly disengaged, culpably unheroic. After beginning "When with pale cheek and sunken eye I sang / . . . How in these days no hero was abroad, / but puny men," the complaint turns back self-punishingly on himself. He hears a "reproachful" strain, sees, in imagination, a great "embattled host" and concludes bitterly, "For I alone had slumbered at my post, dreaming of peace when all around was war." This mood produced one fine poem. Called "Sic Vita," it is direct, colloquial, elegantly rhymed, and carelessly formal:

> I am a parcel of vain strivings tied
>> By a chance bond together,
> Dangling this way and that, their links
>> Were made so loose and wide,
>>> Methinks,
>> For milder weather.

As Emerson so shrewdly saw, Thoreau's biography—or at least one part of it—is in his poems, for he was still dreaming of verse when all around was prose. His 1840 poems reveal the self-doubt and dejection his prose works and even his journal jottings seem determined to overcome. He still believed that "the highest morality . . . is rhymed," that the greatest writings and scriptures would always be poetry, but even now his own poetry was mainly confessional; through it he took himself to task and worked out his doubts and feelings of weakness. His prose was already the medium with which he could fight back. Individual phrases and sentences, better now than anything in his verses, appear in the journal with increasing frequency. "All fair action in man is the product of enthusiasm," or "I find myself always in the rear of my eye," or "for I measure distance inward and not outward. Within the compass of a man's ribs there is space and scene enough for any biography." Writing poetry revealed the emotions and the wishes Thoreau could not help feeling, but his prose lays down direction for the life he willed, the life he was setting out to create.[5]

Around the third week in August he began to make notes about the life and writings of Sir Walter Raleigh, that symbol of Elizabethan romance and daring. Thoreau liked Raleigh's courage, especially when cornered or challenged in a courtroom. He liked his soldierly self-confidence, his ability to be both fighter and writer. His writing had a boldness it could only have gotten from life, Thoreau thought, and from a life that was, above all else, active. But he made only a few preliminary notes on Raleigh now; his main prose piece this year was an essay called "The Service." Called earlier "A chapter on Bravery," Thoreau had written and rewritten it, filling his journal with material for it even after it was finished. The subject was a good one for him, that of heroism, by which he meant the autonomous, courageous, self-reliant, freestanding individual. From one point of view, it is Thoreau's only major theme. But his early treatment is too Emersonian, too abstract, too much a tissue of forced cleverness and elusive sayings all trying to capture and describe a very vague, completely generalized figure, the recruit or new soldier entering the service for the wars of life. The essay, like that on Persius, is too gnomic, too cryptic, and impossibly hard to follow. Eventually, the Raleigh notes would suggest that a better way to handle the subject would be to use a real tangible historical person as the center, rather than a vague abstraction. But however forced the organization, however precious the writing, there can be no doubt that the subject of courage held Thoreau fascinated, almost fixated, for most of 1840. Emerson too was working on the same subject all this fall; it would eventually be his essay on "Self-Reliance." Emerson had also been invited by George Ripley to become a charter member of his new experiment in communal living, and he was having an unusually hard time deciding whether to accept.[6]

Thoreau too felt caught between things. There was family, there was Ellen, there was Emerson, there were others such as Alcott. What did he owe to others, what to himself? His essay bristles with assertions of the need for bravery, with the utter contemptibleness of cowardice. Despite the ill-advised soldier metaphor that he could not bring himself to drop, this essay too is on self-reliance, quoting as epigraph Virgil (Each one his own hope) and starting out with oracular, Vedic pomp. "The brave man is the elder son of creation, who has stept boyantly into his inheritance, while the coward, who is the younger, waiteth patiently till he decease."[7]

On the first of November, 1840, the younger son in the Thoreau household got up his courage and wrote a proposal of marriage to Ellen Sewall.

> I thought that the sun of our love should have risen as noiselessly as the sun out of the sea, and we sailors have found ourselves steering between the tropics as if the broad day had lasted forever. You know how the sun comes up from the sea when you stand on the cliff, and doesn't startle you, but every thing, and you too are helping it.

On November 9 Ellen received instructions from her father and wrote rejecting Thoreau. The letter, arriving on or about the eleventh, found him with a new leveling device surveying places near the river, and measuring and recording heights. Only two days earlier he had written, "I measure distance inward and not outward." Now, suddenly, everything was reversed. Outward measurement was less painful. His journal appears to have dried up; there are no entries for the last half of November. On December 1, Margaret Fuller wrote a letter rejecting "The Service" for *The Dial*. He had had, interestingly enough, some premonition of these losses or setbacks. On November 7 he had written, "I did not think so bright a day would issue in so dark a night." Only a short while before he had been convinced that "joy was the condition of life." Now, in his dismay at being rejected as a lover by Ellen and as a writer by Margaret Fuller, he might feel that the major metaphor of "The Service" was more apt. Life was perpetual warfare, he had just lost two major battles, and what was needed now, as always, was courage.[8]

20. December 1840

Having the essay rejected hurt Thoreau's pride, and perhaps his self-confidence as a writer; losing Ellen Sewall was a deeper, more serious loss, hitting him emotionally, on a side of his nature for which he had no satisfactory outlet, no ready means of expression. He could not turn, as he had often before, to poetry—or if he could, he didn't. As if to compensate for losing her and for the injustice he felt, he turned, this December, not inward but outward to the natural world for the emotional support that was missing in his human world. This compensating turn was not a sweeping rejection of the human. All through December his journal records frequent observations of obvious sincerity on such topics as friendship, the feminine, society. But added to these now is a strongly felt and, more important, a powerfully expressed understanding of external nature as it appealed to the senses and as it made a claim on his emotions.

With exuberance and a joyous, almost physical hunger he went for long walks in the winter woods, and avidly took in the migrating otter tracks, the young pines springing up in the corn fields. Everything was striking, beautiful, sustaining. "In the fields lights and shadows are my diet. How all trees tell of the sun. . . . Nothing is so beautiful as the tree tops." He had always loved the out-of-doors, had always felt literally dependent on it. In college and after, he had to have his walk every day. It was a physical and an emotional necessity for which he now began to find adequate words. "I should wither and dry up if it were not for lakes and rivers," he wrote. He thirsted for the pond up there in the woods. He felt literally "invigorated by the cones and needles of the pine seen against the frosty air."[1]

He had every right, this December, to feel let down, unsupported, and misjudged. Nature alone seemed constant, supportive, able in some way to return his affection and trust. "When most at one with nature," he wrote, "I feel supported and propped on all sides by myriad influences." The Schellingian and Emersonian idea that nature is the externalization of the mind, mind the internalization of nature, now had new appeal for him. "The opposite shore of the pond seen through the haze of a September afternoon, as it lies stretched out in grey content, answers to some streak in me," he wrote in his journal. He has more than a theory of nature in mind. It is the green world itself—leaf, wing, ripple, and reed—that he cares for and responds to. But nature itself means nothing, says nothing except to the perceiving mind. "Beauty is where it is perceived," Thoreau wrote carefully in mid-December. "When I see the sun shining on the woods across the pond, I think this side the richer which sees it." Nature is not an escape from humanity. Nature mirrors and returns his acceptance, giving him back his own projected humanity. When he looked out he saw nature plain, but he also saw himself. "So the forest," he concluded, "is full of attitudes, which give it character. In its infinite postures I see my own erectness, or humbleness—or sneaking."[2]

Nature was always real and tangible for Thoreau; it was also always a text to be read and enjoyed in all its aspects. Even the blank whiteness which so frightens Melville's Ishmael is something Thoreau relishes. "This plain sheet of snow which covers the ice of the pond," he noted on the nineteenth of December, "is not such a blancness as is unwritten, but such as is unread. All colors are in white. It is such simple diet to my senses as the grass and the sky."[3]

Thoreau's other text in the closing days of 1840 was Virgil. The *Georgics* has lost much of its once-great popularity. Dryden could call it the best poem by the best poet. Thoreau never showed much interest in the *Aeneid*, always preferring the *Georgics*. It was for him the great poem of Earth. So detailed that it has often been mistaken for a farming manual, it is the praise of farming, and it is easy to see why Thoreau loved it. It tells how to distinguish good soil from bad, how to make plow handles (bend an elm sapling into the desired shape and let it grow thus to the desired thickness), how to graft fruit trees (insert a scion into a knife cut at the point where a new shoot is coming out of the trunk), how to plow, weed, irrigate, make a hard threshing floor, how to plant and tend vines, how to keep bees, and much more. It is a cornucopia of vivid detail and plain examples, and the agricultural world it describes is remarkably similar to that of the American farmers Thoreau knew. It was certainly a more immediately recognizable world than that of the *Aeneid*.[4]

The *Georgics* is also the great poem of labor. Jove brought the Golden Age to an end so that man might have to work in order to earn and savor the good things won through work. What is really celebrated in the poem is humankind's whole laborious tenure and tillage of the earth. Virgil is a realist who believes in work, and in the rewards and satisfactions work brings. Virgil's farmer is hardworking, thisworldly, self-sufficient, and content. Thoreau's own attitude toward labor is in general much closer to this Virgilian work ethic than to the more famous, more ascetic, Protestant work ethic. Virgil was useful to Thoreau in other ways too. The *Georgics* used a seasonal organization, and more than any other single work, it showed Thoreau just how much detail was required to sustain a literary work designed to convey the feel of the land. He was very well aware of what Virgil had achieved. "It is great praise in the poet to have made husbandry famous."[5]

This December Emerson was slowly "and I may almost say penitentially" bringing himself to say no to George Ripley's pressing invitation to join the Brook Farm experiment, which was about to be launched. Margaret Fuller was giving another of her brilliant conversation courses in Boston this winter; this one was on mythology. Thoreau's thoughts this month kept turning to Walden Pond. Early in December he wrote how "the thought of Walden in the woods yonder makes me supple jointed and limber for the duties of the day." And by the end of the month he was playing lightheartedly with the idea of Walden as his cup of tea and writing an introduction that, with its Hawthorne-like or fairy-tale tone, reads like the start of something to be called The Legend of Walden Pond.

In a little hollow between the hills, some twenty feet higher than the village, lies Walden pond, the expressed juice of the hills and trees whose leaves are annually steeped in it. Its history is in the lapse of its waves, in the rounded pebbles on its shore, and the pines which have grown on its brink.[6]

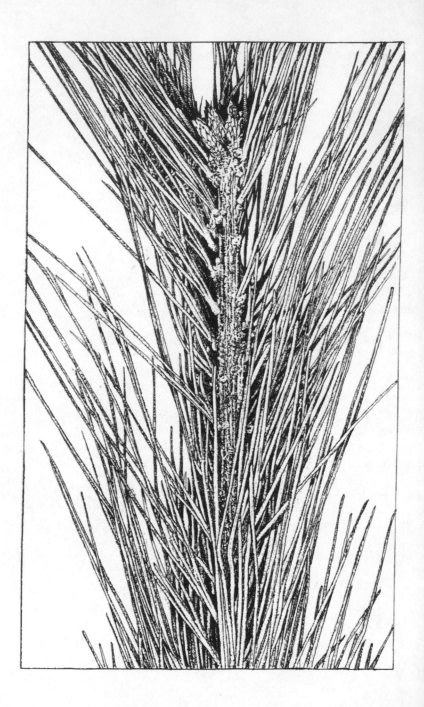

III. 1841-1843

American Reformation

21. Writing

By EARLY 1841, THOREAU was having his poems accepted and published in *The Dial* on a more or less regular basis. Margaret Fuller might be less than wholly enthusiastic, Emerson would soon cool about his young friend's verse, but for all that, Thoreau could now regard himself as a poet. He was faring less well with his prose. His essay on Persius had been published in July of the preceding year; it would be two years before another prose piece saw print. The rejection of "The Service," on which he had worked for almost a year, was a setback, but it had one side benefit. It set Thoreau seriously to work on his writing style. In the early months of 1841 his journal began to expand considerably on this subject. He also began to keep a separate notebook for copying down passages from his reading.[1]

The journal was for his own observations and original thoughts, the place in which he made, he said, "a huge effort to expose my innermost and richest wares to light." The other notebook was for memorable bits from his reading; he would record such things as Raleigh's "to the perfection of men three things are necessarily required; nature, nurture, and use," or from the *London Monthly Magazine*, "And take this with you, ye wretched doctrinaires . . . that all conclusions are heartless, of which the heart is not the premises." Ever attentive to both subject and expression, he noted thoughtfully in his own journal for January, "a perfectly healthy sentence is extremely rare." In addition to the new notebook and the expanded journalizing, Thoreau went back over and recopied into a new notebook all that remained or all that he wished to keep—still hundreds of pages—of his earlier journals. Mechanically at least, he did an enormous amount of writing during January and February, in the course of which he was moved frequently to reflect on the process of writing itself.[2]

Looking at some examples of daguerreotyping early in February, he compared the infant art of photography to that of writing. "We may easily multiply the forms of the outward," he noted, "but to give the within outwardness, that is not easy." Thoreau never abandoned his earlier insistence that, in descriptive writing, we must see the object being described, not merely hear the feelings of the describer. But appearances, however accurately described, could only be *significant* if they were in some way related to inner experience. Commenting on his own shortcomings as a writer later in the same month, he observed, "in composition I miss the hue of the mind." External, detached, objective, or photographic detail was not enough by itself. True to the conviction he now shared with Emerson, Thoreau struggled hard to articulate the connection between inner and outer worlds. "There is a relation between man and nature so that whatever is in matter is in mind," Emerson had written. Pursuing the connection in his journal for January, Thoreau could see that from a writer's point of view the primary impulse came from the mind. "It is more proper for a spiritual fact to have suggested an analogous natural one, than for the natural fact to have preceded the spiritual in our minds." Whatever problems this idea of correspondence posed as a theory of nature, it made great practical sense as a description of the writer's relation to his material and to his audience, as Emerson had seemed to recognize when he said in the "Language" chapter of *Nature*, "Particular natural facts are symbols of particular spiritual facts." Since it was also true for Emerson that words were signs of natural facts, his theory of language held that words were signs of signs. In other words, both language and nature were symbolic.[3]

However much this transcendental aesthetic pointed to the primacy of mind over both things and words, Thoreau never lost interest in words themselves. He loved language, loved to play with words. He owned a whole shelf of dictionaries, etymological, historical, pronouncing, dictionaries of Americanisms, of provincialisms, and of obsolete words. This zest and his genius for wordplay have reminded readers of James Joyce. Like Joyce, Thoreau labored at the craft of making language by breaking it down and building it up again. His fondness for paradox was carried so far so often it exasperated Emerson, who grumbled about Thoreau's trick of always using the opposite of the expected word. He would talk about the white darkness in the winter woods, or the household warmth of a snow-covered tree or claim "the most upright man is he that most entirely reclines." Thoreau might insist that he was expressing the paradoxical quality in human nature itself, but the expression comes close to being a predictable perversity, a mannerism, making stiff or querulous judgments by routinely standing things on their heads. More playful and less predictable was Thoreau's agile fascination with puns. There is a relaxed and sunny quality about these; he describes the "blancness" of a snow-covered scene, turns pansy into pensee, talks about "soular rays." It is the poet in Thoreau that pays such scrupulous attention to syllable and sound. "A true happiness never happened, but rather is proof against all haps." The practice, which became a habit, of roping in all available meanings would give his best writing a richly allusive texture asparkle with humor.[4]

He was also now beginning to try for a figural richness. Thoreau thought of metaphor and simile not as ornament but as a way to bring personal experience into one's writing. "The unpretending truth of a simile," he notes in his February journal, "implies sometimes such distinctness in the conception as only experience could have supplied." His literary images during these months ran to economics. The language of income and outgo, cost, profit, capital, and property was impossible to avoid during these depression years, and Thoreau took to using it, generally in fun, as a metaphor for the business of life. "The capital wanted," he wrote with mock solemnity, "is an entire independence upon all capital, but a clear conscience, and a resolute will."[5]

Thoreau was learning a great deal from Emerson and became closer to him during January and February of 1841. He now calls Emerson "master" and he talks engagingly and unguardedly about their friendship and his "recent growth." Thoreau was stirred by the flashing epigrammatic brilliance of Emerson's best work, but where the younger man already differed—and crucially—from Emerson was in the very high value he assigned to the written word. It has been said of Emerson with some justice that he distrusted language, found it always coming up short of the thought or feeling behind it. Thoreau almost never talks about the inadequacy of language. He tended to blame the poverty of the thought behind the language rather than the inadequacy of the language. When he had nothing to say, and that was often, he was silent, no matter how Emerson teased him about it or tried to draw him out. Thoreau wrote constantly, regularly; he was under no illusions about the ordinary quality of most of it. "Though I write every day," he confided to his journal, "yet when I say a good thing, It seems as if I wrote but rarely." He wanted to write "as well as the farmer talks," and he was only too aware that "very few men can speak of nature with any truth." But he was unencumbered by the illusion that a good style is innate or that it comes by itself, easily and naturally. He was (and Emerson here was a great help and a healthy example) willing to labor over his writing. He was also willing to be judged by the result. "Nothing goes by luck in composition," he noted warily, "it allows of no trick. The best you can write will be the best you are." No style in the living, no style in the writing.[6]

22. Thoreau and Emerson

During the winter months of 1841, Thoreau came under the spell of Emerson more completely than ever. Now thirty-seven, Emerson was at the peak of his early career. He was a popular and successful lecturer with one book out and another on the way. His addresses touched off public controversy, his fame spread rapidly. In England, Carlyle took pleasure in relating that Emerson's writings were being lumped together with Goethe's *Wilhelm Meister* and Schleiermacher's *Reden über Religion* as "aiming at an unchristian apotheosis of man." Emerson was now reckoned, said Carlyle, "among the chief Heresiarchs of the world," and he added, with obvious relish, "Perfectly right." Always in the middle of things, Emerson was handling Carlyle's American editions, bringing along young poets such as Jones Very, and coaxing contributions from everyone for *The Dial*, now an established magazine with its third number coming out in January. As for his own work, Emerson celebrated the new year by sending his volume of *Essays* to the printer. For the next two months he would be engaged in correcting batches of proofs.[1]

A young boy named Alex McCaffery had been living at the Emersons', helping out with chores. Emerson was not keen on having servants. He was, he said, trying to ameliorate or abolish menial labor in his household, and in its place he was trying to school himself to regular manual labor. He talked about getting a smaller house, for as things stood, he and Lydia needed some sort of help with the house and garden. The idea of a small company of friends living and working together was attractive to Emerson. There was some talk that Alcott might come to live with them.[2]

Thoreau this winter was more active than ever in the public affairs that were an increasingly lively part of Concord life. He and John were still conducting their small academy, but despite frequent ads in the newspapers, there were very few students. Both brothers were also active in the Lyceum; together they took the affirmative in a debate late in January with Alcott on "forcible resistance." A week later Thoreau went to see Tyrolean dancers; a day or two later he heard Adin Ballou (the founder of Hopedale, a utopian community in Mendon, Massachusetts) talk about "Non-Resistance." As he looked ahead, Thoreau must have guessed that the school would not long be a full-time matter for him. He began looking at farms, and considered renting some land. He was putting in long hours on his journal, his prose, and his poetry, and still thought of himself as primarily a poet. This winter he was reading Ben Jonson and Coleridge. He admired the tough moral thinker in Jonson; the Coleridge he admired was not the poet of "The Ancient Mariner" but the religious thinker and moralist, the transcendental idealist and author of *Aids to Reflection* and *The Statesman's Manual*. This was the Coleridge who had so deeply impressed Hedge and Emerson, the Coleridge who was the single most important interpreter of German idealism to the English speaking world.[3]

In Thoreau's reading and in his writing at this time the imprint of Emerson is everywhere. Emerson was reading and thinking about Goethe's *Theory of Colors* (Goethe was interested in the subjective aspects of color phenomena, in color as a function of the medium through which light is transmitted and received, in such things as how the blackness of space appears to us as blue sky), and Thoreau makes repeated references to white light and color in his journal. Emerson was correcting proofs of "History," "Self-Reliance," "Love," and "Friendship"; Thoreau's journals are filled with parallel observations. Emerson's themes were becoming Thoreau's. "The present seems never to get its due," Thoreau noted early in February. "All the past plays into this moment, and we are what we are." On another occasion he remarks on the concept of integrity and self-reliance: "There is something proudly thrilling in the thought that this obedience to conscience and trust in God, which is so solemnly preached in extremities and arduous circumstances, is only to retreat to one's self, and rely on our own strength." He wrote much more on self-reliance and history during January and February, but by far the dominant theme in Thoreau's journals for those months is friendship. Much of what he wrote sounds like Emerson's own essay on the subject, but it is also very clear that the ideas about friendship (what is wanted in a friend is not a double but a complement, friends should seek out the distances between them) were given emotional substance by the actual and now rapidly developing friendship between the two men. Thoreau's admiration for Emerson was, this winter, literally without bounds. He is entirely without his usual armor of bristling objection and defensive quirk, and is content for once to use the plain language of master and pupil. He refers to "my recent growth" and to how he is always having to "reach up" in order to take the good things offered by "my friend." And behind the admiration, the esteem, the frank and delighted recognition of Emerson's "greatness," a word Thoreau never used easily, lay a genuine acknowledgment of affection on both sides. Early in February Thoreau noted with wonder that "the world has never learned what men can build each other up to be— when both master and pupil work in love."[4]

Concord had a stretch of bitter winter weather in mid-February, the mercury not rising above twenty degrees for five days starting on the eleventh. By the thirteenth, Thoreau was down with a bad case of bronchitis, confined to bed and trying, as he said, not to let the sickness spread beyond the merely physical. Emerson too was low, if not actually down sick this month. He hated the drudgery of correcting proofs, "parsing and spelling and punctuating, and repairing rotten metaphors and bringing tropes safe into port." His children had the flu, Aunt Mary was ill, a maternal aunt had just died. Late in February Emerson came to visit the still-sick Thoreau; Thoreau was profoundly moved. His thoughts had been running on Emerson, on his "greatness," his generosity, on "the debateable ground between love and esteem," on how "nothing will reconcile friends but love." He had a sense of overwhelming good fortune in being Emerson's friend, knowing as well as he did how high Emerson held friendship. Emerson's visit—there must have been many, but this one was special—left Thoreau with the unutterable security and exaltation that comes when someone the world loves loves us. He wrote serenely, "Life looks as fair at this moment as a summers sea." He was content to be the pupil, the disciple of Emerson, because he was so much more. Emerson's essay on friendship maintains that there are two great requirements for friends. One is truth; friends must somehow avoid lies and deceptions even when these comfort. The other great requirement, Emerson says, is tenderness. Emerson wanted his friendships high and noble, but he also recognized and insisted on this essentially emotional quality in real relations between friends. Emerson gave Thoreau more than help, advice, and ideas, more even than a model of the writer with strong convictions—he gave a tender and affectionate concern. Thoreau recorded it all in his journal, which is for once emotionally wide open. Emerson's friendship was for Thoreau "an infusion of love from a great soul."[5]

Emerson and Thoreau both had complex ideas about what friendship should be. Both made such demands as to make it all but unattainable. But despite the nearly impossible ideal of comradeship and all their theorizing about the subject, it was not an abstract or literary or purely intellectual matter. Behind the ideas about friendship lay real friends. The writing was grounded in life. In friendship as in all else, the only writing that was worth doing would be anchored immovably in character. Two days after Emerson's visit, and with a reference to his friend's current labors, Thoreau wrote, "The best you can write will be the best you are. Every sentence is the result of a long probation—The author's character is read from title page to end—of this he never corrects the proofs."[6]

23. Brook Farm

Of the social and political issues that claimed the attention of the reading public in the early 1840s—and they included the English war with China, the American war with the Indians in Florida, the economic hard times, the condition of the laboring classes, the movement for women's rights, the question of resistance or nonresistance to government, and abolition—none was more attractive, more hopeful in tone than what was called the Association movement, the founding of new model communities by utopian socialists. Perhaps society could be reconstructed along better lines. After all, the grandparents of the 1840s generation had themselves taken part in the radical reshaping of society brought about by the French and American revolutions. The first historian of American utopian communities, John Humphrey Noyes, was the founder of one of the most famous of them, Oneida. He recognized the underlying significance of the movement when, in the 1860s, he wrote that "a yearning toward social reconstruction has become a part of the continuous, permanent, inner experience of the American People."[1]

Discontent with industrialism was already strong on both sides of the Atlantic. Marx and Engels would soon be heard from. The American phenomenon, not even approached in Europe, of more than forty model communities founded during the 1840s alone, was very much part of the times. The impulse to create communities was linked with the cause of nonviolence; most of the founders were more interested in building models, which would be emulated because they succeeded, than in the destruction of the existing order. Still, American utopian socialism had much in common with the spirit of 1848.

When Emerson's good friend, the Reverend George Ripley, seriously proposed to leave his church and set up a new community on a

160-acre milk farm in West Roxbury on the Newton line, he urged Emerson to join. Ripley wrote in November of 1840:

> Our objects are to insure a more natural union between intellectual and manual labor than now exists; to combine the thinker and the worker, as far as possible, in the same individual; to guarantee the highest mental freedom, by providing all with labor adapted to their tastes and talents, and securing to them the fruits of their industry; to do away with the necessity of menial services, by opening the benefits of education and the profits of labor to all; and thus to prepare a society of liberal, intelligent, and cultivated persons, whose relations with each other would permit a more simple and wholesome life than can be led amidst the pressures of our competitive institutions.

The project had strong appeal to Emerson. His own thought had a latent streak of communalism ("the mind common to the Universe is disclosed to the individual through his own nature"), and Ripley was a very close friend, a member of that "class of persons" for whom Emerson felt prepared to "go to prison if need be." Ripley had many claims on Emerson. He had written the best, most intellectually respectable defense of Emerson—linking him by still-impressive scholarship to Spinoza, Schleiermacher, and De Wette—when the Divinity School address had created havoc among Unitarians. Emerson was genuinely tempted; Ripley's plans were congenial, and Emerson's own letters for the coming month contain many echoes of Ripley's forthright statement of purpose. Yet, in the end, after much hesitation and soul-searching, Emerson said no. It was central to his own thought and writing that all significant reform must be a personal reform before it could be widened, and he did not want to lose the impulse to personal reform in a communal setting. Emerson finally made up his mind not to go in mid-December of 1840.[2]

On March 3, 1841—the eve of the actual beginning of the experiment—Thoreau was invited to join Brook Farm, as the community became known. In strong contrast to Emerson, the invitation posed no great problem for Thoreau. Though his school was failing and he did not know what he was going to do next, he rejected the invitation apparently without a moment's hesitation. "As for these communities," he wrote tartly to himself, "I think I had rather keep bachelor's hall in hell than go to board in heaven." He imagined (accurately, as it would turn out) the new community as a large boardinghouse sort of arrangement. Since his own home was as often as not a boarding-house in atmosphere and in fact, what with aunts, uncles, visitors, meetings, and actual boarders, Ripley's project held no novelty for Thoreau. Indeed his boardinghouse metaphor for Brook Farm is also another eloquent description of the side of him that already wanted to escape, to get off on his own. "The boarder has no home," he went on in his snap rejection of Ripley's project. "In heaven I hope to bake my own bread and clean my own linen. —The tomb is the only boarding house in which a hundred are served at once—in the catacomb we may dwell together and prop one another without loss."[3]

The first party of Brook Farmers—including Ripley and his wife Sophia (author of an insufficiently known essay in *The Dial* on woman's role) and the little-known short story writer Nathaniel Hawthorne—set off on April 1, 1841, in the midst of a terrific unseasonable snow-storm. The same day in Concord, the Thoreau brothers closed their school. Thoreau spent the next few weeks flirting with proprietorship, "inspecting my neighbor's farms . . . and chaffering with the land holders." He almost bought the Hallowell place, even though he had no money, no capital, and was reduced to odd jobs. One April day he made seventy-five cents shoveling manure, a substance widely and soberly referred to by solid citizens at the time as "the farmers' capi-tal." Out at Brook Farm, Hawthorne was shoveling manure too, en-joying the same joke, calling the pile his "gold mine." It is hard to imagine Thoreau as a steady farmer, just as it is hard to see him work-ing in the fields with the Brook Farmers, wearing their blue peasant blouses, held in with belts, and their small, visored, European peasant caps. Yet he was undoubtedly drawn, to some degree, by both possi-bilities. He wanted very much to be independent, but he wanted, with equal intensity, not to be tied down by responsibility. Indepen-dence won this time. "When the right wind blows or a star calls," he wrote with obvious feeling, "I can leave this arable and grass ground, without making a will or settling my estate." So he neither bought a farm nor went to live in the Brook Farm boardinghouse, "the Hive" as its inmates called it with approving affection. It was precisely this communal life Thoreau was leery of.[4]

In other ways, insofar as Brook Farm was a serious effort at reform of farming and landholding practices, Thoreau was sympathetic. Brook Farm was a joint stock company and had Fourierist plans to vary the working day with short stretches at a variety of attractive jobs. As he made the rounds of Concord farms in April he confessed himself "startled to find everywhere the old system of things so grim and assured. Wherever I go the farms are run out, and there they lie, and the youth must buy old land and bring it to—Everywhere the relentless opponents of reform are a few old maids and bachelors, who sit round the kitchen fire, listening to the singing of the tea kettle and munching cheese rinds." He was more than a little disillusioned with the old, set ways, and, in theory at least, he was all for the reformers and dreamers. "The mind which first contemplated the present order of things at some remote era must have been visionary and Utopian," he had written in his journal. He could talk warmly of a community of friends or of love and he was not in theory opposed to the basic communalism of the Brook Farmers. "Is not this the age of a community of goods?" he asked himself.[5]

On the twenty-sixth of April, Thoreau solved for the time being his problem of where to live, if not the problem of what to live for, by moving into Emerson's house. The arrangement turned out to be a good one and it would last for two years, a sojourn almost equal in length to his later stay at Walden Pond. Thoreau was to look after things while Emerson was away on his now-frequent lecture tours. Thoreau helped out with the work, but he was far more than a hired hand. His was a very special position, the friend who is closer than many members of the family, an addition to the inner family group, certainly not a "hired man" or a "boarder." Thoreau's ultimate model reform community would be at Walden and would have a very select membership. Meanwhile the move to Emerson's was not so drastic as a move to Brook Farm would have been, and both Emerson and Thoreau felt that their own world and immediate community were improved and reformed by the new arrangement. Emerson wrote to Carlyle, "One reader and friend of yours dwells now in my house—and as I hope, for a twelvemonth to come,—Henry Thoreau,—a poet whom you may one day be proud of—a noble manly youth full of melodies and inventions. We work together day by day in my garden, and I grow well and strong."[6]

24. Self-Reformation

Organized reform and professional reformers usually rubbed Thoreau the wrong way. He was annoyed by "the injured man with querulous tone resisting his age." He maintained bluntly, "I don't like people who are too good for this world." If he was self-righteous in his contempt for self-righteousness, perhaps it was because he disliked seeing certain traits he disapproved of in himself reflected back to him, for it is abundantly clear that, despite his protesting, Thoreau shared, from an early age, the general hunger of the times for reform, renewal, and regeneration.[1]

Noyes's *History of American Socialisms* reflects one contemporaneous analysis of the evolution of the reform impulse as it showed itself in the commune movement of the 1840s. Observing that since the War of 1812, "the line of socialist excitements lies parallel with the line of religious Revivals," Noyes cites the early-nineteenth-century division of Puritan Congregationalism into orthodoxy and Unitarianism; the first party, he says, "was set to defend religion, the other liberty." Orthodoxy, he goes on, "had for its function the carrying through of the Revival system; the other the development of Socialism." "The Revivalists had for their great idea the regeneration of the soul. The great idea of the Socialists was the regeneration of Society." Both impulses took institutional form; there were revivals on the one hand and there were new communities or communes on the other, and both required frequent meetings.[2]

While Thoreau could and did sympathize with both reformational impulses, he would not associate himself with the institutional form of either. He was interested in the reformation of the self. He did not see this as an exclusively religious matter, certainly not just a Christian one, nor did he think of it as essentially a social matter. Nevertheless he was drawing on several long traditions of reformational zeal. One certainly was Protestant. Thoreau's ultimate reformed community of one at Walden would be an example of the extreme results of the tendency of Protestants to splinter away from any parent body. Thoreau's interest in individual reformation also led him back to the Greek ethical schools, and particularly to Stoicism—the search for self-rule or autarky—and the same interest should also be seen as a practical consequence of a serious immersion in the new, Kantian, subjectivism.

All three impulses, Protestant, Stoic, and Kantian, lay behind and fed into the increasingly clear logic of his own personal life, his search for personal reformation, the discovery and fulfillment of his own destiny as an autonomous individual. Of course his dependency on his family, on his school, and on his friends only served to sharpen his growing hunger for independence. "We can render men the best assistance," he wrote in January, "by letting them see how sore a thing it is to need any assistance." He was struck, he said, with the "inexpressible privacy" of each life. Over and over, in endless self-admonishing journal entries, Thoreau tries to hold himself to an almost impossible standard. "Be resolutely and faithfully what you are—be humbly what you aspire to be . . . man's noblest gift to man is his sincerity, for it embraces his integrity also."[3]

As he sought, during this winter and into the spring of 1841, to nourish his sense of self (what Emerson would call his integrity and what we would call his identity), he found within himself a stubborn streak of resistance. Emerson noted that Thoreau required some opposition before he could shine in conversation. "He wanted a fallacy to expose, a blunder to pillory." And indeed Thoreau took a real joy in controversy and paradox; he really only felt himself in opposition, and he relished it. "Resistance," he noted this January, "is a very wholesome and delicious morsel at times."[4]

Personal inclination seconded the ideas about the integrity of the self that were then part of the intellectual climate. Thoreau's own individualism was becoming increasingly better thought out. To start by reforming society or the age was to start from the wrong end of the problem. A little more than a month after the first contingent of Brook Farmers had launched their new era, Thoreau observed that "this lament for a golden age is only a lament for golden men." It was for each one alone to make a beginning. His own response to the challenge was becoming clearer. "I only ask a clean seat. I will build my lodge on the southern slope of some hill and take there the life the gods send me." How and when the chance would come he did not know, but the needle in his inner compass was settling on a consistent heading. The energy, clarity, and simplicity of his comments suggest the calmly growing conviction that the only way for him was self-renewal, self-regeneration, self-reform. Four days after the comment about building his lodge comes this: "The times have no heart. The true reform can be undertaken any morning before unbarring our doors. It calls no convention. I can do two thirds the reform of the world myself."[5]

The only less than ideal aspect of Thoreau's move into the Emerson household was that the increasingly restless Thoreau was no more independent than before. On the very day he moved, and in the first journal entry written "at RWE's," part of him was still resisting, still chafing at being dependent and housebound. The house of the civilized man, he declared, "is a prison in which he finds himself oppressed and confined, not sheltered and protected." But even as he wrote, the gentle influence of Emerson was drawing out the best in him. As Thoreau took shelter at Emerson's, his thoughts turned to the figure of the American Indian, the charm of whom, Thoreau said, "is that he stands free and unconstrained in nature—is her inhabitant—and not her guest." Thoreau himself had to make do with guest status for a while longer.[6]

25. The Orient

Spring turned into summer as Thoreau worked beside Emerson in the garden and taught him grafting in the orchard. Days were long and peaceful; Thoreau found plenty of time to get off by himself to the barn, a large, pleasant-smelling, open building within sight of both house and road, but removed from the busyness of both, a good place to read and write. Chief among the books he read this summer was Sir William Jones's translation of *The Laws of Menu*, one of the great scriptures of ancient India. This renewal of excitement about India may have come about because Emerson was increasingly interested in Indic ideas, but Thoreau's interest in India went deeper than Emerson's, and Thoreau may well have sparked the renewal of excitement about India himself. It was not the first time the book had caught his attention; he had seen it and had made admiring comments the previous summer. It was becoming a habit with him now to work back over his journals and to reread books, to reengage old subjects in the light of new interests, to revise and recopy his own earlier journal work, measuring, weighing, culling, and sorting his materials. He continually reached backward to the Merrimack trip, to the brave man thesis, to familiar books, ideas, and perceptions, to metaphors of music and seeing, taking up earlier threads, reweaving and combining them, moving in slow circles, now forward, now backward, testing earlier perceptions, searching out what it was in each that made it of lasting rather than passing interest.

Often called *The Laws of Menu* (or Manu), the actual title—echoing Calvin—of the volume was *Institutes of Hindu Law; or, the ordinances of Menu, according to the Gloss of Culluca, Comprising the Indian system of duties, religious and civil*. Jones, one of the great jurists and linguists of the late eighteenth century, had been entrusted by Warren Hastings with devising a legal code for British India. Jones had found the book and translated it because he wanted to base modern law as far as possible on ancient and accepted Hindu legal principles. *The Laws of Menu* was quickly and widely recognized, after its translation and publication, as a very ancient code, as venerable as the Bible, and older even than the Pentateuch. The very word *menu*, Jones noted, comes from the ultimate Indo-European root for our words *mind* and *man* both. Here, then, was another great original dispensation, another scripture, harking back to the very dawn and birthplace of Western civilization, a sacred code (or, as Thoreau had learned to call it, Dherma Sastra) older than Hebrew Scripture, preceding poetry, as old as myth itself. The version Jones chose was the text that had been amplified and glossed by an ancient commentator named Culluca; the resulting composite text Jones praised as "the shortest, yet the most luminous, the least ostentatious, yet the most learned, the deepest, yet the most agreeable, commentary ever composed on any author ancient or modern, European or Asiatick."[1]

Thoreau's response to this book was as warm and as immoderate as Jones's. "In the Hindu scripture the idea of man is quite illimitable and sublime—there is nowhere a loftier conception of his destiny." He was deeply, repeatedly, and lastingly moved by the book; his response was that of a strongly religious nature to a great revelation. He responded to Indic Scripture as others of his time responded to the Bible. "There is," he said, still speaking of the laws of Menu, "no grander conception of creation any where." Nor is there, anywhere in Thoreau, a comparable response to the Bible. He saw the Hindu scripture as a primal expression of both natural and human law, and since his assent to it was not required, he offered it all the more freely. "That title—The Laws of Menu—with the Gloss of Culucca [*sic*]—comes to me with such a volume of sound as if it had swept unobstructed over the plains of Hindostan, and when my eye rests on yonder birches— or the sun in the water—or the shadows of the trees—it seems to signify the laws of them all. They are the laws of you and me."[2]

He also found the book an impressive example of what he called "the conservative conscience," and he quotes approvingly Menu's "immemorial custom is transcendent law." This may sound odd in the mouth of a young man, a social liberal with strong reformist impulses. But Thoreau was beginning to face up to a troubling contradiction, which is that the primitive societies in which man lives close to nature, societies such as those of South Pacific Islanders or American Indians, require of their members a powerful anti-innovative, antireform conservatism. Since substantial technical advances or social reforms would disrupt the balance between man and nature, or man and man, adherence to the law of accepted custom, which is conservative by definition, is required, not only for stability, but for survival.[3]

Thoreau's enthusiastic response to Menu shows not only how much he was disposed to regard the book as authoritative but how much he consciously compared its authority to that given the Bible by certain of his literal, prophecy-hunting contemporaries. "It is now easy to apply to this ancient scripture such a catholic criticism, as it will become the part of some future age to apply to the Christian—wherein the design and idea which underlies it is considered, and not the narrow and partial fulfillment."[4]

Thoreau did not get new ideas from Menu. A modern commentator on Thoreau has rightly said that "there cannot be any borrowing in the higher realms of knowledge. There we cannot take what does not belong to us." But Thoreau did find a number of his own ideas reflected back at him, with the added luster of a venerable tradition thousands of years old. *The Laws of Menu* thus arrived as a massive corroboration of Thoreau's interest in austerity, withdrawal, and purification. "The very austerity of these Hindoos is tempting to the devotional as a more refined and nobler luxury," he noted. He also saw that the transmigration of souls was another way of talking about the fundamental natural principle of metamorphosis or change. He read in *The Laws of Menu*, "All transmigration, recorded in the sacred books, from the state of Brahma to that of plants, happen continually in this tremendous world of beings; a world always tending to decay." He found himself agreeing with the concept of god in Menu, which considers "all nature both visible and invisible as existing in the divine spirit," and with the concept of man as participating in the divine. That man, says Menu, "who perceives in his own soul the supreme soul present in all creatures . . . shall be absorbed at last in the highest essence, even that of the Almighty himself."[5]

Thoreau read this book, as he read all books, personally convinced that "one may discover the root of a Hindoo religion in his own private history." *The Laws of Menu* was for years one of his wisdom books. He was open to it as few Westerners have been. But ultimately he aspired to be more than a reader of such books. His own deepest ambition, like Blake's, like Whitman's, was to write such a text. He wondered, "Will this bustling era detain the future reader longer?" He compared his own times with the past and asked himself,

"Who is writing better Vedas?"[6]

26. Fall 1841

By September 1841, Thoreau had come to feel, as he wrote a friend, that he was "living with Mr. Emerson in very dangerous prosperity." The prosperity was obvious; there was companionship, books, good talk, a widening circle of friends. The danger was to his independence. He was now, for all intents and purposes, an integral part of two households. He worked at Emerson's, but he also helped his father make pencils. To escape from both he would, on occasion, go out on the river at night with his flute. He was corresponding this year with Lucy Jackson Brown, the sister of Lydia Emerson, nineteen years older than

Thoreau and for years a boarder with the Thoreau family. Thoreau wrote poems for her and his letters to her have an ease, a warmth, and an intimacy made possible by the age difference between them.[1]

He was also in correspondence this fall with a young man named Isaiah Williams, who had passed through Concord, then moved west, and was now writing long earnest letters beseeching Thoreau's help in grasping the meaning of transcendentalism. The reading list Thoreau recommended is an excellent index to Thoreau's own understanding of "the movement" to which he clearly now feels he belongs. He told Williams to read Emerson's *Nature, Essays*, and "The Divinity School Address," and Carlyle's *On Heroes, Hero-Worship and the Heroic in History*. He also recommended Alcott's 1836 *Doctrine and Discipline of Human Culture*, a twenty-five-page manifesto reprinted as the introduction to *Record of Conversations with the Children on the Gospels*. This too-little-known piece is the essential Bronson Alcott; it sets forth a modern liberal Christian paideia, an ideal of education. "Human Culture," said Alcott, "is the art of revealing to a man the true Idea of his being. . . . It is the art of completing a man," and he makes it clear that his concept of education starts with Jesus, whom he considers a "type of our common nature," or, as Emerson would have said, a representative figure. The achievements of Jesus "are a glimpse of the Apotheosis of Humanity . . . a glorious unfolding of the Godlike in man . . . a worthy symbol of the Divinity, wherein Human Nature is revealed in its Fulness."[2]

The other book Thoreau mentioned to Williams is *Selections from German Literature* (1839), edited by B. B. Edwards and E. A. Park, both professors at Andover Theological Seminary. The selections are exclusively from modern German theological writings by Frederic Koster, L. J. Ruckert, J. P. Lange, F. A. G. Tholuck, W. G. Tennemann, and C. Ullmann. The significance of the volume is its reflection of current German thought, particularly that of Schleiermacher, the greatest theologian of the nineteenth century, a translator of Plato and a powerful influence on American transcendentalism. George Ripley, in his defense of Emerson after the "Infidelity" attack of Norton, relies heavily on Schleiermacher and on Ullmann, whom he calls "one of the most independent, moderate and discriminating followers of Schleiermacher." Believing with Schleiermacher that one could recognize "in the nature of man, the same signatures of divinity which authenticate the Gospel of Christ," Ullmann's position is that "the highest and most comprehensive truth of the divine life in the soul of man reposes in Christ. He, in his complete personality, divine and human at once, in the untroubled undiminished fulness of his being, is, in the highest sense, the true Medium, the mediator between Divinity and Humanity, the central point of the world's history, the exhaustless fountain of all progressive spiritual life."[3]

Thoreau's own transcendentalism did not dwell much on its Christian side, but his choice of texts for poor Williams shows his awareness of its importance, and prepares one for Thoreau's comment to Williams that "If any soul look abroad even today, it will not find any word which does it more justice than the New Testament."[4]

The center of Thoreau's efforts this fall was not, however, transcendentalism, but poetry. He wrote Mrs. Brown in September that he was "in the mid-sea of verses." Three poems, "Sympathy," "Sic Vita," and "Friendship" had appeared in three different issues of *The Dial*. He was working on more, had just sent a three-hundred-line poem on the mountains, "With frontier strength ye stand your ground," to Margaret Fuller and was corresponding with Rufus Griswold, the Louis Untermeyer of the day, about having his poems reprinted in one of Griswold's innumerable anthologies. Beyond this, he was by late November hard at work on what seems to have been intended as an anthology of his own. He had copied many pages of English poetry out of one of Emerson's commonplace books, and Emerson had loaned Thoreau fifteen dollars "for expenses at Cambridge in account of his book." He made lists of poets, and worked his way through Harvard's collection of early English poetry. He read Anglo-Saxon poetry, Chaucer, the Scottish Chaucerians, and indeed everything down to Milton. He read histories (Turner on the Anglo-Saxons, Warton on English Poetry, Sibbald's *Chronicle of Scottish Poetry*), other anthologies and collections (Conybeare's *Illustrations of Anglo-Saxon Poetry*, Chalmers's vast collection, Evans's *Old Ballads*, Headley's *Select Beauties*, Ritson's *Ancient English Metrical Romances*, Hartshorne's *Ancient Metrical Tales*, Park's *Helconia*, Edwards's *Paradise of Dainty Devices*), as well as volumes of individual poets. All through December, and at intervals off and on for several years, Thoreau literally immersed himself in early English poetry. It is difficult to say what the guiding principle of the anthology was to be; no doubt it had something to do with his lifelong admiration of the sinewy energy of earlier, less polished verse. But he found the work of "looking over the dry and dusty volumes" unrewarding. He felt "oppressed by an inevitable sadness." He felt that early English poetry, taken as a whole, did not hold up, and he found himself admiring the "human and wise" Chaucer more and more as he surveyed "the very meagre pastures of saxon and ante-Chaucerian poetry."[5]

Although he labored diligently at the task (which may have been suggested by Emerson, who later did publish an anthology called *Parnassus*), and although the work no doubt helped him feather his own poetic arrows, it wasn't what he really wanted to be doing. It was a long way from writing Vedas. "The best poets, after all, exhibit only a tame and civil side of nature." What he wanted to do was to write poetry himself. "I think I could write a poem to be called Concord," he noted in September, and all through the fall, indeed all through his journal of this year, from April on, runs the yearning to express the growing sense of wildness he felt within, which he associated with westering and with his need for independence. He hungered for some "simple unquestioned mode of living," for a "directer relation to the sun." He admired William Bradford's description of earliest New England: "For summer being ended," said the pilgrim, "all things stand in appearance with a weatherbeaten face, and the whole country full of woods and thickets represented a wild and savage hue." He noted the "fantastic wildness" of the pine and how "the earth is a wild unexplored." In mid-July he wrote Mrs. Brown, "I grow savager and savager every day as if fed on raw meat, and my tameness is only the repose of untamableness." From his dangerous prosperity and taut repose he dreamed, he said, "of looking abroad summer and winter, with free gaze from some mountain side." Fall only deepened the mood. On Christmas eve day he wrote, "I want to go soon and live away by the Pond where I shall hear only the wind whispering among the reeds." He badly needed to make some move, some gesture of independence to counter his sense that he was wasting time, that he was somehow not living. "I don't want to feel as if my life were a sojourn any longer," he wrote on Christmas Day. "It is time now that I begin to live."[6]

27. Tragedy

With the new year, 1842, came the sudden deaths of Thoreau's brother John and Emerson's five-year-old son, Waldo. On the first of January, while stropping his razor, John cut a little piece from the end of his left-hand ring finger. Thinking nothing of it, he bandaged it up. But eight days later, he found the replaced skin "mortified." On the morning of January 9, he complained of stiffening in the jaws. That night lockjaw set in, with terrible spasms. (Emerson wrote later about lockjaw convulsions so violent they bent a man backward so that his head almost touched his heels.) A doctor was called from Boston; his conclusion was that there was nothing to be done. John accepted the fact that he was going to die calmly and with a fortitude that was both Stoic and Christian: "The cup that my Father gives me, shall I not drink it?" Thoreau came over from Emerson's to look after his brother. He was a devoted and attentive nurse, but there was nothing that he could do. John died a day and a half later in the arms of the helpless Thoreau.[1]

The suddenness of John's death left little time to prepare for it; Thoreau took it very hard and, moreover, he held his emotions inside. His family remarked how his strange initial calm sank into complete passivity. Even his interest in nature was gone; he was "denaturalized," as he later admitted to a correspondent. Then to the incredulous horror of his family and friends, on January 22 he came down with all the symptoms of lockjaw himself. He had not cut himself; it was purely an emotional—a sympathetic—reaction that had produced the physical symptoms. By the morning of the twenty-fourth, however, he was better, as a relieved Emerson wrote his brother William. But that same night Emerson's son Waldo developed scarlet fever or scarlatina, and three days later the little boy, the pride of his father's heart, was dead. From accounts left by those who came to the house and from the letters he wrote the night Waldo died and the following day, it appears that Emerson gave immediate expression to his grief, reaching out to others, sharing and articulating his loss in ways Thoreau did not or could not. Partly for this reason, Emerson recovered more quickly from his initial grief and shock, though this loss never really left him for the rest of his life. He also had a lecture schedule to keep, a trip to New York that had to be made, a wife and two baby daughters to be cared for. Thoreau was without similar demands on him; his health was worse than Emerson's anyway, and the result was a protracted illness that kept him in bed for one month and left him too weak to work outdoors for another.[2]

His articulated response to the catastrophes of January, when it finally came to the surface in early March, was still very strong. His physical collapse suggests the depth of his initial shock; his journal, silent entirely from January 9 until February 20, and his letters of early March show him fighting for a philosophic acceptance of death, a position that, however admirable, could only drive simple grief in further. To Lucy Brown he indeed wrote at some length about grief itself, but it was in his complicated and customarily paradoxical way, concluding "only nature has a right to grieve perpetually, for she only is innocent." He dealt with John's death mainly by idealizing him. In the same letter to Mrs. Brown he wrote, "I do not wish to see John ever again, I mean him who is dead—but that other whom only he would have wished to see or to be, of whom he was the imperfect representative." He dealt with Waldo's death and with Emerson's loss by an almost Keatsian acceptance of death as a natural culmination, an emotionally rich and yearned-for state of being. "I was not startled to hear that he was dead;—it seemed the most natural event that could happen. His fine organization demanded it, and nature gently yielded its request. It would have been strange," he concluded, with a turn that reminds one of Emily Dickinson, "if he had lived." A week later he wrote a similar letter to Emerson, now off in New York, only in more philosophical tones and intended, clearly, as consolation; "How plain that death is only the phenomenon of the individual or class. Nature does not recognize it, she finds her own again under new forms." He also wrote a third letter in early March, this one to Isaiah Williams—more philosophical and affirmative still, which dealt with his losses with the resigned courage of a Seneca or a Marcus Aurelius. "I feel that I could not have done without this experience."[3]

There is no way to know how much this acceptance of death cost Thoreau. He could try to talk down his grief, but one cannot deny it permanently, and in some ways it kept coming back all his life. Meanwhile, there was tremendous cold courage, and at least a touch of bravado, in his standing to embrace the angel of death and in his continuing to assert, as he did, his superiority to mere chance. Isaiah Williams had written with well-intentioned meekness that "man's ends are shaped for him." Thoreau fired back "though I am weak, I am strong too. If God shapes my ends—he shapes me also—and his means are always equal to his ends. . . . I am my destiny." A post-Freudian era may be inclined to regard such an assertion not as a statement of faith in the power of an idea, but as a mask for an emotion. In Thoreau's case, both are true. The deaths of John and Waldo called out a response in Thoreau that dealt with grief by means of a powerful willed affirmation of the life principle. Death is "a law and not an accident—It is as common as life," he wrote Emerson. "When we look over the fields we are not saddened because the particular flowers or grasses will wither—for the law of their death is the law of new life. . . . So it is with the human plant."[4]

This steady sounding, life-affirming response was not won or maintained easily. Thoreau's journals and even his letters for March are unusually full of uncharacteristic references to God—God's work, God's palm, God's hands—they are also marked by plaintive and despairing outpourings: "Why God did you include me in your great scheme?" or "How trivial the best actions are," or "I do not know but my life is fated to be thus low and grovelling always." But the strong Stoic response that dominates the letters gradually took the upper hand. And with the affirmation there came, by some curious mechanism, a resurgence of energy. The first indication of this is the way in which his journal, from mid-March on, runs back over a whole series of familiar subjects: Chaucer, Raleigh, Carlyle, friendship, love, music, writing, history, the Orient, natural law—almost as though he was running through his repertoire or picking up and making sense of the threads he had let drop in January.[5]

By March 28 he felt himself running over with "superfluous energy." Emerson must have noticed this, for he picked up in Boston a stack of scientific surveys on the flora, fauna, and natural resources of Massachusetts and on April 10 set Thoreau "on the good track of giving an account of them in *The Dial*, explaining to him the felicity of the subject for him as it admits of the narrative of all his woodcraft boatcraft and fishcraft." It was the right assignment at the right time. Thoreau plunged in and within a month's time, by early May, had fifty or sixty pages ready for Emerson to look at. The essay, called the "Natural History of Massachusetts," published in the July 1842 *Dial*, was in several important ways a major step for Thoreau.[6]

It was the beginning of a very creative six months of work, it was a big step toward staking out his own special subject matter, and it was a significant move away fom "Dialese" and the Emersonian manner to a style of his own. His characteristic form and his characteristic style both emerged over the remaining months of 1842. By one of those little ironies that make life harder to believe than fiction, Thoreau had been writing in his journal on the two days before John cut himself about how books of natural history restored one to a sense of health. Thoreau now went back to those notes to open his new essay, the completion of which marked not only his own recovery that spring, but the beginning of the productive burst in which Thoreau found his true vein, his own voice. His discovery of himself came directly and rapidly out of the tragic losses of January. It is almost as though John's death freed him. The final effect on him of such terrible losses was to confirm, by the very starkness of the contrast, his own continuing life, the vitality of which was now increasingly urgent, increasingly less something to be complacently taken for granted.[7]

28. Excursions

That Emerson did not think much of the "Natural History of Massachusetts" is indicative of the fact that Thoreau was now coming into his own, and that his way of writing was beginning to diverge markedly from Emerson's. He would share some of Emerson's ideas all his life, but the form, the style, and the characteristic subjects of his writing begin now to be distinctly his own.

Hawthorne, on the other hand, admired the essay and thought it "gives a very fair image of his mind and character—so true, minute, and literal in observation, yet giving the spirit as well as letter of what he sees, even as a lake reflects its wooded banks." Emerson had taken over the editorship of *The Dial* this spring, and while he was still interested in pushing Thoreau's poetry, he did print the "Natural History" essay in the July issue. Thoreau did little physical work during the spring, but indoors he functioned as Emerson's editorial assistant. Eighteen forty-two was an eventful year. Brook Farm was flourishing. Emerson and Margaret Fuller made extended visits. In New York, Emerson met Horace Greeley, influential editor of the reform-minded *New York Tribune*; Albert Brisbane, disciple of Fourier and staunch proponent of socialist reform; and Henry James, Sr., the gentle and perceptive Swedenborgian whom Emerson thought the best head in New York. Greeley had begun a daily column on the first of March, trumpeting Fourier and the Association movement. Brisbane was brimming over with his ideas and, with Greeley, was intensely interested in Brook Farm. Parker in Boston was reaching his full power as a preacher, addressing a regular audience of 3,000 persons, while excited reports were coming back from Charles Wheeler in Germany about Schelling's much-heralded lectures in Berlin. The New England circle was widening, coming into touch with other centers.[1]

Back in Concord, the change in editorship of *The Dial* brought Frederic Hedge and Parker in closer to the center. Hedge traveled to Concord, hoping to find a way to move there. Alcott went off to England to visit admirers and disciples, returning in the fall with Charles Lane and his son William and Henry Gardiner Wright, all filled with enthusiasm for yet another New World model community that would combine reformed agriculture, vegetarianism, and high Platonic dialogue and that would be called "Fruitlands." In the middle of the summer, Hawthorne, who was so handsome a man that people stopped in the street and stared at him, married Sophia Peabody of Salem and they came to live in the Old Manse by the Concord River, next to the old battleground. Emerson and Thoreau paid a formal call that went off with comic stiffness, but Hawthorne and

Thoreau were impressed with each other and spent time together subsequently, walking and boating on the quiet river. The Concord Athenaeum, a reading club, was started this summer. Just after his twenty-fifth birthday, Thoreau set out on a four-day walk to Wachusett Mountain between Worcester and Fitchburg with Richard Fuller, Margaret's younger brother. They read Virgil (the *Georgics*), and Thoreau talked about India and the American Indians. Margaret Fuller and Ellery Channing both came to stay for several weeks in August with the Emersons. Thoreau looked, vainly, for other employment, and continued to help Emerson with *The Dial*. Emerson held an evening gathering in November devoted to Alcott's new scheme; the Brook Farmers showed up in force. Thoreau was elected curator of the Concord Lyceum this month and he organized an impressive series of lectures—six in the following four weeks—for the town.

Despite all this external busyness, Thoreau's main energies during the summer and fall were engaged in an amazing variety and number of his own literary projects. There was the volume of English poetry, encouraged by Emerson who was this year working on his essay on "The Poet." During April and early May, Thoreau worked on the "Natural History of Massachusetts." In July came his walk to Wachusett, which he soon after began writing up as an essay, and which he printed during the coming January. At some point during 1842 he recopied out a notebook full of Indic material, mostly apropos of *The Laws of Menu*. He made another try at the river trip material, which would reach final form in *A Week*. Before mid-December he had completed a translation of Aeschylus's *Prometheus Bound* for *The Dial*. In October, eight of his poems appeared in the same magazine. He was also working up material that would become "A Winter Walk" and he was working on a lecture on Raleigh which he would give the following February. This is an impressive amount of work, to say nothing of its range; it amounted to eight substantial projects, three that were completed by year's end, and three more that were finished early in the new year.[2]

Eighteen forty-two, from April onward, was the year when the work of the five previous years finally began to fall into place. From the "Natural History of Massachusetts" through "A Walk to Wachusett" to the early jottings for "A Winter Walk," the excursion form quickly clarified itself. The "Natural History of Massachusetts" began as a review of unpromising books, T. W. Harris's *A report on the Insects*, C. Dewey's *Report on the Herbaceous Flowering Plants*, D. H. Storer's *Reports on the Fishes, Reptiles and Birds*, A. A. Gould's *Report on the Invertebrata*, and E. Emmons's *A Report on the Quadrupeds*. The finished review-essay transcends its origin. It was Emerson's eye that saw the possibilities. Facts, details, lore, woodcraft are subsumed into an essay the theses of which are the healthfulness of nature, joy as the chief condition of life, the seasonal cycles of all natural life, the mythical method of nature, and the unexplored wildness that remains in less obvious as well as in obvious animals and places. Toward the end of the essay Thoreau reaches out for nothing less than a theory of nature, for which he went back to his 1837 reading and journal work. He recovered his earlier observation that both ice crystals and leaves "were the creatures of but one law." He remarked, thinking of Goethe, that "vegetation has been made the type of all growth," then went on with his own idea, "but as in crystals the law is more obvious, their material being more simple, and for the most part more transient and fleeting, would it not be as philosophical as convenient to consider all growth, all filling up within the limits of nature, but a crystallization more or less rapid?" Whether or not his observations hold up strictly is less important than their general tendency. Like Schelling's *Naturphilosophie* and like modern physics, Thoreau is interested in a unified nature, one force or one law or one substance that will be found to be the root explanation of all nature. The form of the essay is not adequate to its larger claims. It proceeds, seriatim, through insects, then birds, then animals. Anecdotal and personal experience is important, making the essay concrete and familiar, and there is at least some effort to organize each section seasonally.[3]

"A Walk to Wachusett" comes a full step closer to what would be Thoreau's preferred short form, the excursion. It too reaches back five years to the start of the journal for its thematic center. Telling the story of the four-day walk Thoreau took in July of this year with Richard Fuller, the piece takes its shape from the excursion itself, the trip to Wachusett, the climb, the return. It is all done in close to journal fashion, sticking to facts and details so carefully one feels one could retrace the entire trip. The essay is a celebration of the countryside. The spirit of Virgil's *Georgics* hangs over the essay, as does Wordsworth, who was also valued by Thoreau chiefly as a country writer. Because Virgil described the unchanging countryside of farms and farmers, Thoreau can plausibly repeat now his 1837 observation that one reads Virgil to be reminded of the identity of all ages. What is new in "A Walk to Wachusett" is the clear trip narrative and the gentle, sociable tone of the familiar essay, combining to make a miniature version of the travel book. The piece closes on a comfortable note as Thoreau praises hospitality, but what gives the piece life is the streak of wildness in the landscape and in the writing. Mount Wachusett beckons to him and haunts his dreams. The little essay looks forward to the great "Ktaadn" piece that will focus on the wild, non-human tops of mountains, the raw material of the planet, the gardenless unhandseled globe. "A Walk to Wachusett" is only a beginning, but it is the first fully characteristic Thoreauvian excursion.[4] His next one, "A Winter Walk," began to form in his head in October; it would turn out to be one of his best.

29. January and February 1843

Thoreau's health was poor again this winter. Emerson, away on a long lecture tour, wrote in mid-January hoping that "Henry has recovered from bronchitis and all its kind." In his own journal, Thoreau forced himself to self-description; "I am," he wrote, "a diseased bundle of nerves standing between time and eternity like a withered leaf." This is more than mere rhetoric or self-flagellation, for he adds in a rare moment of flat unguardedness, "healthy I have been—for periods perhaps healthier than most—But these were short." Though he was not a complainer, he seems to have endured chronic poor health; his endless talk of bravery and "the brave man" is in part a sort of whistling to keep up his spirits in the face of numerous and prolonged illnesses. Emerson admired his determination to be well and called him "my brave Henry." But at times the poor health spilled over in anger at the weakness and vulnerability of the body, and in a kind of self-excoriation. By late January he was no better, and his frustration shows in a letter to Mrs. Brown. He goes from saying "we are poor and sick creatures at best" to confessing himself "vexed by a sense of meanness" to admitting that he felt "for the most part I am an idle, inefficient, lingering . . . member of the great commonwealth."[1]

As his health went through its ups and downs, so his spirits went through great swings of mood this winter. In early February, Emerson, still off lecturing in New York, wrote Henry about the forthcoming number of *The Dial*. In addition to asking (as usual) for various contributions from him, Emerson asked Thoreau to read a piece sent in by Charles Lane and make the decision on whether to take it. "If you see and say decidedly that it is good for us you need not send it to me." Thoreau's response to this gesture of trust was an unrestrained, overemotional burst of gratitude that reminds one of Melville's famous response to Hawthorne's generous reading of *Moby Dick*. "I feel," wrote Thoreau, "addressed and probed even to the remote parts of my being when one nobly shows even in trivial things, an implicit faith in me." The letter to Emerson goes on, "this mild trust translates me. . . . I am no more of this earth." Even though the knowledge that Emerson really trusted him and had confidence in his judgment was indescribably precious to Thoreau, his reaction seems excessive. One may gauge the restraint with which he generally kept his feelings in check by the almost abandoned outburst that occurs when he does give way. "Other chains may be broken, but in the darkest night, in the remotest place, I trail this thread."[2]

As his moods thus swung suddenly from the depression of January to this elation in early February, his literary energies this winter were being scattered over a series of projects, each one pulling him in a different direction. *The Dial* for January had his translation of *Prometheus Bound* and his selections from *The Laws of Menu*. His first piece to be placed outside *The Dial*, "A Walk to Wachusett," appeared this January in the *Boston Miscellany of Literature*, and he was at work on his Raleigh lecture to be given February 8 for the Concord Lyceum.

The translation of Aeschylus's *Prometheus* was the sort of thing

Emerson had concluded Thoreau to be good at, and he therefore actively encouraged this and other projects in Greek translation for Thoreau. It is a good, not a brilliant translation; Hedge admired it, and it compares favorably with the nearly contemporaneous translation by Elizabeth Barrett Browning (1833, revised 1850). Thoreau was drawn to the play partly by his interest in early poetry, in the strong, energetic writing he associated with the early periods of national cultures. His attraction to the rebel Prometheus as a hero is also very much in tune with that of Goethe, Shelley, Margaret Fuller, Elizabeth Browning, and many others in the Romantic era, for whom Prometheus was replacing—or at least joining—Solon, Orpheus, and Apollo as an ancient Greek culture hero and symbol. Thoreau did do something unique with the figure of Prometheus, but it was not until later, when he internalized or subjectivized the story of the chained Prometheus in the "Ktaadn" essay, in what became the first part of *The Maine Woods*.[3]

Thoreau did not read Sanscrit, so his selection from *The Laws of Menu* was a straightforward job of selecting and editing from Jones's translation. In the months ahead he would work up similar selections from other great national scriptures. No doubt he approached Menu as poetry and as wisdom, but he also realized that since these were sacred writings, there was a theological side to his piece, a not very subtle challenge to the Christian assumption that the Old and New Testaments were the only true scripture of the only true God. Later this same year Thoreau wrote Emerson, "Is it not singular that while the religious world is gradually picking to pieces its old testaments, here are some coming slowly after on the sea-shore picking up the durable relics of perhaps older books, and putting them together again?"[4]

For the lecture on Raleigh, Thoreau went back to a familiar subject, the hero, or "brave man." By centering his thoughts around the historical figure of Raleigh, Thoreau avoided the abstract intricacies of "The Service," his earlier effort in this line. The Raleigh lecture is Thoreau's first successful venture into the heroic thumbnail biography or admiring biographical sketch—the new Plutarchian lives exemplified by Carlyle's heroes, Emerson's representative men, and Fuller's representative women. It was to be a moderately successful genre for

Thoreau; over the years he would work ever closer to his own time and place, writing such sketches of Carlyle and John Brown, Joe Polis, and Alek Therien. Thoreau's admiration for Raleigh is wholehearted; he loves his courage, his range, his wit. He admires him, as he had admired Persius, as a supreme example of the kind of writer and poet whose own life is his major work. "But he wrote his poems, after all, rather with ships and fleets, and regiments of men and horse."[5]

Of all his projects that came to fruition this winter, "A Walk to Wachusett" lay nearest his own true path, though it is unlikely that he recognized it yet. Emerson had started him on the "Natural History of Massachusetts," but had not cared much for the result; nor did he much like the Wachusett piece (or its successor "A Winter Walk"). The Wachusett essay was not even published in *The Dial*. Even his longer works would be based on modest outings and trips, although disguised as epics of exploration. The subject, the tone, even the eventual title, "Excursions," all remind one of Wordsworth, as do Thoreau's emphases on the moral life, the growth of the poet's mind, and the quality of joy. In England, Wordsworth is the great spokesman for the sanative, health-giving power of nature; in America that spokesman is Thoreau.

Thoreau did not see his way ahead so clearly. He was, this January, working several different directions. He was doing translations and editing from other writers and times, he was pursuing his interest in the heroic individual, and he was working out a form for nature essays. He was also increasingly involved in editorial work and in lecturing. The past ten months had seen a remarkable burst of creative activity; he could take pride in having finished most of what he had started. He was beginning to have an impressive body of work in print. Yet despite all this, he felt unsure about himself, his talent, his vocation. In a letter to the Emersons later this year he wrote that he was sorry Mrs. Emerson was no better. "But let her know that the Fates pay a compliment to those whom they make sick—and they have not to ask what have I done?" Obviously he did not regard himself as one of the sick, and was determined to do something. But one serious problem with the literary life so far was that despite increased writing, great improvement, and rapidly expanding publication, there was, so far, no money at all in it for him.[6]

30. Staten Island

Early in May 1843, Thoreau left Emerson's house and Concord to go to Staten Island where he was to live with Emerson's brother, William, as the children's tutor. As early as January, Thoreau was preparing himself to leave his home of the past two years. They had been important, pivotal, productive years for Thoreau, and he was appropriately grateful. "I have been your pensioner for nearly two years, and still left free as under the sky," he wrote Emerson. What Thoreau treasured, and wanted Emerson to know he treasured, was the "long kindness" of both Emerson and Lydia, and the free nature of the gift of that affection.[1]

Emerson had done other things of almost equal importance for him. During the two years at Emerson's, Thoreau's interest both in English poetry and in Indic scriptures was deepened. From helping with *The Dial*, he learned a good deal about the practical workaday side of writing and publishing. He returned to lecturing as an invaluable means for trying out a draft on an audience, he became more involved in town life, and he learned to write better, more informative, less self-absorbed letters. When he moved into the Emerson household he had been a young man who vaguely aspired to the literary life; when he left he was rapidly becoming a prolific, practiced, self-assured writer, realistically intent on literature as a profession. When he went to Emerson's the best piece he had written was the highly Emersonian "Persius." When he left he was working on the first of his fully characteristic and very un-Emersonian pieces, "A Winter Walk." John's death had freed Thoreau to write, perhaps spurred him to write, as though he now felt responsible for the articulation of two lives instead of one. Emerson had freed him from imitating Emerson. Emerson did not really care for some of the best things Thoreau was now writing, but this divergence only strengthened Thoreau's emerging confidence. His apprenticeship, his time of reliance on the judgment of others was coming to an end. Thoreau sensed it as he gravely thanked Emerson, by letter, in January, just as he was moved a few months later to a rare unscornful, unsatirical confession of gratitude to Harvard. He told Richard Fuller, who had been his companion on the walk to Wachusett, that what he had learned in college that was valuable was "to express myself," and "sincerity in our dealings with ourselves." His most pressing debts thus acknowledged, he prepared for what he clearly thought of as a major departure. "I expect to leave Concord," he wrote Richard Fuller, "which is my Rome, and its people, who are my Romans, in May, and go to New York, to be a tutor to Mr. William Emerson's family."[2]

He took the great step in early May. Nothing of the trip is recorded except the arrival, by boat, at a wharf near Castle Gardens. Thoreau was struck by the crowds of people in New York and by its built-up, utterly urban atmosphere. He landed amid a swarm of noisily competing cab men and his first impressions of New York were of "a confused jumble of heads and soiled coats, dangling from flesh-colored faces—all swaying to and fro, as by a sort of undertow," each one pointing at prospects with his whiplash and calling out continually.[3]

The Emerson household on Staten Island was rural enough. Seven and a half miles from the city—about half as far as Concord was from Boston—the house was surrounded by farms and woods. Thoreau made four or five trips to the city in his first month there, and continued to be fascinated by the "faces in the street," by "the hum of the city." "The crowd is something new and to be attended to,'" he told Emerson. "It is worth a thousand Trinity Churches and Exchanges," and, he added ominously, "will run over them and trample them under foot one day." New York was full of energy and growing rapidly. Streets were laid out, Thoreau noted, as far as 149th Street, and it was already built solid from the Battery to 15th Street. Manhattan already had its man-made aspect. It was, Thoreau wrote his parents, "clear brick and stone and no give to the foot."[4]

Thoreau continued to be plagued with poor health. He had a severe cold, complicated by bronchitis, for the first two and a half weeks after his arrival. He had trouble getting acclimated; it was a multitude of little things, which he found it hard to account for. He was better by the end of the first week in June—or at least he told his parents he was better—but a month later he was reporting an attack of sleeping sickness. This was a family affliction on Mrs. Thoreau's side, coming from her maternal grandparents, the Joneses. Thoreau wrote in *Walden* of his uncle Charlie Dunbar "who goes to sleep shaving himself."

Thoreau's form of the disease—called narcolepsy—was not severe, but it was recurrent, and the present attack made him so sleepy that it was a daily triumph just to stay awake until nightfall. This affliction adds a sly and touching twist to Thoreau's repeated use of wakefulness as a metaphor for consciousness and spiritual life.[5]

As usual, he held himself to strict standards, struggling against drowsiness to keep on with his literary projects, noting that "most men lead a starved existence like hawks that would fain keep on the wing, and catch but a sparrow now and then," and admonishing himself that during the English Renaissance "the men of genius were at the same time the merriest and most full of life."[6]

His letters this year are more informative and numerous than those of any previous year. And more than ever before, he let himself go in his letters, some of which are so effusive and strained they must have been overpoweringly sincere at the time. "There is a tide which pierces the pores of the air," he wrote in the February letter of thanks to Emerson. From Staten Island he wrote openly affectionate letters to his sisters and family and made no secret of missing Concord. And to Lydia Emerson he wrote an extravagant and emotional letter that looks very much like a love letter. Thoreau had written to her a couple of weeks after his arrival in New York, saying "I think of you as some elder sister of mine," and going on very much in the manner of one of the family. Lydia wrote back a letter, now missing, which triggered a confiding burst of almost tearful gratitude, as had Emerson's trusting letter earlier this same year. "The thought of you will constantly elevate my life," he wrote Lydia, "it will be something always above the horizon to behold, as when I look up at the evening star," which Thoreau knew well enough was the planet Venus. Lydia was not at all well this year—neither was Lucy Brown when Thoreau wrote tenderly to her—and the note of adoration is real enough in the letter to Lydia. No doubt he loved her. The overlapping circles of friends, which had for their twin centers Emerson and Fuller, put an enormous premium on their loving each other and on not hiding either the affection or its expression. Thoreau was less afraid of sounding mawkish or overemotional than he was of seeming cold. He owed the Emersons a great deal, and was on affectionate and intimate terms with them. He was away from home, homesick, and Lydia was ill. The letter says a great deal about the strongly affectionate nature Thoreau usually kept concealed, but it does not say that he was "in love" with Emerson's wife.[7]

Thoreau did not find the William Emersons congenial. There was no intellectual life at the house, and he was not particularly drawn to his young charge. Staten Island itself he enjoyed; things flowered earlier than in Concord and he was pleased by such flora as gum trees, tulip trees, and wild garlic. The high point of his stay was his "discovery" of the ocean. He compared the roar of the sea with the hum of the city and enjoyed walking on the beach. "Everything there is on a grand and generous scale—sea-weed, water, and sand; and even the dead fishes, horses and hogs have a rank luxuriant odor." The city itself he came to dislike as too crowded, and reversing the usual judgment, he thought it a good place to live, but a difficult one to visit. But he had not come for the city itself, or the shore, or Staten Island, or to be a tutor to rich men's sons. Thoreau had come to New York in active pursuit of his literary career.[8]

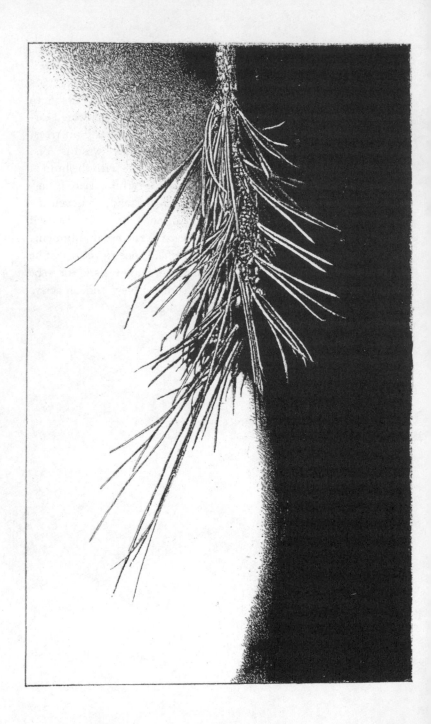

IV. 1843-1845

The Road to Walden Pond

WHAT THOREAU WANTED TO do was to establish his "literary labor" on a paying basis in New York. Living with the William Emersons and tutoring their boy in exchange for board and room was just a means to this end. As soon as he was well, he began making frequent trips to the city, going the rounds of the publishers in an effort to place his writings. Writing for and helping edit *The Dial* had been good experience, but it had paid nothing, and the one piece that had been placed in another Boston periodical also came to nothing financially, as the publisher shabbily went back on his promise to pay Thoreau despite much dunning by Emerson and others. There were more opportunities in New York, then a city of over 300,000 people, or more than three times the size of Boston. Thoreau's vaguely stated plan was "to earn a certain sum before winter." He frequented the New York Society Library and the Mercantile Library, and went to the picture gallery of the National Academy of Design. He tried *The New Mirror*, *Brother Jonathan*, and *The New World*; all were "overwhelmed with contributions which cost nothing, and are worth no more," he reported to Emerson. "*The Knickerbocker* is too poor, and only *The Ladies' Companion* pays." He concluded, glumly, that "even the little that I write is more than will sell." He even went so far as to try selling subscriptions to *The American Agriculturist* door to door. This too failed.[1]

He did meet interesting people. Some young and recent friends of Emerson, Giles Waldo and William Tappan, took Thoreau around, showed him the sights and entertained him. He met the nephew of the great William Ellery Channing, W. H. Channing. Then thirty-three, and ardent for socialism, the one-time member of Brook Farm was about to start, in September, his own socialist periodical, *The Present*. To Thoreau's eye Channing was a man of doubts: "You feel as if you would like to see him when he has made up his mind to run all the risks." There was Albert Brisbane, the American Fourierist, thirty-four years old and author of *The Social Destiny of Man* (1840) and *Association* (1843). Brisbane had laid his axe to Emerson's root the year before; Thoreau now kept his distance, commenting acidly, "he looks like a man who has lived in a cellar, far gone in consumption." There was Horace Greeley, then thirty-three, with "white soft hair." Emerson had found him a man of "sanguine temper and liberal mind." Greeley had founded the *New York Tribune* just two years earlier. Only six years Thoreau's senior, he would become a tireless and loyal promoter of Thoreau's work. Thoreau found him "cheerfully in earnest—at his office of all work—a hearty New Hampshire boy as one would wish to meet." Greeley had come to New York in 1831. He was a Free-Soiler, antislavery, and his cause of the moment was Association, that is, Fourierian socialist communes.[2]

Best of all was Henry James, Sr., then also thirty-two, with a son William just over a year old and another, the future novelist, Henry, just born in April. James had not yet undergone his conversion to Swedenborgianism or to living in Europe, but was already a gently persistent seeker. "I know of no one so patient and determined to have the good of you," Thoreau wrote of him after a three-hour talk. "He is a refreshing forward-looking and forward-moving man, and he naturalized and humanized New York for me."[3]

These men were all just slightly older than Thoreau. All were successful: James had family money, the others were writing with energy and publishing to general acclaim. The other thing they all had in common was a passion for sweeping social reform, specifically the planting of exemplary new communes. Thoreau did not feel at home in New York, he was not successful in finding a way to make his writing pay, and the most interesting company around him was devoted to an issue about which he had the most serious reservations. Despite, or perhaps because of the fact that he found himself out of place and out of step, he continued to work in his own room on his own writing.

His letter writing improved under the need to describe new sights and acquaintances for his family and for the Emersons. When he could keep himself awake, he worked on more Greek translations. This time it was Pindar, and he continued to read for his English poetry anthology project. He was working seriously on his prose, the difficulties of which he increasingly appreciated. He remarked in his journal in April, "It is harder to write great prose than to write verse." And in mid-summer, measuring his prose now not against the rhymed but the spoken word, he observed to Emerson, "In writing conversation should be folded many times thick," and he went on to explain that one ought to write carefully enough so that a piece would need at least three readings before its full beauty could be apprehended. These comparisons show Thoreau with a new self-consciousness about prose, a newly realistic estimate of the difficulties of writing well, and a bright turn of phrase in talking about such things. He was now settling into prose as his proper medium. He was also beginning to be concerned with the emergence of an American idiom in language. He looked to the West for new words, such as "diggings," and he remarked "many others also which now look so raw slang-like and colloquial when printed another generation will cherish and affect as genuine American and standard."[4]

He completed two pieces within six weeks of arrival, "Paradise (to be) Regained" and "A Winter Walk." The first of these is a long review of a book by J. A. Etzler outlining a utopian scheme and called *The Paradise within the Reach of all Men, without Labor, by Powers of Nature and Machinery.* Surrounded in New York as in Concord by reformers, Thoreau found the 1842 reprint of Etzler's book timely, and indeed his review was the only piece he managed to place during his eight months in New York. Etzler's enthusiasm was unfettered by modesty or caution, and his opening was irresistible. "I promise to show the means of creating a paradise within ten years, where everything desirable for human life may be had by every man in superabundance, without labor and without pay." Sober social analysis was not Etzler's forte and there is inevitably a good deal of irony in Thoreau's review. Etzler's scheme depended wholly on machinery and on concerted human action; he had no place for individuals, declaring flatly "nothing great . . . can ever be effected by individual enterprize." Thoreau, of course, took exception to this, chiding Etzler for his "want of faith in . . . a man." But there was a side to the book that caught Thoreau's imagination. It gave him, he said, "enlarged ideas," it represented

"Transcendentalism in mechanics." Etzler began by cataloguing the sources of renewable energy—the wind, the tides, the sun. He thought it possible to develop solar "burning mirrors" to boil water and produce steam; he foresaw huge windmills and tide mills; he imagined large-scale desalinization, pumped-storage water mills, heavy earth-moving and -leveling machinery; he called for the encouragement of mass immigration to provide cheap labor, land grants, and federal subsidies for massive projects such as railways, canals, and power plants. Etzler wrote a sequel called *The Mechanical System*, which Thoreau says he didn't see, that is full of drawings for a central powerhouse (wind-driven) with outlying, cable-driven "Satelites" very much on the principle of the old San Francisco or Denver cable car systems, in which a number of independent cars are driven by mechanical linkage from a central powerhouse.[5]

Thoreau was impressed almost against his will by Etzler's mechanical cleverness and by his painstaking calculations of the natural energy available from wind and tide. "No doubt," Thoreau conceded, "the simple powers of nature properly directed by man would make it healthy and paradise; as the laws of man's own constitution but wait to be obeyed, to restore him to health and happiness." It was only Etzler's headlong conviction—that in the new world of cheap power and large machines the individual would count for nothing and would no longer even have to work—that Thoreau found objectionable. No doubt nothing great could be accomplished without enthusiasm, but Thoreau was sure that nothing at all would ever be accomplished without work.[6]

32. "A Winter Walk"

"A Winter Walk," put together "very hastily" during Thoreau's first month in New York, is his first fully mature piece of writing. He drew on earlier journal entries for some of his material, but the essay was essentially written in late spring and early summer. The writing conveys not only a quality of felt experience, but the selective intensity of remembered experience. It begins very quietly; the reader is made to listen. "The wind has gently murmured through the blinds, or puffed with feathery softness against the windows, and occasionally sighed like a summer zephyr lifting the leaves along, the live long night." The essay's opening is reminiscent of Keats's "Eve of St. Agnes" in the careful alliteration, the control of linguistic sound in a paragraph centering on natural sounds. "The meadow mouse has slept in his snug gallery in the sod, the owl has sat in a hollow tree in the depth of the swamp, the rabbit, the squirrel, and the fox have all been housed." Thoreau's opening begins with natural observation and ends with myth. "But while the earth has slumbered, all the air has been alive with feathery flakes descending, as if some northern Ceres reigned, showering her silvery grain over all the fields." As Thoreau would later observe, the writer who aspires to a language adequate to nature must be able to link fact with myth.[1]

Thoreau's newly scrupulous care in phrasing gives this essay a well-crafted quality. "The river flows in the rear of the towns, and we see all things from a new and wilder side," or "it is the outside and edge of the earth," or "the unexplored grandeur of the storm keeps up the spirits of the traveller." There is a good deal of Thoreau's characteristic paradox. "What would human life be without forests, those natural cities?" he asks, and elsewhere he calls the "deserted woodman's hut . . . a civilized and public spot," while in another place he describes snow "warm as cotton or down upon the window-sill."[2]

When Thoreau sent "A Winter Walk" to Emerson, the latter edited it down by at least two pages, and he wrote Thoreau a candid letter objecting, not for the first time, to Thoreau's mannerisms. Emerson did not like what he said was the mere trick of calling "a cold place sultry, a solitude public, a wilderness *domestic* (a favorite word) and in the woods to insult over cities, whilst the woods, again, are dignified by comparing them to cities, armies, etc." Thoreau accepted Emerson's "pretty free" editing with a grace surprising in one who later became notorious for his objections to even small verbal changes by editors. He must have felt that Emerson was right about his overdoing paradox until it sank into a predictable and therefore irritating rhetorical device. But oppositions and unexpected inversions were already central to Thoreau's thought and wit and were therefore an inevitable aspect of his writing. "A Winter Walk" doesn't merely play with warm snow and civilized woods. It asserts the necessity of the woods to the spiritual well-being and health of a civilized people and it celebrates the powerful life force of nature even when that force seems dormant. "There is a slumbering subterranean fire in nature which never goes out, and which no cold can chill. It finally melts the great snow, and in January or July is only buried under a thicker or thinner covering. In the coldest day it flows somewhere, and the snow melts around every tree."[3]

"A Winter Walk" is the first of Thoreau's excursion essays that is centered on a season and in which all his characteristic concerns are brought together into a whole dominated by the natural scene in all its urgent and immediate detail. The essay strikes the religious note; it ends preferring a personal religion of nature to the Hebrew Bible. It also strikes, if rather faintly, the social note in its account of the woodchopper as the common man. The essay also shows Thoreau's new mastery of the narrative techniques that give his best writing so much authority and so much intimacy. Every reader feels that Thoreau is speaking directly to him or her. This is because Thoreau makes his narrator a vivid presence, an accurate reporter whom we trust. It is also because Thoreau casts the reader as his walking companion. He rarely mentions those people with whom he actually went walking, but he never excludes the reader from the walk. Even in the least hospitable places, it is the reader who is invited to share both risks and insight through the Thoreauvian "we":

> A cold and searching wind drives away all contagion, and nothing can withstand it but what has a virtue in it, and accordingly, whatever we meet with in cold and bleak places, as the tops of mountains, we respect for a sort of sturdy ignorance, a Puritan toughness. All things beside seem to be called in for shelter, and what stays out must be part of the original frame of the universe.[4]

In most respects, Thoreau's stay in New York seemed at the time a failure. He found living with the William Emersons dull, and he did not succeed in breaking into the New York literary world. On the positive side, Greeley would prove a great friend and advocate; Thoreau had managed to write the splendid "A Winter Walk," and he had learned that his heart really was in Concord. He had been willing to leave it, now he was more than content to return. The New York experience both reconciled him to his home and gave him a new realism about his own work. In August he wrote his mother:

> It is still a cardinal virtue with me to keep awake. I find it impossible to
> write or read except at rare intervals, but am, generally speaking, tougher
> than formerly. I could make a pedestrian tour round the world, and some-
> times think it would perhaps be better to do at once the things I *can*,
> rather than be trying to do what at present I cannot do well.

Late in October, he made a comment in his journal that catches
perfectly the sense of instructive failure he felt about his time in New
York:

> Though I am old enough to have discovered that the dreams of youth are
> not to be realized in this state of existence yet I think it would be the next
> greatest happiness always to be allowed to look under the eyelids of time
> and contemplate the perfect steadily with the clear understanding that I
> do not attain to it.[5]

33. *The Railroad Comes to Concord*

Henry Adams remarks in *The Education of Henry Adams* that eighteenth-century Boston came to an end in the 1840s with "the opening
of the Boston and Albany Railroad, the appearance of the first Cunard
steamers in the bay, and the telegraphic messages which carried from
Baltimore to Washington the news that Henry Clay and James K.
Polk were nominated for the Presidency." Eighteenth-century Concord came to an end about the same time and for the same reasons.
When Henry Thoreau came home from Staten Island to Concord first
for Thanksgiving in 1843 and then on December 17 to stay, he was
returning to a town that was rapidly and visibly changing. The most
obvious sign of change was approach of the railroad, but the railroad
was indicative of other changes as well.[1]

Massachusetts as a whole was to grow 34.8 percent during the
1840s. Boston had been chosen as the Cunard terminus in 1840, and
for the next few years Boston was at its height as a port city. Its first
grain elevator was built in 1843. Despite the growth, times were
hard. During the six years from Thoreau's leaving college in 1837 to

his return from Staten Island in 1843, the wholesale price of wheat had fallen from $1.77 a bushel to $.98. Wool had fallen from $.42 to $.30 a pound. The wholesale price index, if one sets 1835 at 100, had risen to 115 by 1837, then fallen to 75 by 1843. Skilled workers such as carpenters still commanded in 1843 the same $1.25 they had in 1837, but the wages for unskilled laborers (on the Erie Canal, for example) fell from $.88 a day in 1837 to $.75 a day in 1843.[2]

Just as Thoreau was leaving for Staten Island in April 1843, he heard that "The Boston and Fitchburg railroad passing through this town [Concord] is to be contracted for directly." The railroads had already been a mixed blessing to Concord. When the Boston to Lowell line had been completed, in 1836, even though it did not run through Concord, it had cut into traffic on the Middlesex Canal, and thus into Concord's hopes for increased water traffic. By 1843 the Lowell railroad had cut canal traffic by two-thirds, the canal was in precipitous decline, could no longer finance repairs, and would soon petition for a change of charter in order to transform itself into an aqueduct for the growing population of Boston. The Fitchburg railroad had begun buying land in 1842, rails had reached Waltham in 1843, the same year preparatory work reached Concord. Emerson's letters to Thoreau described the scene. "The town is full of Irish and the woods of engineers with theodolite and red flag singing out their feet and inches to each other from station to station." In September, Emerson described how the eighteen-foot-high earth embankment, or mole, for the tracks advanced thirty-three feet toward the depot every day. The work moved rapidly; it was of course all done by manual labor, not by Etzler's new world of mechanical aids. There were a thousand Irish workmen on the project, earning $.60 or even $.50 a day for a sixteen-hour day. It reminded Emerson of slave driving; he noted that the town's charitable impulse was moved by "the poor Irish," but he felt helpless in the face of impersonal economic forces. "What can be done for their relief as long as new applicants for the same labor are coming in every day? These of course reduce the wages to the sum that will suffice a bachelor to live, and must drive out the men with families." The railroad was a lesson in economics. When the first train arrived in Concord in June of 1844, the fare to Boston was $.50, a day's wages for one of its builders, a third cheaper than the stagecoach, and it took one hour instead of the stage's four.[3]

Emerson, looking ahead, accurately foresaw that the coming of the railroad would change everything; specifically that it would bring Concord so close to Boston that it would drive him from his peace and quiet. He thought of moving, had doubts about making further commitments in Concord. But even as construction proceeded during the summer of 1843, Ellery Channing found Emerson's end of town still very quiet indeed. Channing, another of Emerson's poets, whose poems had just been published in book form, had moved to Concord in the spring of this year. Thoreau had helped arrange repairs to the little red farmhouse Channing was to rent for $55 a year on the Cambridge turnpike adjoining Emerson's garden. Outside on the road, Channing observed, there were about four carts a day, and two men "in red faces and bundles, just to keep us from forgetting there are other towns." Otherwise it was as peaceful as one could wish. "The old world lolls its tongue sleepily," said Channing.[4]

But the other end of town, out by Walden Pond, was anything but peaceful. The new railroad line passed so close to the pond that an arm of it had to be filled in for the high and still quite visible embankment on which the rails were laid. One could see the new railroad from almost any point on the pond. Concord and Walden were thenceforth much more closely tied, and *obviously* closely tied to the outside world. This alone would have justified calling it the end of eighteenth-century Concord. If the Old World still seemed to Channing to loll its tongue over by the Cambridge turnpike, out at Walden one might hear across the surface of the pond the sounds of the New World of industrial capitalism, first shovels, then hammers, then steam engines.

34. Inside the Civilized Man

Thoreau's fall of 1843 was marked by one last flurry of efforts in September to make his writings sell somehow in New York. Next came an unsettled couple of months as his thoughts turned more and more to Concord. Despite or perhaps because of his growing sense of alienation and frustration in New York, his writing this fall, while not extensive, reached down and tapped some deep springs in him. In his journal for September 29 there appears for the first time a sketch on "the first sparrow of spring" that was to evolve into one of the most famous passages in *Walden*. Just as "A Winter Walk" had been written in early summer, so this famous description of the coming of spring was written as fall approached. This is not as paradoxical as it may seem. Much of Thoreau's best writing, like Wordsworth's, came from feelings recollected in tranquillity, his glad spontaneous response to the seasons was filtered through the imagination over a period of time, reaching expression only when the inner season was right. Increasingly, as the years passed, Thoreau's sense of the seasons is marked by either reminiscence or anticipation. He begins to think of spring returning almost as soon as it is gone.[1]

It is also interesting that this great passage on spring began not with nature itself but with Thoreau thinking about music, and a decidedly man-made music at that. His account begins: "I am winding up my music box and as I pause meanwhile the strains burst forth like a pent up fountain of the middle ages. Music is strangely allied to the past—every era has its strain. It awakens and colors my memories." And now, with no other transition, we get: "The first sparrow of spring. The year beginning with younger hope than ever. The first silvery warblings heard over the bare dank fields."[2]

Thoreau was still several years from even the first short tentative draft of *Walden*, but ideas, images, passages were already in his head and would precede and even influence the nature of the book when it was finally conceived as a book. Thoreau's way of writing was that of a poet. He started with jottings, perceptions, phrases, short bits often written on the backs of envelopes or other scraps of paper, and often while out walking. Later, back in his room, he would expand the jottings in journal or notebook or, sometimes, letter. Later still, he would work up a lecture or an essay, or return to a familiar subject, pulling together bits, some of which could be quite a few years old. He kept indexes for his notebooks so he could find things in what became an increasingly complicated multivolume writer's storehouse of material. From jottings to journal or notebook, to lecture, to essay was the usual pattern of development, with much of the creative work, the phrase polishing, coming in the journal and notebook stage, as he worked on one passage or image or sentence at a time.

He also returned this fall to some of the material that would end up in *A Week*. In his journal and in a notebook he called the Long Book, he worked on a pair of paragraphs that described the walking part of the trip, after the brothers had left their boat and set out for the White Mountains. This was a section of the trip he ultimately left out of the book, and this fall he seemed unsure how to handle this part of the trip. In the Long Book he tried to weave in the idea of "an epic to be called the leaf" (an ambition Whitman, not Thoreau, would fulfill), and he returned to his old interest in how crystallization resembled foliage, citing this time "mildew on a jar [that] had taken the form of perfect leaves." As he reworked the same materials in his journal, he seemed on the verge of leaving it all out. After a brief description of following the Merrimack up until it becomes the Pemmiggewasset, he suddenly stops and wonders "why should we take the reader . . . through this rude tract?"[3]

Also this October, "A Winter Walk" appeared in *The Dial*. Far from protesting Emerson's changes, Thoreau seemed grateful, almost eager for them. Only part of Thoreau's original manuscript survives, but as Emerson left it, it is indeed a good piece, especially when compared with Thoreau's "The Landlord," a Charles Lamb-like familiar essay on a hospitable old Yankee innkeeper, published in the *Democratic Review* this October, and surely the least characteristic piece Thoreau ever allowed into print. In November appeared his review of Etzler, which also had to be revised, but on substantive rather than stylistic grounds.[4]

When Thoreau came back for Thanksgiving, he gave a lecture on "Homer, Ossian, Chaucer," which he worked up during November. He had been reading English poetry over the past few months, and with the notable exception of Quarles, with whose work Thoreau was fascinated, found it not fully satisfying. Drummond is a "quiddler—with little fire and fibre." He wishes Spenser hadn't used "an antique style" in *The Fairie Queene*. He found Marvell good only in parts, and frivolous and mean at other times. Marlowe had "many of the qualities of the great poet." He said in a letter that he rode "along the ranks of the English poets casting terrible glances," and when it came time to do the lecture, he turned back toward earlier poets and times. Homer he praises again as so natural "it is as if nature spoke," and because natural, timeless. Later poets, Thoreau noted, "have done little else than copy his similes," and he insisted that Homer's are the "earliest, latest production of the mind."[5]

Ossian he finds comparable to Homer. He had only discovered Ossian this fall, and he was very much taken with it. It does little good for us to cluck condescendingly at Thoreau's (or Goethe's or Jefferson's) admiration for the Ossianic poems of James McPherson. Authentic as the poems are or are not, McPhersons's work was fruitful for many a greater writer than he himself. What Thoreau—and many others— saw in Ossian was a world that was primitive but noble, the possibility of a society with primitive strength and heroic will, but without squalor, destructiveness, brutality, or meanness of spirit. Ossian rebutted Hobbes and ratified Rousseau; the poems were read as the indigenous Northern equivalent of Homer, poems founding the literature of Northern Europe. Thus Ossian occupied for Thoreau the place Beowulf occupies for us. "Compared with this simple fibrous life [of Ossian's heroes], our civilized history appears the chronicle of debility, of fashion, and the arts of luxury." In a fine phrase Thoreau summed up what Ossian taught him. "Inside the civilized man stands the savage still in the place of honor. We are those blue-eyed yellow-haired Saxons, those slender, dark-haired Normans."[6]

But the lecture—subsequently printed in one of the last issues of *The Dial*—does not rest on this note of longing for older and grander times. Thoreau moves on to Chaucer, whom he treats at greater length than his first two figures, as the founder of English poetry. By contrast with Homer, Chaucer is no longer a sacred bard, a heroic poet. "No hero stands at the door prepared to break forth into song or heroic action, but we have instead a homely Englishman, who cultivates the art of poetry." What Chaucer loses in heroic stature, though, he more than makes up for, Thoreau says, by his great humanness. "There is no wisdom which can take the place of humanity, and we find *that* in Chaucer." Thoreau's appetite for the raw, the primitive, the stern, the desolate is now counterbalanced by a less dramatic but more mature admiration for the wit, gentleness, good sense, the "remarkably trustful and affectionate character" of Chaucer. Thoreau is moved by admiration for what he sees as the preeminently civilized aspects of Chaucer's poetry. Thoreau's relish for the primitive and his growing admiration for the truly civilized do not really mesh in this lecture; the obvious problem is not resolved, but the theme is, as it were, announced. The savage may have the place of honor inside the civilized person, but both are necessary to true integrity.[7]

35. Spring and Summer 1844

The year 1844 did not start well for Thoreau and got worse as it went along. After more than two and a half years living with different sets of Emersons he was back with his own family in the Parkman house on Main Street. His literary career was, for the moment, stalled, and he was instead spending a good deal of time working with his father making pencils. Not that there was anything wrong with either arrangement, it was just that he was going on twenty-seven with two major problems unresolved. Where would he live and how would he support himself as a writer? In early 1844 the answer to both seemed to be home and family.

There was a large socialist convention in Boston in January. The Fourierist reform spirit was still rising, new communes were being established at a record rate. If this was the spirit of the times, Thoreau did not feel part of it. Emerson lectured on "The Young American" in February. As he talked with Thoreau this winter, the differences between them became increasingly apparent. Emerson described the excitement he felt in lecturing, the emotional urgency "not for reading . . . miscellanies, but for painting in fire my thought, and being agitated to agitate." The physical presence of the audience stirred in Emerson the "desire . . . to express myself fully, symmetrically, gigantically to them. . . . Art," said Emerson in one of his triumphant aphorisms, "is the path of the creator to his work."[1]

Thoreau would have none of this, did not find the relation of lecturer to audience "natural," saw only "Art in a sinister sense." Plainly he was not ready to throw himself into lecturing. Thoreau's path to his own work was not through art but was through pencil-making. He was working hard, designing new ways to improve both the production process and the finished product. The problem was that he could do only one thing at a time. Although his evenings were free for study, he told Emerson that "if he was in the day inventing machines for sawing his plumbago, he invents wheels all the evening and night also." It was another difference between Thoreau and Emerson; Emerson said he could only do one piece of work well when another was due. Like Walter Scott, he wrote only to avoid writing something else.[2]

There are long gaps in Thoreau's journals for the winter of 1843–44. Then in April *The Dial* came to an end. This had been his major place of publication; indeed the few pieces he had managed to place outside *The Dial* came to very little indeed: "A Walk to Wachusett," the Etzler review, the Landlord piece.

Also in April, there came to live with the Thoreau family a young man named Isaac Hecker who had been trying Brook Farm and then Fruitlands in a search for a better life. The restless Hecker soon got Thoreau thinking of travel—real travel—a European trip. But before that became a concrete possibility requiring serious consideration, he took a much shorter trip that ended in catastrophe. On the last day of April 1844, Thoreau and Edward S. Hoar, a senior at Harvard whose father was a leading citizen of Concord, were out on a rowboat expedition to explore the upper reaches of the Sudbury River. They caught a mess of fish, and to cook them built a fire in a decaying pine stump on the shores of Fair Haven Bay. It was the worst imaginable place to light a fire; the woods were dry and the fire spread quickly and uncontrollably from the fatwood of the stump. Before it was put out, the fire burned over three hundred acres. The town's reaction can be imagined, as can Thoreau's chagrin. It was six years before he could bring himself to write up—or write out—the incident in his journal, though he would sometimes dream about fire and wind-whipped showers of sparks, and would write about such dreams in his "Ktaadn" essay.[3]

There were no further disasters this year, but the months passed in an undirected, purposeless, thoroughly unsatisfying manner. In May, Ellery Channing moved to New York, having been settled in Concord for less than a year. In June, as the first trains began service from Boston to Concord, Isaac Hecker too moved off to New York. (In New York this May, William Cullen Bryant, poet turned newspaper editor, was calling for the creation of a five-hundred-acre park in the middle of New York City.) In July, Thoreau set off on a walking trip. The idea was for him to meet Channing at the foot of Saddleback Mountain in the Berkshires and proceed thence to the Catskills. Thoreau went by way of Mount Monadnock. He climbed it and Saddleback (now Grey-lock), then met Channing, with whom he walked west to the Hudson, then went by boat down the Hudson to the Catskills. Though Thoreau wrote up parts of the trip and though he used a few pages on the mountain climbing in *A Week*, this seems to have been one of his least productive excursions. It left him, he wrote Hecker in August, with "a slight sense of dissipation," and he amplified his response. "I mean that I constantly return from every external enterprise with disgust to fresh faith in a kind of Brahminical Artesian, Inner Temple life." In general, Thoreau's most eventful, most literarily productive excursions would in the future take him east or north, to mountains or to the sea. His trips west and south, his ventures inland, would come to much less.[4]

Back from the Catskills, Thoreau was invited by Hecker to "work our passage to Europe, and to walk, work, and beg, if needs be, as far when there as we are inclined to do." Thoreau was tempted, and he felt, he told Hecker, "a decided schism between my outward and inward tendencies." He wrote a long letter to Hecker, declining gently and with a good show of hesitation. Perhaps the invitation and the necessity then to decline it helped his own needle to settle. He had to explore the inner world first. "The fact is," he wrote Hecker, "I cannot so decidedly postpone exploring the *Farther Indies*, which are to be reached you know by other routes and other methods of travel."[5]

36. Fall 1844

Thoreau returned from his Berkshire and Catskill trip just in time to witness Emerson's public conversion to the antislavery movement. On the first of August 1844, at the urging of Henry's mother Cynthia Thoreau, among others, Emerson gave a talk in Concord to assembled representatives of thirteen towns. Called an "Address on Emancipation in the British West Indies," it marked the tenth anniversary of the 1834 act by which England had finally abolished slavery in all her colonies. It is a strong, vivid speech, commencing with a dramatic account—complete with names, dates, and a wealth of incidents—of the history of the English movement to abolish slavery. Emerson traced the line from the judicial decree in 1772 which outlawed slavery in England itself, to the 1807 abolition of the slave trade, to the act of August 1, 1834, a day, Emerson called it, of "reason" and "clear light, . . . a day which gave the immense fortification of a fact of gross history, to ethical abstractions." This speech, which is too little read now, is written in a style meant to underline this transition from ethical generality to concrete political fact. It is a historical essay, straightforward, urgent, and full of details and dates. Not only does Emerson compare the Americans unfavorably with the English but also, shrewdly, makes much of the economic argument that English businessmen saw every slave in the West Indies as a potential customer. Emerson's aim is to persuade and convince, not simply to preach to the converted, or air a smug moral superiority.[1]

This was a new public commitment for Emerson, indicative of the expanding and increasingly public sphere of the transcendentalists. No longer a village circle of intellectuals, they were, in Boston, in New York, in the West, and on the communes, increasingly committed to testing their convictions by actual experiment and by writing and publishing. This transfer of energy from the study to the larger world can be glimpsed in the contrast between Emerson's staunch and effective antislavery address and his new Monday evening club designed during the early fall of 1844 for the choice spirits of Concord. The Address was a great success; the club fell flat after three awkward meetings.[2]

Emerson's long hoped-for conversion to active abolition stirred Thoreau strongly. When the sexton of the First Parish Church refused to ring the bell for the meeting, Thoreau "rushed to the church, grasped the rope vigorously in his hands, and set the bell to ringing

merrily until it had gathered a whole crowd for Emerson's speech."
Later he helped arrange for the piece to be printed.[3]

It was a busy fall. The day after the Emancipation speech was published (September 9), John Thoreau bought a lot and his son began to build a house on what was then Texas Street, now Belknap Street, in Concord. It was the first house the family had owned or built; all the earlier ones had been rented. Thoreau dug the cellar, and stoned it. Working with his father took much of his time this fall, but he was learning how to build a house. What he could do for his family he could do for himself.

He was also starting to construct a book. In the inner circle of transcendentalists, Thoreau was almost alone in not having published one. He had copied over into a special notebook (the Long Book) all his earlier notes and jottings on the Merrimack River trip, and by the fall of 1844, he was going through the material for at least the third time. The principle of going day by day, rather than topic by topic, was emerging in the Long Book, and the amount of material to be included was beginning to expand. One of the numerous "models" for the book as it finally emerged was Margaret Fuller's *Summer on the Lakes*, which had just been published the first week of June 1844.[4]

During the first days of October, Emerson bought a pasture on the shores of Walden Pond. He and his group of "gossips" went to look at it, and his friends persuaded him that the pasture was incomplete without the adjoining stand of pines. Emerson bought the woodlot as well, and he wrote Carlyle, "One of these days, if I should have any money, I may build me a cabin or a turret there high as the treetops and spend my nights as well as days in the midst of a beauty which never fades for me."[5]

In mid-October Emerson's second book of essays was published, and though this is the volume that begins with the great essay on "The Poet"—an important essay for Thoreau, too—Thoreau seems to have been much more interested, just at the moment, in the "Address on Emancipation," copies of which he was requesting on October 14. In Boston, on this day, a young seaman named Herman Melville had just returned from four years of wandering and was being paid off at the Navy Yard. What with the antislavery excitement, the housebuilding, and the growing manuscript of *A Week*, the fall was big with promise and excitement. According to William Miller of Pittsfield and his followers, October 22, 1844, was to be the last day of the world. As the time approached, the Millerites waited on hilltops and in roofless churches built for this day. In and around Concord, people abandoned crops, or gave up their work to others. Eggs had been retailing for eighteen cents a dozen, and a turkey cost a dollar on October 18. When October 23 dawned on the shaken Millerites, eggs were still eighteen cents a dozen, and a turkey still sold for a dollar.[6]

37. Spring 1845

"Near the end of March, 1845, I borrowed an axe and went down to the woods by Walden Pond, nearest to where I intended to build my house, and began to cut down some tall arrowy white pines, still in their youth, for timber. It is difficult to begin without borrowing." The pond lies south and just a little east of Concord center. It is a mile and a quarter from the town railroad station to the northern edge of the pond by the shortest route, which is along the tracks. Walden is a good-sized lake, covering about sixty-one acres. It is a half-mile in length, with the railroad running across one end and the Walden road running parallel across the other. It is a walk of nearly a mile and three-quarters around the shoreline of the pond. The whole area was much less densely and completely wooded then than it is now. Despite the railroad embankment that had cut off the pond's southwest arm and an eleven-acre pasture full of old stumps on the north side of the pond, it was a lovely place, though probably not as pretty as it is today.[1]

Thoreau liked to compare it to a mountain lake, and with some justice. It is deep and clear, its shoreline is clean and sharply defined, and it is surrounded not by the low lands and marshes so common around Concord, but by high ground, sloping up from the waterline. In those days most of the area around the pond was covered, but more with pine trees than with the deciduous trees which almost entirely surround the pond today. It deserved to be called "the chief ornament of this town," as Emerson once described it to Carlyle.[2]

Late in September of the previous year, Emerson had bought the eleven-acre field on the north shore of the pond for $8.10 an acre, and then the adjacent woodlot "of three or four acres," also shorefront, for another $125.00. Thoreau associated the pond with his earliest memories. "When I was four years old," he says in "The Bean-Field" chapter in *Walden*, "as I well remember, I was brought from Boston to this my native town, through these very woods and this field, to the pond." He had always loved it, and had gone there frequently, as had Emerson, who claimed to have had "a sort of daily occupancy in it." The idea of building a cabin and living there had long appealed to Thoreau, but it had only become a real possibility in the fall of 1844, when Emerson acquired the land, and Thoreau acquired his house-building skills.[3]

Thoreau's intention was clear by early March. He had even told others of it. Channing responded from New York on March 5, "I see nothing for you in this earth but that field which I once christened 'Briars'; go out upon that, build yourself a hut, and there begin the grand process of devouring yourself alive." It might be Emerson's land and someone else's axe, but it was Thoreau himself who went out and made what he and Channing both obviously saw as something more than just another move. From the start, it was a significant experiment, a new beginning.[4]

Thoreau's move to the woods was clearly related to inner, personal drives and convictions. But, as George Eliot observed, there is no private life without its public context. Thoreau's Walden experiment is no exception, and it gains a good deal by being seen against the backdrop of its time. It was a private experiment, but it had at least three distinct public contexts.

A group called the National Reform Association, located in New York and led and championed by Horace Greeley, was actively involved this spring of 1845 in the growing debate over how to dispose of the vast new federal lands in the newly created states of the expanding West. One suggestion was to give anyone who wanted it a quarter-section—160 acres—of public land free. Greeley and his friends foresaw that this idea, which eventually became the Homestead Act of 1862, would only encourage speculation and would lead to wealthy individuals buying out others and thus acquiring private rights to huge tracts of once-public land. Greeley's association wished to keep the new public land out of the hands of speculators and in the hands of individual farmers. The National Reform Association held a large national meeting in New York City on May 5, 1845. Its fundamental assumption was well put by Alvan E. Bovay, secretary of the Association. "Probably the discovery will soon be made that if a man has a right to life, he has, by inevitable consequence, the right to the elements of life, to the earth, the air, and the water." The NRA proposed that land be sold, not given, to individuals, that it be made immune to seizure for debt, and that no one be allowed, now or later, to acquire more than a single quarter-section. This proposal, which would have kept the land in the hands of the small farmers, and would have made the bonanza farming or agribusiness of the late nineteenth and twentieth centuries all but impossible, was a gesture on behalf of the old Jeffersonian ideal of subsistence farming. Thoreau's recent efforts to buy a farm had convinced him of the need for land reform, and his own sympathies were clearly with the small subsistence farmer, rather than with the large commercial farms.[5]

In the second context, Thoreau's going to live at Walden seems clearly intended as the self-reliant individual's answer to the challenge posed by the utopian communes such as Brook Farm, Hopedale, and Fruitlands. Together with the founders of these and many other new communities—thirty-three new utopian communities were founded in the years 1843 to 1845—Thoreau questioned the competitive quality of American society, the factory mode of production, and the general waste and extravagance in then-current practices regarding the provision of housing, clothing, and food. Thoreau's stay at Walden was the ultimate reform commune, reduced, for purposes of emphasis, to the simplest possible constituent unit, the self.

The third context is the most clearly political. On March 1, 1845, President Tyler signed the bill annexing Texas. It was understood at the time that this meant war with Mexico. Mexico had announced that it would regard American annexation of Texas as cause for war. This was regarded as a major victory for the slave states, as was the admission of Florida to the Union two days later. In this superheated climate, scarcely a week later, Wendell Phillips came to Concord to speak. Phillips was a passionate, committed, and eloquent abolitionist, and his invitation to Concord was strenuously opposed. The conservative curator of the Concord Lyceum resigned over the incident, and Emerson, Thoreau, and Samuel Barrett were elected instead by the victorious proabolition faction.

Phillips spoke in Concord on the eleventh of March denouncing the annexation and the impending war. His speech stirred Thoreau to compare Phillips to Spenser's Red Cross Knight and to write up the speech the following day in a long letter to the *Liberator*, printed on March 28. One of Phillips's topics was a young ex-slave named Frederick Douglass, who was just then making a stir as a speaker and was talking about his intention of writing his own life. Thoreau shared Phillips's indignation that Douglass was being urged to keep silent, lest he compromise people.[6]

Going to Walden was Thoreau's liberation, his experiment in freedom, and his account of himself in *Walden* is an interesting parallel to Douglass's account of his liberation, which was published and reviewed in June 1845, three months after Phillips's speech in Concord and just shortly before Thoreau's move out to the pond.

38. I Went to the Woods
to Live Deliberately

The tall arrowy white pines Thoreau cut down were fashioned into the framing for a small ten- by-fifteen-foot one-room cabin. In early May, Edmund Hosmer and others came out and raised the frame. Thoreau bought a shack and used its boards to sheathe the cabin, which was carefully sited on the north side of the pond. The cabin stood midway between the railroad and the Walden road, facing the water, with its back to the railroad, which was about five hundred yards away. Also in May and while working on the cabin, Thoreau hired a horse and ploughed up two and a half acres of the eleven-acre field. This field had been cut about fifteen years earlier, and it was full of stumps, which Thoreau now cleared out for firewood. Early in June he planted most of the two and a half acres with common small white bush beans, adding some corn and potatoes.

Every aspect of the move to Walden was symbolic or representative. The move itself was an emancipation from town and family, building the cabin was proof of his ability to shelter himself, growing beans showed he could feed himself, and have something left over. In "The Bean-Field" chapter in *Walden* he said he worked in the field "only for the sake of tropes and expression, to serve a parable-maker one day." On July 4, 1845, six weeks after Sir John Franklin set out from Greenhithe on the Thames, just below London, with the ships *Erebus* and *Terror* on his last voyage to find the Northwest Passage, Henry Thoreau took up residence at Walden Pond.[1]

He went to the pond for several reasons. For one thing, he had wanted for years to be independent, on his own. He was twenty-eight this July and he had always lived either at home, at college, or with Emersons. With no money and no steady job, he had few prospects of ever being able to afford a place of his own. And coming as late as it did, this getting away inevitably appeared to him in an exaggerated light, the small sense of personal freedom became an emancipation of the spirit as he groped for a subjective correlative in his own life experiences that would help him to understand the slavery issue. What he sought, he commented in his journal two days after moving in, was "Self-emancipation in the West Indies of a man's thinking and imagining provinces, which should be more than his island territory. One emancipated heart and intellect—it would knock off the fetters from a million slaves."[2]

The Walden Pond experiment was also a small scale social reformation, an effort to see what Brook Farm or Fruitlands (which had in 1843 almost decided to settle very near the pond, over on Fair Haven Bay) meant, not for a group, but for a single person interested in the reformation of society, the reform of agriculture, and the attainment of greater simplicity in domestic arrangements, together with the consequently greater liberty for the householder.[3]

It was not a very adventurous move, certainly not when compared to other contemporary ventures, to Ellery Channing's sojourn on the Illinois prairie, to Melville's four years of seafaring, to Sir John Franklin's doomed efforts this same summer to sail from Greenland to the Pacific via the subarctic waters of Baffin Bay, or to the westward moving Mormons who left Nauvoo, Illinois, for Utah in 1846, or to John

Charles Fremont, or to innumerable small groups such as the Donner party, which left Fort Bridger on the last day of July 1846, bound over the mountains to California. Thoreau was well aware that what he was doing was not braving wilderness, but simulating its conditions in a sort of symbolic or laboratory experiment. On July 16, he commented that he imagined "it to be some advantage to live a primitive and frontier life," and he pointedly added "though in the midst of an outward civilization." Thus it was clear to him at the very outset that what he was doing could be done anywhere, by anyone. It did not require a retreat from society. Thoreau's venture was in no sense a retreat or a withdrawal. He himself thought of it as a step forward, a liberation, a new beginning, or as he put it in the second chapter of *Walden*, an awakening to what is real and important in life.[4]

Another pervasive theme of *Walden* is the getting down to essentials. "I went to the woods because I wished to live deliberately, to front only the essential facts of life, and see if I could not learn what it had to teach, and not, when I came to die, discover that I had not lived." This desire to simplify, to find out how much or how little food, shelter, clothing, and furniture one really needs is one of the main points of the book, and it is important to note that this motive was explicit and clear in Thoreau's mind at the beginning of his stay. On his third day at the pond, in the light and airy cabin, in "the very light and atmosphere in which the works of Grecian art were composed," he wrote in his journal, "I wish to meet the facts of life—the vital facts, which were the phenomena or actuality the Gods meant to show us,—face to face, And so I came down here. Life! who knows what it is—what it does?"[5]

Thoreau went to Walden Pond for earnest, elevated reasons. He was in search of Life. He was also in search of simple living conditions that would permit him to concentrate on his writing.

39. The Epic of the Leaf

The experience of the two years and two months Thoreau stayed at Walden has become a permanent feature of the inner landscape of every educated American. We can no longer help regarding it as the high point of his life, and there is good reason to think that, at the time he went, Thoreau did too. His health had never been better, he was extraordinarily alive and open to his surroundings, his life had for the moment a free and satisfying simplicity and, from the point of view of writing, it was an astonishingly productive stay. In addition to the twelve bushels of beans and eighteen bushels of potatoes "besides some peas and green corn," he produced more writing of higher quality over a greater range of subjects while he was living at Walden than at any other period of his life. In twenty-six months he wrote two complete drafts of A Week, a complete draft of Walden, a lecture on his life at Walden, a lecture essay on Carlyle, and the first third of The Maine Woods that is the "Ktaadn" essay. This is an amazing output; the fundamental shape and substance of two books and a good part of a third, written in a variety of prose styles and recording a period of intense personal growth and awareness, from the elegiac and pastoral mood of A Week, through the balancing of man with nature at Walden, to the one-sided encounter with the primitive savagery of nature on Ktaadn. Thoreau once noted that "it is not easy to write in a journal what interests us at any time, because to write it is not what interests us." But during the stay at Walden, Thoreau managed, for once, to lead a life of extraordinary intensity, to provide a sustained record of that life and, crucially, to give that record adequate literary shape. Thoreau managed to bring to publication only two unified and sustained book-length pieces during his lifetime. Both were essentially shaped during the years at Walden Pond.[1]

Thoreau's first concentrated effort to assemble, flesh out, and then rearrange material about the trip he and John had taken on the Concord and Merrimack rivers dates back to August and September of 1842. Half a year after John's death, and in the extraordinary burst of literary activity that was released by that event, Thoreau began the notebook called the Long Book, the first 177 pages of which, dating from this period, constitute something halfway between rough notes and a first draft of A Week. Now, three years later, the first major task Thoreau took up at Walden was writing a proper draft of the book. This was accomplished by the fall of 1845. A second, expanded draft, the basis for the printed version, was written during the winter and spring of 1846–47. As the book grew, it also changed. The 1842 version is a voyage, held together by the theme of friendship. The 1845 draft has an even more detailed account of the excursion itself, but to the theme of friendship has been added that of the laws of nature and that of the congruence between man's life and nature. With the 1846–47 draft and the addition of a great deal of literary material, much of which had already been published in *The Dial*, the theme of literature itself—the poet's problem of how to express both oneself and nature—was added, diminishing the importance, and even partly obscuring the earlier focal points.[2]

As Thoreau worked on the first draft in 1845, one of the persistent problems in shaping the book was his shortage of detailed notes on the trip itself. Though his memory was remarkably good and though there is a reasonable amount of seemingly fresh description in the book, this paucity of detailed notes may have been one reason why, as the book grew, it came more and more to consist of inserted poems, essays, and meditations. When he took his next excursion—to the Maine woods the following year—he would take copious notes on the spot, and he would return and work them up quickly while they were still fresh.

Another problem with *A Week* was its form, or structure. Its form had not been predetermined. It literally evolved from Thoreau's materials at hand. It is an example, as is *Walden*, of the Coleridgean idea of organic form: it grew like a pear on its branch, not like a bowl on the potter's wheel. It is the first of the many American books shaped along a river trip, the first in which the river becomes a stream, not just of water or even of time, but of consciousness itself. *A Week* owes something to the old chronicles such as Hakluyt's *Voyages*, to new ones such as Shattuck's *History of Concord*, and to modern books of travel and exploration such as Thomas L. McKenney's *Sketches of a Tour to the Lakes, of the Character and Customs of the Chippeway Indians* . . . (Baltimore, 1827)[3]

The first draft proceeded day by day, with dates, giving a circumstantial account of the trip, and adding in supplemental comments and observations that eventually grew into a vast miscellany—almost an anatomy of friendship, like Burton's *Anatomy of Melancholy*.

Thoreau compressed two weeks into one, essentially cutting out the middle week he and John had spent traveling on land and merging the first Thursday with the second, shaping the book into chapters, one for each day of the week, the whole being in this respect a modern, secular version of Guillaume du Bartas's sacred *Week*, a seventeenth-century poetic account of creation.

A Week is also very close in spirit to several books of its own time. It is an American answer to Longfellow's 1835 *Outre-Mer: A Pilgrimage Beyond the Sea*, described by its author as "a kind of Sketch-Book of France, Spain, Germany, and Italy; composed of descriptions, sketches of character, tales illustrating manners and customs, and tales illustrating nothing in particular." Just as Longfellow inserted, for example, a previously published article on "Old English Prose Romances" into *Outre-Mer*, so Thoreau eventually inserted his "Persius," his "Homer Ossian Chaucer," and much more into *A Week*.[4]

Thoreau's *Week* is also close in tone and in subject to Margaret Fuller's 1844 *Summer on the Lakes*, a travelogue miscellany in prose and verse, genial, observant, colloquial, and unhurried, a book asserting the beauty of Niagara against anything Europe might offer and deeply interested in the American Indian.

Of all the books to which it can be compared (Wordsworth's *Excursion* and Gilbert White's *Natural History of Selbourne* should not be forgotten) Goethe's *Italian Journey* is the most important. It is the only such book mentioned in *A Week* by name and treated there at length. Goethe's splendid objective eye, his sense of self-growth, the casual epistolary and occasional shape of the narrative, and its great climactic discovery of the principle of the metamorphosis of plants, all these had made a deep impression on Thoreau years before and now exerted an influence on the long narrative he wrote out in the fall of 1845.[5]

40. The New Typology of the Leaf

"My purpose in making this wonderful journey is . . . to discover myself in the objects I see," Goethe wrote at the start of his *Italian Journey*. Whether or not it had been Thoreau's purpose when he took the trip, it certainly was what he sought now in 1845 as he wrote it up during the long fall days by the pond. It was an act of daring to assume that the mass of material he had gathered for *A Week*, scattered journal notes and insights spread over many subjects and written over many years, could ever arrange itself into a whole, unless the life that had produced and witnessed it all had itself some formative wholeness. What Thoreau explored in *A Week* was the extent to which the laws of his own nature were akin to the laws governing streams, crystals, and leaves. If one carried the organic theory of art to its logical conclusion, then literary form would follow after and be created by the character of the writer.[1]

"While walking in the Public Garden of Palermo," Goethe recalled in the *Italian Journey*, "it came to me in a flash that in the organ of the plant which we are accustomed to call the *leaf* lies the true Proteus who can hide or reveal himself in all vegetal forms. From first to last, the plant is nothing but leaf." Further, he thought that "The same law will be applicable to all other living organisms."[2]

Thoreau took all this up in his draft. "What an impulse was given some time or another to vegetation that now nothing can stay it," he noted. "Every where it is nature's business constantly to create new leaves and repeat this type in many materials." Nature is "a vast manufactory of leaves.—the leaf is her constant cipher. It is grass in the field . . . it flutters on the oak,—it springs in the mould on a jar— and in animal, vegetable and mineral—in fluids and in crystals— plain or variegated—fresh or decayed it acts how large a part in the economy of the universe." And the implications of this for the writer? Thoreau went on to draw a conclusion that would be true for Walt Whitman as well as for himself. "Whatever Coleridge thought of Tasso's having chosen the last remaining topic for an epic poem in the Delivery of Jerusalem—I think his critic was right who thought one could write an epic to be called the leaf."[3]

Throughout the first draft of *A Week* we find these themes: the law of the leaf and its manifestations in everything, and the relations between human nature, individual character, and the rest of nature. Early in the draft, Thoreau gives a catalogue of the fishes in the Concord River—not a Homeric listing or even a Whitmanesque accumulation, but an ordered, taxonomic description like Melville's classification of whales. In the midst of the pickerel, pout, eels, salmon, shad, and alewives, Thoreau pauses to exclaim how "though nature's laws are more immutable than any despots yet to our daily life they rarely seem rigid, but permit us to relax with license in summer weather."[4]

Later, on the third day, comes an extensive discussion of laws, beginning with an allusion to their timeless quality. Off in the country beyond the riverbank men live as they always have. "There dwelt the subject of the Hebrew Scriptures and the Esprit des lois." Thoreau extends this idea, suggesting that

> the hardest material obeys the same law with the most fluid. Trees are but rivers of sap and woody fibre flowing from the atmosphere and emptying into the earth by their trunks, as their roots on the other hand flow upward to the surface. And in the heavens there are rivers of stars and milky ways. There are rivers of rock in the surface of rivers of ore in the bowels of the earth. And our thoughts flow and circulate—and seasons lapse into the current year.

Rivers, like leaves, occur everywhere. The law of currents holds everywhere. The stream of water and the stream of thought are similar; geology offers hints about the landscape of mind. In this same section, Thoreau begins to bring in Eastern, Arabian, and Indic materials and by concentrating on those aspects of nature common to all eras, i.e., the laws, he dechronologizes history much as Emerson had. Thoreau takes up the ancient theologies only to leave them behind. What he is concerned with is the new typology of the leaf, not the old Christian typology of the history of redemption. Insofar as Thoreau is interested in redemption, it is now the newer idea, familiar from English and Continental Romanticism, of natural redemption.[5]

In the account of the sixth day occurs another long section on nature's laws, linked now explicitly to human laws and morals. "It is wholesome," Thoreau tells us, "to contemplate the natural laws—gravity—heat—light—moisture—dryness. Though to the indifferent and casual observer they are mere science, to the enlightened and spiritual they are not only facts but actions—the purest morality—or modes of divine life." Easy enough to assert, perhaps, and we are justified in asking what this might mean in practical terms. Thoreau's reply, a page later, throws light on his fact-gathering side and even offers a glimpse of the great project that would fill his later years long after *Walden*:

> Facts must be learned directly and personally. The collector of facts possesses a perfect physical organization . . . the philosopher possesses a perfect intellectual one—But in the poet they are so fairly—but mysteriously balanced that however frail he may be—that he can use the results of both—and generalizes even the widest deductions of philosophy,—seed—stalk—flower—for as yet the fruit eludes our grasp.[6]

With Friday, the seventh and last day, comes the homeward trip, a lovely stretch of writing on autumn (the season in which he was writing at the moment), and a final extended section on his sense of his relation to nature, as opposed to history or Christianity. "I feel that I draw nearest to understanding the great secret of my life in my closest intercourse with nature. There is a reality and health in present nature which cannot be contemplated in antiquity. I suppose that what in other men is religion is in me love of nature." From this passage we can gather that Thoreau now knew what such a life might be, but he is careful to qualify and explain that he does not think any of us have yet attained this perfect life in nature. "Men no where, east or west, live as yet a natural life, round which the vine clings, and which the elm willingly shadows. A life of equal simplicity and sincerity with nature, and in harmony with her grandeur and beauty."[7]

The laws that had led him through the writing of *A Week* led on to *Walden* then, to his reason for being there, and to his efforts to articulate as well as live this new life in nature.

V. 1846-1849
The Profession of Letters

41. Winter 1846: Carlyle

$\mathbb{E}$ARLY IN FEBRUARY 1846, Thoreau gave a public lecture on the works of Thomas Carlyle; it was a settling of accounts with one of the important early influences in his life, and it was the last conventional critical piece he ever wrote. Carlyle, now fifty, had just finished his large work on Oliver Cromwell, a work made up half of Cromwell's own letters and speeches, and half of Carlyle's "elucidations." Cromwell was, for Carlyle, the "soul of the Puritan Revolt," and English Puritanism was "the last of all our Heroisms." Cromwell had been treated badly by eulogists and enemies alike, provoking Carlyle to ask, "Is human writing, then, the art of burying heroisms?" The Greeks, said Carlyle, had had their *Iliad*, but all England had produced was *Collins' Peerage*. This he proposed to remedy, in a manner, with a vast documentary *Cromwelliad*.[1]

Carlyle had been corresponding steadily with Emerson, who continued to act as Carlyle's American agent with various publishers, "wretched hungerstruck hyaenas" Carlyle called them. Emerson was also busy with his own parallel project, the lectures and essays that would form *Representative Men*. Carlyle's *Cromwell* arrived in Concord in mid-December 1845 and Thoreau took, or was given, the occasion to do a major study of the man who, in Thoreau's estimation, "alone, since the death of Coleridge, has kept the promise of England."[2]

Inevitably, he began with Carlyle's style, defending it against charges of obscurity, mysticism, and Germanic mannerism. It was, said Thoreau, a style for the young; to the older reader Carlyle was "hopelessly sealed." He praised too Carlyle's use of "all the aids to intelligibility which the printer's art affords," adding, "You wonder how others had contrived to write so many pages without emphatic or italicized words, they are so expressive, so natural, so indispensable here." His conclusion, that Carlyle's was "the richest prose style we know of," is not unmixed praise from a man who strove himself for simplicity and naturalness. The judgment shows Thoreau able now to be fair to a Carlyle whom he no longer wished to imitate. As he put some distance between his own and Carlyle's style, so Thoreau was also able now to coolly assess some of the Carlylean ideas which had been so important to his own development. The essay shows Thoreau's familiarity with almost everything Carlyle had written, but it concentrates on *Cromwell* and, especially, on *Heroes, Hero-Worship and the Heroic in History*, since, for Thoreau, that volume—an "altogether wild and original" book—embraced essentially all of Carlyle's other works.[3]

He still found in himself large areas of agreement with Carlyle, for example in the insistence on the overriding importance of the problem of heroism—of heroic endeavor. "Universal History," said Carlyle, "the History of what man has accomplished in this world, is at bottom the history of the Great Men who have worked there." And Thoreau felt, even more strongly than Carlyle, that "Nature is still divine . . . the Hero is still worshipable," and he enjoyed thinking of Carlyle as possessing "the constitutional vigor of one of his old Norse heroes," a "rugged, unwearied" writer of "rich sincerity," who "answers like Thor, with a stroke of his hammer, whose dint makes a valley in the earth's surface."[4]

Thoreau would always be sympathetic to Carlyle's insistence on the plausibility of the actual worship of nature, to such statements as:

The young generations of the world, who had in them the freshness of young children, and yet the depth of earnest men, who did not think that they had finished-off all things in Heaven and Earth by merely giving them scientific names, but had to gaze direct at them there, with awe and wonder; they felt better what of divinity is in man and Nature; they, without being mad, could *worship* Nature, and man more than anything else in Nature.[5]

That last phrase, though, holds a hint of the main problem Thoreau now had with Carlyle's conception of the great man. For all his vividness and persuasiveness, his ability to convince us that in the case of paganism or any other religion "we, had we been there, should have believed in it," Carlyle felt at bottom that the important point was that the hero or great man was better than we are, and he did not shrink from saying so. "No nobler feeling than this of admiration for one higher than himself dwells in the breast of man." Hero worship, for Carlyle, was "heartfelt, prostrate admiration, submission, burning, boundless." The problem, then, with Carlyle's conception of heroes and hero-worship is that it is undemocratic, objective, external, historical, and drawn largely from men of action, men such as the historical Odin, Mahomet, Cromwell. Emerson, on the other hand, had a list of worthies that was better in some respects, Thoreau thought, for Emerson dealt with heroes of thought such as Plato, Shakespeare, and Goethe.[6]

But there was something missing from both Carlyle's and Emerson's treatment. Neither took up Christ, neither took up the "peaceful practical hero" such as Columbus, nor, most important "the Man of the Age, come to be called working-man." "It is obvious," Thoreau insisted, "that none yet speaks to his condition."[7]

Thoreau parts company with Carlyle because the latter's heroes are better than we are, and he finds Emerson coming short because his great men—even though they are representative or symbolic of traits in all of us—are still objective and historical figures. For Thoreau (and after him, Whitman) the problem of how to lead a heroic life in the busy modern nineteenth century would involve a subjective, not an objective hero; an internal, not an external heroism; a present-centered, not a historical context. "Are we not all great men?" Thoreau asks, and so the nineteenth-century hero must be the representative self, the ordinary individual working person, as good as and standing for everyone.[8]

"I wish you would take an American Hero . . . and give us a History of him," Carlyle had written to Emerson. Emerson did not take it up, but Thoreau did. Working himself slowly free of the still-admired friends, Thoreau's next book presented himself as American hero. But from now on, he avoided the easy use of such words as "heroic" or "heroism," as he found increasingly that the American nineteenth-century experience of what Carlyle called "the heroic" and what Nietzsche would call "the Dionysian spirit" lay in what he recognized, named, and celebrated as the "wild."[9]

42. The New Adam (Smith)

Thoreau's life and Concord's were impoverished this fall of 1845 by the departure in early October of the Hawthornes for Salem due to Nathaniel's new position at the Custom House there. Economic issues intruded everywhere. To the continuing effects of the depression in America was added the terrible news of widespread famine in Ireland following the failure of the potato crop. Robert Owen, the economic reformer who had founded New Harmony back in the 1820s, came to Concord this November. His presence was a reminder, if any one needed it, that economic reform was still a major issue.

During parts of November and December, Thoreau was living with his family in Concord while he was plastering the cabin, and this fall his mind too ran on such subjects as money, capital, and economic necessity. As fall turned into winter, Thoreau turned from his draft of *A Week* to the first draft of what would become *Walden*, the first part of which is full of information on Thoreau's domestic economy, detailing and summarizing his initial eight months at the pond. The account has a lighthearted side. There are jokes about his not having the usual capital, about his always endeavoring to maintain strict business habits. When taken together with the scrupulous, even fussy accounting, it is easy to see how the opening of *Walden* has been read as a parody of Benjamin Franklin and *The Way to Wealth*. But Thoreau's main interests here were only partly satiric, and he had others besides Franklin in mind. Ridiculously light as his expenses now seem to us, they were in fact reasonable for the time. He calculated that it cost him, in round figures, $60 to set up house and live at Walden Pond for eight months, while his income, from day labor and the sale of his crops, brought him in $40. An ordinary agricultural laborer in Massachusetts at this period could expect to make between $120 and $140 a year, or, in the case of Michigan, between $50 and $120. What Thoreau's figures show is that one could set up a modest house for something between half a year and a year's salary as a day laborer or about what a student could then expect to pay for a year's rent at college, living the usual way. (This is still true. One can buy a second-hand mobile home for about what it costs to rent a room at college for a year.)[1]

The extent of Thoreau's interest in economics may be gauged by the fact that the chapter of *Walden* called "Economy" was from the beginning the longest as well as the first subject treated. Beyond the satiric jabs at Franklin and the implied humor of absurdly meticulous accounts ($1.0475 for rye meal) and the ironic appropriation of business terminology (trading with the Celestial Empire), Thoreau was seriously interested not just in the economics of everyday life, but in the economic ideas that were visibly transforming his world.

The opening chapter of *Walden* is a thoughtful and informed meditation on economics which gains greatly by being read as a response to the new economics and, particularly, to Adam Smith. Thoreau was not interested in the wealth of nations so much as he was in the wealth of the individuals who made up the nation, but he was familiar with Smith's work—and that of Say and Ricardo—and much of his opening chapter is an application of Smith's ideas and terminology to the individual case.

Thoreau is in agreement with Smith's fundamental premise that it is not gold or silver, but productive labor that is the real basis of wealth. Smith's famous book begins:

> The annual labour of every nation is the fund which originally supplies it with all the necessaries and conveniences of life which it annually consumes, and which consist always either in the immediate produce of that labour, or in what is purchased with that produce from other nations.

Smith's basic terms provide many of Thoreau's main topics. Much of *Walden* is an inquiry into what is necessary and what is convenience, how much labor does each call for, how much must one produce and consume? Thoreau's idea of the cost of something as "the amount of what I will call life which is required to be exchanged for it, immediately or in the long run," is a virtual paraphrase of Smith's "What everything really costs to the man who wants to acquire it, is the toil and trouble of acquiring it." Neither Thoreau nor Smith favors going into debt; both wryly refer to the same Latin saying about having the temporary and expensive custody of someone else's copper, *aes alienum*. Above all, Thoreau agrees with Smith's basic emphasis on labor as "alone the ultimate and real standard by which the value of all commodities can at all times be estimated and compared. It is their real price, money is their nominal price only."[2]

But where Thoreau's inquiry into the economics of individualism begins to diverge from Adam Smith's analysis is over such things as the definition of *true* wealth, or the desirability of the division of labor. Smith says, "Every man is rich or poor according to the degree in which he can afford to enjoy the necessaries, conveniences and amusements of human life," while Thoreau sees in this only an endless cycle of getting and spending, producing and consuming, and therefore is prepared to claim that "a man is rich in proportion to the number of things which he can afford to let alone." Behind the humor is a serious disagreement with Smith as to what constitutes real well-being, and this crucial problem is linked by Smith to the division of labor. "In every improved society," Smith says, "the farmer is generally nothing but a farmer; the manufacturer, nothing but a manufacturer." Thus, "after the division of labour has once thoroughly taken place, it is but a very small part of [his necessities, conveniences, and amusements] with which a man's own labour can supply him. The far greater part of them he must derive from the labour of other people."[3]

Smith is all for this division, of course, since specializing increases production, but this is precisely the point at which Thoreau—like Emerson before him—draws the line. From this division comes dehumanization and alienation. Emerson objected that the sailor became a mere rope of the ship. Thoreau's whole experiment at Walden is a protest against the dogma that the division of labor is beneficial to the individual. Where Adam Smith waxes lyrical over how many more pins can be made if the job is parceled out eighteen ways, one to draw the wire, the next to straighten it, the next to cut it, and so on, Thoreau approves only those ventures in which you "oversee all the details yourself in person: to be at once pilot and captain, and owner and underwriter."[4]

Walden is critical of too much material accumulation, of the factory mode of production, of schemes such as the railroad, where many work so that a few may ride. Behind all these arguments is his major disagreement with Adam Smith. Where Smith wanted to see consumption maximized, Thoreau wants it minimized and simplified. Thoreau emphasizes not how much one can consume, but how little. He stresses this theme with production as well. Instead of increasing production, Thoreau planted fewer beans his second year and he closed his economy chapter with a story about the only tree that could be said to be truly free, the cypress, because it produced nothing and thus was free of the cyclical and tyrannical process of getting and spending.

The answer in the old catechism to the question "What is the chief end of man?" is "To glorify God and enjoy him forever." This, Thoreau thought, was "somewhat hastily concluded." But the gospel of wealth as set down by Adam Smith and by Jean Baptiste Say in a *Catechism of Political Economy* had no better answer. Surely it was also too hasty a conclusion that the chief end of man is producing and consuming.[5]

43. Spring 1846: Walden

If Thoreau is critical of the economics of national production, he is on the other hand eager to explore the economics of individual subsistence. From the beginning, his experiment at Walden had been an effort to find out just what were his true necessities. Rather than increase production and multiply wants, he sought to simplify his material wants so as to minimize the labor needed to satisfy them. And though he was generally careful to point out that the simple life could be lived anywhere, it was more dramatic and satisfying to try the experiment by oneself, out in the open air. Going to Walden, his "place of pines," was an experiment to bring economic and philosophical ideas to the test of practical life. "To be a philosopher," he noted, "is not . . . to have subtle thoughts and found a school—but . . . to live a life of simplicity—of independence—of magnanimity and trust—such as all men should live."[1]

Such a life, for Thoreau, would have to be in nature, not near the depot, the post office, or the barroom, but near "the source of our life." He observed that in Concord as in Boston "the prevailing tendency is to the city life," and he thought that "of all the inhabitants of Concord," he knew "not one that dwells in nature." And as the town bent his thoughts away from nature, so his reading, if he was not careful, pulled him away from living in the present and toward the historical past. Reading *The Crescent and the Cross* one day at Walden, he became indignant with himself. "Am I sick, or idle—that I can sacrifice my energy—America—and today—to this man's ill remembered and indolent story?" And leaving aside the material remains, the "hideous ruins," he asked, "Where is the *spirit* of that time but in this present day?" "This is my Carnac," he asserted, with the emphasis on the "my." "Here grow around me nameless trees and shrubs each morning freshly sculptured."[2]

Economy, philosophy, history, everything led to the present day, to the single self living in an unchanged and ever-changing nature. Theory fell in with inclination. The true artist, said Henry James, is one on whom nothing is lost, and as James missed no nuance of social life, so Thoreau, of all Americans, is the one on whom least in nature is lost.

Sitting in his doorway, looking out and down to the water's edge, he watched the colors in the pond, green in the deeps, blue in the shallows. Thinking of Wordsworth and the great nature poetry of the English he observed "this is our lake country." It was a place of pines, especially in the winter, but there were also oaks and johnswort, sumac and hickory around the hut—the sumac a sure sign that Thoreau's shore was more open then than now. And at all seasons there were birds: brown thrashers, wild pigeons flying in twos and threes, wood peewees, and martins. In mid-March the song sparrows and blackbirds returned, in late March came the robins and flights of geese and ducks low over the water in the dark. There were chickadees, called *mezezence* by his Canadian woodchopper friend Therien, wood thrush, veery, and chewinks. Sometimes he saw a fishhawk dive for a fish, sometimes heard a loon's wild burble and whoop. In the summer, after the rattle of the evening train died away, the whippoorwills sang, just at 7:30 for half an hour, and when all was still at night, the dismal owls began "like mourning women," reminding the watcher by the pond of "the dark and tearful side of music."[3]

Simple and natural as life by the pond could be, there were certain basic aspects of it that stubbornly refused to yield a simple pattern. Early in his stay at the pond he came to realize as never before a fundamental split or division within himself. "I find an instinct in me conducting to a mystic spiritual life," he observed, "and also another—to a primitive savage life." A great modern physicist has said that everything should be made as simple as possible, but no simpler. Thoreau never "solved" the contradiction between the urge to a contemplative spiritual life and the impulse to an active physical existence; indeed part of his greatness comes from his constant effort to do justice to both impulses. He could ask, "Why not lead a hard life?"; he could claim that he had come to the woods "because I wished to live deliberately, to front only the essential facts of life," but he was not one to delude himself that his present abode was actually in a wild or primitive place. He might be leading a primitive life, but it was being led in a backyard laboratory. The value of the Walden stay is its experimental, representative or symbolic character. "I imagine it to be some advantage to live a primitive and frontier life—though in the midst of an outward civilization," he noted in his journal, and over the years he repeated the observation at intervals. None of his statements of purpose says more than this one, the all-important point being that the primitive and frontier life is an inner, personal attitude toward life, an attitude that does not require a primitive physical setting on an actual frontier. Thoreau's friend Channing had tried the real primitive life on the Illinois prairie, but got no advantage, certainly no literary advantage by it. It is not what you look at that matters, it's what you see.[4]

Life at Walden was, in one way, very complex indeed. Reading and writing in the mornings, according to his habit, and going for long walks in the afternoon, he was living simultaneously a thoughtful and intellectual life, and a relatively primitive, outdoorsy existence. He was writing one book and gathering material for a second. *A Week* has strong, if frequently overlooked, social themes: friendship, settlement, Indian life, oriental law. The material being laid up for *Walden*, meanwhile, was more intensely personal. The artistic problem that would need to be solved before *Walden* could be written was the problem of how to express nature itself, whether thought of as the green world, or as the internal, wild, and natural self.

Thoreau began now at Walden to wrestle extensively with the idea that in Homeric times myth had been the language of nature. The subject matter of myth was nature. If true then, it should be true still. The question was how to make modern myth express a modern vision of nature. He included a discussion of this in *A Week*. By the time he was ready to begin *Walden* he was trying not just to discuss modern myth, but to make it.[5]

44. The Great Awakening

Very early in March of 1846, Thoreau did his accounts and worked out the economics of his daily life at the pond. On March 3 the new unfinished central building at Brook Farm burned down, effectively ending that imaginative experiment in reforming the world. By the middle of March, Thoreau had seen song sparrows and blackbirds, but the ice was still a foot thick on the pond. The spring rains began, but by the twenty-sixth they were over, the ice was gone and the first robin had been heard. Spring had come with the shift in the weather; it was, Thoreau noted, no longer the end of a season, but the beginning of one.[1]

By now he had a draft of *A Week* behind him. He was still tinkering with the Carlyle piece, turning it from a lecture into an essay. But most importantly this spring the materials of *Walden* were beginning to come together. His townsmen had, at the February Carlyle lecture, wished to know about his life at Walden. His first response was to give the reply as a piece on economics. But much more than that was now accumulating in the various notebooks he was keeping. One can recognize in his notes, besides the interest in economy, the germs of chapters on reading, on sounds, and on visitors. There is much on his woodchopper friend Therien, and above all this April there is the material that became the center of his great second chapter, "Where I Lived and What I Lived For."

By mid-April, Thoreau was back at his Greek, reading Anacreon, Alcaeus, and Homer on the flight of birds and the coming of spring, and noting the association between spring and the worship of beauty, and how the Greek children greeted the swallow "as the herald of the spring in a little song." It was now time for Thoreau to think about plowing again, and here too the example of Greece rose before him. Thoreau thought husbandry should be a sacred art; it had been so for the Greeks. The plowing ox, "this faithful ally of the labors of the husbandman" had been sacred, and could only be slaughtered after being consecrated or devoted as a sacrifice. But the modern farmer cared only for large farms and large crops.[2]

It was by now a habitual reflex of Thoreau's to seek to attach to the present whatever stirred him in his historical reading. On the day after he had made all these notes on the Greeks, he made one of his happiest connections, finding the vivifying spirit of ancient Greece in the simple experience of the New England morning. On April 18 he noted, "the morning must remind everyone of his ideal life—Then if ever we can realize the life of the Greeks. We see then Aurora. The morning brings back the heroic ages." Heroic because in the morning, things seem possible, and our will revives. "I know of no more encouraging fact than the unquestionable ability of man to elevate his life—by a conscious endeavor." Heroic because morning restores, renews, reinvigorates. "All memorable events in my experience transpire in morning time," he wrote. This connection is the center and key of the second chapter of *Walden*. As the actual morning is the time of simple physical waking, so Thoreau makes morning the general symbol for awakening. Thoreau understood myth to have been for the Greeks a language used to express things in nature. What the myth of Aurora expressed, he now felt and strove to reexpress, directing attention to the phenomenon and its significance rather than to the classical form of the myth. Thoreau deliberately extends morning to the idea of morning, the myth of morning. "It matters not what the clocks say or the attitudes and labors of men—morning is when I am awake and there is a dawn in me."[3]

From notebook jottings to the first draft of *Walden*, written within a year of the April entries already quoted, to the later drafts of the second chapter, Thoreau expanded and developed the section on awakening. The long first chapter was on economics. The short second one emphasized imagination; the word is used repeatedly at the start of the chapter. The first chapter is a critique of ordinary lives as defined by classical (for Thoreau it was modern) economics. The second chapter offers an alternative, a positive program, not how he lived, but where, and what for. The first chapter is overwhelmingly material; the second summons the reader from the material to the real. The awakening Thoreau calls for is a spiritual, perhaps even a mystical awakening, no doubt. But it is more effective than most such calls because it is anchored in the concrete physical freshness of morning and because it calls us to awake from illusion to reality. Reality is not the slumber of our "daily life of routine and habit every where." That, says Thoreau, is exactly the illusion:

> Men esteem truth remote, in the outskirts of the system, behind the farthest star, before Adam and after the last man. . . . But all these times and places and occasions are now and here. God himself culminates in the present moment. . . . And we are enabled to apprehend at all what is sublime and noble only by the perpetual instilling and drenching of the reality which surrounds us.

This urgent call to seize the day, and live in it only, is the major point of the second chapter, and the pivot, so to speak, of the book. The opening chapter seeks to get beyond the economic illusion. The second chapter awakens us to the realities which form the subjects of the following chapters. The experience of awakening is crucial. Thoreau's language emphasizes renewal, reinvigoration, purification. Significantly, he does not use or suggest the language of redemption. The awakening he seeks is Greek, not Christian, and certainly not Puritan. No hint of Calvinist revival is intended or allowed. The awakening is a religious experience in the broad sense of the word, and the language turns to Hindu, Chinese, and above all Greek religion to the pointed exclusion of Christianity.

> I have been as sincere a worshipper of Aurora as the Greeks. I got up early and bathed in the pond; that was a religious exercise, and one of the best things which I did. They say that characters were engraven on the bathing tub of King Tching-thang to this effect: "Renew thyself completely each day; do it again and again, and forever again." I can understand that.

The chapter records Thoreau's great awakening, but it is an awakening to daily renewal, not to eternal redemption.[4]

45. Summer 1846:
Resistance to Civil Government

The agricultural aspect of the Walden experiment was dealt a blow, about which we hear very little in the journal or in *Walden*, when an unseasonable frost on June 12, 1846, killed Thoreau's beans, tomatoes, squash, corn, and potatoes. But he had much else to occupy him. He finished the Carlyle essay and sent it to Horace Greeley. He was keeping up with the adventures of John Charles Fremont in the West, reading much on the Hindus, especially in the *Bhagavat Geeta*. He had been at Walden a year now. Brook Farm had ceased to function after the phalanstery burned down, but domestic innovation was still in the air. Emerson's house was now reorganized, astonishingly, into a boarding house under the management of one Mrs. Marston Goodwin, Emerson and Lydia being just two of the boarders. The arrangement lasted sixteen months, during which there were often as many as sixteen to eighteen boarders. During this time, and for reasons perhaps similar to Thoreau's, Emerson thought of building a house at Walden, on the high ground across the pond from Thoreau.[1]

On July 12, Thoreau turned twenty-nine. Not quite two weeks later, on July twenty-third or -fourth, he was detained in Concord for nonpayment of the poll tax, and he spent the night in the Concord Jail. Someone, it is not known who, paid the tax and he was released in the morning. All sorts of legends have grown up around this, the single most celebrated incident of Thoreau's life. There is no basis for the still repeated story about Emerson seeing Thoreau in jail and asking what he was doing in there and being asked in reply, "what are you doing out there?" But the episode behind this and so many other stories deserves its celebrity, since from it came Thoreau's most often read—and taught essay and one of the great Western statements on the importance of conscience.[2]

It was characteristic of Thoreau that the essay should have its immediate cause in the night in jail, characteristic because Thoreau's best writing always illuminates abstractions and validates moral arguments by means of concrete and personal experiences, graphically reported and pungently phrased. It is also characteristic that the leading issues of the essay were very much issues of the times. Indeed, Thoreau's essay, first called "Resistance to Civil Government," is all the more impressive because it offers a fresh perspective—and one that has lasted—on an issue much debated, discussed, and written about in the 1830s and 1840s. Raymond Adams has pointed out how Thoreau's basic championing of the individual over the state is similar to the position Emerson had just put forward in his essay on "Politics," how Thoreau's essay is cast as a reply to chapter three of book six of Paley's *The Principles of Moral and Political Philosophy*, called "The Duty of Submission to Civil Government Explained" and to a reform movement called Non-Resistance, associated with abolition, with William Lloyd Garrison, and with Adin Ballou.[3]

Non-Resistance is the idea that one should not resist force with force. It had been part of Garrison's platform since the founding of *The Liberator* in the early thirties, but the issue came to the fore just as Thoreau was leaving college. After the abolitionist Elijah Lovejoy was killed defending his press with a gun in his hands by an angry mob in Alton, Illinois, on November 7, 1837, Garrison brought out in December a new prospectus for *The Liberator* in which the familiar call for immediate emancipation was strongly coupled with a new declaration that it was wrong to oppose force with force. This stand split the abolitionists, and those for whom the peace movement outweighed the emancipation issue began to go their own way. In September of 1838 a Peace convention met in Boston, out of which Garrison wrote a "Declaration of Sentiments," which is still regarded as a major document of the Peace movement. "Our country is the world," Garrison wrote,

> our countrymen are all mankind. We love the land of our nativity, only as we love all other lands. The interests, rights, and liberties of American citizens are no more dear to us, than are those of the whole human race. . . . We register our testimony, not only against all wars, whether offensive or defensive, but all preparations for war.

From the nation, Garrison moved to the individual. "If a nation has no right to defend itself against foreign enemies, or to punish its invaders, no individual possesses that right in his own case."[4]

Garrison kept his Non-Resistance and his abolitionism in an uneasy

176

but effective balance for some years; but for Adin Ballou, Non-Resistance became the all-important issue, leading to the founding of a new community, Hopedale, for the exemplary practice of the peace principle. Ballou led a breakaway movement; in September of 1839 he was addressing the first annual meeting of the new Non-Resistance Society.

Interest in the issue reached a peak in Concord in January 1841, when two successive debates were held in the Concord Lyceum on "Is it ever proper to offer forcible resistance." Alcott took the negative both times, the second time he faced the Thoreau brothers arguing the affirmative, that is, in favor of forcible resistance. In early February, Ballou came and lectured on the subject. Non-Resistance remained very much an issue through the 1840s. In 1846 Ballou wrote a book on *Christian Non-Resistance*, which was reviewed by Charles Hudson in *The Christian Examiner* for January 1848, the month in which Thoreau himself first lectured on the subject.

As printed the following year, 1849, in Elizabeth Peabody's *Aesthetic Papers*, the essay was called "Resistance to Civil Government" and it distinctly breathed the spirit of Non-Resistance. Thoreau uses the language of noncompliance and noncooperation. He speaks of *receding* from government, *resigning* from office, *refusing* to pay taxes to support war and slavery. In the essay, he does not advocate or even mention forcible resistance—and he will use the phrase only in rejecting the idea in *Walden*. He was, of course, familiar with the debater's position in favor, and later, during the heat of the John Brown affair, he would come out advocating violent or forcible resistance to the United States government.[5]

"Resistance to Civil Government" is, in good Garrisonian fashion, both abolitionist and pacifist at the same time. The essay is essentially an antiwar, antislavery piece, not a theoretical defense of individual rights and not primarily an autobiographical document. The Mexican War comes up in the opening paragraph. Thoreau ridicules the war and the army. The soldier is no longer the Stoic recruit in the battle of life, no longer a hero and symbol of courage, but a machine "at the service of some unscrupulous man in power." Thoreau also no longer sees American government as self-government or representative democracy, but as machinery that "a single man can bend to his will."

Thoreau's concept of government here is very close to Ballou's idea that government is "the will of man exercising absolute authority over man."[6]

Although Thoreau was at great pains to sound practical and reasonable, claiming that he was not a "no-government man," the essay exhibits a strong tendency in the direction of dissociation from the current American government. It has the moral absolutism of a piece by Garrison. Paley, according to Thoreau, "resolves all civil obligations into expediency," and Thoreau adds that "Paley appears never to have contemplated those cases to which the rule of expediency does not apply." Thoreau leaves no possible doubt about his meaning. "If I have unjustly wrested a plank from a drowning man, I must restore it to him though I drown myself. . . . This people must cease to hold slaves, and to make war on Mexico, though it cost them their existence as a people." This is Thoreau the genuine radical, castigating as "the most serious obstacle to reform" those liberals who personally disapprove of slavery or the war yet still support the government. Observing that "action from principle . . . is essentially revolutionary," he seeks, like Garrison, to block compromise and force the issue. "Unjust laws exist: shall we be content to obey them, or shall we endeavor to amend them, and obey them until we have succeeded, or shall we transgress them at once?" His going to jail is one small example of the latter course and its consequences. "Under a government which imprisons any unjustly, the true place for a just man is also a prison."[7]

The major difference between Garrison and Thoreau is not so much in the basic position as in the ultimate grounds invoked for the position. Thoreau changes the emphasis, in logic and rhetoric, from the religious to the moral. It is not God's law but conscience; not so much respect for the law, civil or canon, as respect for the right, though the essay breathes a strain of Christian ethics—balanced to be sure by a strain of Confucian ethics—which will recur in Thoreau's John Brown writings later. Yet the main thrust of Thoreau's argument is to reach beyond both Bible and Constitution to the individual conscience. The essay is Jeffersonian in its moral and stylistic clarity and it remains one of the landmark defenses of individual conscience as the ultimate source of moral authority and political legitimacy.

Though it was not printed till 1849, and though it has important roots in the late thirties and early forties, the essay springs immediately from events of 1845 and 1846, from the annexation of Texas, the Mexican War, the heating up of abolitionism and the night in jail of July 1846. On these issues, Thoreau was very acutely tuned to his times. Bernard De Voto, in *The Year of Decision*, observes that "somewhere between August and December 1846 the Civil War had begun."[8]

46. North Twin Lake and "Ktaadn"

By midsummer 1846 Thoreau had been living at Walden for a year, and while it gave him unrivaled privacy and freedom for writing, it was by then as much his headquarters as his hermitage. A week after his night in jail, on August 1, he stood host, at the cabin, to the antislavery society's annual meeting in commemoration of West Indian Emancipation, a pointed reminder that there was still no American Emancipation to be celebrated. At the end of August, he left Walden for a two week excursion to the Maine woods.

He took the train to Boston, then another train to Portland, where he caught the night steamboat for Bangor. This was his second sea journey along the shelving granite shore of Maine, less densely forested with evergreens then than now, but still wholly different from the sandy shores of Cape Cod or the inhabited shores of the Boston area. The Maine seacoast in those days was only a commercial artery used mostly for the transport of lumber and firewood. There were no summer folk at Mt. Desert or anywhere else. The coast stood for nothing in the public imagination then, which helps explain why it held no romance and left no impression even on so good an observer as Thoreau. It is true he saw it mostly by night and true also that the steamer's noise and speed induced in him, he said, a dreamlike state that made the trip seem utterly unreal. But it is also true that Thoreau was no sailor. At a time when many young New Englanders still grew up looking to the sea for a future and a living, Thoreau grew up facing inland, looking west instead of east, to rivers, mountains, lakes, and woods instead of the "cold salt running hills of the Atlantic," in Sylvia Plath's phrase. A few years later, when he wanted to front the ocean and learn what it had to teach, he went, not to sea like Dana or Melville, but to Cape Cod.[1]

Arriving by boat in Bangor, Thoreau traveled with his cousin George Thatcher and two other Bangor men with lumber interests by stagecoach north to Mattawamkeag, which was as far as the road went. They then took a batteau for the trip up the Penobscot River, which led through a chain of lakes and streams toward Mount Katahdin. Twenty-five miles upriver from Mattawamkeag, they entered North Twin Lake, which was, for Thoreau, the beginning of the real wilderness. He first saw it by moonlight. There were no cabins and no roads. It was "completely surrounded by the forest as savage and impassable now as to the first adventurers." It had, he noted "a smack of wildness about it as I had never tasted before." It is reported that even now in the 1980s, North Twin Lake is, with trivial exceptions, still as lovely and unspoiled as it was in Thoreau's day.[2]

The party left the batteau at Sowdahunk deadwater and proceeded on foot to Mount Katahdin. They had taken care to make the trip late in the summer, when most of the insects are gone, but this part of the trip was still difficult and wearying travel through old, tangled, pathless spruce forests. Thoreau left his companions to climb alone and when he got there he found the top of Katahdin a cold, misty, windy, utterly primitive place. The ascent of Katahdin was the central experience both of the trip and of Thoreau's subsequent account of it. It was an experience of nature as vast, drear, and indifferent to humankind. Up there in the driving winds of the cloud-factory with rocks on all sides, he felt, he said, like Prometheus chained to the rocks of the Caucasus. Up there, nature was not bound to be kind to man. This discovery was a cold Caucasian epiphany for Thoreau.

Thoreau returned with a few pages of terse jottings such as "climb tree—torrent—camping ground—leave party—go up torrent—fir trees—lakes—rocks—clouds—sick and weary—camp—green fish—fire at night—wind up ravine." In marked contrast to his Merrimack River trip he quickly worked up these notes (which seem intended to preserve things in sequences, but not to give shape or outline to the experience), into a hundred-page chronological account of the trip, an account prefaced however in the earliest draft by two pieces that tell us a good deal about his original thematic intentions.[3]

The first of these pieces starts us out at North Twin Lake, with Thoreau's sense that *here*, at last, he was leaving civilization and entering the true wilderness, a country uninhabited by man. North Twin Lake stood in marked contrast for Thoreau with the pastoral, inhabited, farmed, and lumbered shores of Walden Pond. "It was," he wrote, "the first time I had realized my conception of a secluded lake in the woods." The contrast stuck in his mind, and found its way into both books. "It is difficult," he wrote of North Twin Lake, "to conceive of a country uninhabited by men—we naturally suppose them on the horizon everywhere—and yet we have not seen nature unless we have once seen her thus vast and grim and drear—whether in the wilderness or in the midst of cities."[4]

The problem at the center of "Ktaadn" is the problem of primitivism, of wildness and man's relation to it, and it is this formulation that follows and largely subsumes Thoreau's earlier interest in heroes and heroism. The traditional hero is defined by his exemplary relation to society, the man of the wilderness is defined by his relation to nature, that is to external nature, the green world. In *A Week*, as in most of his early excursions, man lives in harmony with a gentle and benevolent nature that guides and protects. But on Katahdin, Thoreau said, "I first most fully realized that this was unhanselled and ancient Demonic Nature, natura, or whatever man has named it . . . nature primitive—powerful gigantic aweful and beautiful, Untamed forever." On Katahdin nature was at best indifferent to human life. In one sense perhaps, this view of nature contradicts his earlier view of nature as benign, pastoral, and civilizing. But it is not a real contradiction. What Katahdin taught Thoreau is that while man is part of nature, he is not the lord of nature. Nature may indeed smile on man in the valleys, but there are also places where man is not welcome. In short, there are limits. Man is still very much a part of nature, but he is only one part; he is not everything. Nature will support and nourish him, but only if he respects and acknowledges the limits.

Thoreau had always been interested in the problems and the attraction posed by primitivism, but until now, his experience was more with what anthropologists call "soft primitivism," with the easy, undemanding (as we imagine it) primitive life of the South Sea Islands. As he worked up his Katahdin material, Thoreau was reading and was deeply impressed by Melville's first book, *Typee*, which had just appeared and was being reviewed and noticed in all the literary papers. *Typee* is focused squarely on just this issue of the attractions of South Sea Island primitivism for the northern white man. Thoreau actually included a longish discussion of *Typee* in this draft of "Ktaadn," and it is the only book so discussed therein. Life in the Maine woods was, by comparison, "hard primitivism," a yearning for a strenuous, physically demanding confrontation with nature. Thoreau thought that North Twin Lake and Katahdin were wilder for him than the Marquesas had been for Melville, but the differences should not obscure for us the underlying similarity. For both Thoreau and Melville, it was the confrontation between civilized man and the primitive world—both natural and human—that was of interest. This theme, the relation of civilized man to nature, is the central and organizing theme of the first version of "Ktaadn." The emphasis on the American Indian so evident in the published version came later, shifting the focus in part to the subject of primitive man's relation to nature.[5]

The second prefatory piece in Thoreau's first draft of "Ktaadn" concerns myth. Calling myth a version of history and an approach to a universal language, Thoreau looks to myth for a way to express the nature he experiences. We are not then surprised to find Thoreau comparing his experience on Katahdin to that of Prometheus. By now Thoreau understood that one need not so much try to invent new myth as try to attune one's experience to that expressed in older myths, and then try to add a little something to a myth whose ability to contain and communicate meaning has been tested by time. But of course one wants one's own writing to evoke the substance, the inner experience of the myth, not the external shell, the mere classical trappings.[6]

47. Second Year at Walden

Thoreau's second year at Walden somehow managed to sustain the already prolonged burst of creativity and productivity begun the year before. His stay at the pond is the hardest part of his life since college to follow on a day-to-day basis, since his notebooks for this period are not true journals or day books. It must also be remembered that he was absorbed almost continuously for two years in drafting and shaping longer kinds of work that required sustained efforts. He accomplished a phenomenal amount on his major projects and it is little wonder that there was neither energy nor inclination for a full day-by-day account of life as well.

During the fall of 1846, soon after his return from Maine, he wrote out his hundred-page treatment of "Ktaadn," and at some time, perhaps this fall, he must also have begun work on "Resistance to Civil Government." Taken together, these pieces show Thoreau reaching out for extreme, indeed radical positions, confidently expressed in clear strong prose, with less metaphor and ironic play than was usual for him. "Resistance to Civil Government" argues for individual conscience as the ultimate basis of political life, and "Ktaadn" balances this with its contention that human life, whether individual or collective, is not the highest thing in nature, but is merely one—admittedly important—part of it. Extreme individualism in social matters is tempered by a sense of the limits of the individual in nature. This was a crucial insight for Thoreau; it stayed with him as he labored over the long second draft of *A Week* during the winter and spring of 1847, as he gave his February 1847 lecture on "The History of Myself," and as he wrote out the first draft of *Walden* during the summer. Four pages prior to the end of this first version he begins his conclusion, a conclusion to which he would make only trifling stylistic changes over the years:

At the same time that we are earnest to learn and explore all things, we require that all things should be mysterious and unexplorable by us that land and sea be infinitely wild, unsurveyed and unfathomed by us. We can never have enough of nature. We must be refreshed by the sight of inexhaustible vigor, vast features and titanic—the sea coast with its wrecks, the wilderness with its living and its decaying trees the thunder cloud—and rain that lasts three weeks and produces freshets. We need to witness our own limits transgressed, and some life pasturing freely where we never wander.

By the time he was ready to leave the pond in early fall of 1847, he could look back on a year in which he had written the 100-page "Ktaadn," the 117-page *Walden*, and the entire enormous second draft of *A Week*, not to mention other shorter bits and pieces. To his energy, at least, there seemed no limit.[1]

Concurrently with all this writing, Thoreau's interest in science grew rapidly this year. He noted in a letter that he was "not so attentive an observer of birds as I was once," but this may only have been because he was becoming a more attentive observer of fish. He was enlisted this year by James Elliot Cabot to find and ship specimens of fish and other wildlife to the laboratory of Louis Agassiz. A Swiss naturalist who at forty already was a world-famous ichthyologist, Agassiz had just arrived in America. Thoreau found a few specimens previously unknown to Agassiz. Watching gangs of men cutting ice commercially on Walden Pond this winter, he became interested in water temperature and undertook the first of what would be many statistical studies, this one of water temperature in various ponds. He was also newly interested in astronomy, going with Emerson to look at the skies through the Concordian Perez Blood's 85-power telescope. (Galileo's 32-power instrument made clear the craters on the moon. Blood's showed "sunlight on the spurs of the mountains in the dark portion" of the moon.) Harvard now had a telescope of some 2000-power. The college was also taking an interest in mathematics, chemistry, and other branches of science, would shortly appoint Agassiz to a professorship, and was, in Thoreau's opinion, "really beginning to wake up and redeem its character and overtake the age." The same was true of Thoreau himself. He would never be a scientist in the specialized way in which an Agassiz was a recognized authority on fish classification or on glaciation, but Thoreau would always be open to science, hospitable to its basic way of understanding things. "This world," he noted now in his journal, "is not a place for him who does not discover its laws." Nor was Thoreau's rising interest in classification, statistics, and telescope power at odds with his transcendental or idealist side. His concern for material things was still healthily balanced by his concern with mind, his eagerness for facts was offset by his interest in meaning and in myth. "All matter indeed, is capable of entertaining thought," he noted down. He liked astronomy because it "is that department of physics which answers to Prophesy the Seer's or Poet's calling . . . to see more with the physical eye than man has yet seen." As astronomy was linked to poetry, so history was now linked to myth. "Mythology is ancient history or biography. The oldest history still memorable becomes a mythus. It is the fruit which history at last bears—the fable so far from being false contains only the essential parts of the history."[2]

His heavy writing schedule and his fresh scientific interests meant less time than usual this year for reading. But he reread Homer, Ovid, Anacreon, the *Bhagavadgita*, some Chateaubriand, and reports of Fremont's adventures in the West. If he did little new reading, he was however writing about reading; the earliest version of the *Walden* chapter on reading dates from this year.[3]

There were strains associated with the year's heavy concentration on literary output. Publication, always a problem, was very difficult just now. On one side Emerson was urging him to publish *A Week* and on the other side there was Greeley, ever helpful but also exasperating, urging him not to think about books but to concentrate on writing biographical articles. Greeley had managed to place Thoreau's Carlyle essay but he had a very difficult time getting it paid for. Emerson could move no one to publish *A Week*. It had been turned down four times when Thoreau left the pond in the fall of 1847. This shook Thoreau's self-confidence. He had turned thirty this summer, and he had now been out of college for ten years. Living alone, as a bachelor, he was becoming set in his ways now and he was increasingly capable of a kind of tart defensive superiority which, when not laced with wit, could irritate—and continues to irritate—his detractors. His reply to his Harvard class questionnaire prickles and bristles beneath labored cleverness. "I beg that the class will not consider me an object of charity," he added in a postscript, "and if any of them are in want of pecuniary assistance, and will make known their case to me, I will engage to give them some advice of more worth than money."[4]

On September 6 he left the pond. Within a month he was installed back at Emerson's while Emerson started off on his second visit to Europe. Though he would talk brightly about leaving the pond for as good a reason as he went there, and about having several more lives to live, he may have left the pond for no better reason than that Lydia Emerson had invited him to spend the winter helping out while her husband was away in Europe. Thoreau was by no means sure what he was going to do next. Emerson had recommended him for a post with a Michigan survey team. There is frustration written all over his Harvard class tenth annual report, and there is considerable restlessness in his letters. To one correspondent he spoke in the late spring of being on the point of taking a long journey.[5]

48. The Letters to Blake

Before he inserted in the growing manuscript of *Walden* the now famous line "I do not propose to write an ode to dejection, but to brag as lustily as chanticleer in the morning, standing on his roost, if only to wake my neighbors up," he had written in his journal a little prose ode to dejection. "I could tell a pitiful story respecting myself, with a sufficient list of failures, and flow as humbly as the very gutters." And there is a grim-faced, poor-jack tone to the Harvard report he wrote some weeks after leaving the pond. Answering the question "What is your profession?" he wrote, "I don't know whether mine is a profession or a trade or what not. It is not yet learned, and in every instance has been practiced before being studied."[1]

In another week, on October 5, he moved back in at Emerson's. He made efforts to be cheerful, but his general mood this fall was somber. He took walks with Channing and Alcott; he shook off an unwanted proposal of marriage from an enigmatic and, one gathers, totally ineligible Miss Foord, also a boarder at Emerson's. He declared that "winter is the time for study," and he spent many hours at his green desk in the little room at the head of Emerson's stairs, preparing lectures on "Ktaadn," on the relation of the individual to government, and on friendship.[2]

The unsatisfied soul in him divined the same condition in others. Of a poor Swedenborgian he said, "he is insane with too large views," and of a visiting lecturer, H. N. Hudson, he observed that he had a "dark shadow in the core." To Emerson he wrote in mid-November, "the world is a cow that is hard to milk, life does not come so easy."[3]

Thoreau's letters to the absent Emerson were newsy, family-filled, forthcoming about his own moods and feelings, warm and admiring toward Emerson. To date, Thoreau's best letters were those written to Emerson, but they are not impressive, as the letters of great writers go, and Thoreau knew it, confessing to his friend and patron, "I have almost never written letters in my life." But in mid-March 1848, he received a remarkable letter from a thirty-two-year-old Worcester man he had once met named Harrison Gray Otis Blake. Blake had been reading the 1840 *Dial* piece on the Stoic poet Persius and was reminded, he said, of the "haunting impression" Thoreau had left on him. Blake's letter went straight to the heart of what most readers still regard as the central meaning of Thoreau's life. "When I was last in Concord," Blake wrote,

> you spoke of retiring farther from our civilization [perhaps the long journey he had mentioned in a letter of the previous May]. I asked you if you would feel no longings for the society of your friends. Your reply was in substance, "No, I am nothing." That reply was memorable to me. It indicated a depth of resources, a completeness of renunciation, a poise and repose in the universe, which is to me almost inconceivable. . . . If I understand rightly the significance of your life, this is it: You would sunder yourself from society, from the spell of institutions, customs, conventionalities, that you may lead a fresh simple life with God. Instead of breathing a new life into the old forms, you would have a new life without and within. . . . Speak to me in this hour as you are prompted. . . . I honor you because you abstain from action, and open your soul that you may *be* somewhat. Amid a world of noisy, shallow actors it is noble to stand aside and say, "I will simply *be*."[4]

This direct assault on the main gate evoked from Thoreau the first of a series of remarkable, though currently undervalued, philosophical letters he wrote to Blake over the years. His first letter sidestepped the challenge set by Blake's emphasis on withdrawal, renunciation, and abstention, and begins with what is perhaps Thoreau's most thoughtful analysis of the journey metaphor as he understood it. "I do believe that the outward and the inward life correspond," he wrote, but this transcendental commonplace was not followed up with an optimistic conclusion about harmony, but rather with the cold observation that

> if any should succeed to live a higher life, others would not know of it; that difference and distance are one. To set about living a true life is to go

a journey to a distant country, gradually to find ourselves surrounded by new scenes and men; and as long as the old are around me, I know I am not in any true sense living a new or a better life.

The letter has the essential Thoreauvian credo—"I do believe in simplicity"—and the essential Thoreauvian challenge:

I know many men who, in common things, are not to be deceived; who trust no moonshine; who count their money correctly, and know how to invest it; who are said to be prudent and knowing, who yet will stand at a desk the greater part of their lives, as cashiers in banks, and glimmer and rust and finally go out there. If they *know* anything, what under the sun do they do that for?

The letter expresses his fundamental belief in the connection between literature and life. Standing a truism on its head he said, "What can be expressed in words can be expressed in life." There is his basic advice in hard straight nails of language. "Do what you love. Know your own bone; gnaw at it, bury it, unearth it, and gnaw it still. Do not be too moral. You may cheat yourself out of much life so. Aim above morality. Be not *simply* good—be good for something." In one matter he corrected Blake: "I have no designs on society—or nature—or God. I am simply what I am." This letter and the next, written a short five weeks later, on May 2, reaffirm also his fundamental view of nature: "What Nature is to the mind she is also to the body. As she feeds my imagination, she will feed my body." In general the letters to Blake are the letters of a man who knows his own mind. They have a new repose and sureness, and a new directness of expression. They are the most revealing, the least ironic and playful of all his writings, written as they were, not for a general audience, but for a kindred spirit, a disciple, a recruit to the service.[5]

In 1862, the year of Thoreau's death, appeared George Long's translation of the *Meditations of Marcus Aurelius*. It was an important and influential book; it has been described as the book responsible for first introducing Marcus Aurelius to a wide English-speaking public, and for generating a widespread revival of interest in ancient Stoic thought. A year later Matthew Arnold wrote a major essay on Marcus Aurelius, and the year after that, 1864, the American edition came out from Ticknor and Fields and a copy was sent to Emerson. It is an attractive little book, and it seems possible that when Emerson came, very shortly thereafter, to do a volume of Thoreau's letters, the example of Long's *Marcus Aurelius* came to mind and he set out to produce a similar kind of volume.

49. *A Perfect Piece of Stoicism*

The result, the book Emerson put together around the letters to Blake, was called *Letters to Various Persons* and is the neglected masterpiece of Thoreau's American Stoicism. For the transcendentalists generally, Stoicism meant much more a body of ideas than it did a personality stereotype. Stoicism, like Zen, is a body of philosophical doctrines, a group of perceptions, and, also like Zen, it is more than that. It has aspects of a religion and is, in fact, a way of life with a certain perennial attractiveness.

Stoicism dates back to the collapse of the Greek city-state and the undermining of Greek reliance on the polis or state as *the* authoritative context and ultimate justification of moral action. Unable any longer to turn to the polis for reliable answers to the question of how one's life should be lived; unable to find such answers in the forms of traditional religion; and unable to trust society, such as it was, for the answers, Zeno, the first of the Stoics, turned to Nature as the one remaining source of trustworthy moral principles. This turning not to the state, not to God, and not to society, but to nature is the essence of the Stoic way.[1]

From Zeno to the more famous Roman Stoics—Cicero, Seneca, Epictetus, and Marcus Aurelius—the center of Stoic inquiry was the search for a firm support for the moral life, not epistemology, but ethics. Not, what can I know? but, how should I live? was the great and overriding question. And from Zeno to Marcus Aurelius the aim was to answer that question by providing a basis for moral action and a means to personal well-being in the natural endowments of any person, irrespective of social status or personal circumstances.

Stoic thought has three main divisions: physics, logic, and ethics, and its great strength lies in its subordinating everything to the last of these. Zeno held, as William James would hold later, that theoretical inquiry was without value unless it had significance for the moral life. This is the stubbornly practical side of Stoicism; everything is to be judged by whether or not it has concrete implications for our actual and daily lives. Stoicism held that true morality was impossible without knowledge, particularly the knowledge of the natural world which has come to be called science.[2]

Stoicism drew from Heraclitus the idea that all individual things in the world are manifestations of one primary substance. "Always think of the universe," says Marcus Aurelius, "as one living organism, with a single substance and a single soul." From this is drawn the central and basic Stoic perception that "there is a law which governs the course of nature and should govern human actions."[3]

Since Stoicism held, centrally, that there is one law for man and for nature, it followed that one might indeed study nature in order to learn that law for men. "Reserve your right to any deed or utterance that accords with nature," says Marcus Aurelius. "Do not be put off by the criticisms or comments that may follow . . . those who criticise you have their own reason to guide them, and their own impulse to prompt them; you must not let your eyes stray towards them, but keep a straight course and follow your own nature and the World Nature (and the way of these two is one)." And in another place Marcus Aurelius says, in what is one of his most extreme and provocative observations, "nothing can happen to any man that nature has not fitted him to endure."[4]

Stoicism also has a decidedly religious quality. In contrast to Epicureanism, which held that the universe is made up of atoms and empty space, the Stoics held that God is immanent in all created things, but has no separate existence outside them. There is in much Stoic writing a marked sense of gladness or joy quite in contrast to the popular notion of the grim Stoic sage with stiff upper lip. "O world," says Marcus, "I am in tune with every note of thy great harmony. For me nothing is early, nothing late, if it be timely for thee. O Nature, all that thy seasons yield is fruit for me. From thee and in thee, and to thee are all things."[5]

Most important of all is the Stoic insistence upon the individual and upon things that lie within reach of each individual will. Time and again in Marcus Aurelius's notes to himself (usually called the *Meditations*), we find such things as, "No matter to what solitudes banished, I have always been a favorite of fortune. For Fortune's favorite is the man who awards her good gifts to himself," or, "what is the very best that can be said or done with the materials at your disposal? Be it what it may, you have the power to say it or do it; let there be no pretense that you are not a free agent."[6]

Thoreau does not mention Marcus Aurelius. For all Emerson's interest in the Roman emperor, Thoreau may not even have read him. Yet despite the fact that he had read other Stoic writers—Cicero, Seneca, Persius—and despite an early journal entry on Zeno which starts "Zeno the stoic stood in precisely the same relation to the world that I do now," despite these and other traces of Greek and Roman Stoicism in Thoreau, his Stoicism was not derivative in any important way. As has been said so often, he had a genius for living out what others only speculated about. Ellery Channing came near the mark when he said Thoreau's was a natural Stoicism, "not taught from Epictetus" or anyone else. But wherever it came from (and why should we utterly rule out the classics?) the habitual center of Thoreau's personal energy certainly included some major Stoic perceptions. His thought has a strong ethical center—he aimed, early and late, to find a firm support for the moral life in the ordinary nature of man himself. His was always the practical question, how best can I live my daily life? Then too, Thoreau is probably the greatest spokesman of the last two hundred years for the view that we must turn not to the state, not to a God, and not to society, but to nature for our morality. He also stands as the most attractive American *example*—as Emerson was the great proponent—of the ageless Stoic principle of self-trust, self-reverence, or self-reliance, as it is variously called. Thoreau's life can be thought of as one long uninterrupted attempt to work out the practical concrete meaning of the Stoic idea that the laws ruling nature rule men as well.[7]

50. The Apollonian Vision

Blake put forth fundamental questions. He asked Thoreau if there was no "doctrine of sorrow" in his philosophy and Thoreau replied, a touch self-accusingly, that he knew but little of acute sorrow, its place being taken by regrets and chagrins. These he dealt with, as did Goethe, by making poems. It is ridiculous to suggest that a man who knew loss, disease, disappointment, and death on all sides, and whose known responses were strong enough to break his own health from time to time, should actually know nothing of sorrow. Of course he knew it—the question for him was how to surmount it. What Nietzsche said of the Greeks was true for Thoreau as well. Nietzsche observes in *The Birth of Tragedy* that

> The Greeks were keenly aware of the terrors and horrors of existence; in order to be able to live at all they had to place before them the shining fantasy of the Olympians. . . . The Apollonian need for beauty had to develop the Olympian hierarchy of joy by slow degrees from the original titanic hierarchy of terror, as roses are seen to break from a thorny thicket.[1]

The conclusion of Thoreau's reply to Blake's query is down the same avenue. "My only integral experience is in my vision. I see, perchance, with more integrity than I feel." This is a key statement, reminding us that Thoreau's mature outlook is fundamentally Apollonian. In his brilliant discussion of the Apollonian spirit, Walter Otto writes:

> Dionysian nature desiderates intoxication and hence proximity; Apollonian desiderates clarity and form, and hence distance. The first impression this word gives is of something negative, but implied in it is the most positive thing of all—the attitude of cognition. Apollo rejects whatever is too near—entanglement in things, the melting gaze, and, equally, soulful merging, mystical inebriation and its ecstatic vision. He desires not soul but spirit. . . . The sense of his manifestation is that it directs a man's attention not to the worth of his ego and the profound inwardness of his individual soul, but rather to what transcends the personal, to the unchangeable, to the eternal forms. . . . In Apollo there greets us the spirit of clear-eyed cognition which confronts existence and the world with unparalleled freedom—the truly Greek spirit which was destined to produce not only the arts but eventually even science. It was capable of looking upon world and existence as form, with a glance free alike of greed and of yearning for redemption.[2]

Thoreau actually identified himself with Apollo and shared those religious values he understood as Apollonian. His life was far more an imitation of Apollo than of Christ. It does sound a little silly to be talking about "Apollo shining in your face" as Thoreau wryly put it, "in the presidency of James K. Polk," but Thoreau knew a great deal about Apollonian religion. If he did not have Walter Otto or Nietzsche, he did have something far superior to the Victorian simplifications and trivialities of Bulfinch. He had a thorough knowledge of Homer and the so-called Homeric hymns, and he also had K. O. Müller's *The Dorians*, the general source of authoritative information on Doric Greek ideas, values, and culture, the *Paideia* of its day. In its 150-page treatment of Apollo, Thoreau would have found his favorite mythic alter ego, that of Apollo serving Admetis, treated as a preparation for expiation. He would have found the emphasis on expiation and purification that marks his orphic poem "Smoke"; he would have found Apollo as the patron of agriculture and lover of all groves, the god of joy and gladness who could also be hawk or destroyer. The Apollonian year begins, as does Thoreau's, in spring. In Müller too Thoreau would have found Apollo seriously treated as standing for the idea of order, the idea that "the essence of things lies in their due measure and proportion, their system and regularity, that everything exists by harmony and symmetry alone; and that the world itself is a union of all those properties (kosmos or order)."[3]

Meeting Thoreau in March of 1847, E. P. Whipple said he was a man who had "experienced Nature as other men are said to have experienced religion." This is literally true for Thoreau. Another way to put it is to say that his religion was more that of Olympian or Doric Greece than modern Christianity. One reason Thoreau will always seem a little distant, somehow different, and never completely approachable, is that he took Apollonian spirituality seriously. In common with the Dorian Greeks, as Otto describes them, Thoreau "comprehended the things of this world with the most powerful sense of reality possible and nevertheless—nay, for that very reason—recognized in them the marvelous lineaments of the divine." He was not interested in a religion that strove to redeem man from this world, or to raise him above it. He sought clarity of mind, not ecstatic transport; knowledge, not grace. Like the Greeks too he was "inclined to seek motivation for moral decision not in will but in cognition." Otto explains the reason for this:

One who understands the objectivity of the ancient Greek view of the world, one who is capable of following its orientation outward instead of inward, towards the myth of the world instead of the myth of soul, can only find consistency in the emphasis laid upon cognition rather than upon will or emotion.[4]

The key to understanding what Apollo really meant to Thoreau is understanding that Thoreau, like his so-admired Greeks, perceived as *form* that which the modern mind understands as *law*. The figure of Apollo *is* the formal expression of clarity of mind, cognition, individual autonomy. Schopenhauer put it well: "Even as on an immense raging sea, assailed by huge wave crests, a man sits in a little rowboat trusting to his frail craft, so amidst the furious torments of this world, the individual sits tranquilly, supported by the *principium individuationis*." Nietzsche cites this passage, adding, "Apollo himself may be regarded as the marvelous divine image of the *principium individuationis*." The foundation for the sense of reverence we find in Thoreau is his Apollonian recognition that the divine is to be found in the natural world, in what Emerson called the "entire circuit of natural forms," and not in miracle, mystery, magic, or the supernatural. Where the Christian yearns to be redeemed, and the Dionysian to be possessed, the Apollonian yearns to know, to see clearly, to perceive. "The most glorious fact in my experience is not any thing that I have done or may hope to do, but a transient thought, or vision, or dream," he wrote in *A Week*, adding, "I would give all the wealth of the world, and all the deeds of all the heroes for one true vision. But how can I communicate with the gods who am a pencil-maker on the earth, and not be insane?"[5]

51. Spring and Summer 1849: "I Have Chosen Letters"

Though he gamely insisted that getting things published was not so much the problem as getting them written, publication was a major headache for Thoreau. Of the work done at the pond he had least trouble placing "Ktaadn," next easiest was *Walden*, and hardest of all was *A Week*. Back in the fall of 1847, just after leaving the pond and moving in at Emerson's, Thoreau wrote Emerson that *A Week* had made the rounds of four publishers and all had declined to print it, unless at his own expense.[1]

At the end of March 1848, just as the correspondence with Blake was beginning, Thoreau sent the "Ktaadn" piece to Greeley, who had placed the Carlyle essay. Though he thought "Ktaadn" too long for the magazines, Greeley accepted it by return mail, saying that he would "take it and send you the money if I cannot dispose of it more to your advantage." Thoreau wrote back in mid-May gratefully acknowledging Greeley's efforts and including in the letter a long splendid paragraph about himself, beginning "For the last five years I have supported myself solely by the labor of my hands." The paragraph was a small gem on the subject of getting a living. Greeley was immediately struck by it—he was deeply sympathetic with Thoreau's experiments in self-sufficiency—and printed it in the *Tribune* as an example of American self-reliance. "Ktaadn," thanks entirely to the tireless New York editor, began appearing in *Sartain's Union Magazine* starting in July 1848 and running in five installments through November.[2]

Emerson returned home in late July. Thoreau took a short four-day walk with Channing to southern New Hampshire, to Mount Uncanunuc, Goffstown, Hookset, Hampsted, and Plaistow. In November the Alcotts moved to Boston. At Hawthorne's request Thoreau did a lecture in Salem on "Student Life in New England and its Economy." He did two more lectures this winter in Concord, a repeat of the Salem lecture and one on "White Beans and Walden Pond," but mainly he worked, during the fall of 1848 and the winter of 1848–49, on expanding and revising *A Week* and on the second and third drafts of *Walden*. *Walden* was still a relatively short piece, roughly the length of "Ktaadn," but polished up now, while *A Week* continued to rank as his big book, being several times longer.[3]

By February 1849 Thoreau was again sending out *A Week* and dickering in his abrupt fashion with publishers. He also thought well enough of his *Walden* manuscript to be offering it for publication as well. It was exasperating, but Ticknor and Company was willing to publish *Walden* at its expense, but would only take *A Week* at Thoreau's. Unwilling to drop *A Week*, Thoreau tried Monroe, whose offer was little better. They would publish it, but Thoreau would have to guarantee costs if the book didn't sell. After a year and a half of trying and of rewriting, he must have concluded that he was unlikely to do better. He accepted the offer and was busy with proofs by mid-March. It is sad and ironic that just as the book intended to memorialize his brother John was finally to be published, another member of the family, this time his older sister Helen, began to fail. Only thirty-six, she never had been in strong good health and she had had tuberculosis for some time. She was desperately ill by the winter of 1848; by February of 1849 Thoreau said he was afraid for her life.[4]

In mid-May, "Resistance to Civil Government" appeared in Elizabeth Peabody's short-lived periodical, *Aesthetic Papers*. Then, on May 30, at long last, Thoreau's first book was finally published. He had gone to Boston four days before to pick up his author's copies. He gave one to Bronson Alcott, who thought it "An American book, worthy to stand beside Emerson's Essays on my shelves." The first public notice was on nothing less than the front page of the faithful Greeley's *Tribune*, written either by Greeley himself or by the Reverend George Ripley, founder of Brook Farm, whose own dream had now failed and who was making a living with his pen in New York.[5]

The *Tribune* review, appearing on June 13, was essentially fair. It praised the book's observations of nature, and it preferred the prose to the poetry, noting that "nearly every page is instinct with genuine poetry except those wherein verse is haltingly attempted, which are for the most part sorry prose." The review printed generous samples of Thoreau's work and then zeroed in, quite properly, on his pantheism. Unable to appreciate or tolerate Thoreau's serene Apollonian view of religion, the reviewer saw only a "misplaced Pantheistic attack on the Christian Faith." Melville's first book, three years before, had a similar side and got a similar reception, except that Melville went after missionaries, not after Christianity itself. The review, if not completely favorable, should at least have raised interest and sold books.[6]

On June 14, the day after the *Tribune* review, Helen Thoreau died. The funeral was held at home and, at the close of the service, Thoreau got up and set a music box to playing. Everyone sat quietly until the music was over. Both the commencement and the final preparation for the publication of *A Week* were associated intimately with deaths in the family, but the book itself is not death marked. Yet there is a wealth of research to show that Thoreau was very close to his family,

which makes it reasonable to suppose that in somewhat the same way in which John's death had freed Thoreau to be himself, so Helen's death seven years later—expected for months, if not years—seems to have strengthened the sense of purpose that had faltered a little what with leaving the pond and being rejected by publishers. Helen's death may even have spurred Thoreau to accept and announce his ordinary working identity. Now that two of the four Thoreau children were dead, he felt all the more keenly the need to somehow compensate for the others by making his life count. To Blake in late July Thoreau wrote, "we must act with so rapid and resistless a purpose in *one* direction, that our vices will necessarily trail behind. The nucleus of a comet is almost a star." And in September of 1849, he wrote to Harvard president Jared Sparks to ask for borrowing privileges at the Harvard library. His tone, in marked contrast to that of his class report the year before, now was firm and committed even on the touchy subject of getting a living. With unaccustomed emphasis he wrote Sparks,
"I have chosen letters as my profession."[7]

VI. 1849-1851
The Language of the Leopard:
Wildness and Society

52. Shipwreck and Salvation on Cape Cod

On October 9, 1849, Thoreau set out with Channing for a week's tour on Cape Cod, wishing, as he said, "to get a better view than I had yet had of the ocean." Before he was done with the Cape, he would have a better view not only of the ocean and the shore but of early New England and its Calvinism. Full of Ishmaelean humor on the subject of faith, *Cape Cod* is Thoreau's exploration of salvation, of how, if at all, man is (to be) saved.[1]

The account begins, as did the trip itself, with a shocking disaster.

> On reaching Boston, we found that the Provincetown steamer, which should have got in the day before, had not yet arrived, on account of a violent storm; and, as we noticed in the streets a handbill headed, "Death! one hundred and forty five lives lost at Cohasset," we decided to go by way of Cohasset.

They arrived two days after the brig *St. John*, laden with immigrants from Galway, had hit an offshore rock, the Grampus, and then broken up in the gale on the rockiest part of the entire Massachusetts coast. When Thoreau and Channing arrived, the waves were still high, and bodies were still coming ashore. Thoreau described the scene so graphically and so unsentimentally that Robert Lowell could lift the passage almost intact a hundred years later for the opening of his great "Quaker Graveyard in Nantucket." Thoreau saw

> many marble feet and matted heads as the cloths were raised, and one livid, swollen, and mangled body of a drowned girl,—who probably had intended to go out to service in some American family,—to which some rags still adhered, with a string, half concealed by the flesh, about its swollen neck; the coiled up wreck of a human hulk, gashed by the rocks or fishes, so that the bone and muscle were exposed, but quite bloodless,— merely red and white, with wide open and staring eyes, yet lustreless,

dead-lights; or like the cabin windows of a stranded vessel, filled with sand.[2]

Cape Cod starts where "Ktaadn" left off. This is nature in her most savage aspect, indifferent or hostile to human life. The "owners" of these bodies "were coming to the New World, as Columbus and the Pilgrims did," but all they found was death. The shipwreck raises the question the rest of the book tries to answer. From such catastrophe, what salvation? Thoreau entertains three different viewpoints. For a Christian, the body may die, but the soul be saved. From a natural point of view, "if this was the law of nature," and if "to toss and mangle these poor human bodies was the order of the day," the merely natural effects of winds and waves, "why waste any time in awe or pity?" But a third point of view exists, which distinguishes a person's purpose from his physical fate. "A just man's purpose cannot be split on any Grampus," Thoreau wrote in the grim and extended conclusion to his account of the wreck, an account which sets the tone for the entire book. The "unwearied and illimitable ocean" is no more bound to be kind to man than the top of Katahdin. The ocean is a vast wilderness, stretching all the way to Europe. Yet the book's real focus is not so much on the ocean as on the shore, the coast, the beach, the region between the ocean and the land, a region Thoreau finds wild and strange, comparable to Milton's chaos (which he also invoked in "Ktaadn") and which prefigures the land's edge of T. S. Eliot's "Dry Salvages." It is an area "only anomalous creatures can inhabit." The seashore is "a sort of neutral ground," a "wild, rank place, and there is no flattery in it." It is "naked Nature,—inhumanly sincere, wasting no thought on man." All this is seen and recorded in a prose which varies from Melvillean jocularity to the detailed, sad valediction of an Ecclesiastes. "I saw" is repeated over and over, giving biblical solemnity to the opening and to certain other scenes. There is even a terrible beauty in the wreck, and Thoreau notes explicitly his agreement that sublimity is rooted in terror. No mere theory, this.[3]

Thoreau insists on the bleakness, ugliness, and barrenness of the Cape and on the utter commonness of shipwreck. It was a time when everything went by water, when one might see a hundred schooners of the mackerel fleet at once, a time before the Cape Cod Canal, when all ships between Boston and points south had to go the exposed and dangerous outside route. Wrecks were part of daily life on the Cape, salvage part of its economy, as Thoreau noted with his Braudelian eye for economic detail.

In the third chapter, Thoreau goes into a long and amusing account of the Cape's religious life, from early preachers to modern camp meetings, an account which seems like a digression until one recognizes that the entire section is a satiric examination of theological salvation. Thoreau connects Calvinism with the sublime ("the doctrine of terror, which is naturally productive of a sublime and impressive style of eloquence"), but mocks its theological hair-splitting: "So, far in the East, among the Yezidis, or worshippers of the Devil, so-called, the Chaldeans, and others, according to the testimony of travellers, you may still hear these remarkable disputations on doctrinal points, going on." In the end, Thoreau rejects the old minister's message. They may have been "the best men of their generation," but Thoreau can no longer "hear the 'glad tidings' of which they tell." There is no salvation in that quarter.[4]

Chapter four returns to the beach, concluding the first part of *Cape Cod*, and establishing a pattern for the rest of the narrative, which also returns again and again to the beach. Once more we see the dark and stormy sea, the "savage ocean," the "wreckers looking for drift-wood and fragments of wrecked vessels," the wreckers themselves tough and enduring, "too grave to laugh, too tough to cry; as indifferent as a clam." And the chapter ends with a long, apparently lighthearted fantasia on the Charity Houses or Humane Houses placed at intervals along the coast to shelter shipwrecked seamen. Thoreau describes one in great detail, with much Ishmaelish burlesque, looking inside through a knothole darkly. Even these Humane Houses, designed for a very practical, this-worldly salvation, seem not only cheerless, but ill-equipped for their purpose. Looking in, Thoreau could see that "it *was not* supplied with matches, or straw, or hay, that we could see, nor 'accommodated with a bench,' [as regulations specified]. Indeed, it was the wreck of all cosmical beauty within." Not only is the Christian promise of saving souls no longer credible, but even the practical measures of modern charitable societies for saving bodies are ineffectual. There is no salvation, there is only salvage. The final reality in the book, the idea of order at Cape Cod, is expressed in a scene brought in from another and later trip to another wreck-strewn shore by Thoreau, a scene announcing that the final dominion is death's. "That dead body had taken possession of the shore, and reigned over it as no living one could, in the name of a certain majesty which belonged to it."[5]

53. Fall 1849, Spring 1850:
Hindu Idealism

Thoreau had been living back at the house on Texas Street with his family since Emerson returned from Europe in late July 1848. If reading and writing were his real work, his real profession, his apparent living came from making pencils and from an increasingly substantial amount of surveying. In the fall of 1849 he began keeping a separate notebook for surveying. At the same time, his father bought a new house at 73 Main Street in Concord, and by winter Thoreau was at work renovating it. But just as surveying, pencil making, and carpentry were making increased demands on his time, as if by some law of compensation, his interest in Hindu thought now also rekindled. At some point, probably in the fall of 1849, he read and made extracts from an article on "The Philosophy of the Ancient Hindoos" by James Elliot Cabot in the fourth number of the new *Massachusetts Quarterly Review*, edited by Cabot and Theodore Parker.

Cabot was a lifelong friend and, eventually, a biographer of Emerson. As a young man he was interested in architecture, worked as an assistant to Louis Agassiz, and wrote an excellent, clearheaded piece on Kant that had been the lead article in the last issue of *The Dial*, back in 1844. His 1848 piece on Hinduism or as he suggestively calls it, "Hindoo Idealism," draws heavily on contemporaneous scholarship, especially that of H. H. Wilson. It stresses the broad pantheist conception of the world ("the unity and identity of all things in the Deity"), and puts the essence of Hindu thought as "the reduction of all reality to pure, abstract Thought." Cabot takes pains to show the similarity between Hindu idealism and that of Kant and Fichte, especially the latter. Cabot, in other words, understands Hinduism as a major version of transcendental idealism, couched in different terms and originating in another culture. But Cabot notes important differences too. Where Western thought works in terms of antitheses (thought and being, mind and nature), oriental thought, Cabot contends, reflects a prior way of thinking. The Hindus were:

> prone to consider Reality as pure Thought. The highest Reality to them is Mind, from which all trace of the Material is removed,—abstract Soul. The most important theological dogma to us is that God exists. But to the Hindoos the highest description of God is as the One Soul which does not admit of incarnation, and to whom Existence is the illusive show with which He disports himself. The Deity here is pure introversion; mere homogeneousness and equality with himself, that is, pure abstract Thought.[1]

Cabot gave Thoreau an added impetus to explore Hinduism as a powerful independent corroboration of the central concept of Idealism, and it is important to emphasize that his heavy course of Hindu reading in the winter and spring of 1850 show that the naturalist, the surveyor, and the statistician were not driving out the transcendentalist. As his practical pursuits and scientific and mechanical interests grew, they did not displace, but were accompanied by a corresponding reawakening of his interest in idealist thought and ethics.

He began to read systematically and, at the same time, to look for certain familiar and expected things. He had long been familiar with *The Laws of Menu*, a late scripture or code. Now, in September of 1849, he read parts of the *Mahabarata* or Great Epic, and Garcin de Tassy's *Histoire de la littérature Hindui et Hindoustani* (Paris 1839) for an overview. By January 1850, he was reading some of the major early texts such as the *Vishnu Purana*, a central compendium of Hinduism, in the great 1840 translation by H. H. Wilson, which is still in print and regarded as authoritative in India itself. Thoreau was also reading at this time the *Icvara Krsna* or *Samkhya Karika*, as well as *Sacontala, or the Fatal Ring*, the dramatic masterpiece of Calidasa, in the Jones translation. By April 1850 he was working backward into the earlier Vedic literature, such as the *Sama Veda*, in the Stevenson translation, and the collection and translation of early Vedic material—including four Upanishads—by Ramohun Roy. Roy was a contemporaneous Indian religious thinker and reformer who, beginning in 1816, tried to revive the old philosophical monotheism of Vedanta and the Upanishads. His work had long been familiar in New England Unitarian circles and there are strong parallels with Emerson.[2]

Thoreau's earlier interest in Hindu thought had centered on Menu, and had revolved around concepts of cosmic order and universal law. His interests now were somewhat different; they were in philosophical idealism to some extent, but most important they were in Hinduism as a practical path to individual freedom. The central problem that had bothered him in the *Bhagavadgita*—and which he had dealt with in the final version of *A Week*—was that it seemed to him that Krishna did not really give Arjuna a sufficient reason to fight. "Arjoon may be convinced," Thoreau wrote bluntly, "but the reader is not." This concern continued, and now the two dominant motifs in his Hindu reading for 1849–50 are withdrawal (the refraining from action preached also by the Non-Resistance movement) and liberation.[3]

From the Vedas he drew a kind of Hindu Stoicism. "A command over our passions and over the external senses of the body, and good acts, are declared by the Ved to be indispensable in the mind's approximation of God." From the *Harivansa*, he translated a longish piece called "The Transmigration of the Seven Brahmins," in which, as in other notes, he was interested in "how to obtain final emancipation." From the *Samkhya Karika* he began with an observation that might have been made by Epictetus; "the inquiry is into the means of precluding the . . . pain of life," but goes on to something quite different. "The true mode [way] consists in a certain 'discriminative knowledge'—not a doing but a knowing—doing is partial and one-sided, knowing is universal and central. What you see you are, but what you do without seeing helps you not."[4]

From the *Vishnu Purana*, upon which he drew most heavily, he made a few extracts from Cabot and thirty pages more from the text itself. Here too, and almost as though he were formulating the "doctrine of sorrow" Blake had inquired about, he begins with the perception that "as long as man lives he is immersed in manifold afflictions." Here too he swiftly moves to liberation. With true liberation "discriminative knowledge ceases. When endowed with the apprehension of the nature of the object of inquiry, then there is no difference between it and supreme spirit; difference is the consequence of the absence of true knowledge." The *Vishnu Purana* also yielded Thoreau important practical ethical insights. "That is active duty, which is not for our bondage; that is knowledge, which is for our liberation; all other duty is good only unto weariness; all other knowledge is only the cleverness of an artist." The withdrawal, the standing back from action Thoreau sought was not so much a socially negative desire as a positive desire for individual freedom. The great aim is always liberation, which stirs a gladness in us beyond that inspired by the Stoic goal of autonomy. It is no accident that the last note Thoreau made from the *Vishnu Purana* was a confirmation of his own major metaphor for true spiritual awakening: "all intelligences awake with the morning."[5]

54. Spring 1850

The water level of Concord's rivers and ponds was higher than usual this spring, and so were Thoreau's spirits. He went to Haverhill in the middle of May to do some surveying, and in late June he went, alone this time, back to Cape Cod, concentrating on the outer shore from Provincetown to Chatham and back, and spending a good deal of time at the Highland Lighthouse. His mood this season was expansive and relaxed. He allowed his driving sense of purpose to subside a little. "It is wisest," he noted in his journal, "to live without any definite and recognized object from day to day." In looking backward and taking stock of his life, he now recalled and for the first time came fully to grips with the fire he had accidentally set in the woods. And though he would be only thirty-three in July, and was opposed on principle to looking backward, he was sufficiently at ease with himself to be able to do so now. "My imagination, my love and reverence and admiration, my sense of the miraculous is not so excited by any event as by the remembrance of my youth."[1]

But his dominant mood this spring was not retrospective; he was filled with a forward-looking sense of being fully alive in a smiling and all-sufficing present. "Shall not a man have his spring as well as the plants?" He paid close attention to the greening of the countryside, observing that there are more seasons than we commonly notice; that there is one, for example, near the first of June, between spring and summer, when the grass greens and the cows are driven to pasture. His notes are filled with his heady responses to spring: "I was intoxicated with the slight spicy odor of the hickory buds." There is buoyancy and hope in his claim that it is a "sweet wild world which lies along the strain of the wood thrush."[2]

He had been keeping his journal for years, but this spring he kept it with increasing regularity. It is filled with detailed descriptions of natural phenomena, but does not make, at least not yet, any pronounced swing away from the philosophical to the factual. Though the journal record is full and sequential from here on, it is not a diary, and it should not be expected to give a complete account of his life. Thoreau was keeping many other running accounts besides the journal. His letters to Blake, which in many ways are the successors to his poems as the record of his inner biography, continue to be dominated by such problems as the real versus the apparent world, and being versus doing, while his broad philosophical reading is reflected in his *Literary Notebook* and its successors. Indeed, his life this spring seems harmonious and integrated as rarely before. He was reading extensively on all aspects of Cape Cod and balancing that with his own trips for new firsthand impressions. His journal began to grow again with stories—the story of the fire, a long narrative of "the various kinds of life which a single shallow swamp will sustain," a story about a turtle catching a pout ("There he had lain, probably buried in the mud at the bottom up to his eyes till the pout came sailing over"), stories exploring fresh voices and personae ("Well, as I was saying, I heard a splashing in the shallow and muddy water.")[3]

At the same time that Thoreau was working on ways to record detailed natural phenomena in his microcosm, he was reading widely in several new books on the grandest themes imaginable: the *Vishnu Purana*, Alexander von Humboldt's *Aspects of Nature* and his majestic *Kosmos*, and Coleridge's irresistibly titled *Hints toward the Formation of a More Comprehensive Theory of Life*. The *Vishnu Purana*, subtitled *A System of Hindu Mythology and Tradition*, covers a great deal, including the creation of the universe, its destruction and recreation. From Humboldt's charming and vivid *Aspects of Nature*, Thoreau had gone on to *Kosmos* (or *Cosmos*), the newly translated five-volume survey of the material universe in which Humboldt strove, he said, to "represent nature as one great whole, moved and animated by internal forces." One of the most ambitious undertakings of the nineteenth century, *Kosmos* surveyed not only the physical earth and the heavens, but, at great length, the history of man's interest in nature from earliest times. Part I of volume two is called "Incitements to the Study of Nature." From the first subsection of this, devoted to "the difference of feeling excited by the contemplation of nature at different epochs and among different races of men," Thoreau copied out a passage from a lost work of Aristotle illustrating, in an imaginative way, a possible natural origin of our sense of the divine:

> If there were beings living in the depths of the earth, in habitations adorned with statues and paintings, and everything which is possessed in abundance by those whom we call fortunate, and if those beings should receive tidings of the dominion and power of the Gods, and then should be brought from their hidden dwelling places to the surface which we inhabit, and should suddenly behold the earth, and the sea, and the vault of heaven; should perceive the broad expanse of the clouds, and the strength of the winds, should admire the sun in his majesty, beauty and effulgence, and lastly when night veiled the earth in darkness, should gaze on the starry firmament, the waxing and waning moon and the stars rising and setting in the unchanging course ordained from eternity, they would, of a truth, exclaim "there are gods, and such great things are their work."

It was a description commensurate, for once, with Thoreau's own sense of wonder this spring.[4]

In between work on the *Vishnu Purana* and *Kosmos*, he made several pages of notes on Coleridge's *Theory of Life*. Coleridge here defines life, Thoreau noted, as "the principle of individuation, while its 'most general law' is 'polarity'. . . . Life then we consider as the copula, or the unity of thesis and antithesis." This spring Thoreau was applying his reading. The sense of wonder suggested by Aristotle in a book was the same sense of wonder Thoreau found in nature itself, and the key to his work and reading this spring might be termed the principle of individuation. A survey of cosmology and cosmos was only as meaningful as one's own stock of particular detail. On one side Thoreau noted the grand theory of life as individuation. Outside he admired the fresh foliage in the woods in May, which he individualized by adding, "when the leaves are about as big as a mouse's ear."[5]

55. July 1850:
The Wreck of the Elizabeth

Spring brought Thoreau renewal, gladness, revived energy, expanded thoughts, and a general mood of well-being and hope, an attitude he called "a sort of home-made divineness." But it all quickly changed one day in July when the terrible news came from New York that Margaret Fuller had drowned in a shipwreck off Fire Island, and Thoreau undertook, at Emerson's request, to go to the scene and help conduct the grim business of searching for her remains, both physical and literary.[1]

Margaret, recently married to the Marchese Ossoli, had been on the way home from Italy with her husband and her infant son, following the collapse of the Roman Revolution, in which she had taken an active part and about which she had written a book. The manuscript was with her. The *Elizabeth*, a stout brig of 530 tons and only five years old, loaded with marble and other goods, was under the uncertain command of first mate H. P. Bangs, the captain having died of confluent smallpox in Gibraltar. On July 18, the ship was running before a freshening southeast breeze between Bermuda and the New Jersey coast. At 2:30 in the morning on the nineteenth, the wind had increased and the ship was laboring under close-reefed sails. Mr. Bangs had a sounding taken, found 21 fathoms—126 feet—of water, and assumed all to be well. He thought himself to be somewhere between Cape May and Barnegat, off the New Jersey coast near what is now known as Atlantic City. He was headed north, and had, by his reckoning, sixty or seventy miles of open ocean before him. Why did he not, at the very least, heave the ship to and wait for daylight? How could he have been so sure of his position as to keep going in the dark, with the wind increasing? One account suggests he may have seen a light, and thought it was the powerful lighthouse on the highlands of

Navesink, south of the entrance to New York Harbor, when in fact what he saw was the Fire Island light, marking the long, low sandbars that lie parallel to the shore a quarter of a mile off Fire Island, well to the northeast of the entrance to lower New York Bay. Perhaps he thought the storm would blow him into the bay where he would be able to find shelter behind Sandy Hook. Whatever the reason, Bangs let the ship keep going, and the result was that at 3:30 in the morning the *Elizabeth* struck an offshore sandbar five miles east of the Fire Island lighthouse with a head-on jolt that threw the passengers out of their bunks.

The next wave picked up the stern, swung it around and slammed the brig broadside onto the bar. This broke loose the 150 tons of rough Carrara marble in the hold and drove it through the ship's side. Somehow, ship and passengers survived the pounding of the seas until dawn showed them they were only a few hundred yards from shore. The gale continued, increasing its force as the morning wore on. High wind and rain hampered rescue efforts, which were slow getting started. Between 12:00 noon and 1:00 in the afternoon the coast guard surfboat and line gun arrived on the beach. Five shots were fired, but no line could be gotten more than halfway to the ship against such a wind, nor could the lifeboat be launched through the surf. Ordinary means of rescue failed because it was no ordinary blow. It was in fact a hurricane. The New York papers carried accounts of trees torn up by the roots, chimneys toppled, and boats driven ashore or sunk where they lay at dockside.

On the *Elizabeth*, some of the crew and one of the passengers jumped in with planks; only the captain's wife, Acting Captain Bangs, and some of the crew made it to shore alive. All through the morning, those on the ship could see scavengers picking up salvage that had washed up on the beach from the wreck in which they were still trapped. Margaret Fuller Ossoli refused to be separated from her family, and probably realizing that the two year old Nino had no chance whatever in the surf, she could not be persuaded to try for the shore. At last, toward 3:00 in the afternoon, as the rising tide increased the weight of the seas crashing into the ship, the *Elizabeth* began to break up. In the tumult, the steward took Nino and struck out for the beach.

They did not make it; both bodies, still warm, washed ashore a few minutes later. Margaret and her husband were swept overboard at the end. Their bodies were never recovered.[2]

The news reached Concord three days later on the night of Monday, July 22. Emerson's instant response to Greeley was that the best thing he could think to do was "to charge Mr. Thoreau to go, on all our parts, and obtain on the wrecking ground all the intelligence, and, if possible, any fragments of manuscript or other property." (Bayard Taylor got there the day after the wreck; he reported that as many as a thousand people were on the beach by Sunday, and that the shore was littered for three or four miles with fragments of planks, spars, boxes and merchandise.) Thoreau left Concord at once on the twenty-third, and was in New York in time to catch a 9:00 morning train to Long Island on the twenty-fourth, a Wednesday. Arriving five days after the wreck, Thoreau discovered that there was little left. Many others had arrived or were arriving; Arthur Fuller, Ellery Channing, W. H. Channing, and Charles Sumner, Jr., whose brother Horace had also drowned in the wreck. Thoreau's letter to Emerson, written the next morning from the Smith Oakes house, where all the survivors had been brought initially, conveyed the story he had pieced together in abrupt, shaken phrases:

> The ship struck at 10 minutes after 4 and all hands, being mostly in their night clothes made haste to the forecastle—the water coming in at once. There they remained, the passengers *in* the forecastle, the crew *above* it doing what they could. Every wave lifted the forecastle roof and washed over those within. The first man got ashore at 9. Many from 9 to noon. At floodtide about 3½ o'clock when the ship broke up entirely—they came out of the forecastle and Margaret sat with her back to the foremast with her hands over her knees—her husband and child already drowned— a great wave came and washed her off.[3]

Four bodies were still missing, those of Margaret, Ossoli, Horace Sumner, and a sailor. Nino had been buried. A broken desk, some unimportant papers, a few books were all the effects that remained at the Smith Oakes's. But the wreck pickers, many apparently from Patchogue, had made off with much, and Thoreau intended to hire a boat and go there to "advertize etc. etc." The trip produced nothing except—later—some Dickensian sketches of drunken Dutchmen coasting about blindly but with eerie accuracy in foggy shallows. Thoreau returned to the beach. A few more garments were found, including a coat of Ossoli's, from which Thoreau took a button. On Friday, "a portion of a human skeleton" was reported ashore. Very early Saturday morning Thoreau went to look. As he wrote two days later to Charles Sumner, Jr., whose younger brother's body was also still missing, there was so little left that he found he had "not knowledge enough of anatomy to decide confidently, as so many might, whether it was that of a male or a female." Walking out on the now-empty beach early Saturday morning, in search of that wreck of a body, made a lasting impression on Thoreau. He wrote it up in his journal and eventually put it into *Cape Cod*.

> I expected that I should have to look very narrowly at the sand to find so small an object, but so completely smooth and bare was the beach . . . that when I was half a mile distant the insignificant stick or sliver which marked the spot looked like a broken mast in the sand. . . . There lay the relics in a certain state, rendered perfectly inoffensive to both bodily and spiritual eye by the surrounding scenery, a slight inequality in the sweep of the shore. . . . It was as conspicuous on that sandy plain as if a generation had labored to pile up a cairn there. . . . It reigned over the shore. That dead body possessed the shore as no living one could.[4]

From the wreck of the *St. John* and the bodies all over the rocks of Cohasset the previous October to this lone scrap of corpse five miles west of the wreck of the *Elizabeth*, Thoreau had recently seen a good deal of death by water. The material remains were pitiful—a few bones, a few clothes, a button, some papers and books—nothing really. A week later Thoreau wrote to Blake, "Our thoughts are the epochs in our lives: all else is but as a journal of the winds that blew while we were here."[5]

56. August and September 1850: *The Material of a Million Concords*

The grim business of this sad errand, like the wreck of the *St. John*, tested Thoreau's Stoicism and challenged his idealism, but destroyed neither. It forced him again to confront the reality of death, and this time he came directly to terms with it in his writing as he never had done when his brother died. Yet the same strained, paradoxical, and nervous assertiveness that marked his writing to Emerson on the death of Waldo, marks his journal, the opening chapter of *Cape Cod*, and his letter to Blake after the wreck. It is as though he knew what his intellectual position should be, but he could not accept death emotionally, neither his own nor anyone else's. "I do not think much of the actual" he noted in his journal, adding "it is something that we have long since done with. It is a sort of vomit in which the unclean love to wallow." But he edited this strange, strong reaction out of the finished letter to Blake, which opens calmly with "I find that actual events, notwithstanding the singular prominence which we all allow them, are far less real than the creations of my imagination." He goes on to speak of the "button which I ripped off the coat of the Marquis of Ossoli, on the seashore, the other day." The button, like the bones on the beach, is a neat, unbloodied, unemotional, and meaningless bit of material reality. "Held up, it intercepts the light,—an actual button,—and yet all the life it is connected with is less substantial to me, and interests me less, than my faintest dream." His conclusion, already quoted, about everything except thought being insubstantial as the wind, reaffirms the higher, prior reality of mind.[1]

And that is all he said to Blake directly about the wreck. But the main body of the letter is still to come and it consists of practical conclusions to be drawn from the meaninglessness of dead bone or button. From death comes a renewed interest in the business of living and working. "I say to myself, do a little more of that work which you have confessed to be good." Samuel Johnson had said, "Be well when you are not ill"; Thoreau showed the same set of mind. "As for health, consider yourself well." Have your own thoughts and your own doubts. "Do not entertain doubts if they are not agreeable to you." Death gave life a new imperative for Thoreau. "Do what nobody else can do for you. Omit to do anything else." Death also had the effect of stimulating Thoreau's need to experience widely and live deeply. "I am glad when I discover, in ocean and wildernesses far away, the material of a million Concords: indeed," he added, revealingly, "I am lost, unless I discover them."[2]

Shipwreck is from now on a major metaphor for Thoreau. It is the key to *Cape Cod* and it is handled in a special way. When Bayard Taylor, at twenty-five already a seasoned traveler and reporter of excursions for the *Tribune*, described the scene of the wreck of the *Elizabeth*, he emphasizes what we expect, the sea, the wreck, the efforts of the insurers to reach and survey the wreck. He details the cargo and general litter of the beach, giving us a wide canvas, showing us crowds of people thronging to see this vast public calamity.

> All the silk, Leghorn braid, hats, wool, oil, almonds, and other articles contained in the vessel, were carried off as soon as they came to land. On Sunday there were nearly a thousand persons here, from all parts of the coast between Rockaway and Montauk, and more than half of them were engaged in secreting and carrying off everything that seemed to be of value.

Taylor's account is vivid, useful, decent, but the emphasis is on crowds and clutter and it makes the central events very public. In Thoreau's hands, just the opposite happens. By focusing on the button and the few bones, he removes the entire public scene, creating a feeling of being alone, lost in the middle of a great empty space. In death as in life the principle of individuation reigns, just as Thoreau, later in his journal, and then for *Cape Cod*, worked out this scene and ended it with the body reigning over the shore.[3]

The sense of being alone, the fate of bare unaccommodated man, the bleak emptiness of death is strongest in *Cape Cod* of all Thoreau's writings. It is the book in which, even more than *The Maine Woods*, he confronts not only a cold and unfriendly nature, but the cessation of life itself. It is ironic that Thoreau's willingness to front the fact of death and the emptiness of redemption and salvation should have been brought on by the death not of a member of the family or a close friend or someone he loved, but by the death of Margaret Fuller. He had never warmed to her in life, but her death stained the landscape for him. Not long after returning to Concord, he recorded "a glorious lurid sunset tonight, accompanied with many somber clouds. . . .

Pale saffron skies with faint fishes of
rosy clouds dissolving in them.
A bloodstained
sky."[4]

57. Fall 1850:
Trip to Canada

In late September, Thoreau was still looking back on the wreck of the *Elizabeth* and reflecting on what T. S. Eliot would one day characterize as a "trip that will be unpayable / For a haul that will not bear examination." Thoreau observed, "It hardly seems worth while to risk the dangers of the sea between Leghorn and New York for the sake of a cargo of juniper berries and bitter almonds." But within a week he and Channing and fifteen hundred other Yankees were off for a week's tour of Canada to take advantage of a special excursion price of seven dollars round-trip. They went by train to Burlington, Vermont, by steamer across Lake Champlain to Plattsburg, New York, by train again to Montreal, by steamer to Quebec, then back, with side trips to St. Anne de Beaupré and the Montmorency Falls.[1]

As they were setting out, the landscape was still disaster haunted for Thoreau, though his metaphor is now military, not maritime. The woodbine leaves suggested bloodshed to him and seemed "dyed with the blood of the trees whose wounds it was inadequate to stanch. For now the bloody autumn was come and an Indian warfare was waged through the forest." In general, Thoreau's account of what he saw on this trip is thin, uninspired, complaining. On Lake Champlain he saw "a few white schooners, like gulls," but, he adds, "it was such a view as leaves not much to be said." The truth was that he was not very open, at the outset anyway, to what the trip had to offer. "What I got by going to Canada was a cold." True, no doubt, but what he could have added was that, eventually, the trip to Canada was to give him a whole new conception of the history of North America.[2]

He found the people unprepossessing and unenterprising, the arrangements for travelers few and inconvenient. A major reason for his dissatisfaction with Canada was that he spent more time in cities on this trip than on any other, and he found the cities, like the country generally, overwhelmed by the red and the black of Army and Church. Everywhere one went there were nuns, priests, and soldiers; the urban landscape was physically dominated by vast stone churches and fortifications. "Huge stone structures of all kinds, both in their erection and by their influence when erected, rather oppress than liberate the mind," he noted toward the end of his account, though at the beginning he had been impressed with the religious atmosphere of the Cathedral of Notre Dame in Montreal ("an atmosphere which might be sacred to thought and religion if one had any"). In general, Thoreau is more anticlerical than anti-Catholic, and he takes no harsher tone here toward Catholicism than he takes toward Puritanism in *Cape Cod* or Christianity generally in *A Week*. What he really found oppressive were the feudal institutions of Canada. "Why should Canada, wild and unsettled as it is, impress us as an older country than the States, unless because her institutions are old?" In his sole venture out of the United States, Thoreau contrasts the feudal setting out of Canada with the relatively freer institutions of New England, thus prefiguring a major theme of Francis Parkman's monumental life work, *France and England in North America*. He reveals, rather surprisingly, a lurking patriotism in his general preference for the way things are done back home. This is not provincialism, since provincialism is, as Matthew Arnold observed, not knowing the standards by which your work will be judged. It is more his customary contrariness. At home, he could dwell on his French background. In French Canada, he was all Yankee.[3]

A Yankee in Canada, a ninety-page, five-part account that Thoreau worked up, after his return, into lectures and then into serial form, is a book in which the reader feels enclosed and oppressed. Beginning with the wide streets of Keene, New Hampshire, the account narrows to a heavy culminating fourth chapter that dwells gloomily on a long discussion of walls and soldiers. The account only comes alive, giving the reader a sense of relief and openness, at the very end, with a moving description of the great St. Lawrence River, which Thoreau calls "the most interesting object in Canada to me." It is, he says, "the most splendid river on the globe," nearly a hundred miles wide at its mouth, with the largest, most navigable estuary in the world, draining half the fresh water on the surface of our planet. As the finest entrance to the North American continent, it was the pathway of the earliest discoverers, most of them French. "Who can say what would have been the history of this continent if, as has been suggested, this river had emptied into the sea where New York stands?"[4]

The English, Thoreau concludes, may have been better *colonists*, but his own sympathies were drawn, he says, to the French and Spanish *discoverers* of North America, an interest that links *A Yankee in Canada* with the last part of *Cape Cod*. Both were written around the same time, after the Canada trip, with the help of extensive post-trip reading in Cartier's *Voyages de découverte au Canada*, in Champlain's *Voyages de la Nouvelle Fraunce*, and his *Voyages du Sieur de Champlain*, and in Lescarbot's *Histoire de la Nouvelle-Fraunce*, all of which Thoreau had out of the Harvard library between late October and mid-November 1850. He noted with some asperity that he could not find "in English any adequate or correct account of the French exploration of what is now the coast of New England, between 1604 and 1608." Pursuing what he called the "ante-Pilgrim history of New England," he notes that while it is often said that John Smith named New England, what he really did was rename it. It had been New France for many years. Cartier came as far as Montreal in 1535, eighty-five years before Plymouth. French exploration of the coast was extensive, their mapping, especially that of Champlain, was superb, and so much preferred by mariners that even long after the English had come to stay, French names still marked the coast: Isle au Haut, Petit Manan, Mount Desert. One French fishing skipper, encountered off Nova Scotia in 1607, said he had made a trip a year for forty years from France for the fish. There were fish settlements up and down the coast, and permanent settlements at Castine, St. Croix, and Port Royal (now Annapolis, Nova Scotia). In short, Thoreau concludes, "the Englishman's history of New England commences only when it ceases to be New France." Thoreau challenged the view, which still obtains to some degree in New England, and despite Parkman's work, that the history of the white man in North America really starts with the Pilgrims. Thoreau's revisionism insists, perhaps with a touch of pride in his own ancestry, on the prior claims of the French. If the English Puritans in New England saw themselves as a chosen people, as Israelites on an errand from God, Thoreau deftly undercuts the English Puritan view of history by putting discovery ahead of colonization, and France before England.[5]

58. The Red Face of Man I

The exact stages by which Thoreau's lifelong fascination with the American Indians evolved remain in question (because of his habit of working in many notebooks all at once and without dating entries), but the main lines of his interest have recently become much clearer.[1]

When he left college, his playful "Indian" letter to John and his sudden ability to find arrowheads suggest a youthful attitude of light-hearted interest in an idealized figure, a heroic stereotype of the red man as noble hunter. But, however much this early interest may have been marked by then-prevailing preconceptions about "savagism," there was always a strong element of sympathetic identification with the Indians. Thoreau was predisposed from the start to want to be like the Indian, and to value what he understood to be Indian values.[2]

In the first draft of *A Week*, written during 1845–46 at Walden, there is a fair amount of material on Indians, most of it about Indians who had figured in American colonial history and were already dead by Thoreau's time. Thoreau tells of Indian hunters driven out by white farmers; the tone is sympathetic and elegiac, and the point is that the Indian has vanished. No longer a present problem requiring hard decisions, the entire subject could be covered with a benign, reverential mist of good feeling.

In 1846, on his trip to Katahdin, he briefly encountered some actual Indians, living what seemed to Thoreau a degraded, semiassimilated existence. The Indian guide, Louis Neptune, never showed up because he had gone on a drinking spree. Thoreau's first draft of "Ktaadn" records these details circumstantially, but makes very little of them. "Ktaadn" is about wilderness, and wildness versus civilization, but Indians figure only tangentially in the first version. Lying in camp beside North Twin Lake, at the edge of the unbroken woods and beneath the bright summer night sky, he had felt, he said, like the first discoverer of the continent, not like the aboriginal inhabitant being discovered.[3]

But at the same time he was working out the first draft of "Ktaadn," he was reading and responding to the primitivist thesis in Melville's *Typee*, and even more important, he was carefully working his way through Chateaubriand's *Itinerary from Paris to Jerusalem* (which is a much better written and less sentimental work than *René* and *Atala*, and which deserves to be more widely read than it now is). *Typee* makes it clear that primitivism is an account not so much of how the South Sea Islanders live, as it is of how modern European man thinks the islanders live, because he himself yearns for an earlier, simpler life. Because primitivism contrasts the "savage" state with civilization, the primitivist is slow to see aboriginal peoples as civilized in their own ways. Melville's book made Thoreau self-conscious about this point of view. Chateaubriand's *Itinerary* was written, said its author, to complement and balance his earlier trip to, and account of, America. As Chateaubriand works his way east, he makes frequent contrasts between Eastern primitives and Western ones, between Arabs and American Indians, always—and this of course is Chateaubriand's notorious bias—in favor of the Indian. The Indian is

> proudly independent . . . not connected by his origin with the great civilized nations; the names of his ancestors are not to be found in the annals of empire. . . . In a word, with the American, everything proclaims the savage, who has not yet arrived at a state of civilization; in the Arab, everything indicates the civilized man who has returned to the savage state.

Chateaubriand's focus is very wide. The point here, and Thoreau's notes show he did not miss it, is not just the contrast between European voyages and American Indians, but European man's view of non-Europeans. Chateaubriand is still utterly ethnocentric; he berates the Arabs for embodying what he fears and dislikes in European man—his decadence—while he praises the American Indian for the qualities he admires in himself. The essence of the position is put thus by Henri Baudet, whose *Paradise on Earth* is the best treatment of this whole problem:

> Nineteenth century social romantics may have protested against a social structure based on the new techniques and new economy [of the Industrial Revolution] and may have adopted slogans of reform, but no part of their rejection, sombreness, and slogan-making seems to me to have had the intention of extolling the virtues of any outside world to the detriment of Europe.[4]

As Thoreau's dissatisfaction with the arrangements of white nineteenth-century America grew, he became increasingly willing to do just what Baudet says no one did at the time, that is, to recognize in his conception of the American Indians, and, as time went on, in the Indians themselves, certain non-European virtues that were not only valuable to the Indians but valuable in themselves and badly needed by the poor white man.

In the revised version of *A Week* and in the finished version of "Ktaadn," both completed early in 1848, this new sophistication about primitivism can be seen, as can new passages specifically arguing that "the Indian"—still a generalized figure to be sure—is what Philip Gura calls a kind of representative man "providing an important example of what virtues Americans needed to retain significance in their lives." Now Thoreau adds the great coda on the Indians to the end of "Ktaadn":

> In a bark vessel sewn with the roots of the spruce, with horn-beam paddles he dips his way along. He is but dim and misty to me, obscured by the aeons that lie between the bark canoe and the batteau. He builds no house of logs, but a wigwam of skins. He eats no hot-bread and sweet-cake, but musquash and moose-meat and the fat of bears. He glides up the Milli-nocket [a far cry, all this, from the hung over Louis Neptune disappearing up this very stream in 1846] and is lost to my sight, as a more distant and misty cloud is seen flitting by behind a nearer, and is lost in space.
> So he goes about his destiny,
> the red face of man.[5]

59. The Red Face of Man II

Back from Canada in the fall of 1850, Thoreau's interest in the American Indians took a new turn as he plunged into a program of reading about the early voyages of discovery. Simply to say "reading" gives the wrong impression. It was more like systematic scholarly research. He made long lists of available works on early Canadian history, then proceeded to make extracts from twenty-six different books. He collated different editions against each other, traced borrowings, tried to separate rumor from fact, compared all available maps in order to trace the history of the names given to newly discovered features of the coast, and so on. In his so-called Canadian Notebook, begun this fall of 1850, he recorded the results of his omnivorous reading in Warburton's *Hochelega*, Bouchette's *Topographical Description of Lower Canada*, Cartier's *Voyages*, Jean Alphonse's *Routier*, de la Potherie's *Voyages de l'Amerique*, Roberval's *Voyage*, Bouchette's *British Dominions in North America*, Lescarbot's *Histoire de la Nouvelle Fraunce*, and a great many other books.[1]

His fascination with the discovery and exploration of Canada evolved into a general interest in all early voyages to the coast of North America, an interest that found expression in the final chapters of *Cape Cod* as well as *A Yankee in Canada*. This inquiry into the earliest European discovery of the New World raised in turn the subject of the confrontation between the discoverers and the discovered. The Canadian Notebook thus records Thoreau's interest in Canada turning into an interest in the early "history of the North American continent,"— Thoreau's own phrase—the chief feature of which came more and more to be the American Indians themselves. The scholarly habits of the Canadian reading were continued and, beginning in good earnest in the fall of 1850, he began to read and make copious extracts from books and articles on the Indians. The Indian Books (as Thoreau called the notebooks now in the Morgan Library labeled "Extracts mostly concerning the Indians"), eventually filled eleven notebooks with material culled from more than 270 different sources. The sheer volume of this work is daunting, but certain facts help keep it in proper perspective.[2]

First, he tended to avoid the better known and most obvious works on the Noble Savage. Chateaubriand, Rousseau, and Bougainville do not appear. He also ignored most poetry and fiction, preferring first-hand accounts by visitors, travelers, explorers, or missionaries, and his own point of view was by now sufficiently sophisticated for him to make due allowance for the bias of each. Second, he came gradually to see that most of the later accounts were built on the earlier ones, and that the earliest accounts, including the vast record of the annual *Jesuit Relations* from 1630 to 1690, were the more valuable, as well as being a largely untapped resource. Finally, and not surprisingly given this knowledge, the quality of his information and the sophistication of his point of view bear comparison with the best work of the time, with Henry Rowe Schoolcraft's monumental *Information regarding the Indian Tribes of North America*, 1851–1857; with Ephraim G. Squier's *The Serpent Symbol and the Worship of the Reciprocal Principles of Nature in America*, 1851; with Squier and Davis's *Ancient Monuments of the Mississippi Valley*, 1848; and above all with the work of his great contemporary, Lewis Henry Morgan, whose *League of the Iroquois* first appeared in 1851, just as Thoreau's interest in the Indians was accelerating. Morgan's book, which Thoreau read, was called by John Wesley Powell the "first scientific account of an Indian tribe," and it is still regarded as "the best general book on this classic people." Morgan, also famous for a later book on the structure of the family, and for its influence on Engels and on Marxism, confined himself almost entirely to firsthand observation, though he acknowledged the value of such records as the *Jesuit Relations*, even though he said he knew them only in part. Thoreau's work, being mostly based on written, historical sources, is not for that reason inferior to Morgan's; it is rather a complement to it. If their methods are different, their aims and sympathies are strikingly similar. The following, written by Morgan, could as easily have been written by Thoreau: "Civilization is aggressive, as well as progressive. . . . The institutions of the red man fix him to the soil with a fragile and precarious tenure; while those of the civilized man, in his best estate, enable him to seize it with a grasp which defies displacement."[3]

Thoreau's vast Indian Book project, gotten under way in the fall of 1850, may have had one other impetus as well. For that fall a group of Indians came and camped in their tents along the Concord River. Thoreau went to visit, and his notes have a different flavor from earlier ones. There are few generalizations, few comparisons with the white man. Most of the notes are simple observations, on a moose-hide canoe, on cooking methods, on animal trap construction, and are put down as if the important thing were to record the Indian point of view, to acknowledge the actual living Indian.[4]

60. November 1850 to April 1851:
Gramatica Parda

As his interest in Indians became more scholarly, more objective, more external this fall, he was also moving in just the opposite direction in his rediscovery and recognition, within himself, of the essential wildness that had made the Indians of interest to him in the first place. As his autumn walks brought him upon wild apples, wild grasses, wild house cats, wild muskrats, and wild men, he became increasingly interested in the nature of wildness itself, or as he called it, "the wild." Through the fall and winter of 1850 and the early months of 1851, his journal records his thoughts on this subject, which he gathered together for a lecture called "The Wild," first delivered in April of 1851. It became a favorite lecture with Thoreau, was given many times, growing until part of it was broken off as another lecture on "Walking." The two talks were ultimately reassembled and published in 1862 as "Walking."

As *Walden* is Thoreau's central book, so "Walking" is his central essay. The quality it identifies, that is, wildness, stands for much of what we still regard as characteristically Thoreauvian. Everyone has felt this quality of wildness or ferity in Thoreau. He himself talks about his occasional impulse to seize a woodchuck and devour him raw; Moncure Conway said Thoreau was the original for Hawthorne's Donatello, the wild youth with faun's ears in *The Marble Faun*; Channing wondered whether Thoreau ever reached "the wildness for which he longed," and Emerson saw the wildness and was afraid of it:

> Henry Thoreau is like the wood-god who solicits the wandering poet, and draws him into "antres vast and desarts idle," and leaves him naked, plaiting vines and with twigs in his hand. Very seductive are the first steps from the town to the woods, but the end is want and madness.

This time Emerson, so often right, was wrong. He was unable to understand or sympathize with this particular quality in Thoreau. Perhaps it was one of the shadows that was growing between them.[1]

Thoreau approached the subject as he approached everything this fall, in language drawn from travel and voyages of discovery. The resulting essay is that ultimate form of the excursion, the sacred excursion or crusade. The holy land he seeks to recover is the essential primitive wildness in himself. "We go eastward," Thoreau says, "to realize history . . . we go westward as into the future." Citing Michaux, Humboldt, Guyot, Head, Buffon, and Linnaeus, Thoreau turns the discovery of the new world of the West into a vast travel metaphor for another, more important process of discovery. "The West of which I speak is but another name for the Wild." It is clear that he puts the highest possible value on this quality. "What I have been preparing to say," he goes on, "is that in Wildness is the preservation of the World." In a nutshell, this is Thoreau's, and after him America's, conservation ethic. But how we understand that ethic depends on what we think Thoreau meant by "wildness."[2]

The essay opens with a set of definitions. "I wish to speak a word for Nature, for absolute freedom and wildness, as contrasted with a freedom and culture merely civil." He is interested then in absolute, not civil liberty, and he understands wildness as the opposite of civil culture, or civilization. Yet at the same time, the wild, occupying the place some have assigned to Eros, is the ultimate source of the energy that builds civilizations. "The story of Romulus and Remus being suckled by a wolf is not a meaningless fable," Thoreau argues. "The founders of every state which has risen to eminence have drawn their nourishment and vigor from a similar wild source." He is at great pains to show that he puts a high moral value on wildness, thereby separating himself as clearly as possible from the long tradition of fear of the wild. He amends a line from Ben Jonson to read "How near to good is what is *wild*," and he says flatly, "Life consists with wildness. The most alive is the wildest."[3]

He has sought, without much success he says, some adequate expression of wildness in literature. He acknowledges the truth in "the wildest dreams of the wildest men," and the "awful ferity with which good men and lovers meet. . . . All good things are wild and free," he concludes. He is utterly clear that this means that the wild is not something outside or foreign to us but that "we have a wild savage in us," and that true knowledge of this wildness is not ordinary knowledge, but the knowledge of the leopard, *gramatica parda*. When we are really in tune with this quintessential quality of wildness, we will have gone beyond what is usually called knowledge. "The highest we can attain to is not Knowledge," says Thoreau, "but Sympathy with Intelligence." When we attain that, we are no longer servile, but can live free. To understand and sympathize with the wildness within, and to act upon it, leads to liberation. This is the core and meaning of the essay.[4]

Thoreau's position is essentially similar to but not derived from that of Vico, the eighteenth-century Neapolitan who insisted that "savagery was both the original and the necessary stage of every form of achieved humanity." Rousseau also came to realize that "the Wild Man exists within us all," though for Rousseau the rediscovery of the wild man was, as Geoffrey Symcox has argued, "the uncovering and rehabilitation of the realm of *feeling* [emphasis mine], which he instinctively felt was essential to an understanding of man and society." Thoreau is very explicit that for him, recovering the wild man means recovering our essential *freedom*, but it is also important to note that recognition of the wildness within has for Thoreau, as for its other champions, the vital, tonic effect of restoring man to emotional and cognitive awareness of his essential innermost self. The rediscovery of the wild is a process the opposite of alienation, restoring contact, via the *gramatica parda*, between man and his best, most vital self.[5]

Thoreau is a great radical, and what Hayden White has claimed for Marx, Freud, and Nietzsche, can be claimed for Thoreau as well. White says, "the problem of salvation is a *human* problem having its solution solely in a reexamination of the *creative* forms of *human* vitality. Each is therefore compelled to recur to primitive times as best he can in order to imagine what primal man, pre-civilized man, the Wild Man which existed before history—i.e., outside the social state— might have been like." This is why "Walking" is so pointedly secular an essay. Thoreau's belief in wildness parodies the Christian credo. "I believe in the forest, and in the meadow, and in the night in which the corn grows." This is why an even "newer testament," "the gospel according to this moment" is needed, and this is why the essay closes insisting that the true "great awakening" is no Calvinist revival, but the necessary rediscovery of what is wild and free in us.[6]

"Walking" closes with an image of enlightenment and awakening, with a picture we might call a secular luminist landscape. "So we saunter toward the Holy Land, till one day the sun shall shine more

226

brightly than ever he has done, shall perchance shine into our minds and hearts, and light up our whole lives with a great awakening light, as warm and serene and golden as on a bankside in autumn."[7]

61. Technological Conservative

The first draft of *Walden* records Thoreau's disapproval of railroads, factories, and other so-called modern improvements. Over the years he sharpened the phrases, but did not change the attitude. Of manufacturing he said, "I cannot believe that our factory system is the best mode by which men may get clothing." Of the railroad, "to make a railroad round the world available to all mankind is equivalent to grading the whole surface of the planet." Sometimes, however, he felt differently. The sounds of the railroad and even its smoke as seen from a distance could add interest to the landscape, and he would become fascinated by the sound of the wind in the telegraph wires—a kind of industrial-age aeolian harp, communicating messages undreamed of by its engineers. But if his general attitude toward modernization and its effects was skeptical or even hostile, it was not because he was unmechanical or unhandy.[1]

He had a gift for the practical, the mathematical, and the mechanical sides of things. He was clever with tools, making a drawer beneath the seat of a chair for Lydia Emerson's Sunday gloves, making claw-covers for her chickens so they wouldn't scratch in her garden, or knocking together a flat-bottomed scow with wheels for ease of portage in river travel. He was both repelled and impressed by the vast science-fictional wind machines of Etzler, he took a detailed interest in telescopes, and he admired the emphasis on practical education that came in with a renewed interest in modern scientific apparatus at Harvard in the 1840s. He became an expert surveyor, much sought after for his skill and accuracy.

In the late 1840s he began to assemble data on such things as the height of the river, not because he was becoming unimaginative, but because he had enough imagination to see what kinds of fresh generalizations were possible through statistics. His later studies of Concord phenomena and of the dispersal of seeds depend heavily on comprehensive detail and carefully assembled volumes of data. And from the time he left college, he was involved with the family business of grinding lead (graphite) and making pencils, to which enterprises he contributed a string of ingenious inventions and improvements, as Walter Harding has so painstakingly demonstrated. Thoreau found a way to mix graphite with fine Bavarian clay rather than the traditional mixture of bayberry wax, glue, and spermaceti to produce a smoother lead; he designed and built a new grinding mill to produce finer and more evenly ground graphite. He developed a way to bake the graphite and clay mixture, invented a saw to cut out individual leads, then conceived the idea of baking leads just the right size so they would not have to be sawn, and finally invented a way of drilling a hole in the wood for the lead, rather than cutting the wood in half, then gluing it back together. He had enough ingenuity to make the Thoreau pencils a match for any made in America, perhaps enough ingenuity to have made a success of manufacturing had he put his heart into it over the long haul. Whatever he thought of the *results* of mechanization, he clearly had a flair for machines and contrivances themselves.[2]

On January 1, 1851, he was asked to give a lecture (about Cape Cod) at Clinton, Massachusetts, and he took the opportunity to visit the large cotton mills there. Mills were everywhere by this date. New England in 1850 had 896 textile mills, and the industry was growing. Concord had its mill, as did surrounding towns. The Merrimack River was one long, managed mill stream as early as Thoreau's 1838 excursion on it. The mills represented "the vanguard of mechanical progress." To a large extent, it has been argued, they "shaped the nation's perception of technology." The machine promised to liberate humanity from needless toil and drudgery, joining its hum with the roar of the waterfall to sing "a song of triumph and exaltation at the successful union of nature with the act of man."[3]

The Lancaster gingham mill at Clinton was particularly impressive. West of Concord and south of Ayer on the Nashua River, the mill's main room covered 1⅞ acres and contained, as Thoreau reported it, 578 looms, powered by between three- and four-hundred horsepower developed from the river, while a two-hundred-horsepower steam engine stood by for use during periods of low water. (This is more power than it now seems to us. The standard for comparison is that "one mill power," defined as power "equivalent to a flow of twenty-five cubic feet of water per second over a thirty foot fall, or approximately sixty horsepower," as it was then calculated, was enough to drive all the machines that could be put into a five-story mill building, of which each floor measured 150 by 40 feet.)[4]

The operators were mostly women, and Thoreau described the whole process in unironic, technically clean prose:

> From a great many spools, the warp is drawn off over cylinders and different-colored threads properly mixed and arranged. Then the ends of the warp are drawn through the harness of the loom by hand. The operator knows the succession of red, blue, green, etc, threads, having the numbers given her, and draws them through the harness accordingly.

Delighted as always to be able to pin a word to its origin, Thoreau recorded with glee "then the woof is put in, or it is *woven*!!"[5]

Thoreau's cool account is in marked contrast to Melville's almost contemporaneous description of a paper mill in western Massachusetts in "The Tartarus of Maids." Melville writes a bitter satire on the mechanization of life using a running analogy between the mill's creation of paper and human childbirth. For Melville the mill is a symbol in a fiction, the mill machinery coming to stand for the reproductive machinery to which women are also tied. Thoreau, on the other hand, reports what he sees, factually—and, if anything, is impressed by the machinery. Emerson, on his second trip to England, had been impressed by what the mills could turn out, but fearful for what they were doing to the operatives. At Rogers's mills in Sheffield, Emerson was told that "there is no luck in making good steel; that they make no mistakes, every blade in the hundred and in the thousand is good." But he also thought that the machines

> prove too much for their tenders. Mines, forges, mills, breweries, railroads, steam-pump, steam-plough, drill of regiment, drill of police, rule of court, and shop-rule, have operated to give a mechanical regularity to all the habit and action of men. A terrible machine has possessed itself of the ground, the air, the men and women, and hardly even thought is free.[6]

Philip Slater has argued that one of America's most unfortunate heritages is the combination of technological radicalism and social conservatism. Thoreau, on balance, must be considered to represent

almost the exact opposite, combining as he does social liberalism, especially about slavery, and a lasting distrust of the effects of technological change on everyday life. He did not lack detailed appreciation of the new machines, and his understanding of things mechanical makes his eventual rejection of too much mechanization an earned opinion. And though he saw the shortcomings of the mills, he could also learn from them. "The arts," he noted a few days after his visit to Clinton, "teach us a thousand lessons. Not a yard of cloth can be woven without the most thorough fidelity in the weaver."
It was as true for writing as for weaving.[7]

62. Myth and Wildness

The "Walking" essay has three main subjects, all of which were substantially in place by February of 1851. They are walking, the wild, and myth. The walker is the person who is best suited to experience the wild. Myth is the most satisfactory expression of such experience. Thoreau's wildness is not synonymous with savagery or ferocity; it is distinguished from raw destructive violence in two ways. First, it can be sought more successfully by a walker or a poet than by a warrior, and second, it can be better expressed in myth than in battle. For this reason Thoreau notes that, in the nineteenth century, "the chivalric and heroic spirit, which once belonged to the chevalier or rider only, now seems to reside in the walker." And he makes clear in "Walking" that the wildness, for which the walker quests, finds its best outlet not in the siege of Jerusalem, but in the literary expression we call myth. This last, crucial insight shows up in Thoreau's journal by mid-January 1851 and it represents his mature view of the function and nature of myth in literature.[1]

In A Week, from the first draft to the final version, Thoreau's understanding of myth is that it is the form, evolved over time, of early history or early theology. In the "Sunday" chapter of A Week, he observes, "to some extent, mythology is only the most ancient history and biography," and, a few pages on, he adds, "One memorable addition to the old mythology is due to this era—the Christian fable."

As a literary form myth is also something a modern poet can reasonably aspire to create. "The poet is he who can write some pure mythology."[2]

By 1848 and the rewriting of "Ktaadn," Thoreau's view of myth had changed somewhat. In "Ktaadn," myth expresses not history or biography but nature itself. Gazing at the lovely colors of the just-caught trout, Thoreau marveled at how, while still alive, "they glistened like the fairest flowers," though they had swum unseen in the dark forest rivers for so long where their colors could not be seen. He added, cryptically, "I could understand better, for this, the truth of mythology, the fables of Proteus." The myths about the ability of Proteus to take different shapes is a way to express in story form such phenomena as the subtle change of colors from living fish to dead. Myth gives a verbal story-shape to phenomena in nature. Also noticeable in "Ktaadn" are references to the titan Prometheus and a general likening of Thoreau's experience on Katahdin to Prometheus on the Caucasus. The analogy is only very lightly urged, yet it already embodies the perception that becomes so clear and explicit in "Walking," that myth is the literary form, not just of nature, but of that special aspect of nature Thoreau calls the wild.[3]

As even this quick glance backward shows, Thoreau had from the start understood myth as an essentially literary form; what changed was his sense of what exactly it was that could be expressed in that form. In the winter of 1851, working on his ideas about walking and wildness, he began to reflect on where one might seek the expression of the wildness he was now so interested in, and thus he backed into the subject of myth once more. "English literature from the days of the minstrels to the Lake Poets, Chaucer and Spenser and Shakespeare and Milton included, breathes no quite fresh and, in this sense, wild strain," he noted. English literature as a whole was, he thought, essentially tame and civilized, informing us "when her wild animals, but not when the wild man in her, became extinct." He goes further, saying that he could not "think of any poetry which adequately expresses this yearning for the Wild, the *wilde*." Most interestingly, at this point, Thoreau's mind jumped in two directions at once. He looked ahead and said "There was need of America" to reintroduce the wild and the wild in us, and he looked back before poetry to myth.

Reading Ovid again, he was moved to jot down a number of lines, concluding "How much more fertile a nature has Grecian mythology its root in than English literature." In the next sentence he is back to America. "The nature which inspired mythology still flourishes. Mythology is the crop which the Old World bore before its soil was exhausted. The West [a specific American version of that old category the wild] is preparing to add its fables to those of the East."[4]

If the best expression of wildness is to be found in ancient mythology, then the challenge, for the modern writer who wants to give literary expression to that saving sense of wildness, is to find the modern literary equivalent of ancient myth. Thoreau's interest in myth was thus focused down onto this specific problem, and it is the root of his interest in the fictional element in literature. His notes on his readings in Greek myth and in Hindu myth now began to concentrate on myth as story-telling technique. He translates the long story about the transmigrations of the seven brahmins in order to study how one gives concrete and narrative shape to the abstract concept of transmigration. (Of course translation itself is a mode of literary metamorphosis or transmigration.) Now, as often before, Thoreau studies the concise, swiftly moving, audaciously detailed metamorphoses of Ovid. Phaeton's sister Lampetie is suddenly held where she is by roots, "subita radice retenta est" as she and her "sisters were changed to trees while they were in vain beseeching their mother not to break their branches." Now that he knew more surely that the best subjects of myth were aspects of that saving wildness he thought would ultimately preserve the world, he could concentrate on myth as a problem in modern literary form.[5]

More and more, in essays and in his journals, he now tries out fables or mythic parables of his own, trying to find ways to cast modern experience into modern mythic forms. So, in trying to imagine "a people who would begin by burning the fences and let the forest stand," he tries out a metamorphosis or transmigration of his own.

I saw the fences half consumed, their ends lost in the middle of the prairie, and some worldly miser with a surveyor looking after his bounds, while heaven had taken place around him, and he did not see the angels around, but was looking for an old post-hole in the midst of Paradise. I looked again and saw him standing in the middle of a boggy Stygian fen, surrounded by devils, and he had found his bounds without a doubt, three little stones where a stake had been driven, and, looking nearer, I saw that the Prince of Darkness was his surveyor.[6]

This is more like Bunyan or Hawthorne than Ovid or the *Harivansa*, but one can see what Thoreau intends. He is trying to give a narrative—indeed a fictional—form to his perception of the many changes wrought by the fundamental wildness in us. And he makes myths out of our losses as well as our gains.

VII. 1851-1852

New Books, New Worlds

ONE OF THE THINGS THAT had dismayed Adam Smith about life without a proper division of labor was that when one man did several jobs, that man, Smith observed, "commonly saunters a little in turning his hand from one sort of employment to another," eventually acquiring not strict business habits, but the "habit of sauntering and of indolent, careless application." In mocking this attitude Thoreau transforms sauntering into the highest, noblest, form of human endeavor. He even sharked up a false or "folk" etymology in which *saunter* is made to derive from *sainte terre*, making the saunterer a crusader. Thoreau's "Walking" has its serious, its wild side, but it also has its funny side and its very simple and mundane meaning as well, grounded as it is in country life, in Thoreau's countless walks in and around Concord.[1]

He had lectured on "Cape Cod" and on "Life in the woods at Walden" back in January, on "Walking" and "The Wild" in April and May. He was also working on the *Walden* manuscript this spring. Early in May, he had all his teeth extracted and a false set made. Typically, he said—or at least recorded—almost nothing about it except to describe the effects of the still-novel anaesthetic ether (first used for tooth extraction in September of 1846 by Dr. W. T. G. Morton of Boston). He felt, he said, a sense of expansion into "a greater space than you ever travelled," but on second thought concluded that no one needed to take ether who was capable of being transported by a thought.[2]

Or by a walk, he might have added, for he was, during May especially, taking a series of walks, some by day, some by night and moonlight, which his careful attention to seasonal change and his new interest in trees made memorable. On May 10, he saw the year's first snipe, on the twelfth the first golden robin and the first bobolink. As he grew older, his eager anticipation of the seasons—particularly spring and summer—leaped ever further ahead, while his increasingly acute powers of observation provided the hoped-for evidence of the seasons' arrival. The signal for each new season reached him early. The first warm day in December would seem to him to herald the spring. In the middle of spring he would suddenly detect the coming of summer. On May 18 this year, it seemed to Thoreau that the landscape had, all of a sudden, "a new life and light infused into it," and that it had taken "but one summer day to fetch the summer in."[3]

He was reading up on trees in May, in Michaux's *North American Sylvae*, a beautiful book filled with striking color plates, and G. B. Emerson's *Report on the trees and shrubs . . . of Massachusetts*, which has been called "one of the neglected delights of nineteenth century American natural history." He took pains to identify all the trees on his walks and he took pleasure in learning the fitness of different woods for different purposes. Locust was best for trunnels, also called tree-nails, which are the pins which held wooden beams together. Black ash was best for oars, white cedar for shingles, black spruce for rafters, white ash for rake heads, mockernut hickory for rake teeth. Arborvitae fence rails would last sixty years. He felt anew the possibility of man living in harmony with nature, and he could say, this spring, in a wonderful outburst that sounds a little like the young Whitman, "I think that the existence of man in nature is the divinest and most startling of all facts."[4]

Nothing in Thoreau's walks gave him more of this sort of pleasure than the wild apples of New England. All through the late fall and winter he had been picking the "wild fruit native to this quarter of the earth, fruit of old trees that have been dying ever since I was a boy and are not dead." Wild apples, both in Europe and America, had, through grafting, been made to produce innumerable varieties of cultivated fruit, much of which went to the making of cider. In those days before refrigeration, cider, like wine and beer, was merely one more means of preserving the nutritional value of grain or fruit for winter consumption in a form that would not spoil. Considered simply as a beverage, cider occupied the place wine does today. There were even more varieties of apple then than there are of grapes now, and Thoreau's audience would have known many of them by their colorful names, all but a handful of which are now gone.[5]

In Thoreau's day there were "summer apples" such as Pearman, Red Astrachan, Benoni, Bevan's Favorite, Bohanan, Caroline Red June, Early Harvest, Early Strawberry, Early Joe, Garretson's Early, Golden Sweet, Keswick Codlin, Lyman's Pumpkin Sweet, Manomet, Oslin, Summer Belle-fleur, Sweet Paradise, Summer Rose, Summer Queen, and Sops of Wine. There were "fall apples" such as Emperor Alexander, Autumn Swaar, Beauty of Kent, Bailey Spice, Clyde Beauty, Duchess of Oldenburg, Cloth of Gold, Fall Pippin, Fleiner, Garden Royal, Sassafras Sweet Cole, Jewett's Fine Red, Queen Anne, Maiden's Blush, Lyman's Pound Sweet, Porter, Pomme Royal, and President. The third category was that of the "winter apples." They are the ones that lasted the longest into the winter, and some of the names of this group are still familiar, though the rest have disappeared as completely as the farm houses that once stood over the cellar holes all through the woods of New England. The winter apples included Siberian Crab, Flowering Chinese, Bourrassa, Bell-Flower, Belle et Bonne, Carthouse, Dominie, Fameuse, Fallawater, Fort Miami, King, Jonathan, Limber Twig, Mother, Pomme d'Api, Minister, Ortley, Peck's Pleasant, Pickman, Pryor's Red, Rawle's Jannet, Russet Golden, Seek No Further, Winter Blush, Winesap, and Wine Apple.[6]

There were at least a thousand different varieties of apple in the United States in the 1850s. By 1870, moreover, it has been estimated that there were four times that many strains under cultivation. Thoreau in 1851 was worried that the temperance movement and the practice of grafting for table apples spelled the end of the wild, spicy New England apples which had mainly gone into cider. The cultivated or table apples had their stately, opulent, gaudy names, but the wild apples had never had their Adam. In a burst of Joycean wordplay, Thoreau made up names this May for his wild, uncivilized apples. He gave them Latin names for Linnaean sobriety and dignity, and good Yankee names for plain village apple eating. The names signified no essence, he knew. Names by themselves were, he admitted, quite accidental, "as meaningless as Bose or Tray." But the very fact that they were arbitrary removed all restraints from the naming. Sweeter natured than Linnaeus, who gave to ugly and poisonous plants the names of his enemies, Thoreau threw off names for his apples with the high spirits of one who could be intoxicated on words as much as transported by thought.[7]

He thought we might call one Blue Jay Apple or *malus corvi cristati*, another Wood-Dell Apple or *malus silvestri-vallis*. Others he named Truant's Apple (*malus cessatoris*), Wayside Apple (*malus trivialis*), Beauty of the Air (*decus aeris*), Wine of New England (*malus vinosa*), Concord Apple (*malus Concordiensis*), Saunterer's Apple (*malus erronis vel vagabundi*), the Assabet Apple, the Railroad Apple, the Apple that grows in an old Cellar-Hole, to say nothing of those hardest to find apples, "the apples whose fruit we tasted in our youth which grows *passim et nusquam*," and finally, "our own Particular Apple" like a cat's own personal name, "not to be found in any catalogue."[8]

64. June 1851:
The Four Worlds of Henry Thoreau

Of the many paradoxes in Thoreau's life, perhaps the most revealing is that this best known of American stay-at-homes, this keeper of "the sitfast acres" of Concord thought of himself as a traveler. In important ways, he was right. Traveling, like paradox, was a vital necessity of his inner as well as his outer life, and it was the informing and the formal principle of most of his published writings, those excursions which, like spokes, go out from and return to the twin hubs of Walden Pond and Concord village. Indeed, Thoreau traveled in not one but four different worlds, each centered on Concord, and like concentric circles, each was larger than the one before, and each had its own particular kind of travel or guide books.[1]

The first of these was the world of Concord itself. With his "long ungainly Indian-like stride," and wearing stout shoes and strong grey trousers, he took long walks in all directions from Concord, carrying, as Emerson noted, "an old music book to press plants; in his pocket, his diary and pencil, a spy glass for birds, microscope, jack-knife and twine." For local walks his guidebooks were many and varied. This summer they included Bigelow's *Medical Botany* and Michaux's *North American Sylvae*. Concord and its surroundings constituted a world

Thoreau felt he would never know completely. In "Walking" he observed that "there is in fact a sort of harmony discoverable between the capabilities of the landscape within a circle of ten miles' radius, or the limits of an afternoon walk, and the threescore years and ten of human life. It will never become quite familiar to you."[2]

Beyond the magic circle of Concord was a second, larger world, that of North America. Going by train or boat or on foot, he traveled, with an umbrella under his arm and his spare clothes in a plain brown parcel tied with twine, to Maine, Canada, Cape Cod, New York, Long Island, the Hudson River Valley and, shortly before his death, Minnesota. For these trips, he read, before and after, guide books, histories, memoirs, and above all the accounts written by explorers, travelers, and naturalists. He read and studied dozens of books on Canada, dozens more on Cape Cod. He also read travel books about those parts of North America to which he himself never traveled. During June of 1851, he was, for example, reading F. A. Michaux's *Voyage à l'ouest des Monts Alleghanys*. Perhaps he was unaware there was a good English translation, but the evidence suggests that his French was so good that translations were not a factor in his choice of reading. At any rate, Michaux had headed west from Philadelphia, had gone on parts of the Susquehanna and the Ohio River, had traveled through Kentucky and Tennessee, then back over the Blue Ridge to end up in Charleston, South Carolina. In a way, the reading in Michaux and other travelers in America (such as Kalm, Lyell, Hall, Lewis and Clark) represents a literary extension of Thoreau's own travels in North America. These books also form a bridge to the next world, to Thoreau as a world traveler.

His North American travels were partly through books; his world travels were all done entirely through books. And while Thoreau traveled in imagination, he never indulged in imaginary travels. As John Christie has shown best, it was in his reading that he covered the world. Over the years he devoured travel books on North and South America, on Africa and Asia, on the Arctic and the Pacific. Just recently he had been reading Layard's account of the discovery of Nineveh. Bits from Layard's account of the "devil" worshiping Yezidis of the Middle East found their way into *Cape Cod*. In June 1851, he read with great care a travel book that was to have a much greater impact than most on him, Charles Darwin's *Voyage of a Naturalist Round the World*.

The fourth world of Thoreau's travels is the world of ideas, what Melville in *Mardi* called the world of mind. It was a world mapped by special, grand, epoch-making books, each introducing a whole universe of thought, books such as *The Laws of Menu*, Humboldt's *Kosmos*, Linnaeus's *Philosophia Botanica*. The world of ideas was, for Thoreau, simultaneously an objective extension and a subjective analogue to the other three worlds, extending his reach, closing the circle, and giving him a major metaphor and structural principle, the adventure in ideas, the voyage of inner discovery, the self as the subjective version of the shores of America. "A traveller! I love his title," he wrote in his journal in early July. "A traveller is to be reverenced as such. His profession is the best symbol of our life. Going from ———to ———; it is the history of every one of us."[3]

So Thoreau traveled in and near Concord itself, around parts of North America, through the world of nature and the world of ideas; all of it from Concord, most of it in Concord. When he said "I have travelled a good deal in Concord," the qualification wasn't, in the last analysis, for irony, it was simple spartan brevity.[4]

65. Thoreau, Darwin, and The Voyage of the Beagle

One of the most dramatic examples of how his travel reading and his intellectual adventures went hand in hand is his absorbed reading, in June 1851, of the narrative now known as Darwin's *Voyage of the Beagle*. Darwin had set out from England on his five-year-long voyage on December 27, 1831, had stopped first at the Cape Verde Islands, gone on to survey the coasts of South America, including offshore island groups such as the Galápagos, eventually going across the Pacific to Australia before returning home. The trip was the foundation for Darwin's life work. In 1837, the year after Darwin got back home and the year Thoreau graduated from college, Darwin began, in July, his "first note-book on transmutation of Species." He noted how he "had been greatly struck from about month of previous March on character of S. American fossils and species on Galapagos Archipelago. These facts origin (especially latter) of all my views." In 1838, Darwin was reading Malthus on population, and the principle of natural selection (that favorable variations in species would tend to be preserved and unfavorable ones perish in the struggle for existence) occurred to him. In 1839, when he was thirty years old, Darwin brought out his *Journal of the Voyage of the Beagle* as the third of the three-volume narrative of the surveying voyages of HMS *Adventure* and HMS *Beagle*. Thoreau read the edition which appeared in New York in 1846 and his copious notes attest to his extraordinary prescient sympathy with many of Darwin's interests, including his minutely detailed observational techniques, his fascination with *change* in nature, even his writing style and the formal construction of the book, which was half travelogue and half naturalist's journal.[1]

He was struck by Darwin's account of fine dust settling on ships hundreds of miles from land, dusts containing many species of exclusively freshwater protozoa. Thoreau's own interest in the dispersal of seeds, if it did not begin with his reading of Darwin, was reinvigorated and redirected by it. As he had moved from island to island, Darwin was most attentive to this problem of the distribution of species, of exactly what grew where. Thoreau was especially attentive, as his notes and extracts from Darwin attest, when he saw Darwin cutting through romantic preconceptions. Thoreau copied the account of how, at St. Paul's rocks, Darwin found "not a single plant, not even a lichen." Instead of the "oft repeated description" of the successive stages of life as starting with "the stately palm and other noble tropical plants, then birds, and lastly man," Darwin found that "feather and dirt-feeding and parasitic insects and spiders" were, in fact, the first inhabitants. Thoreau also followed Darwin's noting that "seminal propagation produces a more original individual than that by buds, layers, and grafts," and he recorded Darwin's interest, when studying the Galápagos Islands, in being "surrounded by new birds, new reptiles, new shells, new insects, new plants, and yet, by innumerable trifling details of structure . . . to have the temperate plains of Patagonia, or the hot, dry deserts of Northern Chile vividly brought before my eyes." Thoreau was struck by Darwin's observation that these islands had not only flora and fauna peculiar to themselves as a group, but also species peculiar to each individual island, even to islands within sight of one another. Thoreau read Darwin's account of his early voyage closely enough so that when the *Origin of Species* appeared in 1859, he was ready for it.[2]

It was not just ideas that made Darwin attractive. He wrote well and unassumingly, describing himself not as a "scientist," like the self-important Agassiz who was producing such a stir in Cambridge, but as "a person fond of natural history." *The Voyage of the Beagle* began by recording the joy and delight Darwin took in his work and his travels. Darwin had an ear like Thoreau's for strange and wonderful sounds, and his writing is often very close to that found in Thoreau's journal, going back and forth from general travel accounts to very minutely detailed descriptions. The mature Thoreau's sense of what exactly constituted the level of significant detail owes something to the Darwin who described, for example, an ant march in a way that combines the most practical and acute observation with a sure instinct for vivid storytelling:

> One day, at Bahia, my attention was drawn by observing many spiders, cockroaches, and other insects, and some lizards, rushing in the greatest agitation across a bare piece of ground. A little way behind, every stalk and leaf was blackened by a small ant. The swarm having crossed the bare space, divided itself, and descended an old wall. By this means, many insects were fairly enclosed; and the efforts which the poor little creatures made to extricate themselves from such a death were wonderful.

Darwin put a stone in the path of a column of ants and watched them attack rather than go around. "Having been attacked, the lion-hearted little warriors scorned the idea of yielding."[3]

This account and another describing a battle between a wasp and a spider are too similar to Thoreau's description of the battle of the ants (which he added to his *Walden* manuscript when he went back to it in January of 1852) to be accidental. Darwin's meticulous observation and his disciplined and vivid descriptive technique did not so much show Thoreau something new as confirm and reinforce his own practice. But there is no doubt that he found Darwin's mind and writing congenial and suggestive. He may even have noted how Darwin reduced a voyage that crossed and recrossed its own track many times in the course of a five-year span, visiting the same places over and over, into a satisfying and unconfusing narrative whole. "To prevent useless repetitions," Darwin wrote, "I will extract those parts of my journal which refer to the same districts, without always attending to the order in which we visited them." Thoreau's eventual shaping his two years and two months at Walden plus the fruits of many subsequent years of going back and forth over the same ground into a single cycle of seasons would involve a similar process of narrative ordering.

Darwin had much for Thoreau. The English naturalist described brilliantly colored landscapes in which "every form, every shade so completely surpasses in magnificence all that the European has ever beheld in his own country"; he carefully describes the strange glass "tubes" created by lightning striking in quartz sand, a geological phenomenon as strange and wonderful—and natural—as Thoreau's thawing clay bank. Above all Darwin was impressed by the change-ableness of everything. Thoreau copied out Darwin's comment, "Daily it is forced home on the mind of the geologist, that nothing, not even the wind that blows, is so unstable as the level of the crust of this earth." Years earlier, coming out of college, Thoreau had served a naturalist's apprenticeship, learning to see with eyes made sharp by Goethe. Now the power and concentration of his observation were confirmed and encouraged by Darwin. Change, individuation, meta-morphosis, transmigration of form—all these pointed toward growth itself, not the grown thing, as the great underlying reality in nature.[4]

66. Summer 1851:
Practical Transcendentalism

Thoreau, like Coleridge, was a chain reader. One book led to others, each of which led on to still others. He had access now to the library of the Boston Society of Natural History, as well as the Harvard College library and Emerson's library. He took copious notes in a variety of extract books, following simultaneously a variety of subjects all going in different directions. His reading of Darwin is a good example of the process. As he read The Voyage of the Beagle, he was reminded of

Kotzebue's and Cook's voyages, and noted that he would like to read those of Azara, Head, and Hearne. As John Christie has shown, of the nineteen travel works referred to by Darwin in the *Voyage*, Thoreau read nine, and all but one after reading Darwin. These included books by Hearne, Head, Back, Park, Lewis and Clark, Buffon, Humboldt, and Tschudi. Every time he came upon a book that stirred him, this process was repeated.[1]

Besides swimming through libraries of travel and natural history this summer, he did a little modest traveling of his own. In late July he went by train to Boston, then by boat to Hull, then on foot to Plymouth via Nantasket, Cohasset (site of the wreck of the *St. John* nearly two years earlier), Duxbury, Scituate and Marshfield. At Duxbury, he caught a ride out to Clarke's Island, three miles away, on a forty-seven-ton mackerel schooner, and though he described their fishing process clearly (they began fishing even as they were leaving harbor), he was fundamentally out of sympathy with a life that often had to simply sit and wait for a tide. Thoreau liked to go when he was ready to go. He was by now habitually attuned to inland life; the rhythms of the sea would always escape him. About all he could say on this occasion was "I had the experience of going on a mackerel cruise," but he made little more of it than he had of Lake Champlain.[2]

Mackerel fishing didn't enter into his writing plans, nor was he moved to read up on it, though in other respects his reading and his walking were going together well this summer. After Darwin in June, he turned to naturalists and to travelers who were primarily naturalists. In August he read Bartram's *Travels through North and South Carolina*, Agassiz and Gould's *Principles of Zoology*, Cuvier's *The Animal Kingdom*, and Peter Kalm's three-volume *Travels into North America; containing its Natural History, and a circumstantial account of its Plantations and Agriculture in general*, an account of a 1748–1751 voyage. In September he read Cato's *De Re Rustica*.

The common denominator of all this reading is not travel so much as natural history. Thoreau, animated in part by his reading in Darwin, loved the detail in these books and filled his extract books with quotations and his journal with similar local detail. "How copious and precise the botanical language to describe the leaves, as well as the other parts of a plant!" he noted. "Botany is worth studying if only for the precision of its terms—to learn the value of words and of system." A three-and-a-half-hour walk produced an account filling nine printed pages. Another particularly rich day yielded thirteen more. Sometimes he almost sank beneath the detail, and he was, this summer, intensely conscious of this as a problem. During one of his periodic moments of gloomy self-examination in mid-August, he wrote:

> I fear that the character of my knowledge is from year to year becoming more detailed and scientific; that, in exchange for views wide as heaven's cope, I am being narrowed down to the field of the microscope. I see details, not wholes nor the shadow of the whole. I count some parts, and say "I know."[3]

Certainly Thoreau was growing more afraid of subsiding into trivial detail; certainly his interest in close observation was increasing at the moment. But it is equally sure that the sterility he fretted about had not caught up with him yet, and while he was articulating the problem, he was, all during 1851 and for some time to come, able to hold the practical and the ideal aspects of existence in harmonious and productive balance.

Back in May, in the midst of thinking about Hindu scriptures, he had noted that "the ethical philosopher needs the discipline of the natural philosopher. He approaches the study of mankind with great advantages who is accustomed to the study of nature." Early in June, he was tilting the other way.

> My practicalness is not to be trusted to the last. To be sure, I go upon my legs for the most part, but, being hard-pushed and dogged by a superficial common sense which is bound to near objects by beaten paths, I am off the handle, as the phrase is, I begin to be transcendental and show where my heart is.

In July, up to his ears in the classificational data of Agassiz, Gould, and Cuvier, as well as local and current affairs, he fumed over "The habit of attending to trivial things." He noted, with Johnsonian pith, "It is so hard to forget what it is worse than useless to remember." Watching the spot at which Heywoods Brook falls into Fair Haven Pond set him thinking—or *trying* to think—of "the pure waterfalls within me, in the circulation of my blood." Searching for town boundaries and surveying them likewise sent him back, he said, "in search of myself."[4]

His thirty-fourth birthday found him feeling thwarted and "almost wholly unexpanded," with a sense of "such an interval between my

ideal and the actual in many instances that I may say I am unborn."
This was overstating the case. And though he had been seesawing back
and forth all summer, in August he reached a balance, or at least a
hope-awakening awareness of the possibility of balance, and his metaphors were all of fruitfulness and fertility. "The intellect of most men
is barren. They neither fertilize nor are fertilized." In his best sum-
ming-up of the relation between the practical and the ideal this summer, he goes on to say

> it is the marriage of the soul with Nature that makes the intellect fruitful,
> that gives birth to imagination. When we were dead and dry as the high-
> way, some sense which has been healthily fed will put us in relation with
> Nature, in sympathy with her: some grains of fertilizing pollen, floating
> in the sky, fall on us, and suddenly the sky is all one rainbow, is full of
> music and fragrance and flavor.

The mood was prophetic. Thoreau was about to enter another of his
great creative phases, undertaking the total revision and reshaping of
the *Walden* manuscript. All the reading and traveling of the last three
years would go into it, but the catalytic factor, the agent that precip-
itated it out, the fertilizing influence was the creative balance between
fact and idea, detail and ideal.[5]

Thoreau's practical transcendentalism is the characteristic American version of Carlyle's Natural Supernaturalism. In his reading, the
travels and descriptions of Darwin, Kalm, and Bartram are balanced
by the high idealism of Hindu scripture, German idealism, and Milton. Similarly in his daily life, the practical and the ideal could har-
monize, when he stuck to his main road, which he described again at
the end of August. "I omit the unusual—the hurricane and earth-
quakes—and describe the common. This has the greatest charm and
is the true theme of poetry."[6]

67. Fall 1851:
This is my Home, my Native Soil

The fall of 1851 was a time when the various threads, social and personal, physical and intellectual, of Thoreau's life were not unraveling,

but pulling closer together. At the end of September, he helped Henry Williams, a fugitive slave fleeing a master who was also his father, escape to Canada. He was out on the rivers frequently this fall, sometimes walking them lengthwise, wading along parallel to the shore, sometimes rowing, alone or with Channing. He clucked disapprovingly over Channing's "sublimo-slipshod" poetry and thought Channing should write in Latin so as to be forced to mend his grammar. He saw Emerson often this fall; there was admiration and affection between them, but there was also, in Thoreau's perception, a great deal of pride on both sides which troubled the friendship. He also spent time with Emerson's Aunt Mary Moody Emerson, "the wittiest and most vivacious woman I know" whose conversation, especially on philosophy and poetry, he found singularly profitable. It was in some respects rather a social fall for Thoreau, while it was also full in other ways. By December 12, he had spent, he said, between twenty and thirty days of the fall surveying.[1]

His increased busyness meant shorter journals for October and November, but even so, they are very full and they show Thoreau in a calm and thoughtful mood, taking stock of himself and his work. One feels, in his writing this fall, a gathering of inner forces and resources, a rising water table of readiness. "I feel myself uncommonly prepared for *some* literary work," he wrote in early September, "but I can select no work. I am prepared not so much for contemplation, as for forceful expression. I am braced, both physically and intellectually. It is not so much the music as the marching to the music that I feel." Everything this fall seemed to reconfirm to him his sense of himself, his identity. His best and most characteristic themes surfaced again, revived and brightened by new experience and new reading.[2]

He came upon Cato the Censor's *De Agri Cultura*, also called *De Re Rustica*, this fall in a volume of *Rei Rusticae*, which contained also Varro, Columella, and Palladius, and which he borrowed from Alcott on August 11 and was reading by September 2. *De Agri Cultura* is the oldest surviving prose work in Latin, a practical manual of farming crammed with technical details and information. ("If you wish to build a pressing room with four vats facing each other, lay off the vats as follows: anchor posts two feet thick, nine feet high, including tenons.") Thoreau was immediately taken with this reformer who wished to recall the Romans to the primitive simplicity of an agricultural state, this champion of the common people who opposed the introduction of Greek culture into Rome, who left out of his now-lost account of the Second Punic War the names of all the nobles, on both sides, "preferring rather to sing the praises of a certain Surus, bravest elephant of the Carthaginian army," and who began his book on farming by pointing out that Roman law preferred even thieves to bankers since the law only required the thief to repay his victim double, while it required a banker who lent money at interest to repay his victim fourfold. *De Agri Cultura* begins with a long section on farm economy, followed by a seasonally ordered calendar of work to be done. In a rough way, *Walden* follows this pattern. Thoreau felt that Cato, like Virgil later in the *Georgics*, brought Roman farming to vivid life, showing country life to be essentially the same in all times and places. He also admired Cato's tough, straightforward, matter-of-fact approach to his subject and the packed, severe style. Cato's *rem tene, verba sequentur* could serve as Thoreau's motto. Grasp the thing, words will follow. He admired, extravagantly, Cato's *patrem familias vendacem, non emacem esse oportet* (the head of a household should have the selling, not the buying habit). "These Latin terminations express better than any English that I know the greediness, as it were, and tenacity of purpose with which the husbandman and householder is required to be a seller and not a buyer." Some of Thoreau's most thoughtful, most detailed reflections on how words work arise from his Latin reading. Translating Cato, he observes "this termination *cious* adds force to a word, like the lips of browsing creatures, which greedily collect what the jaw holds, as in the word 'tenacious' the first half represents the kind of jaw which holds, the last the lips which collect." Thoreau aspired to write the English equal of Cato's Latin style, tough, nutty, condensed, with nothing wasted. Thoreau discovered again in Cato what he had known since his early reading of Virgil. The elements of a good style do not change with the times, any more than the fundamentals of country life change. Cato's prose could be emulated today, as his advice could have come from the most recent farmer's almanac. "*Sterquilinium magnum stude ut habeas*"; "Study to have a great dungheap," Thoreau translates. "Carefully preserve your dung, when you carry it out, make clean work of it and break it up fine. Carry it out during the autumn. . . . It reminds me," Thoreau added, "of what I see going on in our fields every autumn."[3]

For Thoreau, every bit of knowledge and every perception of identity shared across the ages served to strengthen his own identity. His reading of Cato came early in September. For the rest of the fall his feeling of well-being, gladness, and determination rose steadily, as did a renewed sense of literary vocation, and his growing heap of literary capital. He reworked his view of wildness as a trait of original and independent men and the salt of civilized life, emphasizing now "a certain refinement and civilization in nature which increases with the wildness." Yet he acknowledged bluntly that "disease is not the accident of the individual, nor even of the generation, but of life itself. In some form, and to some degree or other, it is one of the permanent conditions of life." Saying this only increased his determination to resist. "Life is a warfare, a struggle," he said again this fall, and he was ready again to fight. The first tentative glimmer of a project that would dominate his life after *Walden* occurs this fall. "Perhaps a history of the year would be the history of the grass, or of a leaf." The wind vibrating the telegraph wire moved him with its strange music, stirring in him the moth's desire for the star. "Know that the goal is distant, and is upward, and is worthy all your life's efforts to attain to," was what he heard in the wind's music.[4]

Work now was all in all to him, raising him "above the dread of criticism and the appetite of praise." He strove for a way to express facts "simply and adequately." Noting that most statements are merely relative, are "said with reference to certain conventions or existing institutions," he still hoped to do better. "A fact truly and absolutely stated is taken out of the region of common sense and acquires a mythologic or universal significance. . . . Express it without expressing yourself." On a walk in early October, he found an Indian gouge on Dennis's Hill, he picked up and tried to eat some white acorns, and through these trifling talismans he felt "related again to the first men." Winter closed down early on Concord this year in late October, but let up briefly in early November. "I feel blessed. I love my life. I warm toward all nature," Thoreau wrote in his journal. And a few days later, he declared his citizenship again. Walking with Channing to Long Pond in Wayland, he sat on the shore to eat lunch. "Dear to me to lie in, this sand," he wrote, "fit to preserve the bones of a race for thousands of years to come. And this is my home, my native soil; and I am a New Englander."[5]

68. December 1851 to February 1852: The Short Days of Winter

Thoreau was by now very much fixed in his ways. He read and wrote every morning in his room, walked every afternoon. Variations in the schedule called attention to themselves. His work, to which he dedicated his heroic morning hours, had become all-consuming. Winter, with its inwardness, further heightened the impulse toward indoor and intellectual pursuits. During the winter of 1851–52, he heard Elizabeth Oakes Smith lecture on Womanhood, T. W. Higginson on Mohammed, one Professor Blasius on tornadoes, and his friend Channing on society. He did some lectures himself on Canada in early January in Lincoln and Concord. He took Greeley's *Weekly Tribune* and though he groaned about newspapers he read it most of the time. He was also reading Samuel Laing's *Chronicle of the Kings of Norway* this winter, taking great delight in finding such names as Thorer Sel, Thorer Hund, and Thorer the Low. He was still reading for Canadian background in Lahontan's *Voyages*, but the great bulk of his winter reading this year was in botany. He was reading from his manuscripts to Mary Moody Emerson, while he maintained the odd, unhappy, fretful, running quarrel with Emerson, mostly in the form of petulant journal complaints that the relationship was not the ideal one he wished it to be. He was capable of saying, with blithe and utter injustice, that he had "yet to hear the first syllable of valuable or even earnest advice" from his seniors, yet he could turn around and use Emerson as an oracle, opening his printed works at random and reading the first sentence his eye lit upon, a *sortes Emersonianae*.

In his walks, he paid special attention to sunsets, trying to catch in words the changing colors and shapes, the luminous glories of the evening skies. On December 20 he climbed Fair Haven Hill. Looking down he "saw a large hawk circling over a pine wood below" him. He compared it to the new schooner yacht *America*, about which everyone was then reading. It had just sailed to England, then beaten all comers in a fifty-three-mile race around the Isle of Wight. The *America* was a new design; its sleek lines and cloud of canvas—it was twice as long and carried three times as much sail as a modern America's cup racer—made it a thing of heart-stirring beauty and grace, one of the few works of modern man fit to sail with the hawks. The hawk was also, to Thoreau, "a symbol of the thoughts, now soaring, now descending, taking larger and larger circles, or smaller and smaller." As his friendships with men and women gave him "difficulties" and made him feel cold ("I am of the nature of stone"), he turned this winter to consider how he stood in relation to the hawks and the white pine. "We are related," he insisted, "to *all* nature, animate and inanimate." He declared that "a pine wood is as substantial and as memorable a fact as a friend." On December 30 he watched two men cutting down one of the tall pines in the township, 4 feet in diameter, ninety years old and 105 feet tall. He described the felling in great detail. But the scene seemed to him symbolic, not of his own fall, but of his remaining when others had fallen around him. As the pine, "so stands a man. It is clearing around him. He has no companions on the hills. The lonely traveller, looking up, wonders why he was left when his companions were taken."[1]

The coming of winter always increased the woodcutting in the woods around Concord. During the winter of 1851–52, they were logging again out at Walden Pond, and as Thoreau reflected on the changing landscape, he returned actively to his Walden manuscript. He had not worked on it in any concerted way since 1849. He had done a little from time to time; in 1851 he seems to have put in a number of Hindu references and passages, and there are occasional phrases and incidents that found their way from the journal to the Walden manuscript during the intervening years. But in January of 1852, Thoreau began to work on the fourth draft, and he would work now on successive drafts almost without intermission until publication two-and-a-half years ahead. What seems to have provided the impetus to return, and this time not just revise but reshape the account of his life at Walden, was his experience in December 1851, with the thawing clay bank in the railroad deep cut near the pond.[2]

He had for years been fascinated with how the heat of the sun, even
in midwinter, could thaw the bank and send streams of sand and clay
bursting forth to pour down the bank in pulpy sprays that looked like
coral or intestines. This December the familiar sight appeared in an
entirely new light to Thoreau, thanks to his current
absorption in botanical books.

69. Lapidae Crescunt

He had read Darwin's book in June 1851. By August he was reading
as many naturalists as he could. He read Kalm and Cuvier, Agassiz
and Gould. By November he was working backward, trying in his
now-habitual way to get a systematic grasp of the field of natural history. At the moment he was more interested in botany than zoology
or geology, but he never lost sight completely of any of the three. He
read Loudon's *Encyclopaedia of Plants*. He had started with modern
botany since Linnaeus. Now he read Stoever's *Life of Linnaeus*, which
gave him a general idea of the history of botany before Linnaeus.
Stoever and Pultenay's *General View of the Writings of Linnaeus*, which
he now also read, pointed clearly to Linnaeus as the central figure in
the whole subject. He was interested in Linnaeus as a namer of plants,
a modern and scientific Adam, and as one who had increased knowledge by the use of system. He could not decide whether Linnaeus was
imposing a system on nature or deciphering the system in nature.
Linnaeus's work seemed to him a "dictionary" and the competing
"natural" system of John Lindley and others a "grammar" of nature.
Botany, like myth, seemed to him to provide a language for nature.
His journal shows his persistent interest in understanding what he
insisted on calling the "grammar of botany," the "grammar" of ice
cracks. On the last day of December 1851, he went again to see the
sand foliage in the deep cut. The flowing streams of a few days before
had left "perfect leopard paws" in places. "These things suggest that
there is motion in the earth as well as on the surface; it lives and
grows. . . . The earth I tread on is not a dead, inert mass. It is a body,
has a spirit, is organic." It showed, he thought, "the fundamental

fertility near to the principle of growth." It was "the frost . . . coming out in the spring."[1]

Ever since he had read Goethe just after college Thoreau had been interested in how crystallization seemed to mimic foliage. Since the railroad's coming he had watched the flowing sand taking the forms of strange vegetation. This phenomenon of the sand foliage would become, in the final version of *Walden*, Thoreau's major, and highly original, symbol of the true springing forth of the earth that precedes the green and flowery spring. This insight, that "there is nothing inorganic," did not come from Linnaeus, but it received a strong corroboration from him when in February, after reading a good deal about Linnaeus over a period of half a year, Thoreau finally sat down to read Linnaeus's central work, the *Philosophia Botanica* itself. He was surpised and delighted with the book, bemoaned having "lost much time reading the florists." "If you would read books on botany, go to the fathers of the science," he wrote. "Read Linnaeus at once. . . . It is simpler, more easy to understand, and more comprehensive, than any of the hundred manuals to which it has given birth."[2]

On page one, which Thoreau studied and took notes on, Linnaeus begins with first principles. He divides everything on earth into elements and natural things. Leaving elements to physics, he declares that natural science is the study of natural things. All natural things belong to one of the three realms of nature: mineral, vegetable, and animal. Minerals grow (come into existence, spring forth); vegetables grow and live; animals grow, live, and feel or think. Linnaeus's crisp Latin says "*lapidae crescunt, vegetabile crescunt et vivunt, animali crescunt vivunt et sentiunt.*" The word that Thoreau could not have missed is *crescunt*, from *cresco*, to come into existence, spring forth, grow. It is the transitive equivalent of *creo*, to create. It was used, not by Aristotle or the schoolmen, but by Lucretius and Cicero in the same way in which Linnaeus used it, to suggest that the whole earth is alive, not inert. "What makes this sand foliage remarkable," says Thoreau in the great "Spring" chapter of the final version of *Walden*, "is its springing into existence thus suddenly. . . . This is Spring." *Lapidae crescunt.*

> The earth is not a mere fragment of dead history, stratum upon stratum like the leaves of a book, to be studied by geologists and antiquaries chiefly, but living poetry like the leaves of a tree, which precede flowers

and fruit,—not a fossil earth, but a living earth; compared with whose great central life all animal and vegetable life is merely parasitic.[3]

This is a central idea of *Walden*, and the cornerstone of the modern conservation ethic, an insight vital enough to use as the climactic point of the book, compelling enough to have forced, as it seems, a major restructuring of *Walden* in the months after February 1852. No doubt he owed something to Linnaeus, but he was moving now in a direction different from that of Linnaeus. "By the artificial [i.e., Linnaean] system we learn the names of plants, by the natural [system associated with Ray, currently represented for Thoreau by Lindley, and the view that Darwin would eventually endorse in *Origin of Species*] their relations to one another; but still it remains to learn their relation to man. The poet does more for us in this department." Travel was well enough, but it served mainly as a metaphor for inner discovery. Thoreau was sure this winter that his real subject lay close to home, and close to the earth. "I think that the history (or poetry) of one farm from a state of nature to the highest state of cultivation comes nearer to being the true subject of a modern epic than the siege of Jerusalem."[4]

As he worked on *Walden*, other projects danced before him. He was now keeping separate extract books, one for natural history, one for poetry, including Indic, and one for American Indian material, in addition to his regular journal. He was still tinkering with a lecture on the Canadian material and in late January 1852 he first conceived of his journal not as a private record or quarry for other works, but as a work by itself, a publishable chronicle of Concord life.[5]

70. A Sufficient List of Failures

Walden is an affirmation of life—not an easy acquiescence, but the earned affirmation of a man who had to struggle almost constantly against a sense of loss, desolation, and decline that grew on him with age. When he chose to crow, it was not for want of alternative voices:

If there are any who think that I am vainglorious, that I set myself up above others and crow over their low estate, let me tell them that I could tell a pitiful story respecting myself as well as them. . . . I could encourage them with a sufficient list of failures, and could flow as humbly as the very gutters.

The themes of failure and loss were present in *Walden* from the earliest draft, in which the subject had already inspired one of Thoreau's better—and more famous—parables.

I long ago lost a hound—and a turtle dove and a bay horse—and am still on their trail. Many's the traveller I have spoken concerning them—describing their tracks and what calls they answered to. I have met one or two who had heard the hound, and the tramp of the horse, and even seen the dove disappear behind a cloud, and they seemed as anxious to recover them as if they had lost them themselves.

When pressed about the meaning of this by literal-minded readers, Thoreau would reply, for example, "I suppose we all have our losses." He spent much of his life seeking such things, yet he was not always glad of what he found. "What you seek in vain for, half your life, one day you come full upon, all the family at dinner. You seek it like a dream, and as soon as you find it you become its prey." When he wrote to Blake about discovering the material of a million Concords, it was typical of him to add, "indeed, I am lost unless I discover them."[1]

During 1851 and increasingly during the early months of 1852, Thoreau was thinking back on his lost and largely unrecorded youth. The old, unused and overgrown roads of New England, punctuated with the empty cellar holes of long-abandoned farms, evoked in Thoreau a powerful nostalgia not so much for lost America as lost youth. In July 1851 he found himself yearning "for one of those old, meandering, dry, uninhabited roads," because there, he thought, he could walk "and recover the lost child that I am." Though he was not yet thirty-five, he felt himself aging. He found it "ominous" that as he grew older he had more to say about evening, less about morning. Sometimes he seemed to peer ahead almost fearfully. On the last day in March 1852, having failed to get out of bed as early as intended he wrote glumly, "perhaps we grow older and older till we no longer sympathize with the revolution of the seasons, and our winters never break up."[2]

Even if we have to discount this a little as the overscrupulous naggings of a postpuritan conscience, there is much in the journal that cannot be dismissed as lachrymose or self-pitying. As he began the revision and expansion of the fourth version of *Walden*, he was recording his acceptance of some dark, almost Melvillean truths. He found it remarkable and significant that while "no man is quite well or healthy, yet every one believes practically that health is the rule and disease the exception," and he proposed that men acknowledge their common platform, and face the truth, that "disease is, in fact, the *rule* of our terrestrial life." Walking in the wet mizzling weather of fall, observing the death of the leaves and the year, he identified autumn with tragedy. Asking himself why he got pleasure from the "moaning of the storm," he thought it was "because it puts to rout the trivialness of our fair-weather life and gives it at least a tragic interest." (Ellen Sewall had once used the phrase the "moaning of the sea.") Disease and tragedy both had become part of the scheme of things for Thoreau. Since 1846 and the ascent of Katahdin, he had acknowledged that there was an aspect of nature that was not bound to be kind to man. This other, darker side of nature was growing in range and importance for Thoreau. "The constitution of the Indian mind," he wrote in October 1852,

> appears to be the very opposite to that of the white man. He is acquainted with a different side of nature. He measures his life by winters, not summers. His year is not measured by the sun, but consists of a certain number of moons, and his moons are not measured by days, but by nights. He has taken hold of the dark side of nature, the white man, the bright side.

Thoreau is no longer inclined, if he ever was, to take the view that evil is the absence of good, not a positive, but a negative quality. In January of 1853, the local powder mill blew up. Thoreau arrived on the scene within forty minutes. The bodies were still strewn about, "naked and black, some limbs and bowels here and there, and a head at a distance from its trunk. The feet were bare; the hair singed to a crisp." The human wreckage, reminiscent perhaps of that of the wrecks of the *St. John* and the *Elizabeth*, left him thinking that "the lives of men were not innocent," and that there was an avenging power in nature. Yet the west wind blew gently on his cheek and "methinks a roseate sunset is preparing." It was hard to reconcile all this with the idea that there was at bottom one unified and unifying power in nature. "Are there not two powers?" he asked.[3]

But worse even than this loss of innocence in men's lives was Thoreau's own sense that, as time passed, he was becoming a colder and more stony person, and that his poetic springs were freezing up. In February 1852, walking over the "frozen snow crust and over the stiffened rivers and ponds," he felt that he was seeing life "reduced to its lowest terms," and he felt "a similar crust over my heart." What bothered him most about this, one suspects, is in the same journal entry, a few lines before. "The strains of my muse are as rare nowadays, or of late years, as the notes of birds in the winter." A month later, in March, as he walked by Walden Pond, newly lumbered off again, he noted, "The woods I walked in in my youth are cut off. Is it not time that I ceased to sing?"[4]

Beyond mere intellectual concessions to entropy, winter brought him a kind of death each year, an emotionally felt loss of energy and sense of decline. The winter of 1851–52 was worse than most in this respect. Of course March would come, the year would spring forth with the vernal equinox, and Thoreau would again be almost literally reborn with the year. Looking on March 12, 1852, at the flowing sands that so moved him, he was caught by the renovating, subjective logic of the spring. "Nature has not lost her pristine vigor, neither has he who sees this."[5]

Strictly speaking, his poetic spring *had* pretty much dried up, but his prose had grown stronger and tougher with time and discipline. He no longer ignored or made light of losses, disappointments, and regrets but made them into songs—prose songs, indeed, but songs nevertheless. The writer of *Walden* is one of our great poets of loss, along with Longfellow, Frost, and Eliot, but his songs are about sustainable losses, and how not to go down beneath them.

71. April 1852: William Gilpin
and the Articulation of Landscape

A foot of snow fell on April 13, followed by the wettest spring in, some said, sixty-three years. It rained for days on end, there were "scarcely two fair days together" all month. A northeast storm, an umbrella breaker, lasted five days. The rivers in Concord rose so high as to make all the bridges in Concord impassable on foot. Thoreau's health held during April, but by mid-May he would be lamenting that his poor health was getting in the way of his close watch on the progress of the seasons. He was out a lot in April, getting drenched and watching the meadows, which he said reflected "moods of the Concord mind." He spent a good deal of time outdoors with Channing. He was doing some lecturing from the *Walden* material and working on the book, which Alcott now wanted him to call *Sylvania*. April was a rich month, Thoreau's journal alone amounts to 120 printed pages. Just how rich and in what way, he expressed in a journal passage a year later:

> He is the richest who has most use for nature as raw material of tropes and symbols with which to describe his life. If these gates of golden willows affect me, they correspond to the beauty and promise of some experience on which I am entering. If I am overflowing with life, am rich in experience for which I lack expression, then nature will be my language full of poetry.

A creative reader as well as a creative writer, Thoreau's reading this year kept providing him with fresh ways to use nature as language to express what was in him. Linnaeus had shown him how to put names to the smallest botanical detail, how to distinguish the most minute differences. In April, Thoreau made the discovery of the books of William Gilpin, the well-known English travel writer who emphasized the picturesque. Thoreau read and studied everything he could find of Gilpin's; his excitement over Gilpin continued steadily from this April until the publication of *Walden*. Linnaeus gave Thoreau a language for each different part of each leaf, Gilpin showed Thoreau the grand and integrative language of landscape.[1]

The Reverend William Gilpin (1724–1804) was and is most celebrated for his championship of the picturesque as opposed to the beautiful. Whereas beautiful objects please the eye in their natural state, picturesque objects please, said Gilpin, from some quality capable of being illustrated by painting. Gilpin argued that "roughness" or "ruggedness" "forms the most essential point of difference between the *beautiful* and the *picturesque*." The beautiful is smooth, finished and regular, while the picturesque is rough and irregular. "The picturesque eye abhors art, and delights solely in nature. . . . art abounds with regularity, which is only another name for *smoothness*, and the images of nature with *irregularity*, which is only another name for *roughness*."[2]

Gilpin was not only a theorist but was an attentive observer and a good writer. He traveled all over the British Isles describing what he saw in a series of books he illustrated himself. He possessed the ability to describe landscape as vividly as any other English writer of his era, and his own writing helped others to see both nature and representations of nature and to put what they saw into language as well as sketches. Speaking, for example, of Salvator Rosa's habit, copied by so much of nineteenth-century American landscape painting, of putting part of a dead tree in the foreground, Gilpin writes in *Forest Scenery*, the first of his books Thoreau read, "these splendid remnants of decaying grandeur speak to the imagination in a style of eloquence, which the striplings cannot reach: they record the history of some storm, some blast of lightning, or other great event, which transfers its grand ideas to the landscape." Gilpin's own style is always vivid and often powerful. Of the larch he writes, "often it is felled by the Alpine peasant, and thrown athwart some yawning chasm, where it affords a tremendous passage from cliff to cliff, while the cataract, roaring many fathoms below, is seen only in surges of rising vapour."[3]

Gilpin was above all a close observer, and while he is remembered as a painter and as an art theorist, he was also a poet and a writer, concerned with the verbalization of landscape as much or even more than its graphic representation. In his *Three Essays on Picturesque Beauty* (which Thoreau read in November 1853, over a year and a half after his first interest in Gilpin), he says, "Language, like light, is a medium: and the true philosophic style, like light from a north window, exhibits objects clearly, and distinctly, without soliciting attention to itself." Even if we cannot sketch, Gilpin says, "yet still a strong impression of Nature will enable us to judge of the works of art. Nature is the archetype."[4]

Gilpin fills his books with wonderfully detailed descriptions. Goethean, objective, external nature is of the first importance. But he is also aware of how nature can be used as symbol. In the first book of *Forest Scenery*, for example, he writes:

As I sat carelessly at my window, and threw my eyes upon a large acacia, which grew before me, I conceived it might aptly represent a country divided into provinces, towns and families. . . . As I sat looking at it, many of the yellow leaves . . . were continually dropping into the lap of their great mother. Here was an emblem of natural decay, the most obvious appearance of mortality. . . . Among the branches, was one entirely withered; the leaves were shrivelled, yet clinging to it. Here was an emblem of famine. The nutriment of life was stopped. Existence was just supported; but every form was emaciated and shrunk.[5]

Gilpin's ability to articulate or interpret landscape has had a profound but little-studied effect on the American imagination. Gilpin's *Forest Scenery* and Uvedale Price's *On the Picturesque* were the books F. L. Olmsted admired "so much more than any published since, as stimulating the exercise of judgement in matters of my art, that I put them into the hands of my pupils as soon as they come into our office, saying, you are to read these as seriously as as student of law would read Blackstone." Gilpin's vision of landscape was a foundation for Olmsted's, and may therefore still be seen in the parks Olmsted planned all over the United States, from Central Park in New York to Lion's Head Park in Milwaukee, and from which so many modern assumptions about what is pleasing in nature in turn derive. Gilpin was also a major influence on Thomas Cole, founder of the Hudson River school of landscape painting, and on his pupil Frederick Church, the greatest luminist painter, who is, more than anyone else, the Turner of American painting. Gilpin has thus had a major impact on American landscape design through Olmsted, on American landscape painting through Cole and Church, and on American nature writing through Thoreau.[6]

72. The Articulation of Landscape

Thoreau's interest in the literary representation of landscape did not, of course, begin with his reading of Gilpin. He had been actively working on it since at least his graduation from college and his earliest notes on Goethe's landscapes. His writings, from "A Winter Walk" on, had come to rely more and more on landscape. It was a long-standing major preoccupation, and that is precisely why Gilpin's work had the impact on him it did in 1852. Gilpin had gone a bit further down the road Thoreau was already on, and his example could therefore extend Thoreau's range, enlarge his palette, sharpen his vision. Thoreau later came to feel that Gilpin was too little the moralist and had too exclusively the eye of the artist, but this late and mild reservation should not be allowed to obscure the great and liberating effect of Gilpin's descriptive genius on Thoreau just as he was beginning the major revision of *Walden*.

Although Thoreau never went for long without describing landscapes, he was not always successful. On September 24, 1851, for example, he recorded the following, surely a failed landscape by most definitions, but the kind of landscape Gilpin would give him language for: "Such near hills as Nobscot and Nashoba have lost all their azure in this clear air and plainly belong to earth. Give me clearness nevertheless, though my heavens be moved further off to pay for it." On March 4, 1852, he was talking about how to "paint the short days of winter," and next day he tried a wet one. "A misty afternoon, but warm, threatening rain. Standing at Walden, whose eastern shore is laid waste, men walking on the hillside a quarter of a mile off are singularly interesting objects, seen through this mist, which has the effect of a mirage." Two weeks after this he got Gilpin's *Foresst Scenery* out of the Harvard College library and his delighted comments reflect his immediate enthusiasm for the book. "What Gilpin says about copses, glens, etc suggests that the different places to which the walker resorts may be profitably classified and suggest many things to be said." Gilpin, like Linnaeus, gave him system and, more important, ways to say things about what he saw. On April 1, Thoreau opened his month's journal with "Gilpin says well that the object of a light mist is a '*nearer distance.*'" He went on, praising the book in terms that remind one of his earlier hopes for *A Week*, finding it moderate, temperate, graceful, roomy, like a gladed wood," and noting again how it converted scenery into language. "Some of the cool wind of the copses converted into grammatical and graceful sentences, without heat."[1]

Thoreau read Gilpin all during April, and either referred to Gilpin or wrote in obvious imitation of him every day. Gilpin's effect on Thoreau was twofold. He gave him language for certain effects and appearances, and by describing them, he made them visible, in the sense that one often sees only what one has been prepared to expect. Gilpin taught Thoreau to expect more. Gilpin gives fresh descriptions of light, distances, mist, haze, and the effects of different kinds of weather, and the characteristics of different trees. His books have lots of good color illustrations, to which Thoreau paid particular attention, and which constituted a significant addition to the visual art Thoreau is known to have studied. Thoreau began sketching more himself, and the poet in him was revived. He characterized an oak tree as an "agony of strength," described the white pine as "the emblem of my life," and observed how "the bluebird carries the sky on his back."[2]

Of all the "separate intentions of the eye" Thoreau found in Gilpin, perhaps none was so new, or so useful, as Gilpin's remarkable sense for color. He had illustrated all his books with wash drawings, many of which were suffused with a single color; he wrote about colors constantly, both those in the landscape and those in representations of landscape. On January 8, 1854, Thoreau would copy the following from Gilpin's *Art of Sketching Landscape*:

. . . when you have finished your sketch therefore with India ink, as far as you propose, tinge the whole over with some light horizon hue. It may be the rosy tint of morning; or the more ruddy one of evening; or it may incline more to a yellowish, or a greyish cast. . . . By washing this tint over your *whole drawing*, you lay a foundation for harmony.

But even from his earliest acquaintance with Gilpin's work, Thoreau began to work more with color in his journal. On April 1, 1852, he wrote, "The prevailing color of the woods, at present, excepting the evergreens, is russet, a little more red or greyish, as the case may be, than the earth, for those are the colors of the withered leaves and the branches: the earth has the lighter hue of withered grass. Let me see how soon the woods will have acquired a new color."[3]

Seventeen days later he saw for the first time what he called "the andromeda phenomenon." A patch of dwarf andromeda, seen in mid-April, from most angles seemed grayish brown, the light being reflected from the leaves. But seen with the sun opposite, and the light shining through the leaves, the whole appeared lit by a "charming, warm, what I call *Indian*, red color,—the mellowist, the ripest, red imbrowned color," though it was the same light, the same hour, day, and place. He described it again and again. From most angles the leaves gave off a "mottled light or grayish aspect," but when the light shone *through* the leaves, they had "a warm rich red tinge, surpassing cathedral windows." He kept coming back to it. "The thing that pleases me most within these three days is the discovery of the androm-eda phenomenon." Thoreau had been walking these woods for many an April, but if he had seen the phenomenon before, he hadn't regis-tered it. In this case and in many others over the next two years, William Gilpin's writings gave him new things to look for in the still-unexhausted woods of home.[4]

As Thoreau began to revise and expand *Walden* again after the two-and-a-half-year lapse since 1849, his most important and inspiring reading was not literary, though he made literature of it. Darwin, Cato, Linnaeus, and Gilpin all have in common an intense focus on the earth and its productions: Darwin on the distribution and differ-entiation of species; Cato, as good as a nineteenth-century farmer's handbook; Linnaeus on minute classification of plants and parts of plants; Gilpin on seeing and describing the larger arrangement of elements in landscape. These were Thoreau's great writers as he turned now to work on the second half of his man-in-nature theme.

Thoreau has taught countless Americans to see nature. Darwin, Cato, Linnaeus, and Gilpin were some of his teachers. With the help of these and others, and by the force of his own synthesizing genius, he created a way of seeing the world that is highly unusual for its era, because it combines the conceptions of nature as force or energy, and nature as landscape. Thoreau revives the ancient Greek religious tra-dition, as Vincent Scully describes it, "in which the land was not a picture but a true force which physically embodied the powers that ruled the world." Ordinarily, one must agree with Scully that "it is only when the gods finally begin to die completely out of the land and when many human beings begin to live totally divorced from na-ture—at the beginning, that is, of the modern age—that landscape painting, picturesque architecture, and landscape description . . . become the obsessive themes of art," and the Greek view of the earth dies out. It is one of Thoreau's greatest accomplishments in *Walden* that both of these views are simultaneously put forward. One reason Thoreau's view of nature remains so attractive is that it sees nature as force, energy, and process, *and* as landscape, view, scene, or picture.[5]

73. The Flowering of Man

From the wet April of 1852 through the summer, while most of his energy was going into the fourth draft of *Walden*, Thoreau was having a difficult time with the friendships that were so hard but so important for him. Emerson found fault with him for walking alone, for having no companion, and called him a "cold intellectual skeptic." Thoreau found this unjust, but he was stung by it and nursed the hurt, writing grimly in his journal that *if* it were true, he prayed Emerson's "curse" would "wither and dry up those sources of my life." Oblivious to all this Lear-like anger and bitterness, Greeley, from his office in New York, was writing frequent and chipper notes of encouragement to Thoreau, and was asking him specifically to provide an essay on "Emerson, his Works and Ways," on the model of Thoreau's earlier "Carlyle." The request could not have come at a worse time. Thoreau refused. He continued to take walks with Channing, and continued to complain privately about Channing's vulgarity. In welcome contrast, the Hawthornes returned to Concord in mid-May. Thoreau's summer letters to his sister Sophia and to Blake were unusually impassioned and personal this year. His mind was running on emotional matters. Sometime, probably in September, Thoreau sent off drafts of essays on "Love" and "Chastity and Sensuality" to Blake.[1]

It is hard to imagine two less Thoreauvian subjects. N. C. Wyeth once said that he considered Thoreau "the springhead for almost every move I can make, exccept in the intimate matters that transpire between a man and a woman. Here he is utterly deficient, as is Christ, on account of his lack of experience." Looking at it another way, a recent writer argues that "Thoreau, Cooper, Melville, and Whitman wrote principally about men, not girls and children, and they wrote about men engaged in economically and ecologically significant activities. When they treated Victorian mores, with a few notable exceptions they either satirized them or lapsed into *pro forma* imitation of conventional models." But for all his lack of direct experience and his disinclination to deal with the then-evolving feminine mass culture and its stultifying and sentimental emphasis on marriage, he did find himself compelled to try to say something about both love and sexuality. He worked on these essays from 1846 on, his reading notes on such books as the Hindu classic *Sacontala* show him collecting material about love, and his journals and notebooks make occasional reference to sexual subjects. The surviving manuscripts for the essays on "Love" and "Chastity and Sensuality" were not tossed off, but were, like all his writings, corrected, revised, and rerevised.[2]

As may be seen by its early title, "Love and Friendship," the essay "Love" was an outgrowth of one of his earliest serious subjects. For love as for friendship, Thoreau had only the highest, and therefore most impossible, not to say frustrating, standards. For friend or lover he wrote "god or goddess." His language slides into pronominal pietism as he asks the impossible. "I require that thou knowest everything without being told anything. I parted from my beloved because there was one thing which I had to tell her. She *questioned* me." If this is, as it seems, a comment on his courtship of Ellen Sewall, the girl he couldn't win has here become the girl he wouldn't have.[3]

Yet along with preposterous self-justification, he has some plain, though uningratiating doubts about marriage in general. "Considering how few poetical friendships there are, it is remarkable that so many are married. . . . There is more of good nature than of good sense at the bottom of most marriages." The essay recalls Margaret Fuller in its opening point that men are commonly supposed to be wise and women loving, but "unless each is both wise and loving, there can be neither wisdom nor love." For all the essay's faults—sentimental language, overblown idealizing, and choppy, unsure paragraphing—it is refreshing in its desire to avoid sentimental cant. "In Love and Friendship . . . it is commonly the imagination which is wounded first, rather than the heart. . . . *Comparatively*, we can excuse any offense against the heart, but not against the imagination."[4]

In his cover letter to Blake, Thoreau said nothing about the "Love" essay, except that it was just sentences and not yet complete. But he said he sent "the thoughts on chastity and sensuality with diffidence and shame, not knowing how far I speak to the condition of men generally, or how far I betray my peculiar defects." The subject of sex was not, of course, treated explicitly in any sort of writing at this time. Hawthorne had been accused of loosing the "French novel" in America because *The Scarlet Letter* (1850) came as close to sex as it did. Whitman would in a few years make sex an explicit subject for poetry, but in 1852, the year of Melville's *Pierre*, reticence was still universal. Thoreau indeed felt the problem, beginning the essay by complaining that though it "occupies the thoughts of all," mankind had agreed "to be silent about it," except for vulgar language, which Thoreau detested. He thought that in "a pure society" the subject of copulation would be "treated naturally and simply." He himself managed no such thing. Neither here nor anywhere else in his writings is there any scrap of explicit sex. And indeed, while he called for open treatment of the subject, he personally shrank from it. He was suspicious of what he thought of as plain animal warmth or heat, even though, in partial contradiction, he chided himself repeatedly in his journal for his "coldness."[5]

In the essay sent to Blake he comes out openly in praise of chastity as "something positive." He speaks of virginity as a flower, and in the rest of this essay as well as in a part of *Walden* first written this same summer, Thoreau treats sex in outrageous botanical language. "Chastity is the flowering of man," he says in *Walden*, thinking no doubt of the common sexual metaphor of deflowering. The bold botanical metaphors and explicit Linnaean references which dominate the second half of the essay are no accident and are much more than paradox. Indeed, the immediate impetus to take on the subject of sex in an essay and in *Walden* is related to Thoreau's new interest this year in Linnaeus rather than to events, or nonevents, in his personal life. The basis for Linnaeus's greatest achievement, his new taxonomy, was his discovery that all plants have sexual characteristics. Before him it had been assumed that sex played a part in only a very few plants. His famous system is based on observable differences in the sexual characteristics of the flowers of plants. Thoreau had been reading a lot in Linnaeus and in his disciples and thus, in the middle of Thoreau's essay on chastity, we find "J. Bilberg, in the *Amoenitates Botanicae*, edited by Linnaeus, observes [I translate from the Latin], the organs of generation which in the animal kingdom are for the most part concealed by nature as if they were to be ashamed of, in the vegetable kingdom are exposed to the eyes of all." That is to say sex in plants expresses itself as flowers. What Thoreau sought, without much success in this essay, was a way to treat human chastity or continence as a paradoxical flowering of man analogous to the flowering of plants in nature.[6]

There is one other way to understand Thoreau's interest in chastity, or as he usually put it, purity. Mary Douglas, the brilliant modern anthropologist, has argued that even after nature has replaced God in a secular society, certain old ritual concerns persist, often taking new forms. "The violent emotions that used to be centered on purity of doctrine, purity of cult, purity of sex," says Douglas, "seem now to be focussed on purity of the environment." In Linnaeus's reordering of the vegetable kingdom along sexual lines and in Thoreau's awkward and primitive efforts to relate that view of nature to human sexuality, we see a crucial moment in the shift from the old religion of God to the new religion of nature, and the beginnings of the modern views of nature as sacred, and her pollution as profane.[7]

74. My Year of Observation

Thoreau spent July 12, 1852, as he spent many days, reading and writing all morning and going out for a walk around two in the afternoon. On this particular day, he took off his shoes and went wading, slumping along in the "genial, fatty mud" of the Assabet. He went out for a second walk at twilight; both times he carried a notebook and made careful detailed notes of what he saw. This, his thirty-fifth birthday, did not bring on a mid-life crisis, but it did give Thoreau some twinges of uncertainty. On July 7 he lamented, "I am older than last year; the mornings are further between; the days are fewer." On July 14 the theatrical note of lost youth occurs again. "The youth gets together his materials to build a bridge to the moon, or perchance a palace or temple on the earth, and at length the middle-aged man concludes to build a wood-shed with them." True enough, no doubt, for most of us, but for Thoreau it should be remembered that the woodshed he was deprecating was *Walden*.[1]

He was complaining again in late June about science affirming too much, being too full of presumption and of being less help than superstition as a guide to essential truth. He was at the time reading Morton's *Crania Americana* and was contemptuous of Morton's efforts to take the measure of man by filling "your cranium with white mustard seed to learn its internal capacity." To Sophia in July he wrote, "I have become sadly scientific." Yet this was the same man whose reading all spring and summer was dominated by Linnaeus, as well as Gilpin, who was drawing the important lesson of the usefulness of system from Linnaeus, and whose own close observation of nature was gaining immeasurably from the detailed observations of botanists from Linnaeus to his own time.[2]

In the same contrary vein, he grumbled to Blake on July 21 about being "too stupidly well these days to write to you," and about his life being "almost altogether outward," while to his sister a week earlier he had written describing himself as so "slackened and rusty, like the telegraph wire this season, that no wind that blows can extract music from me. I am not on the trail of any elephants or mastodons, but have succeeded in trapping only a few ridiculous mice, which cannot feed my imagination." But on the same day, July 13, in his journal he recorded a walk full of delicious detail about the ripening huckleberries, noting some hitherto undescribed varieties, and he prefaced it all rather breathlessly with "A journal, a book that shall contain a record of all your joy, your ecstasy."[3]

The important thing for the summer is not the complaining, which has been too much stressed and emphasized out of context, but the new excited emphasis on the journal. Though he was working continuously on *Walden*, and while his reading was taking in more of Linnaeus, more of Gilpin, some American books on zoology and herpetology, Morton's work on the brain, Carver's and Drake's travels, and even some Schoolcraft on Indians, Thoreau's ideas about what he could do with his journal were coming together this summer and taking on the proportions of a major project.[4]

The journal had originally been started at Emerson's suggestion, and Thoreau still associated it with Emerson. When Emerson had called him a cold skeptic, Thoreau had responded by writing, in his journal, that if it were true he hoped his journal would no longer yield him "pleasure nor life." What Emerson had given, it seems he could also take away. The journal had always been important to Thoreau, but now it was becoming a project in itself, not just the raw material for other projects. Increasingly he sought to capture day by day the "different states of our meadows," as they reflected "moods of the Concord mind." He now saw, for the first time, he said, that the year was a circle, and this year he began the systematic listing of all the trees, flowers, and plants in Concord, together with details of their growth, the times of their leafing and flowering. He began to keep close track of birds, of the water levels in rivers and ponds, of the weather, of all the phenomena of a natural year in Concord. This year Thoreau really began, systematically and in earnest, the vast project of keeping track of every stage of every plant in town, the project that would culminate in 1860 and 1861 in the great charts he would then assemble, large sheets of paper on which he recorded days of a month in a column down the left-hand side and years from 1852 to 1860 (in later months, to 1861) across the top. Then he filled in, during 1860 and 1861, all the squares so he could track the phenomena of each day of each month through seven or eight annual recurrences. Though he did not draw up these charts till 1860, he began in 1852 to compile sufficiently complete notes to make such a project possible. As he said in early July, 1852 was indeed "my year of observation."[5]

The year, he noted a bit later, "is but a succession of days, and I see that I could assign some office to each day which, summed up, would be the history of the year." Again, so close was his attention that he could say "Nature never loses a day." He noticed everything. "I have the habit of attention to such excess," he wrote in September, "that my senses get no rest, but suffer from a constant strain." His journal this summer is full, animated, brilliant. There are dozens of prose cadenzas, brief snatches of passionately and intensely observed phenomena. His life had inner intensity and outer excitement, and these meshed together far better than his frequent complaints suggest. In late August he wrote:

> I live so much in my habitual thoughts, a routine of thought, that I forget
> there is any outside to the globe, and am surprised when I behold it as
> now. . . . There is something invigorating in this air, which I am pecu-
> liarly sensible is a real wind, blowing from over the surface of a planet. I

look out at my eyes, I come to my window, and I feel and breathe the fresh air. It is a fact equally glorious with the most inward experience. Why have we ever slandered the outward? The perception of surfaces will always have the effect of miracle to a sane sense.[6]

This close observation, this habit of attention was reinforced by his continual reading in both Linnaeus and Gilpin this year. The scientist and the artist-poet were equally congenial to him, and his own best work partook of both. "Every poet has trembled on the verge of science," he noted in mid-July. Thoreau had what Alfred North Whitehead said the scientist must have, a "union of passionate interest in the detailed facts with equal devotion to abstract generalities." His writings from this time on are marked by the quality that Whitehead elsewhere calls "the full scientific mentality, which instinctively holds that *all* things great and small are conceivable as exemplifications of general principles which reign throughout the natural order." And in his best writings he now was able to combine the eye of the naturalist with that of the poet. If he knew that general laws held everywhere in nature, he also knew that "all the phenomena of nature need be seen from the point of view of wonder and awe," and that "Nature must be viewed humanly to be viewed at all; that is, her scenes must be associated with humane affections, such as are associated with one's native place, for instance." Thus nature was both objective and subjective. This summer nature even seemed to favor friendship. The passage just quoted goes on: "she [nature] is most significant to a lover. A lover of Nature is pre-eminently a lover of man. If I have no friend, what is Nature to me?"[7]

75. August and September 1852: Country Life

Botanizing was a common hobby in mid-nineteenth-century America, and Thoreau's passion for it was shared, in different degrees, by friends and relations. Channing's sudden new interest amused Emerson, and Emerson himself found and reported a coral root (*Corallorhiza multiflora*) near Brister's spring on August 12. On the eighteenth, Elizabeth Hoar brought lichens and mosses and several kinds of berry bushes back from a trip to the White Mountains. On September 22, Thoreau noted that Sophia had seen three plants in Concord (Whorled Pogonia, Painted Trillium, and Perfoliate Bellwort) which he had not. Though he was caught up by attentive absorption in the smallest details of botanical classification and in the slightest discrepancies between competing systems, Thoreau did not have the same sympathy with similar attention to the details of, say, history. He had only amused contempt for Alcott's new interest in tracing his own genealogy, for example.[1]

August and September were active, social months for Thoreau this year. Alcott was in town on August 9 and 10. Thoreau's relationship with Emerson was improving. Toward the end of August, just on the brink of fall weather, he went river sailing again as he had with John many years earlier. Toward the end of the first week in September, he and Channing made a short trip to Mount Monadnock, where they heard stories of the previous generation when a dense snarl of uprooted trees near the summit provided a haven for wolves until it was all burned off in a spectacular fire. On the last day of September, he went out bee hunting, and wrote up a graphic account of the intricate process.[2]

Eighteen fifty-two was a peak year for Thoreau's journalizing, as Odell Shepard observed almost sixty years ago when he put together an influential volume of choice selections. *Walden* was expanding under revision, numerous old projects were close to publication, new projects were sprouting. His descriptions this year have a new fire and intensity; his journal also shows his growing interest in a kind of narrative which is not fiction but *fabula*, sketches or short stories of country life. He had always had an eye for the details of how to stone a well, or measure a large elm, how to find a bee tree or cut ice from a pond. His private journal eulogy this January for Bill Wheeler, the town drunk found frozen to death one winter morning, is a profoundly moving story of a life. An entire volume of such stories could easily be extracted from Thoreau's journals, and many of the best would be about animals, or encounters between people and animals.[3]

He had a wonderful gift for getting along with animals. He seemed to many to possess King Solomon's ring, which enabled him to talk to the animals. He tells of chasing a fox in intricate circles through deep snow on a hillside. (In later years he could detect a fox's trail by scent alone!) He writes of a struggle between a turtle and a pout, of "talking" with a woodchuck. He would stand in a swamp all day to watch frogs. Mice and birds would eat out of his hand. He loved watching cats. His final journal entry in 1861 is a spirited account of a kitten's first learning to walk, spit, scratch, and mew. Earlier, he had told of his Maltese cat, Min, returning home one February day after having been gone for five cold nights in a row. After being "fed with the best that the house affords . . . and, with the aid of unstinted sleep in all laps in succession," she returned to her "old place under the stove, and is preparing to make a stew of her brains there." In another place he gives an account of his trying to anticipate the surfacings of an elusive diving loon on Walden Pond. "Though the sky was overcast, the pond was so smooth that I could see where he broke the surface if I did not hear him. His white breast, the stillness of the air, the smoothness of the water, were all against him." Still, Thoreau could not get anywhere near him. "At length, having come up fifty rods off, he uttered one of those prolonged unearthly howls, as if calling on the god of loons to aid him, and immediately there came a wind from the east and rippled the surface, and filled the whole air with misty rain."[4]

There are stories about a lost kitten, a hilarious account of trying to catch a loose pig through the streets of Concord, and another about a neighbor, Pratt, firing a shot at a swallow, hitting it, then seeing "a second swallow come flying behind and repeatedly strike the other with all his force beneath, so as to toss him up as often as he approached the ground and enable him to continue his flight, and thus he continued to do till they were out of sight." This story, like some others of Thoreau's best, were not things he himself had seen, but stories he had heard told. Many of the best come from Minott. One of the most vivid in the entire journal is Minott's account of a mad dog that had showed up in Concord when Minott was a boy. Minott's detailed recall and Thoreau's vivid narration are equally impressive:

> The first he remembers a couple of men had got poles and were punching at a strange dog toward night under a barn in that neighborhood [near the old Ben Prescott house]. The dog which was speckled and not very large, would growl and bite the pole, and they ran a good deal of risk, but they did not know that he was mad. At length they routed him, and he took to the road.

Minott followed, watching. After the dog had bitten off the head of a turkey, Minott then raised the cry of "mad dog."

> Minott next saw Harry Hooper coming down the road after his cows, and he shouted to him to look out, for the dog was mad, but Harry, who was in the middle of the road, spread his arms out, one on each side, and, being short, the dog leaped right upon his open breast and made a pass at his throat, but missed it, though it frightened him a good deal; and Minott coming up, exclaimed, "Why, you're crazy, Harry; if he'd 'a' bitten ye, 'twould 'a' killed ye."[5]

The point here is not close observation, at least not his own, but telling a story. The language is clear, economical, colloquial. Nothing impedes the narrative dash. We accept the story as true, not tall, because we trust the narrator who seems so objective, so matter-of-fact. Similar stories and vignettes or sketches occur all through *Walden*, but neither the half-tame mouse, nor the battle of the ants, nor even the wonderful hawk high in the spring sky making all the earth lonely beneath it, have more sheer verve or more of the comic quality than the best of the journal stories. It is hard to improve on the mad dog, or the escaped pig, or this dog and squirrel story, also from Minott:

> When Minott lived at Baker's, B. had a dog Lion, famous for chasing squirrels. The gray squirrels were numerous and used to run over the house sometimes. It was an old-fashioned house, slanting down to one story behind, with a ladder from the roof to the ground. One day a gray squirrel ran over the house, and Lion, dashing after him up the ladder, went completely over the house and fell off the front side before he could stop, putting out one of his toes. But the squirrel did not put out any of his toes.[6]

Thoreau's behavioral realism, if it may be called that, is not of course confined to the journal, though the journal is where he perfected this kind of writing. *Walden* itself is a more concrete, a more believable book, because of its wealth of stories that entertain and amuse and, through sheer narrative verve, celebrate and raise to significance what Whitman called "the concrete and its heroisms,"
the ordinary doings of country life.

VIII. 1852-1854

Walden

or the Triumph of the Organic

76. Ante-Columbian History

Thoreau's creativity was at flood tide for most of 1852. He was working almost exclusively on large projects. In March he sent Greeley the *Yankee in Canada* manuscript. In November he sent off a hundred pages, roughly half the manuscript of *Cape Cod*, to George William Curtis, editor of *Putnam's*. His journal for 1852 runs to over seven hundred printed pages, a major project in its own right this year, a Book of Concord, or Calendar, or Concord Year. His botanical reading gave him a heightened sense of the uses of system, the orderings of nature, both for observation and for composition. He worked on his descriptive prose and on his story telling. He was becoming more and more self-conscious, and self-consciously articulate, about the processes of observing and creating, about moods in which "I am conscious of the presence and criticism of a part of me, which, as it were, is not a part of me, but a spectator, sharing no experience, but taking note of it," much like T. S. Eliot's conception of the self-conscious poet as someone watching over his own shoulder.[1]

Into the journal went all the observed detail of the year, and the details began to gather around certain kinds of general concerns, like iron filings around the feet of a magnet. He was unusually attentive this year to flowers, and noted how some flowers lasted even into late fall. Only on the twenty-third of November would he finally admit that the flowering season was completely over. He was also becoming more interested in seeds, and the process of seeding. On the last day of December, he wrote a long account of how chestnuts seed themselves, with the aid of a thick covering of leaves. Eighteen fifty-two saw the planting, so to speak, of the great, still-unpublished project on "The Dispersion of Seeds."[2]

Thoreau also wrote a fourth draft of *Walden* this year, adding some sixty-seven leaves to his manuscript. New this year was the opening of chapter two, "Where I lived, and What I lived For," with its emphasis on the writer's imagination. New too were large parts of "Sounds," "Solitude," "Visitors," "The Ponds," the sensuality paragraphs in "Higher Laws," and the Ovidian section of "Spring," on how "the coming in of spring is like the creation of Cosmos out of Chaos and the realization of the Golden Age." Especially marked in this revision is the addition of botanical and zoological details, such as the descriptions of the sand cherry and the hoot owl in "Sounds."[3]

Nor was this all he accomplished during this extraordinary year. He was reading and making notes in his Natural History Extract book on Linnaeus, Evelyn, Gilpin, and other travelers and naturalists, and he was reading and accumulating material in the Indian notebooks for the project he called "my own Ante-Columbian History." It is still hard to be sure just what Thoreau intended for this project at any given moment. On a sheet of paper now tipped into the first of these Indian notebooks, he compared his project to Schoolcraft's multivolume *History of the Indian Tribes of North America*. On this same sheet, just below the title ("my own Ante-Columbian History") the next line reads "First aspect of Land and People." In a questionnaire he returned to the Association for the Advancement of Science in December 1853, he listed his special interest as "The Manners and Customs of the Indians of the Algonquin Group previous to contact with the civilized man." In other places, he seems also to have had a major interest in the flora and fauna of the New World. To judge by his scattered comments, his list of topics, and his reading over the years, he seems to have had in mind a volume that would have had something of the detail and scope of Francis Parkman's *France and England in North America*, or Samuel Eliot Morison's *European Discovery of America*, except that Thoreau would have concentrated on what was discovered in North America by Europeans, rather than on the Europeans who did the discovering. Thoreau was to fill ten notebooks with material for this project, yet he never seems to have sketched even a tentative draft or lecture on it. But while he neither wrote nor planned a single great work on early North America and its people, the subject preoccupied him and flowed over, in innumerable ways, into his other projects, such as the *Yankee in Canada* manuscript, *Cape Cod*, the later parts of *The Maine Woods*, and late drafts of *Walden*.[4]

Thus, in the end, very little of the Indian material was finally wasted, since his sympathetic identification with the early North American landscape and its inhabitants colored so much of his mature work. Even the heavy and seemingly arid research tasks he set himself in his North American "project," such as reading through the *Jesuit Relations*, paid off in interesting and sometimes unforeseen ways.

77. The *Jesuit Relations*

Thoreau began reading the *Jesuit Relations* in October of 1852. Every year from 1632 to 1672, a book-length account or *relation* of events concerning the Jesuit mission to the Indians of Canada was sent home from the Father Superior at Quebec to France, and there published. These forty volumes, widely read and discussed in their day, are a major document for the early history of Canada. One cannot read very far at all in Canadian history without coming across references to these accounts. Thoreau must have known about them for years. Charlevoix, an early historian of Canada with whose work Thoreau had long been familiar, says, "no historian can enter fully into an investigation of the circumstances attendant on the first settlement of this country, without being conversant with them." It is not hard to see why Thoreau would have wished to look into them. Why he did more than glance, why he persevered, eventually reading and making extracts from thirty-three of the volumes, is another matter.[1]

The first two volumes, which Thoreau took out of the Harvard library in October 1852, had been written by Father Paul Le Jeune. The *Relation* for 1633 runs to 216 pages and 342 pages for 1634. They are lively books, filled with graphic detail, written with clear attention to style by an observant man who was genuinely interested in the Indians' well-being. Lest we condescend or scoff too quickly at the missionary point of view, it is useful to recall Lewis Morgan's tribute to these particular Jesuits:

> While the English entirely neglected the spiritual welfare of the Indians, the French were unremitted in their efforts to spread Christianity among them. The privations, and hardships endured by the Jesuit missionaries, and the zeal, the fidelity and devotion, exhibited by them, in their efforts for the conversion of the Indians, are unsurpassed in the history of Christianity. They traversed the forests of America alone and unprotected; they dwelt in the depth of the wilderness, without shelter, and almost without raiment. . . . The intercourse of the French Jesuits with the Iroquois furnishes, in some respects, the most pleasing portion of their history.

The *Relations*, especially those written by Le Jeune, are attractive, readable, indeed absorbing books. The Jesuit's focus is almost exclusively on the Indians, their habits, customs, manners, language, clothing, behavior, beliefs, and history. There is nothing even remotely comparable for early New England. Writing in simple journal form and chronological order, Le Jeune describes where he has been and what he has seen. In their comprehensive treatment of one area over forty years, the *Relations* are, collectively, the ultimate travel book.[2]

Père Le Jeune is only a few pages into his account of 1633 when he begins to go into minute detail on how the Indians dry eels: "This work is done entirely by the women, who empty the fish, and wash them very carefully, opening them, not up the belly but up the back; they then hang them in the smoke, first having suspended them upon poles outside their huts to drain." (Thoreau read the *Relations* in the original French.) An eel is roasted for the Father, who continues, "I ate it with the child, of whom I asked some water; he brought me some in a dipper or dish made of bark. The little boy, having handled the roasted eel, which was very greasy, used his hair as a napkin, and the others rubbed their hands on the dogs." Le Jeune notes all the cultural differences between him and the Indians, but he is always trying to learn, not to belittle. He notes in his vivid and concise French: "l'huile, c'est leur sucre, ils en mettent dans les fraises et framboises quand ils en mangent, a' ce qu'on m'a dict: et leur plus grands festins sont de graisse ou d'huile. Ils mordent par fois dans un morceau de graisse blanche figee comme nous mordrions dans une pomme: voila leur bonne chere." [Oil . . . is their sugar. They use it with their strawberries and raspberries when they eat them, as I am told, and their greatest feasts are of fat or of oil. They sometimes bite into a piece of solid white grease as we would bite into an apple: this is their high living.][3]

Le Jeune describes everything, an elegant, full-length, thin, cedar battle shield; how to cook in bark dishes (use hot stones); how the Indians travel down steep snowy slopes (roll, pushing the aged off first on a sled) and across ice; how they make shoes of untanned (and therefore unwaterproof) elk hide; how work is divided between men and women, and the lengths men went to avoid "woman's work"; how the young treat the old, how the Jesuit quarters are so cold the ink freezes in the inkstand as he writes; and a thousand more details. One Indian told Le Jeune how his grandmother used to take pleasure in describing the astonishment of the Indians "when they saw for the first time a French ship arrive upon their shores. They thought it was a moving Island: they did not know what to say of the great sails which made it go; their astonishment was redoubled in seeing a number of men on deck." Later, watching the French eat the food they had brought with them, they "said the Frenchmen drank blood and ate wood, thus naming the wine and the biscuits."[4]

Le Jeune speaks often of the Fathers' efforts to learn the Indian languages. They construct grammars and dictionaries, negotiate shrewdly for tutors, and go off to winter quarters with the Indians in their villages specifically to learn the native languages, which they considered an essential first step in their mission. From the start, the Jesuits were much more interested in translating Christianity into Indian languages than making French speakers of Indians.

The *Relations* are immensely readable even today. The Fathers' pervasive missionary spirit is less intrusive than one might suppose, though it did not escape Thoreau's amused notice. He commented in his journal for October 15, "How Father Le Jeune pestered the poor Indians with his God at every turn (they must have thought it his one idea)." But there was no question of the Jesuits' sincerity. As Thoreau also noted, "they could not be suspected of sinister motives. The savages were not poor observers and reasoners. The priests were, therefore, sure of success, for they had paid the price of it."[5]

In the end the Fathers themselves and their annual accounts must have been almost as interesting to Thoreau as the Indian matters they wrote about. The *Relations* are, after all, rather similar to much of Thoreau's own writing. They take the form of a chronological journal, filled with excursions and close observation. They concentrate on the border area between civilized and savage life with great sympathy for the latter but with ultimate loyalty to the former. It is no wonder Thoreau found the *Relations* interesting enough to pursue for years, since both in form and in purpose he was doing something quite similar. His own books were, in a sense, reports from his own missions to Maine, Cape Cod, and Walden Pond.

78. Pantheism

The winter of 1852–53 was remarkable for having little snowfall. The ground was bare most of the time, and Thoreau did a great deal of work surveying during the last half of December and all through January and February. At the end of February he remarked that he had made a dollar a day for the last seventy-six days. He was working so much primarily to pay off his debt for the publication of *A Week*, and the hired labor made him feel stupid and worthless. By January 21 he was thoroughly out of sorts. Nothing pleased him. He snarled at science, at the idea of the sun being ninety-five million miles away as "a statement which never made any impression on me, because I never walked it, and which I cannot be said to believe." He felt equally gloomy this month about what he called "the rottenness of human relations." He dreamed, he said, "of delving amid the graves of the dead," and complained in his journal that "Death is with me, and life far away." Though he could rejoice at winter with its snow and cold, its frost crystals everywhere, its sounds and sights, still the long winter months of short days depressed him, and he looked forward hungrily, almost obsessively, to spring. Even his journal dried up this year as fall turned into winter, and it only began to flow again as he began to ferret out the premonitions of spring. He had let go of the flowery season with great reluctance, meticulously noting yarrow, tansy, and tall buttercup still hanging on in mid-November. By December 1, he was watching the soft red and brown colors of the wet mild winter and observing, three weeks before winter was officially come, "the form of the buds which are prepared for spring." On January 7 he broke open some male catkins, noting that he was "surprised to see the yellow anthers so distinct, promising spring." And before January was out, he was optimistically recording "something springlike in [the] afternoon," making lists of plants that "wear their leaves conspicuously now," and finding watercress "fresh and green at the bottoms of the brooks."[1]

Also contributing to his despondency this winter was the fact that however well his writing might be going, the business of publishing was still a major problem. He was still paying for *A Week*, and now, in January 1853, he ran into problems with *Putnam's* over their censoring and editing his Canada piece without consulting him. On hearing about the incident, the usually patient Greeley, still energetically pushing Thoreau's work in New York, wrote an exasperated letter to Thoreau pointing out that he, Greeley, thought it a mistake to have the Canada pieces appear anonymously "making them all (so to speak) *editorial*; but *if* that is done, don't you see that the elimination of very flagrant heresies (like your defiant Pantheism) becomes a necessity?" The phrase struck home. Thoreau began using the term *pantheism* with a show of injured defiance. He wrote Greeley, still grateful for his help, but adding petulantly that he didn't know how he could have avoided the problem "since I was born to be a pantheist—if that be the name of me, and I do the deeds of one."[2]

What did he believe now, in the winter of his thirty-fifth year, in the pause between the fourth and fifth drafts of *Walden*? He had no more use than most sensible people for the oversimplifications inherent in labeling, and he himself used labels gingerly and with traces of irony. But he was also coming to accept the essential accuracy of some labels. In early March he was asked to fill out a questionnaire for the Association for the Advancement of Science. He felt that "though I probably stand as near to nature as any of them," he didn't really fit their categories, "inasmuch as they do not believe in a science which deals with the higher law. . . . The fact is," he went on, "I am a mystic, a transcendentalist, and a natural philosopher to boot." He also thought of himself as a scholar, in the broad Emersonian or Fichtean sense, and he kept reminding himself that as a scholar, instead of surveying, one should be doing only those things that "lie next to and conduce to his life, which do not go against the grain, either of his will or his imagination."[3]

He was intensely conscious, as he wrote Blake in late February, that he had no *new* beliefs:

As the stars looked to me when I was a shepherd in Assyria, they look to me now a New Englander. The higher the mountain on which you stand, the less change in the prospect from year to year, from age to age. Above a certain height, there is no change. . . . I have had but one *spiritual* birth (excuse the word,) and now whether it rains or snows, whether I laugh or cry, fall farther below or approach nearer to my standard, whether Pierce or Scott is elected, not a new scintillation of light flashes on me, but ever and anon, though with longer intervals, the same surprising and everlastingly new light dawns to me.[4]

He might bridle at the label "pantheist," but Greeley had not meant it maliciously, nor was it essentially inaccurate. Thoreau was certainly no Christian in any commonly accepted sense. He allowed that he would rather walk to Rutland than to Jerusalem, said pointedly that his system had no place for man-worship, by which religious liberals of the time usually meant worship of Christ, and considered that "God exhibits himself to the walker in a frosted bush today [he was writing in early January, after an ice storm], as much as in a burning one to Moses of old." Much of his love of nature is expressed in language devoid of conventional religious terminology, but no less religious in feeling for that. "I love Nature partly *because* she is not man," he wrote in January. "None of his institutions control or pervade her. There a different kind of right prevails. . . . He [man] is constraint, she is freedom to me. He makes me wish for another world. She makes me content with this."[5]

He did not always avoid religious language. The blossom-bud of the crowfoot plant, observed in early January this year, is described in openly religious—but still not Christian—terms. "There it patiently sits, or slumbers, how full of faith, informed of a spring which the world has never seen, the promise and prophecy of it shaped somewhat like some Eastern temples, in which a bud-shaped dome o'ertops the whole."[6]

Thoreau believed that each era is as good as any other, each life an epitome of all life, his life in Concord symbolic of all men's everywhere. This was his real religion, his deepest belief, not his creed or confession, but the principle which lay closest to his daily life and common usage, the newer testament, or gospel of this moment, as he called it in "Walking." "There are, from time to time mornings," he noted in late January, "both in summer and winter, when especially the world seems to begin anew. . . . Mornings of creation, I call them. . . . A morning which carries us back beyond the Mosaic creation. . . . Mornings when men are new-born, men who have the seeds of life in them. It should be part of my religion to [be] abroad then." If a pantheist is one who worships nature, because nature is life, and life is all there is that matters, then Thoreau was a pantheist.[7]

Out one day in late March by Clamshell Hill, he turned over a bit of sod and saw what at first he thought were "beautiful frost crystals of a rare form." Looking more closely he saw that it was not frost, but "clear, crystalline dew in almost invisible drops" clinging to the tiny fine hairs of the grass roots. "The half is not shown," he wrote. "The process that goes on in the sod and the dark, about the minute fibres of the grass,—the chemistry and mechanics,—before a single green blade can appear above the withered herbage, if it could [be] adequately described, would supplant all other revelations."[8]

79. America

Thoreau's attitude toward America was in some ways more complex than his attitude toward nature. This is at least partly because he thought less often and less intensely about America than about nature. He could be ambivalent, if not contradictory, about American government, character, and values. It depended on the issue, and he was careful to discriminate among the different aspects of American life. The angry young man of "Resistance to Civil Government" makes it pointedly clear by careful repetition that it is American *government* he wishes to oppose. "Visit the Navy Yard, and behold a marine, such a man as an American government can make." More specifically, he disapproves of the position taken on the slavery issue by the American government. "How does it become a man to behave toward this American government today? I answer that he cannot without disgrace be associated with it. I cannot for an instant recognize that political organization as *my* government which is the *slave's* government also." But rejection of the American government did not mean rejection of everything American. It was not the government, Thoreau thought, that had kept the country free, settled the West, or educated people. On the contrary, he was convinced that "the character inherent in the American people has done all that has been accomplished." Thus, in the same essay, Thoreau could be strongly critical of American policy, foreign and domestic, and at the same time warmly enthusiastic about the American people, and about the idea of America.[1]

"Walking" contains his most explicit and extended discussion of the idea of America, which he found best exemplified in certain aspects of the westward movement. "When I go out of the house for a walk . . . my needle . . . always settles between west and south-south-west. . . . Eastward I go only by force, but westward I go free. . . . Let me live where I will, on this side is the city, on that the wilderness, and ever I am leaving the city more and more, and withdrawing into the wilderness." This is not just true for himself. "I should not lay so much stress on this fact, if I did not believe that something like this is the prevailing tendency of my countrymen. I must walk toward Oregon, and not toward Europe. And that way the nation is moving, and I may say that mankind progress from east to west." "Walking" is a classic articulation of the spirit of the westward movement. "We go eastward," Thoreau says, "to realize history and study the works of art and literature, retracing the steps of the race; we go westward as into the future, with a spirit of enterprise and adventure."[2]

But Thoreau's idea of the West is not an affirmation of the westward march of civilization, or the "transit of civilization." For Thoreau the West means almost literally the opposite; it is the impulse to recognize and act on what is wild within us. Thus his praise of America as the West, and his description of the physical beauty of the western American landscape concludes with his great redefinition of the meaning of the West. "The West of which I speak is but another name for the Wild: and what I have been preparing to say is, that in Wildness is the preservation of the World."[3]

Another reason for Thoreau's praising America—which in this essay can at times be mistaken for plain national puffery—is his unwillingness to devalue the present time or his place in it. When he begins, "if the heavens of America appear infinitely higher, and the stars brighter, I trust that these facts are symbolical of the heights to which the philosophy and poetry and religion of her inhabitants may one day soar," he goes on to give as the reason, "I should be ashamed to think that Adam in paradise was more favorably situated on the whole than the backwoodsman in this country."[4]

Thoreau had too much self-respect to permit himself wholesale denunciation of an America which included himself, his family, and his friends. But he nevertheless had a keen eye for the gaps between rhetoric and reality, and he didn't limit himself to political issues. An example is the long, desolate prose elegy in his journal for January 27, 1852, in which he begins by looking "over the plains westward toward Acton," and like Henry the Fifth looking over the ruined countryside of France, begins to speak of "the still, stagnant, heart-eating, life-everlasting, and gone-to-seed country, so far from the post-office where the weekly paper comes, wherein the new married wife cannot live for loneliness, and the young man has to depend upon his horse for society." This is the unromantic countryside we associate with later New England local color writers such as Sarah Orne Jewett and Mary Wilkins Freeman, but Thoreau had seen it first, that countryside where

> none of the farmer's sons are willing to be farmers, and the apple trees are decayed, and the cellar holes are more numerous than the houses, and the rails are covered with lichens, and the old maids wish to sell out and move into the village, and have waited twenty years in vain for this purpose and never finished but one room in the house, never plastered nor painted, inside or out, lands which the Indian long since was dispossessed [of] and now the farms are run out, and what were forests are now grain-fields, what were grain-fields, pastures. . . . I say, standing there and seeing these things, I cannot realize that this is that hopeful young America which is famous throughout the world for its activity and enterprise, and this is the most thickly settled and Yankee part of it.[5]

Thoreau disapproved of much of the national rhetoric, including that which was Puritan-derived. He explicitly rejects the language of redemption ("as long as ideas are expressed, as long as friction makes bright, we do not want redeemers," he noted on April 15, 1852) and that of manifest destiny. To Blake, in February of 1853 he wrote,

> The whole enterprise of this nation which is not an upward, but a westward one, towards Oregon, California, Japan, etc., is totally devoid of interest to me, whether performed on foot or by a Pacific railroad. It is not illustrated by a thought it is not warmed by a sentiment, there is nothing in it which one should lay down his life for, nor even his gloves. . . . No, they may go their way to their manifest destiny which I trust is not mine.[6]

Thoreau did not reject all civic ties, all citizenship, all patriotic attachment to his native land, but he was always asking, of what exactly was it that he was a citizen? His sense of his own identity did not insist much or often on his Americanness. As Henry James was said to have been a citizen not so much of England or America as of the James family, so Thoreau was a citizen of his family, of the town of Concord, of New England, and of nature, and while all of these taken together might make him an American, any one of them by itself took precedence over the grand abstraction of America.

80. Spring 1853: The Golden Gates

Much of January and February were spent not lecturing but surveying in order to raise money. In January, *A Yankee in Canada* began to appear in monthly installments in *Putnam's*. Thoreau broke off the agreement after the third installment in March. As spring approached, he painted his new flat-bottomed boat and fretted over ways to keep his boots from running so rapidly down at the heels. He also turned his inventive Yankee cunning to the problem of his bootlaces, which simply would not stay tied. He tied them and retied them on every walk. His laces came undone with such regularity that he speculated with Channing that a "shoe-ties worth" might be a very reliable unit of linear measurement. He tried laces made of exotic materials, such as "the hide of a South American jackass." He wondered if no better article had appeared at the World's Fair, and he applied himself to the redesign of the standard shoelace as he had to the pencil. Then one day it occurred to him to reverse his usual "two simple knots one over the other the same way." Thus Henry David Thoreau reinvented the square knot in July 1853. His problem, as others were quick to tell him when he talked about it, was that he had been using a plain granny knot all those years.[1]

April saw still more surveying. Emerson, always helpful, offered Channing a hundred dollars to assemble an anthology of writings of the three of them, to be called *Country Walking*. Thoreau took day trips with Channing and with Sophia. He spent time with Alcott and tried again to talk with Emerson. If it was a social spring, it also brought a reconfirmation of the significance, the representativeness of his own life. At the end of May he noted how "some incidents in my life seem far more allegorical than actual," and he was satisfied that such things were "quite in harmony with my subjective philosophy." He even ventured a new, subjective definition of wealth this month, reaching past Adam Smith, and anticipating Henry James's "I call that man rich who can satisfy the requirements of his imagination." Thoreau was more specific, equating riches with the artist's or writer's expressive capacities. "He is richest who has most use for nature as raw material of tropes and symbols with which to describe his life." What he saw in nature simply gave him language to describe what was already going on in him. It was not only spring again in Concord but another springtime of the spirit for Thoreau.[2]

As with nature, so with books, where he found that his reading tended less to inform than to reinforce what he was already thinking or working on. He found things in books *after* he had already begun exploring them himself. Reflecting on this process some years later, Thoreau commented that

> a man receives only what he is ready to receive, whether physically or intellectually or morally. . . . We hear and apprehend only what we already half know. If there is something which does not concern me, which is out of my line, which by experience or genius my attention is not drawn to, however novel and remarkable it may be, if it is spoken, we hear it not, if it is written we read it not, or if we read it, it does not detain us. Every man thus *tracks himself* [the metaphor is from hunting] through life, in all his hearing and reading and observation and travelling.

This is the most astute comment Thoreau ever made on the complex dynamic between his reading and writing. After he had started down a path, he became aware of the same path in others' accounts, and could quickly find it everywhere. Reading confirmed his own ideas and expressions, suggesting new examples or fresh phrasing or a whole new turn of argument. Thus extracts from his reading might go into or influence the next draft of something. Thoreau's reading is more active than passive, more for confirmation than for discovery, whetting existing interests and confirming prior insights.[3]

For example, in January 1853 he picked up Richard Trench's *On the Study of Words*, an English book that became a standard text on language, first published in 1851. Trench was the person responsible for the initial impulse that resulted in the *Oxford English Dictionary*. Thoreau may have picked up Trench's book because he picked up lots of new books on language, or because Trench bases much of his argument on the observation by "a popular American writer" that "language is fossil poetry." Following and extending Emerson, Trench argued that words were fossil ethics and fossil history as well and, like Emerson, Trench enjoyed restoring the lost concreteness of words that had degenerated into abstraction. Thus he reattached "dilapidate" to a "falling house or palace, stone detaching itself from stone"; he points out that "sierra," as in Sierra Nevada, is a name for a ragged ridge and means "saw." Trench taught Thoreau to associate "pagans" with "pagani" as "villagers" or "civilians"; he showed that "rivals" meant dwellers along the banks of the same stream. But what most interested Thoreau in Trench was the latter's treatment of words Thoreau was already interested in, such as "the words we use to set forth any transcending delight. Take three or four of these words," Trench goes on, " 'transport,' 'rapture,' 'ravishment,' 'exstasy.'—'transport,' that which *carries* us, as 'rapture,' or 'ravishment,' that which *snatches* us out of and above ourselves; and 'exstasy' is very nearly the same, only drawn from the Greeks."[4]

Thoreau's response was immediate, recalling in phrasing the famous transparent eyeball passage in Emerson's *Nature*. "These are the words I want. This is the effect of music. I am rapt away by it, out of myself. These are truly poetical words. I am inspired, elevated, expanded. I am on the mount." From Trench, as from the work of Charles Kraitsir on language, Thoreau was finding exciting confirmation of his, and Emerson's, long-held belief that language has a primary relation to nature. Kraitsir, whose work Thoreau began to read seriously late in 1852, argued that the underlying unity of languages was a physiological one, that all languages are composed of a few basic sounds, that these sounds, these basic phonemes are the necessary outcome of the encounter of man, mind, and nature. These basic sounds are prior to all languages, into which they are later elaborated. Thus all the various languages spring from speech sounds common to all human beings, demonstrating once more the essential similarity of all people in all times. Trench and Kraitsir, by their emphasis on *spoken* language, suggested to Thoreau—in Philip Gura's phrase—how "in its deepest core language reflects the natural world." Sound was the key to language. This insight bore wonderful fruit through the next revisions of *Walden*, as Thoreau rewrote parts of "Sounds," "Spring," and much else.[5]

He also found in Trench a bold new connection between wild and will. "Trench says a wild man is a *willed* man. Well, then, a man of will who does what he wills or wishes, a man of hope and the future tense, for not only the obstinate is willed, but far more the constant and persevering." And in a brilliant aside, unusual for its lack of ironic undertow, he suggests that the real legacy of Calvinism to the nineteenth century was to have focused attention on the problem of will. "The perseverance of the saints is positive willedness, not a mere passive willingness." Trench's Emersonian interest in language, his treatment of specific words, are reflected in Thoreau's subsequent writing, but only because Thoreau's books, like his observations of nature, augmented the vision he already possessed.[6]

81. Summer 1853:
Walden Five

In early July the Hawthornes departed for Liverpool, where Nathaniel had been posted as U.S. Consul in return for writing a campaign biography of his classmate—now president—Franklin Pierce. Hawthorne had been an obscure writer when he and Sophia first came to Concord. Now, at forty-nine, he was famous, and his fame had come largely in the last few years. Between 1850 and 1853 Hawthorne had published *The Scarlet Letter*, *The House of the Seven Gables*, *The Blithedale Romance*, and six other books. Thoreau was thirty-six this July, still hard at work on a manuscript that seemed destined never to be finished. July was a sociable month for him this year. He saw more of Emerson; there were more walks and outings with Channing and with Sophia. Moncure Conway, who came to Concord to see Emerson, met Thoreau tending a fugitive slave who had arrived the night before.[1]

Most of his time, however, was spent writing and reading. At midsummer he was spending both mornings and evenings reading, writing, or revising—"arranging my papers," as he called it. There was a lot of arranging to do, because he was working simultaneously on at least four major projects. First and most pressing were the drafts of *Walden*, which he was now turning out one right after the other. Walden Five consisted of 112 new leaves and was written during 1853. Walden Six, consisting of 119 leaves, was started late in 1853 and finished during the winter. The seventh draft, involving 46 new leaves, was written early in 1854, leaving time for one final clean draft or copy of unknown length for the printer, since it has not survived. The book itself was published in August of 1854. In addition to this continuous work on *Walden*, Thoreau was recording new observations, mostly of nature, in his journal at a rate averaging 50 printed pages a month; he was taking copious notes on his still-extensive reading in American Indian history and customs in his "Indian Books"; and he was making lengthy extracts on his reading in natural history in the notebook of "Extracts mainly concerning Natural History."[2]

Walden Four, completed in 1852, had involved extensive work on the "Economy" section and other early sections of the manuscript, and had consisted in good part of expanding and adding observations of nature. Walden Five was a major reshaping, adding a little early material, but concentrating mainly on completing the seasonal cycle and giving the year some symmetry by expanding the later parts of the book. This draft also injected a major social dimension to the account of life in the woods. It also seems probable that he now first broke up the narrative into separate chapters with chapter headings.[3]

Going quickly through the early sections, Thoreau added references to Indians, Eskimos, and the Jesuit missionaries. He revised the already lengthy description of the Canadian woodchopper, Therien.

He made major additions to the section on "The Ponds," setting it in autumn so that it contributes to the seasonal shape. "The Ponds" contains some of his best writing on the appearance of the water, on the effects of light, on different colors. (His journal for early May 1853 is especially sensitive to color also.) His description of the pond this year recalls Cooper's lovely description of the Glimmerglass in *The Deerslayer*. Thoreau insists, as had Cooper, on the calm purity of the scene:

> In such a day, in September or October, Walden is a perfect forest mirror, set round with stones as precious to my eye as if fewer or rare. Nothing so fair, so pure, and at the same time so large as a lake, perchance lies on the surface of the earth. Sky water. It needs no fence. Nations come and go without defiling it.[4]

To the "Higher Laws" section, Thoreau now added material on wildness, including the famous description of his momentary impulse to seize a woodchuck and devour it raw. He added in some material on his views about hunting and fishing. In "Brute Neighbors," he added partridge, loon, and duck stories to the account of the ant war. Another major addition was the bulk of the "Housewarming" chapter, which was about fall, about fire, and about wood.

The most significant additions, besides filling out certain seasons to make a full year, are the social additions. Accounts of Cato Ingraham, Zilpha, and Brister and Fenda Freeman draw attention to the fact that the area around Walden had been where Concord's black people lived. They are not prominent in the book, but neither are they invisible. Thoreau had been reading Henry Mayhew's *London Labour and the London Poor* (1851) in late May 1853. Mayhew's tone, in his "cyclopaedia of the conditions and earnings of those that *will* work, those that *cannot* work, and those that *will not* work" is spirited and indignant. He writes, he says, to inspire those in high places to "bestir themselves to improve the condition of a class of people whose misery, ignorance, and vice, amidst all the immense wealth and great knowledge of 'the first city in the world,' is to say the very least, a national disgrace to us." In the bulk of the book, Mayhew describes in amazing, vivid, statistically overwhelming detail the daily life of all the myriad classes of the poor. Of street folk, for example, he distinguishes with Linnaean classificational rigor "six distinct genera or kinds": street-sellers; street-beggars; street-finders; street-performers, artists, and showmen; street-artisans or working pedlars; and street-laborers. Always seeking both to classify and to specify, he calls up, in hundreds of closely printed pages, the actual daily lives of the people.

> After these we have the street-finders, or those who, as I said before, literally "pick up" their living in the public thoroughfares. There are the "pure" pickers, or those who live by gathering dog's dung: the cigar-end finders, or "hard-ups" as they are called who collect the refuse pieces of smoked cigars from the gutters, and having dried them, sell them as tobacco to the very poor, the dredgermen or coal-finders; the mud-larks, the bone grubbers; and the sewer hunters.

Each of these street-dwellers is carefully described by Mayhew. It is interesting that Thoreau found himself able to identify with some of them. In general, no such classes existed in Concord at the time, but the nearest equivalents—the blacks, the town drunks, ne'er-do-wells, the Irish brought in and left behind by the railroad—are not permitted to escape Thoreau's pages, and they are in general more sympathetically treated than are the mass of good burghers who are seen leading their lives of quiet desperation and who are treated as a group in "The Village."[5]

In Walden Five, Thoreau also added graceful and moving tributes to his friends, to Channing, the "poet" who "came from farthest to my lodge," and to Alcott, "one of the last of the philosophers."[6]

82. Fall 1853: Friends

There is no chapter on "friendship" in *Walden*, though there is more than one on "visitors," and Thoreau has been accused since his own time of being contemptuous of ordinary social behavior, of being cold, withdrawn, stoical, and boorish. But friendship was, in certain ways, vital to him. It was one of his earliest subjects and is a constant theme through fifteen years of his journal. If he treated Concord's most prosperous citizens and certain visiting clerical gentlemen with cool rudeness, he was bound by a tight network of acknowledged ties to his family, to a wide circle of Concord children (who were so deeply impressed with his minute knowledge of everything in town they thought it was Mr. Thoreau who had made Concord), to a small group of disciples, especially Blake and, after *Walden*, Ricketson, to the Irish for whom he once raised money, and to the blacks he helped to freedom. He valued his friendships with Hawthorne and Greeley, as well as those with Pratt, Minott, and Melvin. Above all, he was bound by special ties to a small number of kindred spirits, the transcendental loyalists, fellow writers, and walkers errant: Alcott, Channing, and Emerson.

The four were somewhat closer as a group this year because of a new project. In April 1853, Emerson offered the perennially broke Channing a hundred dollars (a fourth of a year's income for Channing) to prepare a volume to be called *Country Walking*, of "walks and talks about Concord and its region, in which Emerson, Thoreau, Channing, and Alcott should be the recorders and interlocutors." By July 1, Channing was far enough into it for Emerson to be able to read parts of it to Alcott, whose idea it may have been in the first place. By October 1, Channing had finished it.[1]

But in other respects, October was a disaster for Channing. He was, by common consent, moody, boorish, a bad husband, a bad father, given to uncontrollable outbursts of rage at the dinner table and frequent, violent verbal abuse of his wife, Ellen. Early in October, Ellen finally decided to leave Channing, taking the children with her. Channing, alone in the house with an ailing puppy, declined into mawkish despair and whimpering self-pity. "I have thoughts which rack me," he wrote in his journal. "If I can keep these out I can live. Pup is quiet. He may die, but I shall not disturb him. Tomorrow if it stops snowing some milk. . . . Don't think I can walk . . . storm increases, grows dark." Channing had lived right across the street from the Thoreaus since 1850. He had been Thoreau's almost daily walking companion for years. Thoreau did not condone Channing's domestic mess any more than he did his vulgarity of expression, but the two men were nevertheless very close in some ways. Channing wrote a biography of Thoreau later, and he knew him well enough to say his "chief principle was faith in all things, thoughts, and times." Both liked to walk, neither had a steady job other than writing. Both wanted above all to be writers. Channing's biographer thinks that what really formed the deepest bond between them at this time was that both were perceived by the town as failures, "as irresponsible idlers, a trial to their families, and no credit to their town."[2]

Channing had published three books of verse and one of prose by now, but none had done well, despite Emerson's praise. Thoreau had published one book, the unsold copies of which (706 out of an edition of 1,000) were returned to him this October. Though he made a joke out of the incident ("I now have a library of nearly nine hundred volumes, over seven hundred of which I wrote myself"), the fellow feeling of failure must have been very strong. As he revised *Walden*, Thoreau inserted in the section on "Former inhabitants and Winter Visitors" a moving salute to the Channing of happier, Walden days, now moping across the street. "The one who came from farthest to my lodge, through deepest snows and most dismal tempests, was a poet. A farmer, a hunter, a soldier, a reporter, even a philosopher, may be daunted; but nothing can deter a poet, for he is actuated by pure love."[3]

Alcott is the second friend eulogized in *Walden*. Their friendship was also of long standing. The two had, finally, quite different ideas (Alcott believing that man must impress his mark everywhere on nature, Thoreau believing the opposite) but there was between them both affection and a kind of old-fashioned high courtesy common among country-bred people. Thoreau called Alcott "the man of the most faith of any alive," and Alcott called Thoreau "a solid man and valid, sane and salt, and will keep forever—a friend who comes never too often nor stays too long." Alcott cherished a benevolent, approving, fatherly attitude toward Thoreau that made intellectual agreement unnecessary. His biographer, Odell Shepard, says that his journals, still largely unpublished, show him to have taken as much interest and pleasure in the growth of Thoreau's reputation as in the growth of his own daughter Louisa's. Alcott too was widely considered a dreamer, ineffectual, a failed man, a trial to Mrs. Alcott, and a very poor provider. To him, also, Thoreau could be imperially generous. "His words and attitude," he wrote, "always suppose a better state of things than other men are acquainted with, and he will be the last man to be disappointed as the ages revolve."[4]

Thoreau's friendship with Emerson was by far the most important, the most complicated, and as time passed, the least happy. By early

1853 their relations had been strained, often bitterly, for some time. Thoreau complained to his journal on May 24 that he "Talked, or tried to talk, with R. W. E. Lost my time—nay almost my identity. He, assuming a false opposition where there was no difference of opinion, talked to the wind—told me what I knew—and I lost my time trying to imagine myself somebody else to oppose him." Emerson found Thoreau cross-grained, contrary, always criticizing, always in opposition. More seriously, he thought Thoreau lacked ambition, that he pounded beans instead of pounding empires, led huckleberry parties instead of leading parties of engineers. "I fancy it an inexcusable fault in him that he is insignificant here in the town," Emerson wrote in mid-1851, "He speaks at Lyceum or other meeting but somebody else speaks and his speech falls dead and is forgotten." Emerson felt and tried to fight what he perceived as Thoreau's increasing, unreachable, provincial isolation and loneliness. Of an evening's talk with Thoreau in October 1851 he wrote, "we stated over again, to sadness, almost, the eternal loneliness . . . how insular and pathetically solitary, are all the people we know!"[5]

Thoreau appears constantly in Emerson's journals. To the end of his life, Emerson regarded Thoreau as his best friend. Even when Alzheimer's disease had set in and memory disintegrated before wit (unable to call up the word "umbrella," he would say "the thing visitors carry away"), affection too outlived memory. "What was the name of my best friend?" he once had to ask. Emerson also wrote what is still the best single short piece ever done on Thoreau, but Thoreau was never able to do the same for Emerson. Perhaps he felt that Emerson, unlike Channing and Alcott, didn't *need* his good opinion. When Emerson's mother died in November of 1853, a few days before the departure of Channing's family, Thoreau helped in a major way with the funeral arrangements, and in a journal note a few days later, there is this admission: "If there is any one with whom we have a quarrel, it is most likely that that one makes some just demand on us which we disappoint." In his current draft of *Walden*, after the glowing testimonials to Channing and Alcott, Thoreau writes, "There was one other with whom I had 'solid seasons,' long to be remembered, at his house in the village and who looked in upon me from time to time." It is the saddest sentence in the book, because of what it does not, will not say.

Perhaps it is merely the ultrasimple truth of Cordelia, but the most important friendship of Thoreau's life is buried in that flat sentence with no further attempt at a public marker.[6]

Just as sad—no simpler word exists—is the fact that however esteemed and even loved Thoreau was, he was often severely misunderstood by those closest to him. Emerson came to be so out of touch with Thoreau's reading and writing as to think that the man who wanted to create new Vedas lacked ambition. Sophia was so far from understanding what he had been after in *A Week* that she could be reported as having found "parts of it that sounded to me very much like blasphemy," and Channing once admitted that "I have never been able to understand what he meant by his life."[7]

83. Chesuncook

The final drive to fill out and complete *Walden* was interrupted by one other event this fall, his second trip to the Maine wilderness during the latter part of September. Leaving Boston on the thirteenth, the steamer went the "outside" route, which meant leaving the coast and going out of sight of land straight for Monhegan Island, a traditional landfall marking the entrance to Penobscot Bay. Thoreau and his fellow passengers saw it just before dawn. Landing at Bangor, Thoreau joined his cousin George Thatcher and their guide, Joe Aitteon, an Indian lumberman, and they set off up the Penobscot River for Chesuncook Lake, which lies between Moosehead Lake and Mount Katahdin, extending farther north than either. Thatcher wanted to hunt moose, Thoreau to study Indian ways. They went by stage, tying the canoe on top, as far as Moosehead Lake, crosssed the lake by steamer, and entered the woods at the northern end of the lake.

They did get a moose, and Thoreau described the whole process of retrieving the carcass, skinning and butchering, as a bloody, sorry, "tragical" business. They covered a good deal of country. Besides noting the omnipresent evidence of large-scale hunting, Thoreau turned his new botanical knowledge to describing the woods. He wrote some lovely and moving accounts of the forest, especially of the white pines he so loved, and he spent a good deal of time learning as much as he could about Indian languages. One of the high points of the trip for him was lying in the dark listening to the Indians talk in their own "unaltered Indian language." It was, he says, "a purely wild and primitive American sound . . . and I could not understand a syllable of it." It is as though he recognized, and relished the knowledge, that the conquest of the continent by the white man was still incomplete so long as the Indian retained his language. Back in Concord, Thoreau took time to work up his notes for a mid-December lecture on his moose hunt. Later, after the piece had grown somewhat, he would describe it as being about "The Moose, the Pine Tree, and the Indian."[1]

It has sometimes been lamented that Thoreau never wrote his book about the Indians, a book that might have created a more sympathetic, better informed view of American Indians. "A cruel fate robbed the world of a great work," wrote Albert Keiser in 1928. It is true that at one time Thoreau contemplated writing the ante-Columbian history of North America, and at another time "The Manners and Customs of the Indians of the Algonquin Group previous to contact with the White Man." It is also true that he had assembled over the years eleven notebooks with twenty-eight hundred pages of extracts and commentary, mostly the former. But though he was accustomed to doing elaborate historical scholarship from at least the early 1850s on, writing straight historical narrative was not his forte. He must have realized this, since, so far as is known, he never attempted even a draft of this project.[2]

Other factors weighed against his taking up this subject. He was not ahead of his time; at least three other works of major importance—sympathetic, informed books that still command attention—appeared during the years of Thoreau's greatest interest in the subject. They are Squier and Davis's *Ancient Monuments of the Mississippi Valley* (1848), Schoolcraft's massive *History of the Indian Tribes of the United States* (1851–1857), and Morgan's *League of the Iroquois* (1851). The Squier and Davis volume, the first of the new Smithsonian Contributions to Knowledge series, is still an underrated book. It documents the astonishing phenomena of the Indian burial mounds in the Midwest, works of art and engineering that are comparable in many ways to Stonehenge and Avebury in England, and which recent research suggests were built for similar reasons by people at a stage of cultural evolution exactly parallel to the builders of Avebury. Had Thoreau undertaken the Indian book, there is no real reason to believe he would have written anything better than these books, a conclusion he may well have reached on his own.[3]

He had interrupted his stay at Walden Pond for his first Maine trip, to Katahdin. Now he had interrupted his work on the *Walden* manuscript for a second trip. No doubt the timing was accidental, depending as it did on cousin George Thatcher, but it is significant that each of the first two trips to the Maine woods provided an infusion of authentic wilderness into the gentler, tamer, essentially civilized world of *Walden*.

Thoreau's narrative of the second trip is even plainer than the first. "Chesuncook" has the unadorned narrative flavor and easy pace of the *Jesuit Relations* (to which it refers frequently) instead of the Aeschylean, Promethean tone of parts of "Ktaadn." The emotional center of "Ktaadn" is the ecstatic, almost frantically inarticulate enounter with primitive nature on top of the mountain. The parallel emotional center of "Chesuncook" is the killing and skinning of the moose. "Ktaadn" announces the discovery of the truly wild. "Chesuncook" is a calm, balanced rendering of the account of the complicated relation between savagery and civilization. If it is tilted at all, it is in the direction of civilization.

Thoreau clearly retains his great zest for the primitive pine forest with its "wild, damp, and shaggy look, the countless fallen and decaying trees," the surface of the ground "everywhere spongy and saturated with moisture." Seeing from a distance a pair of timber scouts and their camp, he eagerly learns about their solitary and adventurous life searching for timber, and says with rare wishfulness, "I have often wished since that I was with them." But it is not a wilderness *life* but a wilderness *episode* or sabbatical that he craves. "I think that I could spend a year in the woods fishing and hunting just enough to sustain myself, with satisfaction." He does not now yearn to live forever free of civilization but, on the contrary, he is glad to get back to it after two weeks in the woods. "It was a relief to get back to our smooth, but still varied landscape. For a permanent residence, it seemed to me there could be no comparison between this and the wilderness, necessary as the latter is for a resource and a background, the raw material of all our civilization." Chesuncook is one of the founding statements of the conservation movement, remarkable not least for the unimpassioned, plain statement of the value of wilderness not as the opposite of, but as the raw material—in the largest, not just the commodity sense—of civilization. The conservation ethic proposed in "Chesuncook," with its call for "national preserves," is not hostile to civilization, not inspired by a distaste for human society or by a desire to escape it, but by a sense that true civilization will always require infusions of the spirit of wildness from time to time. "Not only for strength, but for beauty, the poet must, from time to time, travel the logger's path and the Indian's trail, to drink at some new and more bracing fountain of the Muses, far in the recesses of the wilderness."[4]

Just as Melville's *Typee* was part of the context of Thoreau's interest in primitivism in the first draft of "Ktaadn," so Gilpin's *Observations . . . on the Western Parts of England* and Evelyn's *Sylva* are important books for Chesuncook and its concerns for reforestation and conservation. *Sylva, or a Discourse of Forest trees and the Propagation of Timber* (1664; third edition 1679) is another neglected masterpiece of English literature of the land. Evelyn, usually regarded as a minor Restoration diarist and foil to Pepys, also wrote *Terra, a Philosophical Essay of Earth*, *Pomona . . . Concerning Fruit trees in Relation to Cider*, and a *Kalendarium Hortense or the Gard'ners Almanac*, all of which were known to Thoreau. *Sylva* shows Evelyn's interest in the utility of forests as well as their beauty. His book ranges from discussions of the usefulness of wood for national defense (the navy) to considerations of how many ancient peoples have held forests sacred. He is primarily interested in the propagation of forests, and his great emphasis on seeds and seeding clearly struck home to the Thoreau who was to spend so much effort on the same subject himself. Evelyn argues for conservation at least partly on utilitarian grounds—timber is needed for building. But he also cares about the forests as such, as his tone everywhere indicates. Evelyn is clearly angry about the general effort "not only to *fell* and *cut* down, but utterly to *extirpate*, *demolish* and *raze*, as it were, all those many goodly *woods*, and *forests*, which our more prudent *ancestors* left standing." Thoreau made copious extracts from *Sylva*, concentrating on propagation, conservation, and Evelyn's vigorous fondness for his subject. "Evelyn is as good as several old druids, and his 'Sylva' is a new kind of prayer-book, a glorifying of the trees and enjoying them forever, which was the chief end of his life." The Evelyn tone is very strong in "Chesuncook," where Thoreau has concentrated much of his own best writing on trees, and it would appear that much of what we think of as Thoreau's conservation ethic either derives from or is closely paralleled by Evelyn's seventeenth-century interest in the same problem.[5]

Citing the kings of England and their parks, Thoreau asks why we cannot have our national preserves, "our forests . . . for inspiration and our own true recreation?" "Chesuncook" is not only our earliest but also our sanest, most balanced call for preservation of the wilderness. And in thinking about parks as an expression of the relation between civilization and nature, Thoreau was only part of his times. In May 1853, New York had authorized the creation of a large central park, and in 1857, F. L. Olmsted and Calvert Vaux would win the design competition with their "Greensward" plan. The impulse behind Olmsted and Vaux's park has much in common with that behind *Walden*. Both appeal, and were designed to appeal, to the value of a primitive and frontier life "though in the midst of cities." Both the park and the book are among the last pre-Civil War expressions of optimism about the possibility of making nature a permanent part of American urban life.[6]

Not only is "Chesuncook" a balanced statement but coming where it did in the revising of *Walden*, it exerted a temperate, balancing effect on the final revisions. At this time in his life, the immense appeal of the wild weighs equally with a strong acknowledgment and acceptance of civilization:

> Perhaps our own woods and fields,—in the best wooded towns, where we need not quarrel about the huckleberries,—with the primitive swamps scattered here and there in their midst, but not prevailing over them, are the perfection of parks and groves, gardens, arbors, paths, vistas, and landscapes. They are the natural consequence of what art and refinement we as a people have,—the common which each village possesses, its true paradise, in comparison with which all elaborately and wilfully wealth-constructed parks and gardens are paltry imitations.[7]

Thoreau's idealism is at this period working in harness with his naturalist's realism and respect for fact, while his interest in nature is, in turn, yoked with his growing social concerns. "Chesuncook" was written and *Walden* finally revised at the moment of greatest equipoise in Thoreau's life. The only thing that was not in moderation at the moment was his driving compulsion to work. His December 19 letter to Blake harps almost exclusively on this iron string. Like muskrats building houses, Thoreau insists, "we must heap up a great pile of doing, for a small diameter of being," and his letter is punctuated at intervals with an impatient drumming ferocity Blake must have wondered about: "work—work—work! . . . Whether a man spends his day in an ecstacy or despondency, he must do some work to show for it . . . make your failures tragical by the earnestness and steadfastness of your endeavor. . . . Work—work—work!" As he badgered Blake to do, he did himself, throwing himself into *Walden* with renewed energy and just a hint of desperation.[8]

84. *January 1854:*
Walden Six

The last days of December 1853 brought the worst snowstorm Thoreau could remember. The wind blew the snow nearly horizontally. It was impossible to go anywhere, and when it was over, two feet had fallen. The new year brought thaws and then freezing rains until there was ice everywhere. Thoreau found it frustrating to try to study the snow, but the coatings of ice, the frost, and the crystals fascinated him as always. He also spent a good deal of time indoors this month, reading and writing. He read extensively in the *Jesuit Relations*, in John Josselyn's *Account of two Voyages to New England*, and in the literature of the picturesque. This month he read Gilpin's *Three Essays on the Picturesque*, which he saw at once to be the "key" to all of Gilpin, and he also read Uvedale Price's *Essays on the Picturesque*.[1]

He also went back this month to Cato's *De Re Rustica*. The thirty-six-year-old Thoreau noted with approval Cato's advice to begin building only when one had reached the age of thirty-six. From Cato he went on to the other Roman agricultural writers, Varro and Columella. Varro especially held his attention this January. Varro, a contemporary of Caesar and a supporter of Pompey, lived an active public life, and was also esteemed the most learned of all the Romans, though most of his works have not survived. His *Rerum Rusticarum*, written when he was eighty, is one of some seventy-four separate literary works he is known to have undertaken. Varro has the same careful attention to detail Thoreau liked in Cato; he has the same tough, earthy, farmer's common sense as Cato, the same practical attention to daily routine. What made Varro special to Thoreau, besides all the things he shared with Cato, was his interest in language and his fondness for speculating on the etymology of words. He could derive *spica* (ear of grain) from *spes* (hope), and *villa* from *veho* (to carry), "because the villa is the place to and from which things are carried."[2]

In mid-January, Thoreau noted how much he preferred "writers of the bronze age" to those of the Augustan age. This preference for the vigorous earthy beginnings over the polished perfections of later and higher culture was not new for him, but it had been getting stronger and is particularly pronounced this month. In preferring the agricultural writers to the epic poets, the *Jesuit Relations* to later, more sophisticated histories, and Gilpin and Price, who wrote mostly about nature, to Ruskin, who wrote mostly about art based on nature, Thoreau was being true to form. He must have hoped that his own current work would one day properly belong to the timeless company of bronze-age books, those vigorous, natural, rural writings. "I will be a countryman," he wrote in his January journal.[3]

But the real work of the winter was the sixth draft of *Walden*, begun late in 1853 and finished some time early in 1854, probably in January. It was the last major revision, adding some 119 leaves to the manuscript, which was now divided into chapters and was beginning to resemble the final book. The emphasis on the word "imagination" was now added to chapter two, as were admonitions to avoid despair and desperate haste. He redid part of "Solitude," emphasizing wild scenes and fall rains. He put in material quoted from Evelyn, and added more references to husbandry considered as a sacred calling. The experience of the Chesuncook trip is reflected now in the rejection of hunting and fishing he wrote into a chapter first called "Animal

Food," later changed to "Higher Laws." He added more animal stories, about dogs and cats, to "Brute Neighbors," and in "Housewarming," he wrote of his dreams of a "golden age but not a gilded one." As Professor Shanley has shown, "two-thirds of [Walden Six] was devoted to a fresh draft of 'Former Inhabitants; and Winter Visitors,' 'Winter Animals,' 'The Pond in Winter,' 'Spring,' and the first draft of 'Conclusion.'" Much of Walden Five had been devoted to giving autumn its proper weight, and now in Walden Six, winter was expanded and emphasized to complete the seasonal symmetry.[4]

Walden follows the seasons of the year, and Thoreau's revisions show his careful attention to this structural center, but he was at the same time working to emphasize other unifying aspects of the book, such as the concept of the imagination, the sense of the sacred, the idea of a prose poem of work and the earth, the double concept of nature as both scenery and force, the transcendental center represented by the chapter "Higher Laws," and the practical, ethical imperative of "Conclusion." Though *Walden* is based on the succession of the seasons, it is a mistake to concentrate too exclusively on that aspect. For one thing, building a book around the seasons was hardly a fresh idea. His recent reading alone furnished him with a variety of ways in which the seasons had already been used to structure a narrative. Varro's attempt to set up a practical schedule for major farm work led him to provide not one but two different seasonal structures. He first divides the year into the four familiar seasons, Spring, Summer, Autumn, and Winter, a division based on the solar year, and using the equinoxes as the seasonal boundaries. Each season is further subdivided in two parts and the whole year commences on February 7. Varro's second scheme was less rigidly fixed to the sun's revolution; it recognized six seasons, which he called Preparing time, Planting time, Cultivating time, Harvest time, Housing (storing) time, and Consuming time. Varro's second scheme is more subjective, more a matter of measuring off the year by human needs. What Varro's second scheme really shows is that the very concept of seasons—whether four or six or twelve or twenty-four, as in old China—is a human one, projected out onto nature.[5]

Columella also devotes a substantial part of his book on agriculture to a calendar of work to be done, which he specifies almost day by day. He begins his year with the period between January 13 and the first of February, the "time between mid-winter and the coming of the west wind." Like Cato and Varro, Columella aims to produce a practical and useful book.

Immediately after January 1st it will be proper to plant pepperwort. In the month of February rue, either as a plant or as a seed, and asparagus, and again the seed of the onion and the leek; likewise if you want to have the yield in the spring and summer, you will bury in the ground the seeds of radish and turnip. . . . For ordinary garlic and African garlic are the last seeds which can be sown at this season.[6]

In the seventeenth century, Evelyn had prepared a gardener's calendar, which directed the gardener what to do in orchard and kitchen garden each month. Evelyn begins with January. Thoreau was familiar with Evelyn's calendar, and he also knew that Linnaeus had prepared a *Calendarium Florae* in which he showed how the blossoming of specific flowers was so predictable that it could be used as a timepiece to calculate when to perform "certain labors of rural economy." Thoreau was familiar with numerous other eighteenth-century calendars. In the last paragraph of *The Natural History of Selbourne*, Gilbert White wrote, "When I first took the present work in hand, I proposed to have added an *Annus-Historico-Naturalis*, or the Natural History of the Twelve Months of the Year." One reason he did not do so was that a Mr. Aiken of Warington had already done "somewhat of this sort." Aiken also later extracted from White's papers a *Naturalist's Calendar with Observations in Various Branches of Natural History* (1795). And before White had published his book, Daines Barrington had issued a form for the observation of periodical natural phenomena, in which he provided "columns for meterological readings, and for the appearances or disappearance of leaves, flowers, insects, and birds." Barrington's blank book was published annually and used by White. Thoreau remained fascinated with exactly this sort of detailed calendar keeping (now called the science of phenology) to the end of his life, and his own prodigious labors at constructing a calendar of Concord phenomena need to be seen in the light of this well-established and to Thoreau well-known tradition of naturalist's calendars.[7]

Meantime he was shaping *Walden*, and it was hardly possible to write a book consisting largely of observations of natural phenomena without paying major attention to the seasons. *Walden* is perhaps the most attractive of all the books that tell the story of a natural year. But Thoreau had another, equally pressing concern, and that was to make sure that *Walden* was not just another naturalist's calendar. *Walden* is unlike any previous book of natural observations. It is closest perhaps to Gilbert White's *Natural History of Selbourne*, which had now become one of Thoreau's favorite books.[8]

White had been born in 1720, almost a hundred years before Thoreau, and the book by which he is remembered appeared in 1789, a year mostly remembered for other occurrences. White had studied Ray and Linnaeus, and from them had learned to understand the study of nature as the study of living things. White, like Thoreau, was a stay-at-home. He never left England, traveling only in the southern and central counties, and spending most of his life in and around Selbourne. His book, written in the form of letters, is filled with patient, clear observations. One of his editors has wisely said that "White is interesting because nature is interesting." White was also interested in writing local history, which he thought ought to include natural productions and occurrences as well as antiquities. His book has remained fresh because of its vivid, local, painstakingly detailed observations. It deserves its reputation, but it is altogether different from *Walden*. In White, there is observation and fact, but there is no observer. We get almost no sense of White himself. He was a man curious about everything, but it is a disembodied curiosity. *The Natural History of Selbourne* suggests that there are limits to the mere reporting of close observation. By contrast, in *Walden*, we get a strong sense of Thoreau the observer on every page. Where White is almost wholly objective, and the Wordsworth of *The Prelude* is almost wholly subjective, the Thoreau of *Walden* has managed both, giving us a strong sense of the observer as well as of the thing observed.[9]

Thoreau was perfectly conscious of this as an aim. It may have been Varro's subjective division of the year that moved Thoreau to write a long journal entry at the end of January on getting the most out of winter. "It is for man the seasons and all their fruits exist," the passage begins. In April his mind was still running on the same theme. "I am not interested in mere phenomena, though it were the explosion of a planet, only as it may have lain in the experience of a human being." And again, in early May, returning to the same insight, he rearticulated the point of view that underlies *Walden* and that distinguishes it from all previous natural history:

> There is no such thing as pure *objective* observation. Your observation, to be interesting, i.e. to be significant, must be *subjective*. The sum of what the writer of whatever class has to report is simply some human experience, whether he be poet or philosopher or man of science. The man of most science is the man most alive, whose life is the greatest event. Senses that take cognizance of outward things merely are of no avail. It matters not where or how far you travel, the further commonly the worse,—but how much alive you are.[10]

We have made too much of the seasonal structure of *Walden*, too easily assuming that the book's message is to accept the seasonal cycle of nature as final widsom. Such a view, essentially objective, conservative, and tragic, is not at last what Thoreau wanted or taught. The book opens not with a season but with the exaggeratedly long chapter on economics, the detailed subjective economics of the everyday life of one individual person. The book ends not with a season but with the passionately flung challenge not to resign oneself to the iron law of seasonal flux, but for each person now to live more fully than those who went before. There is no more tonic or stirring bit of nineteenth-century American writing than the "Conclusion" of *Walden*. Neither Emerson nor Whitman ever wrote a better—or a more carefully prepared for—call to have the courage to live fully. In the end, *Walden* is not about submission to nature, nor is it an effort to exalt the individual above the community. Nature teaches us to want to reach beyond nature. The conclusion of *Walden* is a call to everyone, whatever their present position, whether living alone or in crowds, in the woods or in the city, to have the courage to live a life according to the dictates of the imagination, to live the life one has dreamed.

85. February and March 1854: Triumph of the Organic

That upwelling, spring-returning, victorious sense of life came back to Thoreau himself in full force as the winter edged into spring. January he thought "the hardest month to get through," the only month of pure winter. "December belongs to the Fall; is a wintry November: February, to the Spring; it is a snowy March." Once again, however, in Minott's phrase and like Minott himself, Thoreau "toughed it through the winter." The first days of February were warm, melting days. The sun's heat was great enough to set the sand foliage flowing in the deep cut. As the strangely exciting sand- and clay-bearing streams flowered forth, Thoreau recognized it once more as the truest spring. "This is the frost coming out of the ground; this is spring. It precedes the green and flowery spring as mythology does ordinary literature and poetry." The sand foliage was his best metaphor for spring. The earth literally sprang forth, ex-pressing itself. Together with his interest in crystals and the analogy between crystallization and leaf formation as observed by Goethe, it was one of his oldest interests, and one that never lost its fascination. As time passed, the flowing sand bank seemed ever more apt and exciting as a key to the real meaning of spring. *Lapidae crescunt.*[1]

One of the most significant additions to Walden Six and the cleanup version—the seventh draft, which was probably completed during February—is the dramatic expansion of the description of the clay bank in "Spring." The phenomenon itself appeared on February second. In his journal he wrote "That sand foliage! It convinces me that Nature is still in her youth,—that florid fact about which mythology merely mutters,—that the very soil can fabulate as well as you or I. It stretches forth its baby fingers on every side. Fresh curls spring forth from its bald brow." The real point, and now everything from Linnaeus on, all the gathered force of his new natural history reading and study, lies behind the statement, simplicity itself in its expression, "There is nothing inorganic. This earth is not, then, a mere fragment of dead history, strata upon strata, like the leaves of a book, an object for a museum and an antiquarian, but living poetry, like the leaves of a tree,—not a fossil earth, but a living specimen."[2]

One of the earliest elements of Thoreau's journal when he first began it in the fall of 1837 was his excited reading of Goethe's *Italian Journey*, with its great culminating moment when the importance and centrality of the leaf as the fundamental unit of botany first becomes clear to Goethe. The essence of the insight was that certain laws underlie and guide all natural processes. That same fall, Thoreau had been struck by the similarity between leaves and ice crystals. On a late

November morning in 1837, when everything was covered with a dense hoarfrost, he had marveled at the "wonderful ice-foliage. . . . It struck me," he wrote, "that those ghost leaves [of frost] and the green ones whose forms they assume, were the creatures of the same law."[3]

Thoreau never lost this view of things. His sense of the pervasiveness of law grew only stronger over the years. Later this spring of 1854 he would ask "who shall distinguish between the *law* by which a brook finds its river, the *instinct* [by which] a bird performs its migrations, and the *knowledge* by which a man steers his ship round the globe?" In February and March, watching the flowing sand, it seemed to him also to obey the law of leaves. "You find in the very sands an anticipation of the vegetable leaf. . . . The atoms have already learned the law. . . . No wonder that the earth expresses itself outwardly in leaves, which labors with the idea thus inwardly. The o'erhanging leaf sees here its prototype. The earth is pregnant with law."[4]

This is not only a great affirmative hugging of nature, a clear choice *for* the organic principle of nature, the vital anti-entropic force Whitehead says is best symbolized by spring, but it is also a choice for nature over history and a clear rejection of the burden of history. "Above all," he had written back in December 1853, when he was reading Layard's account of the discovery of ancient Nineveh, "deliver me from a city built on the site of a more ancient city, the materials of the one being the ruins of the other. There the dwellings of the living are in the cemeteries of the dead, and the soil is blanched and accursed." The "Spring" chapter of *Walden*, with its exhilarating description of the flowing clay bank at its center, is finally an affirmation of foliage over fossil, natural fact over historical relic, life over death.[5]

Thoreau's mood this February stayed mostly at the exhaustingly high level of excitement he reached in the first week. The rest of February was changeable weather; snowstorms and intense cold were followed by mild days of "peculiar softness and luminousness." There were, he remarked, "hardly three days together alike." He was working constantly on the *Walden* manuscript, making changes, cutting out substantial amounts now from all parts of the book from "Economy" to "Spring."[6]

At the same time that his most important book, and the longest in incubation, was finally reaching maturity and demanding more and more time for revisions, a larger share of the family graphite business was also falling on his shoulders, as his correspondence shows. He bore it willingly. There was no complaining about this or any other family related work, though when, in early April, he was out surveying for others, he fell into his habitual Apollonian grumbling about keeping the sheep of King Admetus.[7]

March brought its share of "raw, thick, misty weather," with winds strong enough to blow down an old barn over in Conantum. By mid-March arrangements for publishing *Walden* were firm at last, as he wrote Greeley, who was still after Thoreau to do a volume of miscellanies. Greeley, decent man that he was, was quick with his congratulations. On March 28, almost nine years to the day after he had gone out to the pond with an ax to cut the arrowy pines for his hut, the first batch of printer's proofs of *Walden* arrived to be corrected.[8]

86. Spring and Summer 1854:
Anthony Burns

Thoreau worked over the proofs of *Walden* all spring. He was an interminable reviser, and could not stop improving his pages even after they were out of his hands. "When I have sent off my manuscripts to the printer, certain objectionable sentences and expressions are sure to obtrude themselves on my attention with force, though I had not consciously suspected them before." Working on *Walden* took most of his time this spring, but there was also time for business and family and for frequent walks and river trips. In April and May he kept close inventory on the spring, watching the leafing of trees, shrubs, and flowers, establishing, in Linnaean fashion, the precise order in which the leafing of plants occurred. He kept careful track of birds and birdsong. He bought a telescope and it quickly rewarded him by showing a white-headed eagle.[1]

Thoreau had always had very little capacity for boredom; he had less than usual this spring. His health held, only one comment in the journal betrays anything at all. "A little relaxation in your exertion, a little idleness, will let in sickness and death into your own body," he wrote, but he kept stubbornly to his belief that "every human being is the artificer of his own fate in these respects. The well have no time to be sick." He was continually busy. Amid his lists and catalogs he could still complain about the barrenness of most scientific accounts of nature. His own observations, he kept reminding himself, had to be subjective as well as objective. In his best observations, now as always, one can both *see* the thing described and *feel* its effect on Thoreau. For example, he describes a particularly fine day as a "washing day,—a strong rippling wind, and all things bright." On May 9 he planted melons, a specialty for which he was famed locally and with which he gave summer melon parties for favored friends and neighbors.[2]

But even with *Walden* to correct and revise, the spring to record, and the growing demands of the family business, Thoreau found himself drawn into the Anthony Burns affair in Boston. Early in 1854, Stephen Douglas had introduced a bill to open the Kansas and Nebraska territories (essentially everything west of Missouri and Iowa and north of Texas) to settlement. From the Northern point of view, which Thoreau shared, there were serious problems with the bill. First of all, the United States had made prior treaties with the Indians, giving them most of the territory in question for "as long as grass grows and water runs." Second, Douglas had proposed that the issue of whether or not the new states to be made from the territories would be slave or free should be decided by popular vote in those territories. Much of the North was furious at the proposal, since it set aside the Missouri Compromise that had lasted for over thirty years, and it undermined the Compromise of 1850 by permitting the extension of slavery west of Missouri and north of latitude thirty-six degrees, thirty minutes. An important part of the Compromise of 1850 had been a new fugitive slave law, which had not gone down well with most of the North, and had only gone down at all because of Daniel Webster's vast prestige.

Northern resistance to the proposed new Kansas-Nebraska Act took the form of vowing to set aside the hated fugitive slave law if the new bill passed. On May 24, Anthony Burns, a runaway slave, was arrested in Boston. On the twenty-fifth the U.S. Congress passed the Kansas-Nebraska bill. On the twenty-sixth a Boston mob tried to rescue Burns from the courthouse. They failed. Burns was identified, taken to the harbor and put on a ship for return to the South. But it had taken a battalion of U.S. artillery, four platoons of marines, the sheriff's posse, twenty-two companies of state militia, and forty thousand dollars to return Anthony Burns to slavery. He was the last to be returned from Massachusetts. The public was greatly stirred up over the incident, Thoreau along with the rest. He began composing a lecture or speech on the danger of submitting to an unjust law. The subject grew on him, would not leave him alone. Out walking for lilies or for the serenity of a lake, the incident kept rising to mind. Eventually, on July 4, on the ninth anniversary of his move out to the pond for personal liberation, he delivered, in Framingham, his "Slavery in Massachusetts" talk.

It is strong stuff, not quite advocating violent disobedience but coming very close. The lecture was toned down a bit from the journal version in this regard. The question was not, he thought, whether the fugitive slave law was constitutional, but whether it was right. "I wish my countrymen to consider, that whatever the human law may be, neither an individual nor a nation can ever commit the least act of injustice against the obscurest individual, without having to pay the penalty for it." The law was wrong. It should not be obeyed. If the state said obey it, the state was wrong and should be disobeyed. Thoreau's language veered toward the violence he would still not openly call for. "Rather than do this [obey the fugitive slave law] I need not say what match I would touch, what system endeavor to blow up,—but as I love my life, I would side with the light, and let the dark earth roll from under me." The essay is strong in its denunciation of the governor, the courts, the papers ("I have heard the gurgling of the sewer through every column"), but it is important to remember that this essay reflects a wide segment of popular feeling of the time. There is no doubt Thoreau felt strongly about the issue, so strongly that he slipped into some old Christian rhetoric. In his notes as in his speech, Thoreau makes heavy and uncharacteristic use of heaven and hell, angels and devils, adopting, for the time and the cause, the rhetorical style of William Lloyd Garrison, Wendell Phillips, and Frederick Douglass:

> I dwelt before, perhaps, in the illusion that my life passed somewhere only *between* heaven and hell, but now I cannot persuade myself that I do not dwell *wholly within* hell. The site of that political organization called Massachusetts is to me morally covered with volcanic scoriae and cinders, such as Milton describes in the infernal regions.[3]

Freedom is one of the ideas we cannot do without, though various terms for freedom become stale or suspect. But whether called liberty by the revolutionary generation, emancipation by the Civil War generation, freedom in the first half of the twentieth century, or liberation, as now, it is only the terms that change, becoming valorized or discredited by turns. One of the important meanings of Thoreau's life, and of *Walden*, is the imperative of freedom or liberation. It is thus entirely fit that the final stages of the printing and publishing of *Walden* should coincide with Thoreau's renewed involvement in the antislavery movement, and the aftermath of the Anthony Burns affair. Nor is it an accident that the earliest stages of Thoreau's move to Walden coincided with the emergence of Frederick Douglass, and the publication of Douglass's narrative of how he gained his freedom. *Walden* is about self-emancipation, but not at the expense of ignoring the problem of external, physical freedom. The Thoreau who sought his own freedom was, inevitably, involved in the political movement to abolish slavery, and his involvement grew rather than diminished as time went on.

87. July and August 1854:
Walden

Walden modernizes and extends the idea of freedom by reviving the classical, Stoic emphasis on *autarky* or self-rule, by domesticating into an American context the Hindu concept of the "final liberation" of the spirit, and by equating freedom with the wildness he understood to be the source and raw material of all civilization and culture. Thoreau thus transcends what is often said of the Hindu tradition, that the quest for an exclusively inner freedom can lead to acquiescence in outward tyranny. He links, in his life and in his writing, the idea of the free autonomous individual, and the individual taking his stand in the world, marching to a different drummer perhaps, but marching all the same. India in this century has taken back its own tradition improved and made practicable by Thoreau. Gandhi, drawing explicitly on Thoreau, could say in his treatise on *Indian Home Rule*, "Real home-rule is self-rule or self-control. . . . If man will only realize that it is unmanly to obey laws that are unjust, no man's tyranny will enslave him. This is the key to self-rule or home-rule."[1]

Thoreau says near the beginning of *Walden* that he went to the woods to see what the woods had to teach. As we reach the concluding chapter, the stirring, extravagant, Beethoven-like ode to life, we are reminded that this celebration and exhortation to "explore thyself" is intended as an answer to that opening question, what does a life close to nature teach?

It taught Thoreau the imperative of courage, the absolute value of freedom, a conception of nature as law, a respect for the limits imposed on us by that law, and, finally, the necessity of individual wholeness or integrity if one was to avoid a life of despair. "I learned this, at least, by my experiment, that if one advances confidently in the direction of his dreams, and endeavors to live the life which he has imagined, he will meet with a success unexpected in common hours." Courage, then, is the first, most important thing learned by living close to nature. Without courage, the other lessons are useless, they can be learned but not lived. Without courage, freedom is only a word. With courage, freedom becomes the opposite of slavery and the absolute ground of human life. "If slavery is not wrong," said Lincoln, "nothing is wrong."[2]

Thoreau also learned the role of law and the necessity of limits. Law pervades nature, and certain limits and boundaries exist which must be respected. Thoreau's sense of this was not negative, belittling, or admonishing. Law was, in his view, something that connected seemingly isolated phenomena. In accepting the laws of nature, he accepted nature. In accepting nature he accepted not only himself but things beyond himself. From the first draft on, he had insisted

> We can never have enough of Nature. We must be refreshed by the sight
> of inexhaustible vigor, vast and Titanic features, the sea-coast with its
> wrecks, the wilderness with its living and its decaying trees, the thun-
> dercloud, and the rain which lasts three weeks and produces freshers. We
> need to witness our own limits transgressed, and some life pasturing freely
> where we never wander.[3]

Life in the woods also taught integrity, in the sense in which Erik Erikson uses the word when he describes the final stage of a person's life as a struggle between a sense of integrity and a sense of despair and disgust. Integrity consists, for Erickson, in "the ego's accrued assurance of its proclivity for order and meaning. It is a post-narcissistic love of the human ego—not of the self—as an experience which conveys some world order and spiritual sense, no matter how dearly paid for." The alternative, that is, what happens in a life that falls short of this integrity, is put with terrible simplicity. It is simply despair. "The lack or loss of this accrued ego integration is signified by fear of death: the one and only life cycle is not accepted as the ultimate of life. Despair expresses the feeling that time is short, too short for the attempt to start another life and to try out alternate roads to integrity. Disgust hides despair."[4]

One of the important issues Thoreau built into *Walden* itself is exactly this question of integrity versus despair, thus recognizing, long before Erikson, the problem of the final or eighth stage of Erikson's famous life cycle. Thoreau explicitly raises the question of the integrity of the ordinary working person in the seventh paragraph of the first version of *Walden*, and during the 1852 revision, he added, three paragraphs later, the striking assertion that "the mass of men lead lives of quiet desperation," going on to amplify and explain what he means by despair. As the book went through draft after draft, Thoreau added references to depair and desperation and examples of integrity. From his friends, his walks, and his reading he gathered a growing heap of examples on which to build that cumulative assurance of the mind's own predisposition for order and meaning. And in his "Conclusion," he brings us back again to the subject, asking "why should we be in such desperate haste to succeed, and in such desperate enterprises?" To which he replies with the great parable of the artist in the city of Kouroo who was disposed to strive after perfection, "the artist who decides to make one thing right, though he do nothing else in his life." As he searched "without haste but without rest" (Goethe's motto) for the proper materials, "his friends gradually deserted him, for they grew old in their works and died, but he grew not older by a moment. His singleness of purpose and resolution, and his elevated piety, endowed him, without his knowledge, with perennial youth." He labors on the staff, ages pass, his city falls, the dynasty and the race pass away. "By the time he had smoothed and polished the staff, Kalpa was no longer the pole star and ere he had put on the ferule and the head adorned with precious stones, Brahma had awoke and slumbered many times." When at last the staff is done, it "suddenly expanded before the eyes of the astonished artist into the fairest of all the creations of Brahma. He had made a new system in making a staff, a world with full and fair proportions. . . . The material was pure, and his art was pure; how could the result be other than wonderful."[5]

Finishing *Walden* now, after so many years spent collecting the right materials, writing, rewriting, adding and rejecting, was just such an experience for Thoreau himself, the artist of Concord. From 1852 this parable had stood in the manuscript, kernel of the later "Conclusion," and constant reminder to Thoreau that he must be worthy of having the story told about *him*, that this book must be done right, though he should do nothing else. Finishing the book was a triumph of sorts, an assurance of the mind's continuing proclivity for order and meaning, proof that it could be done. Thoreau expresses himself this July in the language of fruitfulness and completion. On July 18, rambling up by Sam Barrett's he felt, he said, "a crisis in the season." Along one road in particular he found so many berries he felt he had "wandered into a land of greater fertility, an up-country Eden."[6]

On August 9, in the *New York Tribune*, under "New Publications" there appeared a ten-inch piece headed "Unprecedented success of the greatest of American Romances, *Fashion and Famine* by Mrs. Ann S. Stephens." This was followed by a two-inch announcement of *Walden* headed "Life in the Woods," which in turn was followed by a three-inch piece on "*Magdalen Hepburn*, A Tale of Scottish History, by the author of *Margaret Maitland*."

This year the first of the soon-to-be-famous Concord grapes were offered for sale. They too had been a long time in preparation. The seedlings had first been planted in 1843, the first grapes had matured in 1849. Now, in the summer of 1854, Thoreau's garden, his book, and his life grew ripe together. On August 10, the day after *Walden* was published, Thoreau carefully noted,

First muskmelon in garden.

IX. 1854-1862

The Economy of Nature

88. Night and Moonlight

THE PUBLICATION OF *Walden* brought Thoreau a sense of completeness which he expressed in metaphors of fruitfulness in his August journal as he turned to consider future projects. A "seed-time of character" might lead, he supposed, to a "harvest of thought. . . . Already some of my small thoughts—fruit of my spring life—are ripe." He thought, for example, that "walking may be a science, so far as the direction of a walk is concerned. . . . There is, no doubt, a particular season of the year when each place may be visited with most profit and pleasure, and it may be worth the while to consider what that season is in each case." A few days later he thought he might "describe some of those rough all-day walks across lots." His notes are full of references to seeds, fruits—especially huckleberries—and early autumnal colors, particularly the purple grasses. He made list after list of birds. All this material would eventually be useful for one project or another, but at the moment of midsummer, after *Walden*, he had no one purpose or project to give direction to his mornings of literary labor, which were now as various as his walks.[1]

As a result, his dominant mood this summer is not one of joy or purpose or accomplishment, but one of culpable aimlessness. He had felt the year come to its high point somewhere in mid-July, and by July 28 he was talking of having "postponed the fulfillment of many of our hopes for this year, and, having as it were attained the ridge of the summer, commenced to descend the long slope toward winter, the afternoon and down-hill of the year." Early in August he did some surveying in Lincoln. The hired work left him feeling ill-employed. July had also been a hot month, so hot that he couldn't work up in his attic room after supper, but was compelled to "sit below with the family at evening." Rather ungraciously he complained (in his journal) of needing to cultivate privacy, of a feeling of dissipation from too much company. He tried taking walks in the evening, but they were not immediately productive.[2]

"July has been to me a trivial month," he noted wearily. He began a letter to Blake with humorless self-accusation. "I have spent a rather unprofitable summer thus far." He berated himself in mid-August for his failure to get up early, for being "overrun" with "society," for having "drank tea and coffee and made myself cheap and vulgar." This mood, which could be called gloomy and bitter if it were not so petty, is hard to account for this month. Perhaps he felt his life to be trivial compared to the intensity of the days that had given him *Walden*. Perhaps he was withdrawing from the politically fevered "Slavery in Massachusetts." Or perhaps he was reacting to his own renewed determination to go on the lecture circuit. He had never been a real success as a lecturer, not compared to Emerson, and it was not something he enjoyed.[3]

His mood this summer may also have been a response to the terrible heat and the long, appalling drought that gripped the land. Before mid-August the leaves had all turned. Those on the maples wilted. The birches dropped their leaves entirely, and many of the younger trees died. Fruit died before it ripened. Anywhere one dug, "you find it all dusty." In one place Thoreau found no moisture at all in a four-foot layer of topsoil. The usual haze of August in New England was intensified with smoke from innumerable fires. Not just woods but meadows burned, with fire going as deep as three feet down into the sod. Brooks's meadows in the northwest part of town burned for "several weeks." On some mountains, Thoreau was told, "it burns all the soil down to the rock."[4]

The drought broke late in August with rains and cooler weather. On September 4 and 7, Thoreau went for long moonlit walks and somewhere about this time he decided to do a series of lectures on night and moonlight. The cool nights of early fall were as different as possible from the dry heats of the summer days. They were, said Thoreau, the "negation of day." He went out on the river, and his evening observations speak of mist, dampness, and coolness. He reveled in water. "The sound of this gurgling water running thus by night as by day falls on all my dashers, fills all my buckets, overflows my float boards, turns all the machinery of my nature, makes me a flume, a sluice-way to the springs of nature. Thus I am washed; thus I drink and quench my thirst." The nights were "medicative and fertilizing," and in the daytime he now combed through his journals and compiled a list of passages on night and moonlight, most of which dated back to a series of night walks during the summer of 1851. Thoreau worked up the moonlight material into a lecture which he gave in Plymouth on October 8. No fully satisfactory text of it has yet been assembled or printed, but the extensive fragments are highly suggestive.[5]

The moon was a familiar subject for Thoreau, identified earlier with Ellen Sewall and Lydia Emerson, with writing poetry and with Diana, sister of Apollo in Greek myth. He identified himself still with Apollo, bound to toil. By contrast, however, "Diana still hunts in the New England sky." Thoreau's moon manuscripts exhibit the usual learning and reach, quoting the Puranas, Ossian, Raleigh, Origen, Augustine, du Bartas, and citing Beulah, Nineveh, and the Incas. Some of the passages are reminiscent of Byron, of Longfellow's *Voices of the Night*, even of the nocturnes of Chopin (1810–1849). Romanticism had favored the form, in music, verse, or prose. Thoreau's quiet, cool moonlight sketches are prose nocturnes. "I turn and see the silent, contemplative, spiritual moon shedding the softest imaginable light on the western slopes, as if, after a thousand years of polishing, their surfaces were just beginning to be bright; a pale whitish lustre. Already the crickets chirp to the moon a different strain, and the night wind blows, rustling the leaves, from where? what gave it birth?"[6]

Like Longfellow, Thoreau sought to express the voices of the night. Moonlight was a language, he thought, a Sanscrit with its "world of poetry, its weird [in the sense of fated] teachings, its oracular suggestions." He worried about how to get the qualities of the night into his own language. "I fear that I have not put duskiness enough into my night and moonlight walks. Every sentence should contain some twilight or night." Thoreau also thought, in this pre-Jungian era, that night could symbolize the unconscious. By mastering the language of night he hoped, he said, to conquer some realms from the night. Night brought him closer to the origins of things, an experience that could be profoundly unsettling. "As the shades begin to gather around us, our primeval instincts are aroused, and we steal forth from our lairs, like the inhabitants of the jungle, in search of those silent and brooding thoughts which are the natural prey of the intellect." The predatory image is comparable to something Henry James the elder once said. "The natural inheritance of everyone who is capable of spiritual life is an unsubdued forest where the wolf howls and the obscene bird of night chatters." Indeed the whole subject of night has, for Thoreau, sinister, tragic, misanthropic potential. Talking of night as the "mere negation of day," he added, "Death is with me and life far away." He found it ominous that, as we grow older, "we have more to say about evening, less about morning." Getting up at midnight also helped him put distance between himself and others. "I do not value any view of the universe into which man and his institutions enter at once and necessarily and absorb a great share of the attention," he wrote.[7]

By undertaking to lecture on night and moonlight, Thoreau was, in part, playing with the view of many of his contemporaries that transcendentalism was mere moonshine. With his usual weapons of irony and paradox he would show them that it was indeed moonshine, but the moon would turn out to be more light than they bargained for. *Walden* had ended "Only that day dawns to which we are awake. There is more day to dawn. The sun is but a morning star." One version of his "Moonlight" paper ends, "So might we walk by sunlight, seeing the sun but as a moon—a comparatively faint and, in fact, reflected light—and the day as a brooding night in which we glimpse some stars still." It is a negative, a passive, and a paradoxical version of the end of *Walden*, an interesting experiment, begun with the uncharacteristic assertion that "men do not make or choose their own paths . . . but what the powers permit each one enjoys," and ending with convoluted cleverness. The moonlight project, conceived as the night piece to balance or complement the sunny moods of *Walden*, was quickly taken up and quickly dropped.[8]

89. New Friends

As the appearance of *Walden* set Thoreau looking for new topics, it also brought him new friends, as well as new attention from old ones.

He had, for once, some grounds for his ritual complaint that he was too much in society. Emerson had written a letter to Richard Bentley, his English publisher, warmly recommending the book. There was a review by John S. Dwight, a letter from Thomas Wentworth Higginson, and an especially warm and admiring one from Richard Fuller. In mid-August, John Russell, the Salem botanist, came for a visit that whetted Thoreau's scientific interests. In early September came Samuel Worcester Rowse, a quiet young portrait painter, born in Maine, an associate of Eastman Johnson, and best known today for his early portraits. Rowse stayed with the Thoreaus, went for outings with Henry, and, at Cynthia's request, drew a crayon portrait of Thoreau which many have thought the best likeness ever done of him. It may be a bit more youthful and idealized than its subject actually appeared that summer of *Walden*. The expression is gentle and the portrait has a soft, open quality not seen in the later photographic likenesses.[1]

Thoreau also wrote another of his philosophic letters to Blake just between getting his first specimen copy of *Walden* and the actual day of publication. He had been corresponding with Blake ever since the latter initiated it with a letter in 1848. Blake, now thirty-eight, was a Harvard alumnus, a sometime minister and teacher, now a leading liberal spirit in Worcester, a town with a strong intellectual community, even though, as Higginson observed, it had an air of country and "the main street is filled all day with country wagons and you buy your firewood from the carts." Blake's Worcester circle included Theo Brown, a tailor and the wit of the city whom Thoreau met first in 1849, Higginson, John Weiss, Edward Everett Hale, David Wasson, and others, who gathered from time to time in Brown's shop. On his occasional visits to Worcester, Thoreau would sit in the back window of Brown's tailor shop at the corner of Main and Pearl streets, "fashioning the habiliments of the soul, while near him Theo would calmly continue cutting out habiliments for the wear of the body, and Harry Blake, with his eyes glistening with delight behind his gold-bowed glasses, would follow the arguments of each."[2]

Thoreau was fond of his Worcester friends. He lectured there, went for walks with them, and something in Blake himself called out Thoreau's most important and most revealing letters, which are filled with an austere intellectual intimacy. Blake later said that their friendship was "almost an impersonal one," mostly conducted on the level of ideas, and mostly on one side. "Our conversation," Blake told an early biographer of Thoreau's, "or rather his talking, when we were together, was in the strain of his letters and of his books." Blake proved a worthy correspondent. When Thoreau's manuscripts came into his keeping, he tried to give the unpublished material the seasonal shape he knew Thoreau wanted. He reread Thoreau's letters all his life and said he was "still warmed and instructed by them, with more force occasionally than ever before; so that in a sense they are still in the mail, have not altogether reached me yet, and will not probably before I die."[3]

Very shortly after *Walden* was published, Thoreau received a congratulatory letter from a Daniel Ricketson. Ricketson was a Quaker and an abolitionist from an old New Bedford family. Though he was married and had four children, he was, like Thoreau, a semidomesticated recluse. He had striven all his life, he informed Thoreau, "to live as free from the restraint of mere forms and ceremonies as I possibly can." Ricketson, now forty-one, had recently built a cozy cluttered rustic shanty with a hard-pine floor on the grounds of his new home "Brooklawn," north of New Bedford, and he spent much of his time and received many of his friends in this lodge or den. Ricketson's feeling for nature was thoroughly sincere. "All through my boyhood," he told Thoreau, "*the country* haunted my thoughts." He read widely, entertained and corresponded with many well-known figures of the day, wrote a *History of New Bedford* (1858), and two volumes of poetry, *The Autumn Sheaf* (1869), and *The Factory-bell and Other Poems* (1873). He became a frequent visitor in Concord and Thoreau felt welcome at the shanty in New Bedford. Ricketson was a crooked stick. He had, in Tom Blanding's nice phrase, a "patchwork personality." He was a hypochondriac, a sufferer, a man in constant spiritual turmoil. He also complained that Thoreau paid him too little attention. Ricketson always thought he wanted more than Thoreau would give. Actually he only wanted more than he was capable of taking. When Thoreau wrote him an introductory letter of thanks in which he tried to share and communicate his enthusiasm for the works of William Gilpin, Ricketson could only see offense. He found the letter "hastily written and hardly satisfactory."[4]

But Ricketson was loyal, a good companion, and an intermittent presence in Thoreau's life from now on, despite his marked limitations. He was, in the jargon of the era, a "seeker," a restless and unsatisfied soul like Isaac Hecker or Ellery Channing, but beneath the surface turmoil was a deeply conventional nature that expressed itself in conventional Christianity and old-fashioned Cowperian verse. *The Autumn Sheaf* has what might be taken as a Thoreauvian frontispiece showing the "feelosopher" Ricketson sitting in the door of his vine-covered shanty, but his poems convey the sensibility of an eighteenth-century vicar reposing "Not in the decorated halls of wealth, / Where flows the goblet round the groaning board, . . . / But in the calmer scenes of Nature's court, / In woodland shades, beside the murmuring rill." Yet this same man had a local reputation for eccentricity and outspokenness, and on subjects that stirred him he was capable of strong feeling and swift logic. "My love of Nature, absolute, undefiled Nature makes me an abolitionist," he wrote Thoreau. He was also sufficiently acute to later say of his friend that "the life of Thoreau was mostly within himself, or rather with the company he entertained there, as he would probably have expressed it." The bond between them was real, though, and the loyalty was not all on Ricketson's side. The last trip Thoreau took in 1862, after he returned from Minnesota, was to visit Ricketson in New Bedford.[5]

In September 1854, there arrived in Concord one Thomas Cholmondeley. He was thirty-one, a friend from Oxford of Arthur Hugh Clough, and just back from a trip to the new English colony of New Zealand, about which he had written a book, *Ultima Thule*, published this same year as *Walden*. Cholmondeley came to Concord for Emerson, but he stayed for Thoreau. He boarded with the Thoreau family, and despite the wide differences in their backgrounds, he got on well with Thoreau, who invited him to go to Westminster and climb Wachusett with him and his Worcester friends. During the Englishman's visit Thoreau withdrew both the *Bhagavadgita* and the *Vishnu Purana* from the Harvard library, making it easy for Cholmondeley to appreciate his interest in the Hindu classics.

The author of *Ultima Thule* was a thoughtful, active, informed man, much interested in the "discovery of a new region" and the founding of a new nation. The English had been officially active in colonizing New Zealand since only about 1838. It was all very new and exciting, and there were innumerable parallels with New England. But Cholmondeley had a far greater interest in the colonies than the country, and wrote much more about the evolving society of the whites than the displaced society of the Maori. Indeed Cholmondely was not interested in the Maori or their way of life, nor does his book show any interest in the natural history of New Zealand. His interest in the land was legal and social, not botanical. He understood well enough that "all the native troubles in New Zealand have arisen from this one source—*disputes about land*." He took a comfortable view of colonization that sounds like Social Darwinism before Darwin:

> Nothing can keep out white settlers, and wherever they come, the natives, as a fact, die away. So, in our woods and fields, even in England, we may observe that a new kind of tree or plant will elbow out another, which flourished before it was introduced. The antagonisms and antipathies of race and society, are but extensions of the phenomena of natural history.

Cholmondeley was clearly an intelligent observer, and he asked interesting questions. "Could our children ever become savages? Were *their* [Maori] ancestors ever civilized? Was the first man civilized, or savage, or either? Which is the nearest to the natural man, we or they? Is civilization first culture, or reclamation?" Thoreau never took up Cholmondeley's later invitations to go traveling abroad with him, but Cholmondeley was, nevertheless, in his book, his letters, and one supposes in his conversation, more than just a rich Englishman who later gave Thoreau a large box of valuable Oriental books.[6]

Also new to Concord this fall was Frank Sanborn, who later became a well-known journalist and Concord figure, writing, among many other things, a life of Thoreau. Like Blake, Sanborn later came to play a major part in presenting Thoreau's unpublished papers to the world, for which he has been heavily criticized by more recent and more careful scholars. But the twenty-three-year-old Harvard student who came to visit Emerson on November 2, 1854, and who became acquainted with Thoreau in January 1855, was then a fiery young radical spirit, soon to be an inside associate of John Brown, and one of the few who knew about Harper's Ferry ahead of time. A photograph of the young Sanborn shows a slim, sharp-eyed, clean-jawed, active young man. He was later a friend of Whitman's, who described him as "one of John Brown's big young men in the old times—was a fighter: up in arms—a devotee . . . the revolutionary crusader sort: gets hot in the collar about the enemy . . . is quick on the trigger; noble, whole sized, optimistic."

In January 1855, Thoreau left a copy of *A Week* at Sanborn's room in Cambridge, intended for the writer of a piece on Thoreau that had just appeared in the *Harvard Magazine*, then being edited by Sanborn. Sanborn was out, but he acknowledged the gift with a letter in which he commented on the "marvelous beauty of your descriptions," then added, with as much cheek as the young Thoreau had ever shown, "If any one should ask me what I think of your philosophy, I should be apt to answer that it is not worth a straw." But Sanborn soon came to live in Concord, where he opened a school, boarded with the Thoreaus, and saw Thoreau almost daily for three years, encouraging Thoreau's interest in John Brown and ultimately becoming a Thoreau loyalist. Whitman also remembered asking Sanborn one day many years later, "who of all men of Concord was most likely to last into the future. . . . Sanborn took his time in replying. I thought he was going to say Emerson, but he didn't. He said Thoreau. I was surprised—looked at him—asked: 'Is that your deliberate judgment?' and he said very emphatically: 'Yes!' I thought that very significant," Whitman concluded. "Considering who Emerson was, Thoreau was, Sanborn was, very, very significant."[7]

90. *Life Without Principle*

Thoreau gave his "Moonlight" lecture in Plymouth on October 8. On the nineteenth, he climbed Wachusett with Blake and Cholmondeley. During October and November he did a good deal of corresponding about possible lecture engagements, and late in November he made a quick trip to Philadelphia where he gave his "Moosehunting" talk ("Chesuncook"), stopping over briefly in New York on the way back home to see Greeley. Early in December he was ready with a new lecture, called, for the moment, "What Shall it Profit a Man."

The entire fall was lived under the shadow of *Walden*. As the book brought him friends, so he expected it to bring him employment as a lecturer. The "Moonlight" talk tries to explore the dark, night side of life that is largely neglected in *Walden*, while the next project, variously called "What Shall it Profit," "Life Misspent," "The Higher Law," and, finally, "Life Without Principle," is the tactical polemical obverse of *Walden*, a forceful, uncompromising piece on getting a living, concentrating on what *not* to live for. Its point is finally the same as *Walden*'s, but where *Walden* exhorts us how to live, and offers a positive vision of what to live for, "What Shall it Profit" is largely a negative, Persius-like attack on business, a protest that getting a living should not be considered an end in itself, but only a means to the real business of living. With its biblical text and sermonic tone, it is Thoreau's most Puritan piece, but it is puritanical without being Calvinist, a jeremiad directed against both the Protestant ethic and the spirit of capitalism.[1]

The dominant note is the same in early and late versions of the lecture. "I think that there is nothing, not even crime, more opposed to poetry, to philosophy, ay, to life itself, than this incessant business. . . . The ways by which you may get money almost without exception lead downward," Thoreau observed in this lecture given for money. This is not a new thought for Thoreau, but it has a new vehemence, a new one-eyed fixity. Thoreau does not see—or chooses not to notice—the humor of his position. Indeed the wonderful, leavening, playful humor of *Walden* is generally missing now. "It is remarkable that there are few men so well employed, so much to their minds, but that a little money or fame would commonly buy them off from their present pursuit," he writes, yet the passage has no application to most of those Thoreau knew well. It does not describe Emerson or Greeley, Ricketson or Blake, Cholmondeley or Sanborn, or his farmer friends Minott or Rice. It is, like much of the essay, a general lashing-out at unnamed and unspecified persons, a diatribe unsupported by his own life and circle of acquaintances. He has of course an excellent point to make, which is that one "may be very industrious, and yet not spend his time well," and he will even put the remedy in a fine short phrase, "You must get your living by loving." Nor is the humor entirely gone. "Thus men will lie on their backs, talking about the fall of man, and never make an effort to get up." But the prevailing tone is stiff, the rhetoric earnestly on the attack. "I believe," he writes, "that the mind can be permanently profaned by the habit of attending to trivial things." And it is only at the end that he pulls back from extravagance and denunciation to plead, more reasonably, "Those things which now most engage the attention of men, as politics and the daily routine, are, it is true, vital functions of human society, but should be unconsciously performed, like the corresponding functions of the physical body. They are *infra*-human, a kind of vegetation." And he ends saying that we should not always meet as "dyspeptics, to tell our bad dreams, but sometimes as *eu*peptics, to congratulate each other on the ever glorious morning." Sometimes regarded as Thoreau's best, most concentrated statement of his major message, his equivalent of Emerson's "Self-Reliance," the piece is also his stiffest moral essay.[2]

The new talk was first given in Providence on December 6, 1854, where it was not a conspicuous success. Thoreau noted coldly, "I would rather write books than lectures," but he gave the talk twice more this month, once in New Bedford, and once to an appreciative audience in Nantucket. But no sooner was the draft completed and the lecture given than Thoreau went back, with renewed energy, to the ante-Columbian North American reading he had been doing back in April and May of 1854. Over the next few winter months, his life began to resettle into familiar patterns. The winter had come upon him unawares, he said, he had been so busy writing. Now he stopped to read Hunter's *Memoirs of Captivity among the Indians*, Cadwallader Colden's *History of the Five Indian Nations. . . ,* the *Jesuit Relation* for 1639, Schoolcraft's *Information Respecting Indian Tribes* (which he had last worked on the previous November, 1853) Sagard-Theodat's *Le Grand Voyage du Pays des Hurons*, and his *Histoire du Canada*, Wm. Adams's *Journal*, and, especially, William Wood's *New England's Prospect*. He felt his spirits reviving, and as usual he expressed it in seasonal terms. He noted on December 26, "I felt the winter breaking up in me," and on January 7 he described "The delicious soft, spring-suggesting air,—how it fills my veins with life! Life becomes again credible to me."[3]

He also found the style of some of the early New England writers credible. He noted the "strong and hearty but reckless, hit-or-miss style" of John Josselyn and William Wood, the "rich phrase" of Cotton Mather, and he observed that, as a group, "they use a strong, coarse, homely speech which cannot always be found in the dictionary, nor sometimes be heard in polite society, but which brings you very near to the thing itself described." "What Shall it Profit" seems to have moved Thoreau to revalue the old Puritan and Colonial writers. He had once complained that "most New England biographies and journals affect me like opening of the tombs." But now, while he still thought that if you read nothing but Mather, "you might live in his days and believe in witchcraft," he concluded that, on balance, Mather's "generation stood nearer to nature, nearer to the facts, than this, and hence their books have more life in them."[4]

This was Thoreau's winter of skating. The river was frozen by December 19. The next day Thoreau was out skating with Channing, who made heavy going of it. The perspiration "actually dropped from his forehead on to the ice, and it froze in long icicles on his beard." Thoreau skated often, once during a snowstorm. He loved the speed of it. It made him feel, he said, "like a new creature, a deer perhaps." He clocked himself one day skating at the rate of fourteen miles an hour. The exhilaration spread through his journal. In mid-January, he observed that "the world is not only new to the eye, but is still as at creation." On January 30 he skated, by his reckoning, thirty miles.[5]

The brief midwinter spring and the accompanying high spirits did not last. In mid-February he gave "What Shall it Profit" at the Concord Lyceum, where it was coolly received as too transcendental and as urging a return to a savage state. Late in March, Frank Sanborn opened his school in Concord and came to board with the Thoreaus. In March the river opened, and Thoreau got his boat out for caulking as usual. But spring returned a little less to him this year, and the change toward spring was, he noted, "mainly in us." By mid-April he was walking without a greatcoat, but also by mid-April he had come down with an odd illness, which was prolonged into "four or five months of invalidity and worthlessness." Whatever it was (and he was unwilling to give it a name), it made him feel good for nothing but to lie on his back. Emerson noted with alarm in June that Thoreau was feeble and languishing. Alcott thought he seemed shiftless for the first time. Channing noted that his cough was particularly bad that summer. Thoreau grew whiskers to try to head off future colds. Perhaps the oddest symptom of this decline was that Thoreau's knees grew weak and not till December of this year would they really improve. Thoreau fretted terribly about the "months of feebleness." In June he was feeling lonely, bereft of friends. In September he wrote, with a touch of desperation, "I do not see how strength is to be got into my legs again." In October he was still planning to get to work after "these long months of inefficiency and idleness," but still groaning over "our awful unsocial ways, keeping in our dens a good part of the day, sucking our claws."[6]

His image of himself as a cross old hibernating bear was apt. Perhaps the illness had something to do with tuberculosis; certainly it was accompanied by a marked depression of spirits. From any point of view, Thoreau's life was in decline for something more than a year after the publication of *Walden*. The new friends did not make him feel less alone. The physical collapse of mid-April and the attendant demoralization ruined his pleasure in the spring and summer, and neither the "Moonlight" nor the "What Shall it Profit" lectures could be developed into longer pieces as Thoreau had planned.

91. Recovery

In mid-April 1855, and coinciding with his physical slump, Thoreau was corresponding with George Curtis, an old acquaintance, a Brook Farmer, and one of those who had helped raise the frame of Thoreau's Walden cabin, about publishing the Cape Cod sketches. Thoreau had first sent them to *Putnam's* late in 1852. Now, just as F. L. Olmsted was acquiring an interest in and becoming the nominal editor of *Putnam's*, interest revived. There is no evidence that Olmsted took an interest in Thoreau; Olmsted seems not to have been intimately involved in day-to-day editorial matters. Curtis was worried that the tone of some of Thoreau's remarks about Christianity and Cape inhabitants might give offense. Publication was scheduled to start with the June number. At the end of April, in another, unrelated effort to capitalize on the modest success of *Walden*, Thoreau wrote Ticknor and Fields about reprinting *A Week*. In late May and early June he did a little walking and a little surveying, but most of the time he felt sick and good for nothing.[1]

Early in July he and Channing made a two-week trip to Cape Cod, commencing with a seven-hour sail to Provincetown. In August, the third installment of *Cape Cod*, "The Beach," appeared, but it was the last. Some time shortly after this, *Putnam's* broke off publication, probably from uneasiness over the indelicate parts of "The Wellfleet Oysterman," which would naturally have come next, and the anticipated problems with the author's unwillingness to tone down any of these indelicate parts. Thoreau disliked having his remarks softened or excised, and though he was capable of concession, he never made it easy for his editors.

Late in September the accounts came in on *Walden*. He had made $51.60 in royalties, the equivalent of a year's tuition at college. In early October he visited Ricketson in New Bedford for a few days, compelled by his continuing weakness to travel about the countryside by wagon. Back in Concord he gathered wood for the winter and read Howitt on the Australian gold fields. Cholmondeley, now patriotically aroused and off to fight in the Crimean War, had stirred Thoreau's interest in Australia as well as New Zealand, and he in turn had been stirred by Thoreau's interest in the Orient. In late November, there arrived in Concord, from Cholmondeley, a "royal gift," as Thoreau quite properly called it, of forty-four books on Oriental subjects. Among the books Thoreau already knew were the *Vishnu Purana*, *The Laws of Menu*, the *Bhagavadgita*, the *Samkhya Karika*, and the *Sacontala*. There were other Hindu texts that were new to him, such as the *Rig Veda*, some Upanishads, two volumes of aphorisms, and two volumes of Hindu drama. There were three volumes of commentary by Thomas Colebrook.[2]

A month later, Thoreau was still referring to the collection as "almost exclusively relating to ancient Hindoo literature," though that is a curious description of a collection that is almost one-quarter (9 volumes) made up of a *History of British India* and one-quarter composed of books on Buddhism, Egyptian chronology, early Christianity, and Universal History. As he told Ricketson, Thoreau was familiar with many of the books and knew how to prize them. Even though the gift came years after Thoreau's most creative engagement with the Hindu classics, the new books could still nourish his habitual circling and widening reading habits. Claude Lévi-Strauss described his own study habits as "the intellectual equivalent of slash-and-burn agriculture." Thoreau worked very differently, returning often to favorite texts, finding renewal and fresh insight on the oldest, most familiar ground. At the same time, he continued to expand his interests. The *Bhagavadgita* was old ground. R. Spence Hardy's *Eastern Monachism* and his *Manual of Buddhism*, and Christian C. J. Bunsen's *Outlines of the Philosophy of Universal History* were new.[3]

Hardy's *Eastern Monachism* is about Buddhist monastic life. It is written from a Christian perspective that finds Buddhistic withdrawal hard to accept, but the book is reasonably sympathetic. An early part tells the story of Rathapala of Kuru. It is a sort of Buddhist *Pilgrim's Progress*, about a man who left his family for the spiritual discipline of the Buddhist priesthood, explaining that he did so because he had come to understand these four aphorisms of Buddha:

1. The beings in this world are subject to decay, they cannot abide long.
2. They have no protection, no adequate helper. 3. They have no real possessions; all that they have they must leave. 4. They cannot arrive at perfect satisfaction or content; they are constantly the slaves of evil desire.

There are obvious points of similarity between Hardy's account of Buddhist spirituality and the Stoicism with which Thoreau was familiar, as there is between Rathapala's withdrawal from society and Thoreau's. Thoreau was familiar with the land of Kuru from the *Bhagavadgita*. It is the land Arjuna is supposed to protect. But Hardy connected Kuru with Buddhism, and Hardy's books together with Burnouf's *Lotus de la bonnes lois* (also part of Cholmondeley's gift), represent one of the few important infusions of Buddhism into American intellectual life before Sir Edwin Arnold's *The Light of Asia*.[4]

Volumes three and four of Bunsen's *Christianity and Mankind* constitute a separate and distinct work, entitled *Outlines of the Philosophy of Universal History, applied to Language and Religion*. Bunsen was a Prussian diplomat who became secretary to the historian Barthold Niebuhr before moving to England for good in 1838. He wrote well, and he took up what were for Thoreau the right causes. In one place, he excoriates the "used-up unintellectual formulas of unexplained tradition," and elsewhere he refers to the "two dark points of Protestant society" as "the Prussian Law of Divorce, and the Law of Slavery in some of the States of the American Union." Bunsen's theory of history is developmental. "There must be," he says, "an Evolution (*Werden*) in a finite form, of that which is in the divine Being (*Sein*) as infinite Thought. . . . Universal History is the totality of that divine evolution."[5]

Bunsen applied this post-Hegelian pre-Darwinian Christian Evolutionism in a most interesting manner to language, claiming, "Every language of which we know the history owes its origin to the decay and decomposition of another." So too with religion. Bunsen's modern Transcendentalism held that "There is no finite life except unto death, no death except unto higher life." Bunsen's great work on *Christianity and Mankind* remains impressive for its effort to create a modern synthesis of developmental and evolutionary ideas with the development of language, and with a late, Schleiermacher-influenced, liberal Christian religious viewpoint. *Christianity and Mankind* is a neglected high point of international transcendentalism.[6]

Thoreau was also reading this September of 1855 Sophocles's *Antigone*, the center of which is the conflict between the state and the higher law as exemplified in the conscience of a good individual. Between Bunsen, the "What shall it Profit" lecture and *Antigone*, it is clear that Thoreau was still in the fall of 1855 actively interested in the higher law aspect of transcendentalism.

Women as well as men could be heroic in that way. Again this fall there was visiting in Concord Mary Moody Emerson, Waldo's paternal aunt, who, though seventy-five this year, was still sound of mind, as tart as a quince in conversation. With admonishing honesty she once signed a letter to Thoreau "Your admirer often and your friend always." She preserved the intense Calvinism of an earlier time, and as Virginia Woolf commented, "her soul was always in conflict . . . and her fervour boiled within her, scalding those she loved best." Thoreau not only took her ministrations in stride but he pronounced her "the wittiest and the most vivacious woman I know."[7]

Thoreau's spirits, health, and power of observation all began to revive in the fall of 1855, even though he would not feel completely restored for another year or so. And just as there is no real indication of what caused the decline, so there is no one thing that reversed it. The physical renewal he experienced this fall was accompanied by a renewal of interest in sense-experience, above all in visual experience. One of the few things he had noted back in April was how the radical greenness, the color of life, spread from the roots to a full, vigorous growing greenness as the month advanced. The journals for the next few months have little of this, though visual culture and stimuli were all around him. In May, Emerson became aware of a new magazine called *The Crayon*, devoted to the graphic arts and to their link with literature. William Cullen Bryant is compared to Kensett and Durand, lines from Longfellow are explicated via Ruskin's *Modern Painters*. In volume 1, number 3, Asher Durand was asking, in "Letters on Landscape Painting," "Why should not the American landscape painter, in accordance with the principle of self-government, boldly originate a high and independent style, based on his native resources?"

On the Fourth of July, while waiting for the boat to Provincetown, Thoreau visited the Athenaeum gallery, where the great "Andes of Ecuador" painting by Frederick Church was on display. Though he left no record of his impressions, Thoreau's future work would have interesting similarities with Church's. The latter's oil sketches of Katahdin and of fall foliage in New England, now in the Cooper Hewitt Museum in New York, are the exact visual counterparts of "Ktaadn" and "Autumnal Tints." In October, Thoreau visited the studio of the well-known marine painter George Bradford. The artist was out but Thoreau met his colleague, the Dutch marine painter Van Best. Also in October Thoreau spent quite a bit of time examining and describing an old picture of Concord battle, mostly from the point of view of local history, and this month he wrote Ricketson another letter recommending the works of William Gilpin, with a careful list of all available titles and insisting that "There *must* be plates in every volume."[8]

No one dramatic event occurred to Thoreau this fall, but it was nevertheless a crucial, pivotal season for him. Dramatic events could be misleading. As he observed in his journal late in December, "In a true history or biography, of how little consequence those events of which is so much is commonly made." In early November, on a lovely Indian summer day, he had noted with interesting emphasis, "This, too, is the *recovery* of the year." His tolerance for social visits increased also. This month he wrote a vivid and generous account of neighbor Rice's mode of getting a living.[9] (Rice was a cheerful, self-sufficient farmer who made it a rule to make his own tools.)

He began to feel his thought concentrating again. "I am all compact," he wrote on November 7. Best of all, he felt his "power of observation and contemplation is much increased." On December 11, studying a "flock of delicate, crimson tinged birds, lesser redpolls," he begins to sound like his old self. "I am struck by the perfect confidence and success of nature," he wrote. "There is no question about the existence of these delicate creatures, their adaptedness to their circumstances." To clarity of perception and taut certitude of phrase is added now the old sense of wonder and enthusiasm. "It is only necessary to behold thus the least fact or phenomenon, however familiar, from a point a hair's breadth aside from our habitual path or routine, to be overcome, enchanted by its beauty and significance." And he concludes with all the verve of the conclusion of *Walden*: "To perceive freshly, with fresh senses, is to be inspired. . . . My body is all sentient . . . the age of miracles is each moment thus returned."[10]

92. The Dispersion of Seeds and the Succession of Forest Trees

The weather during the last month of 1855 was pleasant, but the first month of 1856 brought the beginning of a long, snowy winter. From mid-January to mid-March the snow stood never less than sixteen inches in the open undrifted fields about Concord. There was so much snow on the river there was no skating, though Ricketson reported that boys were wind skating "holding sails in their hands" down in New Bedford. In Concord there was not one thawing day in two months. People wrapped their pumps with straw and rags, and counted the days till spring. The Thoreaus' new kitten, Min, got into a foolish spell one day, rushing up to the attic and leaping (unharmed) "from the attic window to the ice and snow by the side of the doorstep."[1]

At the same time the cold and snow descended in January, Thoreau experienced a creative infusion and his spirits lifted. Watching the snowflakes fall, he marveled at "how full of creative genius is the air in which these are generated. . . . Nature is full of genius, full of the divinity; so that not a snowflake escapes its fashioning hand. Nothing is cheap and coarse, neither dewdrops nor snowflakes." Thoreau was always glad to find he could still take pleasure in the common, and his language now, even in midwinter, emphasized creation and generation. He was forcefully reminded again that "the same law that shapes the earth-star shapes the snow-star." It was his perennial, and perennially valid, belief that every time and place was as good as any other, because all were expressions of the same ordering forces. "As surely as the petals of a flower are fixed, each of these countless snow-stars comes whirling to earth, pronouncing thus, with emphasis, the number six. Order. Kosmos." From now on all his major projects would in one way or another explore the ramifications of this universally observable ordering process at work in nature. It is interesting that this vision of order was now accompanied by a corresponding, Malthusian vision of the fecundity and voracity of nature. On the day after his delighted description of the invariable six-sidedness of all snowflakes, he caught a pickerel that had just swallowed three perch, one of which was in turn just swallowing a minnow, and a week later he was still wondering at it, and calculating that for a thousand pickerel (the probable count for one large pond) to make one meal a day for a year would require 365,000 perch.[2]

His journal also grew this month, and he noted explicitly that it should record his life and growth, not just his past. No doubt the journal was a separate, self-justifying work by itself now, but it also continued to generate other works, functioning as an immense, always-expanding reservoir or preserve, as inexhaustible as Concord or as Nature itself, a vast accumulation of fact and observation across which Thoreau could strike a line of purpose at any time. Into the journal went all his careful measurements of the snows, his observations on the dispersal of pitch-pine seeds, details about bird nests he methodically dissected, descriptions of the contents of crows' droppings studied under a microscope. About half the journal as we have it had now been written. Another seven volumes or a million words

341

were to be written in the next few years. Thoreau worried about the ever-increasing factual quality of the journal, and so have many of his readers. But the heavy concentration on recording concrete observable phenomena does not mean a necessary and corresponding decrease in imaginative or intellectual powers. When Thoreau's other notebooks, essay drafts, and letters are read alongside the journal, they show an increasing objectivity, an attention to fact, and an awareness of what can be done with facts. His intellectual powers were, if anything, expanding with time, and his great life-stabilizing generalizations only grew stronger as evidence accumulated. What William James once said of Louis Agassiz was just as true for Thoreau. "No one," James insisted, "sees further into a generalization than his own knowledge of details extends."[3]

During February, Thoreau watched how cedars are planted by birds, and how a line of willows was planted by the action of the wind on a new railroad embankment. In March he noticed how birch seed, scattered on the snow covering the river, would be carried downstream to new and distant places when the river broke up. In April, amid much relief and rejoicing on the breakup of what had seemed an endless winter, he collected and tested all sorts of birch saps. His father thought it took him away from his studies, but such things were by now part of his studies. He also felt the cruelties of April, noting how old people tend to die on the approach of spring. His own uncle Charlie Dunbar died on March 27. Earlier Thoreau had again despaired of his friendships with Emerson and Channing, speaking of them in the past tense. Yet he himself revived with the revival of the year, and refused to sympathize with any other view. "Hosmer is overhauling a vast heap of manure in the rear of his barn," he wrote on April 3, "turning the ice within it up to the light; yet he asks despairingly what life is for, and says he does not expect to stay long here. But I have just come from Columella, who describes the same kind of spring work, in that to him new spring of the world, with hope, and I suggest to be brave and hopeful with nature." This spring especially, Thoreau fought back his own sense of transiency and loss with this countervailing, classical comforting sense of permanence and solidity. "Human life may be transitory and full of trouble," he concluded, "but the perennial mind, whose survey extends from that spring to this, from Columella to Hosmer, is superior to change. I will identify myself with that which did not die with Columella and will not die with Hosmer."[4]

The long winter had been, literally, a seed time. His interest in generativity, creativity, and the spreading of seeds is evident all through the winter and into the spring. One day in late April he was out walking with a Concord acquaintance. "Observing the young pitch pines by the road south of Loring's lot that was so heavily wooded, George Hubbard remarked that if they were cut down oaks would spring up, and sure enough, looking across the road to where Loring's white pines recently stood so densely, the ground was all covered with young oaks." Thoreau made a note to himself to look into this further.[5]

By mid-May 1856, he had the general outlines of an answer. "If you look through a thick pine wood, even the exclusively pitch pine ones, you will detect many little oaks, birches etc. sprung probably from seeds carried into the thicket by squirrels etc." The hardwood seedlings thus planted annually are annually overshadowed and choked by the pines, but if the pines should be cleared, "the oaks etc., having got just the start they want, and now secured favorable conditions, immediately spring up to trees." The agency of squirrels and birds in such planting was, he thought, not sufficiently appreciated.[6]

Thoreau had long been interested in seeds, as he was in everything else in nature. This new interest in how different kinds of trees follow each other in a natural succession, in the evolution of forests, and in the process Darwin would call natural selection, gave him a new focus for an old interest. His observations this spring form the nucleus of the talk "The Succession of Forest Trees," that he eventually gave on September 20, 1860, by which time it was a part of a much larger work, to be called "The Dispersion of Seeds," which, together with the large bundle of manuscript called "Wild Fruits" or "Notes on Fruits," may itself have been conceived as part of a still larger work, a natural history of Concord. This vast and many-sided project was slowly taking shape this spring. It had a distinct scientific flavor. To Blake, Thoreau wrote that he was working on material that, from a lecturing standpoint, might be thought too scientific and matter-of-fact. He went on to affirm that he was concerned to get "more precision and authority" in his work, and when he finally gave the talk in 1860, he would refer to it, without deprecation, as a "purely scientific subject." A hint of the scope of the project is given in another letter, in which Thoreau wrote, to a young man who had asked what he was working on, "I am drawing a rather long bow."[7]

He pushed the "Succession" idea a bit further in June. He confirmed the observation that squirrels plant acorns in pine woods, which grow into shrub oak when the pines are cut. "If you cut the shrub oak soon, probably pines or birches, maples, or other trees which have light seed will spring next, because squirrels etc., will not be likely to carry acorns into open land." Much more observation would be required before he could be quite sure on this and on other related points.[8]

During June he made a visit to Worcester and another to New Bedford. Events in Kansas crept into his journal from time to time. The Free-Soil legislature and governor elected in January 1856 were opposed by a rival proslavery legislature. President Pierce intervened on the proslavery side. Passions were high; there was much violence. On May 24 John Brown and a small band of followers killed five unarmed proslavery settlers along Pottawatomie Creek. Kansas and Kansans bled all summer. Thoreau was aware of these events, but his day-to-day interests continued overwhelmingly in botany. This summer he was making many lists and notations on plants, and there is a new confidence in his notes now as he more and more frequently cites an authority such as G. B. Emerson or Asa Gray only in order to correct it on a point of detail. He took pleasure in his mastery of the technical language of plants. He saw a new sunflower on August 10, called it the "*tall* rough sunflower" and described it: "leaves opposite except for a few small ones amid the branches, thick ovate or ovate-lanceolate, taper-pointed, three-nerved, obscurely and remotely toothed, rough above, smooth and whitish below, abruptly contracted into margined petioles." In addition to the manuals of Gray, Bigelow, Hooker, and Richardson, he was reading in June the new life of Newton by Brewster. While he took time to write some wonderfully vivid and humorous stories this summer, particularly one about trying to catch his father's runaway pig, his interests are preponderantly scientific.[9]

His journals sometimes seem to drift from subject to subject this year, but he himself was aware of this, and of the need for directing purposes. Only if one had purposes, even small purposes, could one "really take a position outside the street and daily life of men." And he phrased his scientific purposes with an interesting metaphor from current affairs. "For only absorbing employment prevails, succeeds, takes up space, occupies territory, determines the future of individuals and states, drives Kansas out of your head, and actually and permanently occupies the only desireable and free Kansas against all border ruffians." What that purposeful absorbing employment would be for him, he put best at the end of a series of questions this August. "Why don't maples and alders spring up much in the open meadow, though they border the river? Why is the black willow so strictly confined to the bank of the river? What is the use, in Nature's economy, of these occasional floods in August?" As *Walden* opened with an account of human or household economy, the economics of individualism, so now Thoreau was turning outward, beginning to sense the outlines of a project he may not yet have seen with full clarity, but which centered now not on *his* economy but that of Nature. The economy of nature is a familiar phrase from at least the time of Linnaeus. The other word for it is *ecology*, which was not yet coined. Thoreau's vast new project, the "long bow," probably comprising everything he left as the "Dispersal of Seeds" and "Wild Fruits," and sometimes called—or thought of—as his Kalendar or Book of Concord, was beginning to form itself in his walks, his readings, and his notes. Whatever called, it was to be focused on the economy of nature as it could be seen in Concord, or as we now might call it, the ecology of Concord, a contribution to the natural history of the United States. Brooding on his purposes and his subject, he wrote in late August, "It is in vain to dream of a wildness distant from ourselves. . . . I shall never find in the wilds of Labrador any greater wilderness than in some recess in Concord."[10]

93. *Walt Whitman and the Ethics of Intensity*

By early September 1856, Thoreau's already systematic botanical observations were reaching for comprehensiveness. On September 1, for example, he set out to note the exact state of all the asters and golden-rods in the vicinity, and he netted thirteen varieties of aster alone. Similar checklists appear this fall at intervals of two or three weeks. At the end of the first week in September he went to visit Alcott, recently moved to Walpole, New Hampshire, to take advantage of a rent-free house. On the way, in Brattleboro, Vermont, Thoreau missed by a few hours Dr. Elisha Kane, the arctic explorer who had been on the first American expedition in search of Sir John Franklin, and whose first book, about that search, Thoreau already knew. He was told that Kane had compiled a list of arctic plants he had brought home, and he was shown the list. A few days later Thoreau drew up his own list of plants observed on his own most recent expedition. Yet at the same time that he was increasing his concentration on the or-derly accumulation of details, he remained acutely aware that facts alone, even themes, were not by themselves of much use to him. "The theme is nothing," he observed on October 18, "the life is every-thing." The individual recorder of experience was still crucial. "Man is all in all, Nature nothing, but as she draws him out and reflects him." And the most important quality of any life is not its web of detail, but the intensity with which that life is lived and shared. "All that interests the reader is the depth and intensity of the life excited."[1]

A few days later, on October 24, Thoreau left Concord to go to Eagleswood, near Perth Amboy, New Jersey, to do some surveying of a Fourierist commune that had failed and was now to be subdivided and developed for homes. The trip was a social whirl, but for Thoreau it was neither exciting nor intense. First he went to Worcester, saw Blake and Higginson, then to New York and Barnum's Museum. Then he ran into Elizabeth Peabody, also on her way to Eagleswood. Once there, there were dances and talks besides surveying and plant-ing. Thoreau gave his three current talks, "Moosehunting," "Walk-ing," and "What shall it Profit." He felt the community at Eagles-wood crowded him, taking it for granted that he craved society. Meanwhile the work took longer than anticipated. Alcott arrived on the first of November, and soon he and Thoreau went to see Horace Greeley. Alcott, now fifty-seven, had been in New York since some-time in September, was giving "Conversations," and in general felt inspired and renewed by New York after his rustication in Walpole.

He had already met a new poet, another of Emerson's discoveries, named Walt Whitman.

On November 9, Alcott and Thoreau crossed the East River on the ferry to Brooklyn to hear Henry Ward Beecher, the greatest pulpit orator of the age. Thoreau was not impressed with Beecher's self-assured style and emotion-compelling delivery. "If Henry Ward Beecher knows so much more about God than another," he later commented, "I would thank him to publish it in *Silliman's Journal*, with as few flourishes as possible." Next morning, Alcott and Thoreau together with a Philadelphia woman named Sarah Tyndale called on Whitman.[2]

Whitman was now thirty-seven, two years younger than Thoreau, and he already had more gray in his hair and beard than one might expect. *Leaves of Grass* had been published in July of the year before, and it had been a total failure commercially. Whitman later said he doubted if ten copies had been sold, though many were given away. Only one early review had appeared, in Greeley's *Tribune*, and it expressed grave reservations. But within a few weeks of the book's appearance, Emerson had read it and had sent Whitman a jubilant, glowing letter, calling *Leaves of Grass* "the most extraordinary piece of wit and wisdom that America has yet contributed." Emerson spoke of the "great joy" he took in the book. "I find incomparable things said incomparably well," he said, and he hailed the new poet in his best clarion prose. "I greet you at the beginning of a great career." To Emerson's surprise, the entire letter appeared, with Whitman's connivance, in the *Tribune* on October 10, 1855. Whitman sent clippings to Longfellow and others, and he had copies of the letter circulated to editors and critics. Whitman capped everything by having the "I greet you" sentence, complete with Emerson's name, stamped in gold letters on the spine of the second edition, which had just come out. No doubt the whole business was a brash exploitation of Emerson's great prestige, but Emerson *had* written the letter, and, as Thoreau knew very well, he had written nothing comparable when *Walden* appeared.[3]

Whitman led his guests up two narrow flights of stairs to the attic room he shared with his brother Eddie. Alcott noted that "the pressure of [their] bodies was still apparent in the unmade bed standing in one corner, and the vessel scarcely hidden underneath." There were pictures of a satyr, Bacchus, and Hercules on the walls, leading Alcott to comment later that he had been to see "Walt the satyr, the Bacchus, the very God Pan," a modern pantheon unto himself. They talked for two hours, Thoreau feeling a little constrained in talking with Whitman by the two others present. Whitman said something about "representing America." With reflex contradictoriness Thoreau replied—as he reported later—"that I did not think much of America or of politics, and so on, which may have been somewhat of a damper to him."[4]

During the two-hour meeting, Alcott was amused at the defensiveness of both Thoreau and Whitman, each of whom "seemed planted fast in reserves, surveying the other curiously." Whitman never let the conversation "stray very wide away from Walt's godhead without recalling it to that high mark." To something Thoreau said, Whitman replied that Thoreau misapprehended him. Thoreau told Blake later, "I am not quite sure that I do." Thoreau had reservations about the "sensuality" of some of the poems in the new, second edition Whitman now gave him, but when he returned to Concord he wrote two enthusiastic letters about Whitman to Blake, explaining why Whitman "is the most interesting fact to me at present. . . . He is apparently the greatest democrat the world has seen," he told Blake, and he went on, approvingly, "kings and aristocracy go by the board at once, as they have long deserved to." Thoreau returned often to Whitman's Americanness, as though compensating for his quick rejoinder to Whitman about not valuing America much.[5]

Whitman often spoke of Thoreau in later years. He lumped him with Carlyle as too supercilious and disdainful toward the common man, and he said he thought Thoreau's work a little bookish by comparison, say, with that of Burroughs. But Whitman also recalled that Thoreau, in that first and probably only meeting, warmly condemned Whitman's critics, who had by now surfaced, calling them "reprobates" and wanting to call them worse. From Emerson and others, Whitman learned later that Thoreau carried *Leaves of Grass* around Concord "like a red flag," and Whitman came, over time, to value Thoreau's work. In 1888 he concluded that Thoreau was "one of the native forces—stands for a fact, a movement, an upheaval: Thoreau belongs to America, to the transcendental, to the protesters . . . he was a force—he looms up bigger and bigger: his dying does not seem to have hurt him a bit: every year has added to his fame." To this general and generous appraisal he added a personal touch. "One thing about Thoreau keeps him very near to me: I refer to his lawlessness—his dissent—his going his own absolute road let hell blaze all it chooses."[6]

Thoreau had singled out "Song of Myself" and "Crossing Brooklyn Ferry" from Whitman's second edition for special note. In the latter poem, then called "Sun Down Poem," Whitman takes a river crossing experience and uses it, as Thoreau had used his two weeks on the Concord and Merrimack rivers, as the core of a work about how all eras and places are equal and how we, in the present, are as lucky and blessed as any. It is Thoreau's own theme. "On the whole," he concluded, "it sounds to me very brave and American after whatever deductions." And he knew how to value Whitman as compared to Beecher. "I do not believe that all the sermons so called that have been preached in this land put together are equal to it [*Leaves of Grass*] for preaching." Thoreau had reservations about the sexual—he called it sensual—side of Whitman. "He does not celebrate love at all. It is as if the beasts spoke." But he qualified his qualification, adding "even on this side [sensuality] he has spoken more truth than any American or modern that I know. I have found his poem exhilarating encouraging. . . . We ought to rejoice greatly in him." Meanwhile the *Criterion* in New York called the book "A mass of stupid filth" and J. P. Leslie in Philadelphia thought it "profane and obscene." In Cambridge James Russell Lowell, successor to Longfellow as professor of Modern Languages at Harvard, did not feel obliged to read it and said he would take care to keep it out of the way of the Harvard students.[7]

Whitman had an important and an immediate impact on Thoreau, even though Sophia later made Emerson omit mention of it in the funeral address. Whitman's absorption in sense experience excited Thoreau, though he shrank from suggestions of sexuality. Thoreau also responded to Whitman's tremendous capacity for joy, the quality of enthusiasm to which Emerson also responded. Even Whitman's Americanness seems to have won Thoreau over. Most important of all,

Whitman's emphasis on intensity of experience and immediacy of communication coincided perfectly with Thoreau's growing recognition of the central goal of intensity in his own writing.[8]

Thoreau's new interest in Whitman marked some, but not all, of his pursuits through the winter of 1856 and the spring of 1857. Back in Concord from Eagleswood, Thoreau argued with himself in his journal for the next few months about his need for solitude versus the merits of society, almost as though he were continuing the debate begun in Brooklyn. He came down repeatedly for solitude, yet in a letter to Benjamin Wiley, who had written to ask what to read and what to think, Thoreau singled out for emphasis this cardinal Confucian principle, applicable to himself and to Whitman as well: "Conduct yourself suitably toward the persons of your family, then you will be able to instruct and direct a nation of men."[9]

In December he read the newly discovered and published account of Plymouth Plantation by William Bradford, singling out for admiration the great passage where Bradford stops to reflect on the daunting situation of the settlers as they came ashore at Plymouth just as winter was about to set in. "For summer being done, all things stand upon them with a weather-beaten face; and the whole country, full of woods and thickets, represented a wild and savage hue." He was also reading Elisha Kane's new book, the two-volume *Arctic Explorations*, with large detailed maps and vivid engravings of arctic scenes based on Kane's own sketches. The first volume has for the frontispiece a full-rigged ship on its side in an ice field dominated by towering ragged icebergs.[10]

In midwinter Thoreau read more of the *Jesuit Relations*, Winckelmann's famous book on *Ancient Art*, and Richard Burton's *Travels in Arabia*. With the return of the "working days," those bright, windy days between winter and spring "when activity, vitality, change become paramount," his New England reading intensified. He read Thomas Morton's *New England Canaan* and Church's *History of King Philip's War*. He told Wiley that his lecture on the Wild, though a hundred pages long, was not ready for publication. He was also becoming more interested in autobiography. He wrote a few sample passages about his own life, and about his introduction to botany, and he made a list of autobiographies that included those of Goethe, Gibbon, Alfieri, Haydon, Franklin, Cellini, and DeQuincey. Here, as in so many other places, he refused to restrict himself to American writers.[11]

In April of 1857, while on a visit to Ricketson's, Thoreau met and went for a long walk with Kate Brady, a young woman of twenty, a former maid at the Ricketsons who had read *Walden* and now wanted to "live free" by herself in an old farmhouse. Alcott, who was also at Ricketson's this April, later spoke of Thoreau's having fallen in love with her, and Alcott remembered that Thoreau treated her differently from other women. Though twice her age, Thoreau was certainly impressed, perhaps smitten. In a brief burst of admiration a week later he said, in the middle of the longest journal passage he ever wrote on a member of the opposite sex, that he "never heard a girl or woman express so strong a love for nature." Some submerged part of his mind was running to matrimonial imagery. His account of Kate Brady concludes that "all nature is my bride." No doubt he was struck by her, but he was twenty years older, and was, by now, irrevocably engaged elsewhere.[12]

In May, Thoreau worked building an arbor for Emerson. His reading ranged from Bunyan's *Pilgrim's Progress* to Sophocles' *Oedipus at Colonus* to Richard Burton's *Personal Narrative of a Pilgrimage to Al-Madinah and Meccah*. May warmed into summer, now his favorite time of year. "There is really but one season in our hearts," he wrote this year.[13]

When a companion of the moment, probably Ricketson, complained to Thoreau about the sufferings of life, Thoreau's instant retort was that since we were human we were doubtless not complete or round, but torn, "like one of the laciniae of a lichen." The point, he insisted was that "we want not completeness but intensity of life." It has recently been argued that late nineteenth-century fiction in America turned away from ethos to pathos, from ethics to feelings, from character to personality, as fictions of self-discovery and self-realization replaced the Victorian belief in the virtue of selflessness. The intensity with which one lived, not the rules by which one lived, became the measure of value in life. But for Whitman and for Thoreau, the ethics of intensity remained ethics. The poems of Whitman and the prose of Thoreau were meant morally. "That is moral," said

Matthew Arnold, "which teaches us how to live." For Mme de Stael's Germans the key had been enthusiasm. Now, in America, enthusiasm took the new forms of intensity and immediacy, new values both for life and for the expression of that life in literature. Whitman, crossing Brooklyn Ferry with the sun at his back, saw in the water below "the nimbus of light / around the shadow of my / head in the sunset." With a similar sense of homemade divinity Thoreau went out on a clear, bright, cold day in January. Walking on the snow-clad earth with the sun behind him, he saw his shadow in front of him, not black, as one might expect, but "a most celestial blue." Nothing, for either of them, could be any more divine than the intensely experienced present moment.[14]

94. The Indian

From June 12 to 22, 1857, Thoreau took what would be his last trip to Cape Cod. He went via the South Shore and Plymouth, then by rail to Sandwich. In three days he walked the fifty-odd miles to the Highland Light on the outside of the Cape up near Provincetown. He had stopped to see John Newcomb, the Wellfleet oysterman, but found he had died the winter before. Thoreau spent several rainy days around the Highland Light, then sailed for Boston from Provincetown by steamer in a thick fog that had settled in for five days. As always, he noticed everything and asked questions. He found out that one man could haul two hundred lobster traps a day. He paid a dollar each for the traps, and he sold the lobsters for three cents apiece, uncooked. But the trip was not really productive. He had said what he had to say about the Cape, and he never wrote about this last excursion to it.

His health, however, had clearly returned. Two months earlier, in April, despite a cold, he was already referring to his "two-year-old invalidity" in the past tense. In mid-July he wrote his cousin George Thatcher saying that he felt "somewhat stronger than for 2 or 3 years past" and proposing a trip to Moosehead and the Allegash lakes. Thatcher couldn't go, but on July 30, Thoreau, Ed Hoar of Concord, and Joe Polis, a Penobscot Indian, set off on what would be Thoreau's third and last trip to Maine, a 325-mile canoe trip up the West Branch of the Penobscot working north, then across the swampy carries from the headwaters of the West Branch to the headwaters of the East Branch, then down the East Branch, a long, arduous circuit all the way around in back of Katahdin.[1]

Ed Hoar was thirty-four, six years younger than Thoreau, and just back from California. He had been on expeditions with Thoreau before, including the disastrous one when they set the Concord woods afire. Joe Polis, the "chief man of the Penobscot tribe" and forty-eight years old, was their guide. It was a hard, dangerous trip into country which, then as now, becomes very difficult anywhere off the beaten track. They went early enough to be bothered by insects, they made numerous open lake crossings in the heavily loaded canoe against high winds and waves, they made frequent and long "carries" over un-marked, swampy, obstructed routes piled with blowdowns. They were wet for long stretches, they got lost, and one night Ed Hoar got separated from the other two. Thoreau was nearly frantic with worry and with imagining how he was going to break the news to Hoar's family if they never found him. Next morning they did find him and Thoreau shouted repeatedly at the sight of him, moving Polis to say testily to Thoreau, "he hears you."[2]

The dark, shaggy, damp woods of Maine were as wild as anything in Thoreau's experience. He had known that the trip would be too hard for Blake, who had wanted to go, and afterward Thoreau found a tactful way to explain why he hadn't asked Blake to come. In a letter Thoreau commented that Hoar (who was seven years younger than Blake) had "suffered considerably from being obliged to carry unusual loads over wet and rough 'carries,' in one instance five miles through a swamp, where the water was frequently up to our knees, and the fallen timber higher than our heads. He went over the ground three times, not being able to carry all his load at once." Their best nights, he told Blake, were those when it rained the hardest, because it cut down on the mosquitoes. Even the Indian, Polis, who could "find his way so wonderfully in the woods," was impressed with the difficulty of the route and he told the story of how he had been caught out deep in the woods by the coming of winter when he was a boy, and how he traveled for days without food except for one otter he caught, nearly starving before making it home. He had been ill for six months after getting home, and Polis thought the experience had permanently affected his health. Polis was sick before this trip was over, though Thoreau was not.[3]

Thoreau called his account of this excursion "The Allegash and East Branch," but he could equally well have called it "The Indian," for it was more about Joe Polis than any other single subject. Polis had long been an important figure in the Penobscot tribe. He had represented his people in Washington and had met Daniel Webster; he was impressed with city life, unimpressed with Webster. But unlike some of the Indians Thoreau had known, Polis had lost none of his woodcraft, though he had learned to take advantage of civilization. Polis was full of surprises for Thoreau. He was a Christian, he prayed, and he worried about breaking the Sabbath. He was better off financially than Thoreau, and told him he preferred to hire whites rather than Indians because the whites were steadier and "knew how." He and the Penobscots generally were more sociable than the white settlers, and avoided living in lonely outpost cabins when they could. Thoreau got Polis to teach him as much of his language as he could, and while Thoreau botanized he also picked up the Indian names for many plants. Thoreau was fascinated with Polis's canoe-building skills, his ability to track and to find his way, his songs, his beliefs, his stories, his views of the white man, and above all, his language. "The Allegash and East Branch" contains, as a result, the "most realistic and attractive native American" portrayed by a white writer in nineteenth-century American literature. Polis is described in swift, sure, vivid detail. In contrast, for example, to Thoreau's laborious preparations and lists of necessary items for the trip, here is Joe Polis setting out:

> He wore a cotton shirt, originally white, a greenish flannel one over it, but no waistcoat, flannel drawers, and strong linen or duck pants, which also had been white, blue woollen stockings, cowhide boots, and a Kossuth hat. He carried no change of clothing, but putting on a stout thick jacket, which he laid aside in the canoe, and seizing a full-sized axe, his gun and ammunition, and a blanket, which would do for a sail or knapsack, if wanted, and strapping on his belt, which contained a large sheath-knife, he walked off at once, ready to be gone all summer.[4]

Thoreau wrote the trip up during the fall of 1857. "The Allegash and East Branch" is not only the longest part of *The Maine Woods*, forming more than half the book, but also, at 167 pages, almost twice the length of *A Yankee in Canada*. "The Allegash" is a major work in its own right, the last long manuscript Thoreau completed. If anything deserves to be thought of as his Indian Book, it is this narrative, which is both an account of the canoe trip just taken, and in many and complex ways, the culmination of all his years of Indian reading and his thousands of pages of notes on Indian subjects. By February and March 1858, Thoreau was making notes (on Father Rasles's *Dictionary of Abnaki*) in the eleventh of his twelve Indian books of extracts. Thus his immense reading about the Indians was essentially behind him now, and whatever he had learned from it all can be seen, if anywhere, in "The Allegash and East Branch."

There are a few references to other Indians and to earlier times in the narrative but, astonishingly, when one considers the depth and range of backlog reading and note taking he had done on Indian matters over the years, "The Allegash" is the least comparative, the least metaphorical, the least worked-up with material from other times and travels, of any of Thoreau's major writings. It is not that he hadn't learned from the endless reading about Indian life, it is rather that all the reading prepared and educated him to make the most of his time in the woods with Polis. Thoreau was supremely ready for what Polis had to teach. The Indian reading and his own sensibilities had prepared him to see Polis's world. As he noted in mid-July, "We find only the world we look for."[5]

"The Allegash" as it stands (and it was published only after Thoreau's death, partly at least because he did not wish to embarrass Polis) is an account of two worlds. First there is the world of the Maine woods as seen by the Indian, as the Indian was in turn watched and reported by Thoreau. This aspect of the narrative has the peak of Katahdin looming above it, as it looms above the other two parts of the book, much the way the highest mountain peak shows up in every panel of Thomas Cole's *Course of Empire*. "The Allegash" is also full of dark, bear-haunted slopes, lakes of light, innumerable treatments of wildness, and a fair amount of humor. (Thoreau found a dead porcupine on a long carry and speculated that perhaps it had "succumbed to the difficulties of the way.") But wildness is the principal subject. The word occurs on nearly every page and is treated from many viewpoints. "The Allegash" is not, like "Walking," on the meaning of the wild, but is a transcription of the experience of wildness itself.[6]

The other world of "The Allegash" is its botanical, naturalist's report side, the natural history of the Maine woods, complete with appendixes listing trees, plants, birds, animals, temperatures (omitted from the printed version), and Indian names, all comprising the Maine woods as Thoreau the naturalist saw them. He observed how few animals there were in the deep woods, how there were fewer fishes than in Concord River, how wildflower seeds are not in fact widely dispersed in deep forests, how dispersion of most plants seems more limited than in cleared or partially cleared lands. "The Allegash" is the most botanically detailed of Thoreau's Maine woods narratives, and its botanical and Indian aspects are united by the emphasis on wildness and by Thoreau's observation that Indian intelligence, Indian modes of perception, and Indian language all had important lessons for science. Polis had sources of information "so various that he did not give a distinct conscious attention to any one." It was like instinct, but, Thoreau added, "perhaps what is commonly called instinct in the animal, in this case is merely a sharpened and educated sense." To Blake, Thoreau wrote that he had visited the "New World" of the Indian, adding, "He begins where we leave off." He thought that "the Indian . . . possesses so much intelligence which the white man does not,—and it increases my own capacity, as well as faith, to observe it." This is not sentimental adulation. Thoreau found much to criticize in Polis and once observed that Polis understood very well both his own superiority and inferiority to white civilization. Thoreau was interested especially in the observational acuity of the Indian, and in a conversation a year later with Harvard librarian John Langdon Sibley, Thoreau said he thought the scientists had things to learn from the Indians, that the Indians "stand between the men of science and the subjects which they study." He pointed out that the Indians have more than fifty words for cedar, that they could hear a "little whistle" made by a snake, could call a wild muskrat by imitating his notes and sounds, that they knew, though no naturalist mentions, that pout lead their young about as a hen her chicks. If the best naturalist is the closest observer, the Indian had some claims in that direction.[7]

95. Autumnal Tints,
John Ruskin, and the Innocent Eye

There was another financial panic this fall of 1857. The railroads had overbuilt, settlers had not appeared in the necessary numbers, and stocks fell. Things were unsettled, at home and abroad. The Mormons were defying the federal government in Utah, the wounds in Kansas had not closed. Chief Justice Taney of the United States Supreme Court handed down a decision that members of the Negro race "are not included under the word citizen in the Constitution, and can therefore claim none of the rights and privileges" guaranteed by that document. The British were attacking the Chinese at Canton, and in India the Great Mutiny of 1857 flared.

Life in Concord seemed little touched by all this. Alcott returned to Concord this fall to take up residence in Orchard House out near Emerson's on the Lexington road. In Boston James Russell Lowell was starting a new magazine called *The Atlantic Monthly*, titled to recognize the cultural bonds between the Old World and the New as constituting a new entity, an Atlantic civilization. Lowell asked Emerson to help enlist Thoreau for the new venture.

From late September on through all of October and November, it was a glorious autumn. The weather was perfect for weeks at a time; no one remembered a more splendid fall. Thoreau's spirits rose and his entries for October and November of this year constitute one of the high points of his entire journal. He exulted in the season, and in marked contrast with his earlier depression, his energies and spirits were never higher, never in better harmony with his world. Back in December of 1856 he had made, in a letter to Blake, the astonishing accusation that "nature is *emphatically* wrong." Now he was noting how "the seasons and all their changes are in me." And he added that even in his moods he now felt "the perfect correspondence of Nature to man."[1]

As the leaves began to turn in Concord this fall, Thoreau was deep in the writings of the English art critic John Ruskin. Ruskin, who was thirty-eight at the time, had leaped to public notice in 1843 with a book called *Modern Painters*, a passionate defense of modern landscape painting in general, and J. M. W. Turner in particular. *Modern Painters*, volume two, which followed in 1846, was on ideas of beauty; volume three, published in 1856, treated "greatness of style," true versus false ideals, the "pathetic fallacy," and "the moral of landscape." Volume four, also published in 1856, returned to Turner, and to a lengthy and detailed discussion of "mountain beauty." Thoreau made a couple of deprecating remarks about Ruskin, as he had about Gilpin, but he was greatly stirred by Ruskin, as he had been by Gilpin. He read all of the above books plus *The Seven Lamps of Architecture*, and, as his subsequent journal entries show, he learned a great deal from Ruskin about how to see, and how to describe what he saw. It is true that Thoreau said that Ruskin often described not nature but nature as Turner painted it, and he disapproved of Ruskin's Christian views, but there are many Ruskinian passages in the journal, and the unlabeled parallels far outweigh the recorded reservations about Ruskin. He told Blake he had read most of Ruskin's books and found them "singularly good and encouraging," with such themes as "Infinity, Beauty, Imagination, Love of Nature etc.—all treated in a very living manner. I am," he concluded, "rather surprised by them."[2]

Thoreau's Ruskin is not the social and economic reformer of the years following 1860; he is the early Ruskin who was inspired by Carlyle and fired by Turner, the Ruskin who combined a strong moral sense, a passion for nature, an eye trained for close observation, an equal capacity to put it into words, and a prophetic earnestness and prose style:

> About the river of human life there is a wintry wind, though a heavenly sunshine; the iris colors its agitation, the frost fixes upon its repose. Let us beware that our rest become not the rest of stones, which so long as they are torrent-tossed, and thunder-stricken, maintain their majesty, but when the stream is silent, and the storm passed, suffer the grass to cover them and the lichen to feed on them, and are ploughed down into dust.

Ruskin attacked the idea that "utility" was the only valid standard in life, his *Two Paths* became a favorite with the older Emerson for its espousal of the "vital law" of "organic form" as the basis of "all noble design." But Thoreau was interested in Ruskin long before Emerson was, and what really interested him was not so much the grand moral theories of Ruskin as his remarkable technical skill at calling attention to the *processes* by which we take in and register the world around us. Thoreau read a great deal of Ruskin, but the book that made the biggest impression on him and proved the most useful to him as a writer was Ruskin's recently published *Elements of Drawing* (1857).³

This is a short, brilliant book, intended as a practical guide to the beginning painter, still in print and still capable of firing the young artist to acquire essential habits of hand and eye. It is the book the young Georges Seurat read, the one Monet said contained 90 percent of the theory of impressionist painting. Ruskin thought seeing was more important than drawing, insisting that one draw not what one knows, but what one sees. A recommended exercise is

> sitting about three yards from a bookcase (not your own, so that you may *know* none of the titles of the books), to try to draw the books accurately, with the title of the backs and the patterns on the bindings as you see them. You are not to stir from your place to seek what they are, but to draw them simply as they appear, giving the perfect look of neat lettering, which nevertheless, must be (as you will find it on most of the books) absolutely illegible.

Thus Ruskin insists on representing "visual appearances only, never memory knowledge." In the opening exercise he wrote that "everything that you can see in the world around you, presents itself to your eyes only as an arrangement of patches of different colors variously shaded." Ruskin elaborates in a note:

> The perception of solid Form is entirely a matter of experience. We *see* nothing but flat colours. . . . The whole technical power of painting depends on our recovery of what may be called *the innocence of the eye*: that is to say, of a sort of childish perception of these flat stains of colour, merely as such, without consciousness of what they signify,—as a blind man would see them if suddenly gifted with sight.⁴

Ruskin writes vividly, and uses numerous small sketches to illustrate our perception and discrimination of different kinds of light and dark, brilliancy, shade, form, outline, mass, and color. He directs his reader to examine the particular features of individual leaves and branches, and he spends an entire chapter on color. He notices how nature mixes purple and green, purple and scarlet, green and blue, yellow and neutral gray, the basic palette of art nouveau. He insists that color is even linked to health. "When you are fatigued or ill you will not see colours well." Ruskin knew that colors can function as signs, and he could explain why. "Vivid orange in an orange is a sign of nearness," he writes, "for if you put the orange a great way off, its color will not look so bright; but vivid orange in sky is a sign of distance, because you cannot get the color of orange in a cloud near you." Ruskin showed how all colors in nature are gradated, never solid, but always shading lighter or darker, brighter or duller, from one hue to another, and Thoreau copied one of Ruskin's key observations into his natural history notebook. "The victorious beauty of the rose as compared with other flowers, depends wholly on the delicacy and quantity of its colour gradations, all other flowers being either less rich in gradations, not having so many folds of leaf; or less tender, being patched and veined instead of flushed." Thoreau had read the *Elements of Drawing* by late November 1857, and his journals for the months to come are full of Ruskinian observation. On January 26, he followed a careful description of the appearance of lichens and birches with "Nature loves gradation," and on February 13 he was struck with how "the swamp was variously shaded, or painted even, like a rug, with the sober colors running gradually into each other."[5]

Also during the fall of 1857, Thoreau wrote some of the important parts of what would become the essay "Autumnal Tints." Thoreau gave the talk, with specimen autumn leaves mounted on white backgrounds, and he later gave very specific instructions to the *Atlantic Monthly* for reproducing exactly the outline of a large scarlet oak leaf he described in detail. "Stand under this tree and see how finely its leaves are cut against the sky,—as it were, only a few sharp points extending from a mid-rib. . . . The eye rests with equal delight on what is not leaf and on what is leaf,—on the broad, free open sinuses, and on the large, sharp, bristle pointed lobes." In its emphasis on seeing, its attention to visual detail, and above all in its excitement and its reveling in color, the essay owes much of its brilliance to Thoreau's excited reading of Ruskin.[6]

"Autumnal Tints" treats autumn not as a time of death and decay, but as a time of the perfect maturing of the trees, the colored leaves answering to ripened fruits, the high point of ripeness of the year. The essay starts with the purple grasses of August (so does Gerard's Renaissance *Herbal*, another of Thoreau's favorites), goes on to the red maples of late September, the yellow elms of early October, the leaf fall, which Thoreau observed came mainly from October 6 to 16 most years, then the late October sugar maples and the crowning, culminating glory of the scarlet oaks late in October and on into November. The scarlet oak, he says, is

> our chief November flower. . . . It is remarkable that the latest bright color that is general should be this deep, dark scarlet and red, the intensest of colors. The ripest fruit of the year; like the cheek of a hard glossy red apple, from the cold Isle of Orleans, which will not be mellow for eating till next spring! When I rise to a hill-top, a thousand of these great Oak roses, distributed on every side, as far as the horizon! I admire them four or five miles off!⁷

"Autumnal Tints" is Thoreau's poem on October, which, along with March, was always his great month. It is a rare year when his October journal does not burst forth in a kind of verbal richness and color to rival the autumn leaves of New England, that phenomenon so remarkable to English visitors and so unknown to English poetry. "Autumnal Tints" is one of Thoreau's great essays; it is his essay on perception, and it ends on this theme. All that he has described, he tells the reader directly, "you surely *will* see, and much more, if you are prepared to see it,—if you *look* for it. . . . Objects are concealed from our view, not so much because they are out of the course of our visual ray, as because we do not bring our minds and eyes to bear on them." Thus, he says, "the greater part of the phenomena of Nature are for this reason concealed from us all our lives." Thoreau insisted that the "Scarlet oak must, in a sense, be in your eye when you go forth. We cannot see anything until we are possessed with the idea of it, take it into our heads, and then we can hardly see anything else." What he looked for he saw. "A man sees only what concerns him."⁸

Ruskin greatly enlarged these concerns for Thoreau this fall. For not only does *The Elements of Drawing* (especially Letter 3, on Color) underlie "Autumnal Tints," but volume four of *Modern Painters*, about mountain scenery, accompanies Thoreau's renewed interest in mountains this fall of 1857. In late October he said he had thought twenty times of "that mountain in the east part of our town," and this fall saw some of his most imaginative and vivid writing about mountains. Recalling his dreams and a dim childhood experience, he writes, "and then I steadily ascended along a rocky ridge half clad with stinted trees, where wild beasts haunted, till I lost myself quite in the upper air and clouds, seeming to pass an imaginary line which separates a hill, mere earth heaped up, from a mountain, into a superterranean grandeur and sublimity." The Turnerian visual grandeur of landscape, which is evident in much of Thoreau's late landscape writing, does not come from a direct encounter with Turner, but from the visual excitement that rubbed off from the Ruskin whose own early work was so steeped in Turner. But Thoreau was doing something quite different than Ruskin. When Ruskin brought out the fifth and final volume of *Modern Painters* in 1860, it opened with a good-sized monograph on "Leaf-Beauty" which does not go into color at all. "Autumnal Tints" is one of the greatest demonstrations of how Thoreau's immense openness to experience, his capacity for living, both in books and in nature, is always being matched and then exceeded by his creative adaptation and his power of original expression. Thoreau's vision seems very similar at times to that of nineteenth-century landscape painting. Yet he saw, or at least he commented on, very few actual paintings, even though many were available to him. The real training of his eye, and the thing that gave him the verbal equivalent of what Ruskin calls habit of hand, came not so much from landscape painting as from the great writing about landscape in Gilpin and Ruskin.[9]

96. Louis Agassiz and the Theory of Special Creation

Thoreau's interests during the years from 1854 to 1860 were increasingly centered in the botanical, zoological, geological, and geographical sciences. In his public life, he was now as much a naturalist as a writer. He had become a corresponding member of the Boston Society of Natural History in 1850, he was appointed to Harvard's Committee for Examination in Natural History in 1859, and again in 1860, and when he died his occupation was officially listed as that of Natural Historian. During the 1840s and 1850s the language of the natural sciences underwent a dramatic shift. The older terms "naturalist" and "natural history" were increasingly displaced by the new (1840) word "scientist," the confident rhetoric of "scientific objectivity" and "the scientific method." During these same decades the study of the natural world became rapidly professionalized and sharply specialized.

Thoreau had for years been interested in detailed, transcribable, ascertainable facts of all kinds. He had an unambiguous respect for things, as well as for ideas about things. But as time went on he became ever more interested in the question of who is doing the observing of the facts and details. He became increasingly convinced that we see only what we are prepared to see, that we find, not the world as it is, but the world we look for. Ruskin showed him how much more there was to look for in nature's colors, in light and shade, mountain and forest. Polis, the Indian, was also most valuable to Thoreau in enlarging his capacities for observing. In a journal passage on November 5, 1857, he put the matter as clearly as he had anywhere in his writings. "I think that the man of science makes this mistake, and the mass of mankind along with him that you should coolly give your chief attention to the phenomenon which excites you as something independent on you, and not as it is related to you. The important fact is its effect on me. He thinks that I have no business to see anything else but just what he defines the rainbow to be." But, Thoreau objects, "I find it is not [rainbows] themselves (with which the men of science deal) that concern me; the point of interest is somewhere *between* me and them (i.e., the objects)." Coming where it does in 1857, it is highly likely that the problematic scientist challenged in the passage is Louis Agassiz, and much of Thoreau's longstanding ambivalence about science—though not about natural history or botany or zoology—can be understood in the context of his long association with and eventual rejection of the views of Louis Agassiz. Indeed, Thoreau's later life, from 1857 until his death, was lived out at or near the center of some of the most important intellectual events of his era, the birth of the modern biological sciences, including botanical geography, and the emergence of the Darwinian worldview. In all these matters, Thoreau was an informed participant, not just an observer.[1]

In December of 1845 Harvard began to plan for a new school of science. In the fall of 1846 the thirty-nine-year-old Agassiz came to America, and in 1847 was appointed professor of zoology and geology at Harvard's brand new Lawrence Scientific School. Agassiz was already famous, with an international reputation as an authority on fishes and glaciers. He had been appointed professor of natural history at Neuchâtel when he was twenty-five, his *Recherches sur les poissons fossiles* began appearing in 1833, when he was twenty-six, and his *Études sur les glaciers* in 1840. He had met the great Cuvier. As soon as he arrived at Harvard he set to work to classify all North American fauna, especially fishes and turtles, and in the spring of 1847 Thoreau was enlisted (by James Elliot Cabot) as one of Agassiz's many field correspondents and collectors. In November 1847, Thoreau was applauding Harvard's new science initiatives.[2]

In June of 1848 Agassiz published his first American book, *Principles of Zoology*, a book Thoreau would come to know well. It presented the most recent information concerning anatomy, paleontology, geology, and embryology. It also maintained that species were fixed and unvarying, all species having been created, in successive waves over time, by a deity according to a fixed plan of creation. In an 1850 volume called *Lake Superior*, Agassiz again put forward the theory of special creation. "The more intimately we trace . . . geographical distribution, the more we are impressed with the conviction that . . . animals must have originated where they live, and have remained almost precisely within the same limits since they were created." These limits, Agassiz asserted, "were marked out on the first day of creation." Agassiz had believed, as early as his first work on fossil fishes, that species were immutable, that they "do not pass insensibly one into another, but that they appear and disappear unexpectedly, without direct relations with their precursors." If there seemed to be a sort of progress in the succession of beings on earth, as evidenced by the fossil record, the explanation, for Agassiz, was that "this progress consists in an increasing similarity to the living fauna" of the present day. "But this connection," he went on to insist, "is not the consequence of a direct lineage between the faunas of different ages. There is nothing like parental descent connecting them." Darwin would assert the exact opposite, but that was still to come, and Agassiz currently held the field. "The link by which [species] are connected is of a higher and immaterial nature," Agassiz claimed, "and their connection is to be sought in the view of the Creator himself, whose aim, in setting forth the earth, in allowing it to undergo the successive changes which geology has pointed out, and in creating successively all the different types of animals which have passed away, was to introduce Man upon its surface. . . . In the beginning, the Creator's plan was formed, and from it He has never swerved in any particular."[3]

The strict determinism of this explanation sounds remarkably like Calvinistic predestination in biological clothing, and it may be significant that Agassiz's ancestors, Calvinists of Burgundian Huguenot extraction, had been clergymen in Protestant Switzerland for six unbroken generations down to and including Agassiz's father. Agassiz's argument that species do not develop or evolve one from another but were all created separately can in fact be strictly maintained only by positing a comprehensive preexisting blueprint, a plan preordained by God. And the explanation for the unsettling similarity between some now-extinct species and certain living species is not, for Agassiz, because of some as yet undiscovered missing link, but rather in the idea—familiar to theologians and known as typology—that earlier species were purposefully designed by the deity as prophecies of later, currently existing species. In his 1857 *Essay on Classification*, in which he "nailed his colors to the mast," and which Thoreau read, section 26 is devoted to these "prophetic types," showing, in part, "how the embryonic conditions of higher representatives of certain types, called into existence at a later time, are typified, as it were, in representatives of the same types, which have existed at an earlier period. . . . They appear now, like a prophecy in those earlier times, of an order of things not possible with the earlier combinations then prevailing in the animal kingdom." In other words, Agassiz's overarching scheme was theistic, Christian, Calvinist, typological. It depended upon a preordained scheme, rigidly carried out by means including "prophetic" types or species.[4]

Yet Agassiz always claimed to be, and his era always accepted him as, a pure, disinterested, objective scientist, confining himself exclusively to observation. More than any other single figure, he was responsible for professionalizing science in America, and more than any other person, he came to stand for the concept of science in the public mind. He once answered a question about what he considered his greatest work, "I have taught men to observe." Supporting his high claims to being a pure scientist was his attractive, outgoing, dynamic personality. He surrounded himself with tremendous activity. He collected, had scores of people collecting for him, planned new schools, introduced new methods of teaching, founded and raised money for the new Harvard Museum of Comparative Zoology (prototype for the New York Museum of Natural History), held press conferences, staged events, outings, lectures, dinners. His biographer describes him as a man whose *"bonhomie* seems inexhaustible." William James thought him a "commanding presence, a man on the heroic scale." He wielded enormous influence, he had vast prestige. The Massachusetts legislature appropriated money for his projects, he posed with President Lincoln at the founding of the American Academy of Science. The State Department ordered its consulates worldwide to help him. The emperor of Peru ordered his subjects to collect specimens for the great Harvard scientist. He had brought science to Harvard, and Harvard responded by backing him and his views, as did the popular press, the pulpit, the publishing establishment, and the reigning poets, Lowell, Longfellow, and Holmes. Agassiz was also supremely self-confident. In later years he enjoyed telling his friends and foes alike that "Darwin's work was contrary to modern science as he [Agassiz] had defined it."[5]

Thoreau not only collected for Agassiz, finding new species for him, but he read, indeed studied, the *Principles of Zoology.* He had it out of the library for three months in 1851, just a year after he had been elected a corresponding member of the Boston Society of Natural History. Over the years Thoreau made many observations on fishes, turtles, and frogs, contributing to and being properly acknowledged in Agassiz's great comprehensive specialist's study of turtles, which came out in 1857. The study was part of an ambitious but never-finished project called *Contributions to the Natural History of the United States of*

America. The first volume consists of the famous "Essay on Classification" followed by two long, detailed, and rather technical studies of turtles. The appearance of the book coincided with Agassiz's fiftieth birthday. There were celebrations, including a dinner at Emerson's on March 20, which Thoreau attended.

At dinner, Thoreau asked a lot of questions and his account of the conversation suggests he was not really satisfied with Agassiz's answers or, indeed, with his knowledge:

> He had not observed the silvery appearance and the dryness of the lycoperdon fungus in water which I showed. He had broken caterpillars and found the crystals of ice in them, but had not thawed them. When I began to tell him of my experiment on a frozen fish, he said that Pallas has shown that fishes were frozen and thawed again, but I affirmed the contrary, and then Agassiz agreed with me.

Some of this may be attributed to Thoreau's habitual contradictoriness, but he also did not fully trust Agassiz's views, or his methods, which involved, among other things, killing quite a few specimens, especially for the systematic work on turtle embryos. Though one might not guess it from the caterpillars and fishes mentioned above, Thoreau had severe qualms about killing turtles for science. Emerson too had his doubts, and though he once went on an outing to the Adirondacks where he shot specimens for Agassiz, he also said in his journal that "the turtles of Cambridge, on the publication of this book of Agassiz, should hold an indignation meeting, and migrate from the Charles River, with Chelydra serpentina marching at the head, and 'Death to Agassiz' inscribed on their shields." Something in Agassiz called out such sallies, and behind the fun lay a serious critique. Already in 1857 Emerson thought it ill advised of Agassiz to teach theism under cover of science, and Thoreau made impatient comments, long before he read Darwin's *Origin of Species*, on Agassiz's ideas about the subject. In June 1858, while climbing Mount Monadnock, Thoreau found toad spawn in a tiny rainwater pool in the rocks near the summit, wondered how it had got there and remarked, "Agassiz might say that they originated on the top." It was too glib. Thoreau already knew a lot about the dispersion of species, and he looked for other explanations for the presence of the toad spawn.[6]

Beginning in mid-1858, Thoreau undertook a major reading campaign in zoology. From Agassiz on turtles he went on to Bell's *History of British Reptiles* and Hewitson's *British Oology* (on birds). Agassiz's volume seems to have been the initiating impulse, but it was not the last word. Darwin's work on species was not yet published in book form, though he presented his paper on evolution this year to the Linnaean Society. It made so little impression that the president of the society, Thomas Bell, could say that the year "has not, indeed, been marked by any of those striking discoveries which at once revolutionize, so to speak, the department of science in which they occur." Thoreau's inclinations already favored the "developmental" hypothesis that originated with Lamarck, and he had the same misgivings about the idea of special creation that he now had about other eighteenth-century fixed schemes, such as that of Linnaeus. The issue would become increasingly complex, interesting, and heated in the years just ahead, and Thoreau kept up with the new ideas through books, through botanical friends, and through the Boston Society of Natural History. Thoreau was, by comparison with the eminent Professor Agassiz, an amateur country naturalist, known thus far for his writing, not his science. But condescension to Thoreau's scientific habits of mind is no longer possible. If Thoreau did not have the great fame and vast scientific prestige of Agassiz, he also was not burdened by the typological creationism that was eventually to discredit the great man and all his many works. Agassiz's science clung to the Calvinist past, while Thoreau's combination of the new science and the older tradition of natural history led him toward the Darwinian future.[7]

97. *A Plea for Captain Brown*

During April and May of 1858, Thoreau studied and observed frogs; during June and July it was mountains. In early July he went on a trip to the White Mountains with Theo Brown, Harry Blake, and Ed Hoar. The resulting sixty-page journal write-up emphasized the scenery around Chocorua ("ever stern, rugged and inaccessible, and omnipresent") and North Conway. In September and October he returned to his autumnal tints theme. November was a month of wonderful contrasts of light. He thought he might do a piece on "November Lights." "Now a new season begins," he wrote, "the pure November season of the russet earth and withered leaf and bare twigs and hoary withered goldenrods." He watched the light across Fair Haven Pond. "A cool and silvery light is the prevailing one; dark-blue or slate-colored clouds in the west, and the sun going down in them. All the light of November may be called an afterglow." December was, as often, a hard month to get through, as he noted on Christmas day. January of 1859 began with a great northeast storm. Thoreau's father had been sick for two years. In mid-January he was confined to his room, in late January to his bed. On February 3 he died, and Thoreau had one more claim upon the earth of Concord. "How enduring are our bodies, after all!" he exclaimed in his journal obituary. "The forms of our brothers and sisters, our parents and children and wives, lie still in the hills and fields round about us."[1]

Thoreau traveled much less this year, kept home more by business than by bad health. But his March journal sprang to life again. It is filled with observations on the interconnectedness and interdependence of things in nature. He generalized his experience of arrowhead hunting (look for them on high ground, near water, in March) and tried to explain why geese fly in formation. He was sure there was "some advantage" in it, perhaps "they really do overcome [air] resistance best in this way." In April Thoreau set out four hundred pines on two acres at Walden. He was reading Gilbert White once more, noting again how there was a season for everything and reaffirming that one must stick to one's work. "Where the good husbandman is, there is the good soil. Take any other course, and life will be a succession of regrets."[2]

Early in May 1859, John Brown returned to Concord. Ossawatomie Brown was, in the words of Bruce Catton, Michigan-born historian of the Civil War, "a rover, a ne'er-do-well, wholly ineffectual in everything he did save that he had the knack of drawing an entire nation after him on the road to unreasoning violence." Thoreau had met Brown over a year earlier, when Brown had left Kansas and was meeting in Boston with a secret group of prominent men to procure rifles, raise money, and launch a guerrilla raid against "the slave power." Sanborn, just a year out of college, was one of the "secret six." So was

T. W. Higginson, now thirty-six, who had been in the forefront of the effort to rescue Anthony Burns in 1854, "undoubtedly the only Harvard Phi Beta Kappa, Unitarian minister, and master of seven languages who had led a storming party against a federal bastion with a battering ram in his hands."[3]

Brown spoke in Concord in late March of 1857 about his battles in Kansas against the proslavery faction. One of his points, Emerson noted, was "the folly of the peace party in Kansas, who believed, that their strength lay in the greatness of their wrongs, and so discountenanced resistance." Emerson also reported that Brown "believes on his own experience that one good, believing, strong-minded man is worth a hundred, nay twenty thousand men without character." Thoreau was impressed with this Carlylean hero and made a small contribution, though he was annoyed that Brown would not say what exactly he wanted the money for.[4]

Whatever Sanborn, Higginson, and the other secret supporters of Brown knew in advance about the Harper's Ferry raid, Thoreau was surprised by it when he got the news on October 19, 1859. His instant response to the (mistaken) report that Brown had been killed by federal troops was that Brown was right and the government wrong. "When a government puts forth its strength on the side of injustice, as ours (especially to-day) to maintain slavery and kill the liberators of the slave, what a merely brute, or worse than brute, force it is seen to be!" But public opinion began quickly to harden against Brown, and Thoreau, who was instantly, totally caught up in the passion of the moment, decided to make a public speech to try to right the imbalance. As Brown had acted, so must he act now. He announced in Concord that he would speak on John Brown on October 30. The selectmen would not have the town bell rung, so Thoreau rang it himself, then delivered "A Plea for Captain John Brown." He laid his cards on the table at the start. The piece was intended to persuade, to counter—though not to answer—Brown's detractors, to give the other side. Thoreau's general strategy was to praise John Brown as a good soldier. He was careful to use the military title *captain* frequently. He reminds the audience that Brown's grandfather was a soldier, his father an army contractor. Thoreau compared Brown to the Concord minutemen, his band to Cromwell's New Model Army. Brown is the

Puritan soldier in the new world. Everything Thoreau had written in "The Service," that early essay about life as warfare, written long ago and rejected by Margaret Fuller, returns now, no longer metaphor but life.[5]

The "Plea" does not mention the Pottawatomie Massacre, which Thoreau must have heard about, but may not have wished to know about, nor does it dwell on the actual events at Harper's Ferry. Thoreau's indirect, rhetorical defense to charges of murder and insurrection is to treat Brown consistently as a soldier. His other tactic is to defend not the act, nor even John Brown's character, but the principle under which Brown acted. He calls Brown a "transcendentalist above all, a man of ideas and principles." He had recently delivered his "Life without Principle" lecture again, on October 9, and the subject was still fresh for him. Brown is a hero on principle, a hero of principle. He is, for Thoreau, a great man because he acted on the principle that the slaves should be freed. Brown's ethical imperative, for Thoreau, was summed up in this categorical statement he quoted from Brown: "I want you to understand that I respect the rights of the poorest and weakest of colored people, oppressed by the slave power, just as much as I do those of the most wealthy and powerful."[6]

When a young William Dean Howells came to visit Thoreau a few months later, he heard Thoreau speak about John Brown, but "it was not the warm, palpable, loving, fearful old man of my conception, but a sort of John Brown type, a John Brown ideal, a John Brown principle, which we were somehow (with long pauses between the vague, orphic phrases), to cherish and to nourish ourselves upon." The John Brown principle, as argued in "A Plea," takes high ground. Thoreau praises Brown's "respect for the Constitution, and his faith in the permanence of this Union." Above all, Brown followed his own conscience. Thoreau's position is quite consistent, not only with his own "The Service," "Civil Disobedience," and "Slavery in Massachusetts," but with the Jeffersonian position that when governments become destructive of the natural rights of the governed, the latter have a right to revolt, by violence if need be. A similar situation now existed, Thoreau thought. The problem Thoreau saw was that the "government puts forth its strength on the side of injustice." Therefore, the government should no longer be obeyed. "The only government that

I recognize,—and it matters not how few are at the head of it, or how small its army,—is that power which establishes justice in the land, never that which establishes injustice." Slavery was wrong. If all peaceful means of abolishing it, such as "moral suasion," had failed, and if force was now required, then one must not shrink from force. It was only over time, and reluctantly, and with complex qualifications that Thoreau came to accept the use of force. Violence was bad, but slavery was worse. So he framed the John Brown principle and so he endorsed it, as his personal reply to the South's peculiar institution. "It was his peculiar doctrine that a man has a perfect right to interfere by force with the slaveholder, in order to rescue the slave. I agree with him."[7]

Thoreau had calculated the effect of his talk correctly. The speech was reported, reprinted, and discussed in all the Boston papers. He gave it again on November 3. Brown dominated his thoughts and journals through November. And when Brown was hanged on December 2, Thoreau arranged a simultaneous memorial service in Concord at which he and others read elegiac selections. Next day, Francis J. Merriam, one of Brown's men who had escaped from Harper's Ferry to Canada, and had returned, crazily, on hearing of Brown's execution, arrived in Concord. Sanborn enlisted Thoreau to drive Merriam, disguised as a "Mr. Lockwood," to the South Acton Station to get on the next train back to Canada. Thoreau did not know it was Merriam, but he knew enough not to inquire too closely into whom he was helping. Thus the normally unpolitical Thoreau got seriously involved in one of the key events leading to the Civil War.

John Brown's body was brought north by train. He was buried, but not forgotten. In April of 1860 Sanborn was arrested in Concord by federal marshals. He put up a good fight and the incident made the front page of the *New York Tribune* for days. On July 4, Thoreau was invited to speak at a memorial for John Brown. He could not go, but sent the piece now called "The Last Days of John Brown," which he culled from unused journal entries of October and November 1859. Emerson would note in his funeral address on Thoreau that John Brown had had an immense effect on Thoreau's last days. It was certainly so for six weeks from October 19 to December 2, 1859. But Thoreau's absorption in John Brown ceased almost as suddenly as it began. By December 8, 1859, Thoreau had picked up his natural history pursuits again and was absorbed in another rediscovery, this time of Aristotle on animals, and the writings of the Roman naturalist Pliny. Within a month a copy of Darwin's *Origin of Species* would arrive in Concord and Thoreau's own vast natural history projects would take one last turn.

98. Darwin and the Developmental Theory

Thoreau's last major systematic new campaign of reading covered both modern and historical zoology. This December he was following an old pattern. With his interest aroused, no doubt in part by Agassiz, he now went back to investigate the beginnings of the subject in the classical writers. The ancient zoologists included, especially, Aristotle, Aelian, Theophrastus, and Pliny. In mid-December he was working on Aristotle's *History of the Animals*, using a late eighteenth-century French edition and translation by Armand Camus. Aristotle's was the first natural history. Camus regarded it as still one of the best, an attitude Thoreau quickly came to share. In his journal, Thoreau gives Aristotle credit for creating the attitudes and much of the language of what we still call science. Thoreau took fifty pages of careful notes. He admired Aristotle's eye for everyday detail. We know that fishes sleep because "often it is possible to come upon fishes thus without being observed, so as to take them with the hand. . . . At this time they are very still, and move no part but the end of the tail gently." He also admired Aristotle's wonderful power of generalization, evident at the start of almost any paragraph. "The egg of all fishes is not 2-colored, but one-colored." "In the same flight the bee does not go to different kinds of flowers, but it goes as from a violet to a violet, but does not touch another without having been to the hive." Thoreau also made extensive notes on Aristotle's treatment of reproduction and sexuality in animals and on his ideas about creation and generation.[1]

Camus's extensive annotations also provided Thoreau with a comprehensive reading list of zoological writers from classical times on down into the Renaissance (Gesner, Topsell, Belon are included) and on to modern times, listing twenty-seven seventeenth- and eighteenth-century zoologists and ending with Buffon. From here, Thoreau could make his own sequence to Cuvier, Agassiz, and the present. Thoreau's interest in modern zoology was of long standing, but now, beginning with Aristotle, he gave himself a thorough grounding in historical zoology, including the history and development of interest in zoology. In Aristotle's observational and descriptive power Thoreau found another approach to natural history, a counterweight to the modern kind of science, the measuring and weighing he associated, quite rightly, with Agassiz.

Thoreau's careful study of Aristotle also signals a most important shift now going on in Thoreau's outlook. Transcendentalism, particularly in Emerson's version, has its major philosophical roots and allegiances in Plato. The world we see, the phenomenal world, is a product of and therefore less important than the world of ideas or forms behind it. Thoreau still calls himself a transcendentalist, but the term seems now to refer more to ethics than to metaphysics or epistemology. A transcendentalist is now, for Thoreau, one who follows Kant's categorical imperative in matters of ethical conduct. "Act so that you can will that all persons should act under the same maxim you do." This ethical transcendentalism, if it may be called that, could now accommodate a strong infusion of Aristotelian respect for what William James would call "stubborn and irreducible fact."

From Aristotle, Thoreau moved on to Pliny, who, Camus said, "first made what the Greeks called an encyclopedia." Camus put Pliny "a degree below Aristotle, who had at least seen as much as he read." Pliny's *Natural History*, often condescended to as a "storehouse of ancient error," had much for Thoreau. Pliny, a Roman administrator and a moderate and rational Stoic imbued with the Roman work ethic, was killed near Mount Vesuvius in A.D. 79 trying to get a closer look at the eruption that buried Pompeii and Herculaneum. A man of awe-inspiring diligence, he had books read to him while he ate, while he traveled, and indeed at all times except when he bathed. Even then, the reading was stopped only for the actual immersion. The reading resumed while he was being toweled and rubbed. Pliny took notes and made extracts on all he read, saying no book was so bad as to have nothing of value. Like Thoreau, he assembled a large and valuable collection of extract books. His only surviving work, the *Natural History*, fills ten volumes in the Loeb edition. It runs to a million words, or roughly half the length of Thoreau's journal. The table of contents fills seventy pages; the work itself has twenty thousand items culled from two thousand books by a hundred writers. It covers the entire natural world, defined as everything not made by human beings.

Pliny is usually thought of as combining fact with myth, which is one of the ways Thoreau had earlier defined his own purpose as a writer. But his interest now was more in Pliny's natural observations than in stories about dragons or unicorns. Pliny was an example of how the observer and the scholar could be combined. Like Aristotle, Pliny underlined for Thoreau the importance, the centrality of the observer. Thoreau began with Pliny's work on trees, which comprises more than a tenth of the entire work. He copied down Pliny's observations on countries that have no trees, on trees that have no fruit, on the order of events in the spring.

Thoreau was strongly impressed by Pliny's observations and by his vivid style. Many of Thoreau's late works begin with citations from Pliny. The version of "Night and Moonlight" printed posthumously in *Excursions* opens with a reference to Pliny, as does "Huckleberries." "Wild Apples" refers to him, and the "Dispersion of Seeds" manuscript begins:

> Pliny, whose work embodies the natural science of his time, tells us that some trees bear no seed. "The only ones," says he, "among the trees that bear nothing whatever, not so much as any seed even, are the tamarisk, which is used only for making brooms, the poplar, the Atincian elm, and the alaternous." And he adds that "these trees are regarded as sinister (or unhappy, infelices) and are considered inauspicious."[2]

Aristotle and Pliny, together with Ruskin, recalled an increasingly scientific Thoreau to the importance, indeed the centrality and primacy, of the articulate observer. All could describe common sights and creatures so sharply as to make the description interesting—often exciting—after two thousand years. This continuing ability of the classical mind to comment on our own times was what had first attracted Thoreau to Virgil's agricultural writings. With Aristotle and

Pliny this was still true. In addition, both the *History of the Animals* and the *Natural History* had much to teach about the organization of vast projects in natural history.

Thoreau was still very much involved with the classical naturalists when, on January 1, 1860, not quite a month after John Brown's death, a copy of Darwin's *Origin of Species* arrived in Concord. Charles Brace, a New York social worker, had picked up a copy from Asa Gray, the Harvard botanist and ally of Darwin in the coming struggle. Brace, Sanborn, Alcott, and Thoreau had dinner together and discussed the new book, which had been published five weeks before. Thoreau soon got hold of a copy, read it carefully, and made a series of extracts from it.[3]

So many things fail to interest us, says Ortega y Gasset, because they cannot find enough surfaces in our minds on which to take hold. Thoreau's nearly limitless capacity for being interested is one of the most unusual and attractive things about him. That his interests were still expanding, his wonder still green, his capacity for observation, expression, and connection still growing is the most impressive evidence possible that his spirits this January were still on the wing. He had long been familiar with Darwin's *Voyage of the Beagle*; he was already interested in questions of the geographical distribution of animals and plants; he was by now inclined toward evolutionist or—as they were then usually called—developmental ideas about species; and he was correspondingly skeptical about Agassiz's pronouncements on special creation. Thoreau, therefore, was fully prepared for what he was to find in the *Origin of Species*, a work described by a recent editor as "easily the most readable and approachable of the great revolutionary books of the scientific imagination."[4]

The *Origin of Species* is not a specialized work. Darwin was, as Thoreau wished to be, a "polymath in the biological sciences," interested in geology, zoology, paleontology, botany, ornithology, with a special interest in the study of pigeons. His view of science is not a narrow insistence on professionalism, objectivity, or measurement as such, though he was deficient in none of these. "Science," said Darwin in an often-quoted remark, "consists in grouping facts so that general laws or conclusions may be drawn from them." The *Origin of Species* was certain to appeal to Thoreau, being a book very much concerned with "the relations of animals and plants to their environment and to each other," and having much to say about such matters as "the relative size and hairiness of gooseberries."[5]

Where Agassiz believed in the permanent and unchangeable nature of species, Darwin was arguing for the transmutation or metamorphosis of species into one another. Agassiz said there were no variations, only fixed species. Darwin held the exact opposite, that there were only variations, and that no such thing as permanent distinct species could exist. Darwin intended to show that transmutation or metamorphosis, a ruling image in the Western imagination, especially since Goethe's time, was no longer just a metaphor, but a fact.

Darwin started (as did his rival and codiscoverer of natural selection, Alfred Wallace) from Thomas Malthus, whose *Essay on the Principle of Population* opens with striking observations on the immense fertility of living things. "The germes of existence contained in this earth, if they could freely develop themselves, would fill millions of worlds in the course of a few thousand years." Malthus proposed his main subject as "The constant tendency in all animated life to increase beyond the nourishment prepared for it." Reading Malthus gave Darwin his point of departure. "Being well prepared to appreciate the struggle for existence which everywhere goes on from long-continued observation of the habits of animals and plants, it at once struck me that under these circumstances favourable variations would tend to be preserved, and unfavourable ones to be destroyed. The result of this would be the formation of new species."[6]

This process Darwin called "natural selection." The word "evolution," with its suggestion of progress, does not occur in early editions of the book. Natural selection was the process or mechanism Darwin proposed as the basis of "descent with modification," which was, in turn, the concept he proposed in place of "special creation." "As many more individuals of each species are born than can possibly survive; and as, consequently, there is a frequently recurring struggle for existence, it follows that any being, if it vary however slightly in any manner profitable to itself, under the complex and sometimes varying conditions of life, will have a better chance of survival and thus be naturally selected." Perhaps so, but first he had to demonstrate that variations in species in fact occurred, a point flatly denied by Agassiz.[7]

The opening chapter carefully sets this argument up by showing how much variation has occurred in grain, cats, dogs, livestock, and pigeons owing to artificial selection by human breeders. From variation under domestication, he passes to variation under nature. If all the existing varieties of pigeons—pouters, fantails, runts, barbs, dragons, carriers, and tumblers—can be shown to be descended from a single wild species of pigeon, the differences owing entirely to breeders' selections, then why cannot similar small variations have occurred in nature? Thoreau took extracts from this part of the argument. Chapters three and four, on natural selection, talk much about the enormous number of seeds produced by many plants, the severe competition for growing space, the resulting destruction of vast numbers of seeds. Thoreau began doing similar studies, especially of acorns, in the months to come. Chapters eleven and twelve are on the geographical distribution of species. This part of the book is important to Darwin's case against special creation because the more widely species can be shown to be dispersed, the greater the likelihood that similar, neighboring species are connected via common descent. Thoreau quotes liberally from these chapters in his notes.

Darwin repeatedly observes how little we now know. "I do not believe that botanists are aware how charged the mud of ponds is with seeds," he wrote. And again, "how profoundly ignorant we are with respect to the many and curious means of occasional transport,—a subject which has hardly ever been properly experimentised on." Chapter thirteen, on classification, returns to the old debate between the artificial (Linnaean) system and the natural system of botanical classification. Darwin comes down strongly on the side of the natural, with this interesting explanation, repeated several times in the book: "I believe this element of descent [from a common parent] is the hidden bond of connexion which naturalists have sought under the term of the Natural System." Darwin's concluding chapter repeats his conviction, which may have operated as a call to Thoreau over the months ahead, that "we are as yet profoundly ignorant of the many occasional means of transport" of species from one place to another. The dispersion of seeds, then, was a topic that needed attention.[8]

In concluding, Darwin restates his central argument once more: "There is no obvious reason why the principles which have acted so efficiently under domestication should not have acted under nature.

In the preservation of favoured individuals and races, during the constantly-recurrent Struggle for Existence, we see the most powerful and ever-acting means of selection. The struggle for existence inevitably follows from the high geometrical rate of increase which is common to all organic beings." Species, he repeats, are merely strongly marked varieties. Darwin repeats the argument against individual, separate creation, giving yet another example, which Thoreau copied out into his extract book. "Nearly all the plants and animals of the Galapagos archipelago, of Juan Fernandez, and of the other American islands being related in the most striking manner to the plants and animals of the neighboring American mainland: and those of the Cape de Verde Archipelago and other African islands to the African mainland." How closely Thoreau followed the argument and how clearly he grasped the central point may be judged by the simple concluding note he now added to this passage. "Hence not created there." Thoreau had followed Darwin's detailed account, understood his argument and noted where further work remained to be done. The advantages of Darwin's developmental theory would grow on him over the next months.[9]

99. Beyond Transcendentalism: The Natural History Projects

In late December 1859, Thoreau was considering what was required of a natural historian. On the last day of the month he noted that "he who speaks with most authority on a given subject is not ignorant of what has been said by his predecessors. He will take his place in a regular order, and substantially add his own knowledge to the knowledge of previous generations." It is a goal one must respect, a solid acknowledgment of how one should proceed. On the following day came the dinner discussion about Darwin. Three days after that Thoreau wrote the often-quoted description of how the scientist, the scholar, and the writer really proceed:

A man receives only what he is ready to receive, whether physically or intellectually or morally. . . . We hear and apprehend only what we already half know. . . . Every man thus *tracks himself* through life, in all his hearing and reading and observation and travelling. His observations make a chain. The phenomenon or fact that cannot in any wise be linked with the rest which he has observed, he does not observe. The remark is made apropos of his reading something in Aristotle about the spawning of pouts which he had already half observed, but the force of the statement, Aristotelian in its scope, could apply not only to his own patterns of observation but to those of Agassiz or Darwin as well. It is not an apology for preconceptions or blinkered vision, but a recognition of the importance of the prepared eye and mind. Chance might rule in the Darwinian world now dawning, but Thoreau knew, as Pasteur would say, that "chance favors the prepared mind."[1]

In the early months of 1860 Thoreau was prepared and preparing for some major work. "Write with fury, and correct with flegm," he advised a local youth and would-be author. The mood of a February 12 journal entry dominates his reading and observation for the season. "It excites me to see early in the spring that black artery [the river] leaping once more through the snow-clad town. All is tumult and life there. . . . These are the wrists, temples, of the earth, where I feel its pulse with my eye. The living waters, not the dead earth." How different this sounds from earlier accounts of the sleepy currentless Musketaquid or Grass-Ground River. He read Aelian, Topsell, Brand (whom he marked down for ignorance of Theophrastus), and Belon. He lectured on "Wild Apples" in Concord and Bedford. In his journal he sharpened and refined his chosen point of view. He had gained enormously over the years by learning scientific nomenclature, but now he could also see a limit to its usefulness. "We can never begin to see anything as it is so long as we remember the scientific term which always our ignorance has imposed on it. Natural objects and phenomena are in this sense forever wild and unnamed by us." Unnamed perhaps, but not undescribed. Vivid, life-lending description was the great gift and lesson of earlier writers. "We cannot spare the very lively and lifelike descriptions of some of the old naturalists," he wrote. "They sympathize with the creatures which they describe." Gesner, for example, says of antelope living near the Euphrates that they "delight much to drink of the cold water thereof." Thoreau's response is that the animals described by most modern naturalists "do not *delight* in anything." The old naturalists excelled in description; the new, in measuring. Thoreau would make a serious effort to do both.[2]

Taking advantage of his annual upsurge of energy in March, Thoreau began a massive reordering of his journal and extract books. Over the next twenty-two months, extending through January 1862, he worked at rearranging the natural history materials and observations he had been accumulating systematically for ten years. His working procedure now was to run through his journal entries for a single month, say April, of a single year, making a list of observations in a single category, such as leafing, in chronological order. Then he would go on to April of the next year and write down all the leafing data for that month. From nine or ten such lists, generally beginning with 1852, he would then compile a large chart, enabling him to track each item of April leafing across ten Aprils. He repeated the entire procedure for flowering, again for bird sightings, again for different fruits, for quadrupeds, and for fish. Eventually he accumulated over 750 pages of these lists and charts, some of which must have taken many days to complete. It is a huge undertaking, a major effort, the general purpose of which seems to have been the distillation of ten years' observations into an archetypal year, not impressionistic, but statistically averaged, combining the accuracy of a Darwin with the descriptive flair of a Pliny and the eye of a Ruskin.[3]

The large charts are missing for July, August, and September, but these are the months chiefly covered in yet another large pile of manuscript, some six hundred more pages, called "Notes on Fruits," or "Wild Fruits." It seems possible that this represents the next stage beyond the charts, the gathering up, in narrative form, of the vast materials. The "Notes on Fruits" show how not just the journal but all his reading and note taking was being called on for the new project. He quotes heavily from his Indian Books, from his New England and Early Canada reading, and from his classical studies. And everywhere he tries to leaven the mass of detailed observation and exact knowledge with a prose style marked by admiration and delight. Thus he writes, of the first fruits of summer, "wild raspberries begin to be ripe the 25th of June and last into August—being at their height about the 15th (or 20th) of July. The sight of these bright red berries on a comparatively large and leafy bush—as perchance, winding our way through the little groves which they make, we pluck the fruit dripping with rain, surprises us while it reminds us of the progress of the year." The project, which seems to have been conceived as a sort of microkosmos by comparison with Humboldt's *Kosmos*, or as his response to the challenge of Agassiz's *Contributions to the Natural History of the United States*, required the distillation of enormous stores of material filling thousands of pages. Emerson and Blake seem to have had the best sense of the real scope of the work. Emerson noted that "the scale on which his studies proceeded was so large as to require longevity," and Blake, no doubt following what he took to be Thoreau's purpose, edited four volumes from the journals called *Early Spring in Massachusetts*, *Summer*, *Autumn*, and *Winter*. Blake's volumes consist of journal passages only; he did not try to complete Thoreau's consolidating and generalizing process, but the four volumes deserve respect for preserving the shadow of Thoreau's intentions.[4]

His determination was as strong as ever. To Blake he wrote in May 1860 that "if a man believes and expects great things of himself, it makes no odds where you put him, or what you show him." Thoreau had little or no will to power, but he had a very powerful will to expression. Carrying his January remarks a step farther, he now wrote, "whether he wakes or sleeps, whether he runs or walks, whether he uses a microscope or a telescope, or his naked eye, a man never discovers anything, never overtakes anything or leaves anything behind, but himself. Whatever he does or says he merely reports himself."[5]

New emphases mark his journal this year. He became more aware of violence and cruelty in nature. The heron's long beak went in after turtles inside their shells, and Thoreau remarks, with unusual emphasis: "such is Nature, who gave one creature a taste or yearning for another's entrails as its favorite tidbit!!" His reading this spring and summer covered Gosse, Cornuti, Crantz's *Greenland*, and Gerard's *Herbal*, the last now a favorite book. It continued to be true of Thoreau, as Augustine said of Varro, "that he read so much that it was a marvel he ever had time to write anything, and wrote so much that it was difficult to see how he found time to read."[6]

September 1860 was another buoyant month for Thoreau. He discovered a rare Canada lynx wild in Concord and wrote it up for the

Boston Society of Natural History. He gave a talk on the "Succession of Forest Trees" at the Middlesex Agricultural Society, and he lingered over the spell of September. "This is a beautiful day," he wrote on the eighteenth, "warm, but not too warm, a harvest day (I am going down the railroad causeway), the first unquestionable and conspicuous autumnal day, when the willows and button-bushes are a yellowed bower in parallel lines along the swollen and shining stream. . . . A brightness as of spring is reflected from the green shorn fields. Both sky and earth are bright."[7]

All year long the Agassiz-Darwin controversy was being fought out. From February to April, Agassiz had defended his position in a series of debates at the Boston Society of Natural History. In March the *American Journal of Science* published Asa Gray on Darwin. In July came Agassiz's long-awaited (negative) review of the *Origin of Species* in the same journal. Thoreau's "Succession of Forest Trees" was quickly printed and reprinted this fall. Thoreau gave a copy to the Boston Society of Natural History. On October 17, his paper on the Canada lynx was read there. On the following day Thoreau made a long journal entry on the controversy between special creation and developmentalism. "We find ourselves in a world that is already planted, but is also still being planted, as at first. We say of some plants that they grow in wet places and of others that they grow in desert places. The truth is that their seeds are scattered almost everywhere, but here only do they succeed. . . . The development theory [i.e., Darwin's] implies a greater vital force in nature, because it is more flexible and accommodating, and equivalent to a sort of constant *new* creation." This explicit, informed rejection of Agassiz is repeated and freshly stated on January 14, 1861.[8]

Plant dispersion is the aspect of Darwin's work Thoreau chose to concentrate on, and his own contribution to the subject, which he did not live to complete, is the four-hundred-page manuscript, unfinished but clear enough in outline, on the "Dispersion of Seeds," which appears to have taken its present shape after Thoreau's reading of Darwin and after the talk on "The Succession of Forest Trees." This essay or book or "chapter" as Thoreau calls it was intended to remedy some of the ignorance about seed dispersal to which Darwin had called attention, but more important it was designed to counter Agassiz's special creation thesis by showing how universal the phenomenon of seed dispersal is. The more Thoreau could show about plants springing from other plants via seeds transported from one place to another, the less tenable the theory of special creation becomes.

Thoreau's late projects—or project, since even the "Dispersion of Seeds" is called a chapter rather than a separate work—on the natural year are a culmination of lifelong concerns, but they also break new ground. In the closing paragraph of "Economy" in *Walden*, Thoreau had included a short parable from Saadi's *Gulistan* about the cypress which, according to Saadi, bears no fruit and was therefore alone of trees called *azad*, or free. To be without seed was to be free of the relentless biological treadmill of growth and decay, free of the economics of production and consumption, getting and spending. The ideal, then, was to be free of productive involvement with the world. Now, as the "Dispersion of Seeds" manuscript shows, the rare tree that bears no seed is simply sterile. Pliny replaces Saadi, the Stoic replaces the ascetic. Thoreau's interests have shifted to a profound new focus on production and dissemination, in generation and creative effort. The center of *Walden* is the desire to be free. The center of the late work is the desire to connect. The movement is from economy to ecology.

From Christian transcendental belief in a divine ordering principle, to a neo-Greek belief in the preeminence of mind in the universe, Thoreau gradually came to accept a view, for which Darwin was one more confirmation, that any ordering force in the universe must be sought in the developmental principle, most easily observable in the natural world in crystals or in leaves and in the spring of the year. This new view holds that the laws of nature are the laws governing growth, maturation, reproduction, decay, death, and growth again. *Walden* was a testament to the centrality and integrity of the individual mind observing nature. The great new project would testify to the coherence of the observed world. It would form a context for *Walden*'s text,
a magnificent, vast, detailed circumference
to *Walden*'s shining center
of light.

100. One World at a Time

By November 1860, Thoreau was hard at work studying how forests grew. He had recently read Harland Coultas's *What Can be Learned from a Tree*, he had found how much trees' rings show about the history of trees, and he was working particularly on the pitch-pine stands in Concord. A couple of Thoreau's charts measuring pitch-pine growth and printed in the last volume of the Torrey and Allen edition of the *Journal* are the only printed charts by which a reader can gain some idea of the nature and scope of the dozens of similar manuscript charts Thoreau compiled during his last two years. His general subject, which seems as much Malthusian as Darwinian at times, was how plants grow, multiply, and disperse. As far back as *Walden* he had felt the link between death and fecundity. A dead horse in a hollow smelled so badly that it forced him to go out of his way around it, "But the assurance it gave me of the strong appetite and inviolable health of Nature was my compensation for this." Now, in late November, looking at a thick young forest standing where not a tree or a seed of a tree had existed fifteen years before, he repeated the insight, only now it concerns his own death and his own body. "I confess that I love to be convinced of this inextinguishable vitality in Nature," he noted. "I would rather that my body should be buried in a soil thus wide-awake than in a mere inert and dead earth." Four days later, on November 29, Alcott stopped by to talk with Thoreau about a meeting to commemorate the first anniversary of John Brown's death. Alcott had a bad cold at the time—he called it "an influenza"—which he very likely gave to Thoreau, who came down with a severe cold, which he also called influenza, on December 3 while out counting tree rings. He insisted on keeping a lecture engagement in Waterbury, Connecticut, but it was ill advised. The cold deepened into bronchitis and kept him housebound all winter. His journal entries for each month shrank dramatically, from 104 pages in October and 81 in November to 17 in December and 11 in January. But he did not stop working. Cut off from making new outdoor observations, he continued the work of restructuring the journal and notes of the last nine years. In February, Alcott found him hard at work "classifying and arranging his papers by subjects, as if he had a new book in mind."[1]

His March journal returns to the question of "natural succession." In April the Civil War finally broke forth; the bombardment of Fort Sumter began on April 12. Thoreau continued to work and to read. His interest in plant distribution and seed dispersion was leading him into further reading in geography. He read and took notes on Alphonse de Candolle's *Géographie Botanique*, a book often cited by Darwin. Thoreau also read Strabo, the ancient Stoic geographer, and Blodget's *Climatology of the United States*. On April 19, the commemorative heart of the Concord year, forty-five volunteers departed for the war. There was a moving sendoff at the railroad station. War news now dominated life in Concord. Thoreau's health was so bad the doctors insisted he get out to a better climate. The bronchitis had seriously weakened him, but the underlying problem was tuberculosis. Rejecting Europe (too costly) and the Caribbean (too muggy), he decided to go to Minnesota. It seems an odd choice, but it was currently being praised for its dry climate, and besides, Thoreau had recently read about the exploring expeditions of the late 1850s to that part of western Canada adjacent to Minnesota, in Harry Youle Hinds's *Report on the Assiniboine and Saskatchewan Exploring Expedition* (Toronto, 1859). He would be going for the first time to the real frontier, just beyond which explorers were still advancing into unmapped areas.[2]

Neither Channing nor Blake could accompany him, so Thoreau went on this long two-month journey by rail and steamboat with seventeen-year-old Horace Mann Jr., son of the famous educator who had died at Yellow Springs, Ohio, two years before. The trip was a tragic failure in most respects. It was difficult, and Thoreau derived no real benefit from it. He saw Chicago, St. Paul, Redwing, an Indian dance and ceremony, the Mississippi River, Milwaukee, and Mackinac Island, but he noted down disappointingly little about either the frontier or the Indians. His notes for the trip strongly suggest that neither subject was much on his mind, nor was the Civil War a major concern—but botanical studies were. His notes are overwhelmingly concentrated on natural history and here, if nowhere else, there are signs of energy and method. He met naturalists, saw museums, read books and reports, took, with Mann, many notes and specimens, and hunted for a wild apple tree with an eagerness he showed for no other subject on this trip.[3]

A friend of Emerson's in Chicago, the Rev. Robert Collyer, saw Thoreau on this trip and noted how "he would hesitate for an instant now and then, waiting for the right word, or would pause with a pathetic patience to master the trouble in his chest." He came home in worse health than when he set out. Horace Mann went on to Harvard, studied botany with Asa Gray, wrote three books on botany, became curator of the Harvard Herbarium, and seemed headed for a major career when he too died of tuberculosis at only twenty-four. He may have caught it from Thoreau, but it was a common killer. "Consumption" was the leading cause of death in Concord in 1859, with nine deaths; in 1861, again with nine deaths; and in 1863 with five.[4]

Thoreau returned to Concord in early July 1861. In late August he made a last trip to see Ricketson in New Bedford, where a photographer named Dunshee took his picture. It shows a man who looks much older than his forty-four years, and much worn down from the man we see in the Maxham daguerreotype of five years earlier. In November, Thoreau made the last entries of his journal proper, recording with amusement the antics of kittens and noting how storms left telltale aftertraces. When Margaret Fuller had died, Thoreau had grimly concluded that our thoughts are all that matter, everything else being, as he then said, but as the wind that blows. Now he had learned better. Every life, like every wind, was "self-registering."

A visitor in November observed that "by evening a flush had come to his cheeks and an ominous brightness and beauty to his eyes, painful to behold. His conversation was unusually brilliant, and we listened with a charmed attention which perhaps stimulated him to continue talking until the weak voice could no longer articulate." But he was still working on the large projects. His charts tabulating and collating phenomena for the month of November include events from 1861, showing that he was still gathering as well as arranging natural history information, even though it does not appear in the printed journal. December and January were, as always, the hardest months to get through. George Minott, the old farmer who was the source for so many of Thoreau's animal stories, could not tough out this winter. He died in December. Thoreau now came down with pleurisy on top of everything else. January was a month of high winds and cold weather. When Blake and Brown visited Thoreau, they found him "pretty low," but characteristically determined to get the good of his present life, however hard or mean it might be. When Blake asked him how the future seemed to him, Thoreau replied, "just as uninteresting as ever." "He was," Brown noted, "in an exalted state of mind for a long time before his death." A scrap of manuscript now in the Huntington Library shows that he was still collecting and listing "general phenomena" for his project as late as this January of 1862. He resisted giving up on the large-scale projects as long as he possibly could.[5]

In February, James T. Fields solicited Thoreau for articles for the *Atlantic Monthly*, and only then did Thoreau turn away from the large projects to clean up a few earlier talks for present publication, and for money for the family. On February 20 he sent off "Autumnal Tints," on the twenty-eighth "Life without Principle." On March 11 he sent "Walking," and on April 2, "Wild Apples." A new edition of *Walden* was proposed by Fields, who also now bought up Thoreau's library of unsold copies of *A Week* with a view to republishing that book as well. Thoreau was, at the end, a well-known writer. His illness had been reported in the papers; his death at only age forty-four would be widely noticed.

Everyone now knew he was dying. In a letter of March 21, 1862, he wrote to a new correspondent and admirer "If I were to live, I should have much to report on Natural History generally," and he added, "I *suppose* that I have not many months to live." Thoreau had been unable to cope emotionally with his brother John's death many years earlier, but he now fully accepted his own. The autumn leaves "teach us how to die," he wrote. Away from home, the Civil War deepened. A new general named Grant was emerging in the Western campaign. On April 6 and 7 one of the bloodiest battles of the war was fought at Pittsburgh landing near Shiloh church. On May 1 New Orleans fell to the Union.[6]

Thoreau's last days were spent at home, in peace, surrounded by family and friends. His bed was brought downstairs. No longer able to write, he dictated to Sophia. By early April his voice had been only a faint whisper for many weeks. But his mind, wit, and spirits held. He advised Emerson's son Edward, who was about to take a trip to the

Rocky Mountains before going back to college, to carry an arrowhead so as to learn from Indians the secret of making them. Sam Staples, Thoreau's one-time jailer, thought he had never seen a man "dying with so much pleasure and peace." When Ellen Sewall's name came up, Thoreau told Sophia he had "always loved her." To his Aunt Louisa, who asked if he had made his peace with God, he answered, "I did not know we had ever quarrelled, Aunt." His last words came back to his writing. Early in the morning on May 6, Sophia read him a piece from the "Thursday" section of *A Week*, and Thoreau anticipated with relish the "Friday" trip homeward, murmuring, "Now comes good sailing." In his last sentence, only the two words "moose" and "Indian" were audible.[7]

No more satisfying deathbed utterance can be imagined for Thoreau than his reply to a question put gently to him by Parker Pillsbury a few days before his death. Pillsbury was an old abolitionist war-horse, a former minister who had left his church over the slavery issue, a man of principle and proven courage, an old family friend who, like Blake and Aunt Louisa, could not resist the impulse to peer into the future. "You seem so near the brink of the dark river," Pillsbury said, "that I almost wonder how the opposite shore may appear to you." Thoreau's answer summed up his life. "One world at a time," he said.[8]

Henry Thoreau died at nine in the morning on May 6, 1862. Outdoors, where he could no longer see them, the earliest apple trees began to leaf and show green, just as they do every year on this day.[9]

Notes

Principal Sources

Abbreviations

EC .... *The Correspondence of Emerson and Carlyle*, ed. Joseph Slater (New York: Columbia University Press, 1964).

EEM .... *Early Essays and Miscellanies*, ed. Joseph J. Moldenhauer and Edwin Moser, with Alexander Kern (Princeton: Princeton University Press, 1975).

ESQ .... *Emerson Society Quarterly*.

HCL .... "Books Thoreau Borrowed from Harvard College Library," in K. W. Cameron, *Emerson the Essayist*, 3d ed. (Hartford: Transcendental Books, 1971), 2: 191–208.

J .... *The Journal of Henry Thoreau*, ed. Bradford Torrey and Francis H. Allen, 14 vols. (Boston: Houghton Mifflin, 1906).

JMN .... *The Journals and Miscellaneous Notebooks of Ralph Waldo Emerson*, ed. William H. Gilman et al., 16 vols. (Cambridge: Harvard University Press, 1960–1983).

LCR .... "List of Planned Classical Reading" in *The Transcendentalists and Minerva*, ed. K. W. Cameron, 3 vols. (Hartford: Transcendental Books, 1958).

LRWE .... *The Letters of Ralph Waldo Emerson*, ed. Ralph L. Rusk, 6 vols. (New York: Columbia University Press, 1939).

NEQ .... *New England Quarterly*

PJ .... Henry D. Thoreau, *Journal*, ed. John C. Broderick et al., 2 vols. published (Princeton: Princeton University Press, 1981–).

RP .... Henry D. Thoreau, *Reform Papers*, ed. Wendell Glick (Princeton: Princeton University Press, 1973).

SAR .... *Studies in the American Renaissance*, ed. Joel Myerson (Charlottesville: University Press of Virginia, 1977–).

SP .... *Studies in Philology*.

TLN .... *Thoreau's Literary Notebook in the Library of Congress*, ed. K. W. Cameron (Hartford: Transcendental Books, 1964).

TSB .... *Thoreau Society Bulletin*.

Short Titles

BUELL .... Lawrence Buell, *Literary Transcendentalism: Style and Vision in the American Renaissance* (Ithaca: Cornell University Press, 1973).

CHANNING .... William Ellery Channing, *Thoreau, the Poet-Naturalist*, ed. F. B. Sanborn, new enlarged edition (Boston: Charles E. Goodspeed, 1902).

CHRISTIE .... John Aldrich Christie, *Thoreau as World Traveller* (New York: Columbia University Press, 1965).

CLAPPER .... Ronald E. Clapper, "The Development of Walden: A Genetic Text" (Ph.D. diss., UCLA, 1967).

CORR .... *The Correspondence of Henry David Thoreau*, ed. Walter Harding and Carl Bode (New York: New York University Press, 1958; rept., 1974).

DAYS .... Walter Harding, *The Days of Henry Thoreau*, enlarged and corrected edition (Princeton: Princeton University Press, 1982).

DIAL .... *"The Dial" A Magazine for Literature, Philosophy and Religion*, 4 vols. (Boston: Weeks, Jordan, 1840–1844; rept., New York: Russell and Russell, 1961).

HOWARTH .... William L. Howarth, *The Literary Manuscripts of Henry David Thoreau* (Columbus: Ohio State University Press, 1974).

H WORKS RWE .... *The Collected Works of Ralph Waldo Emerson*, 3 vols. published (Cambridge: Harvard University Press, 1971–).

JOHNSON .... Linck C. Johnson, "'A Natural Harvest': The Writing of *A Week on the Concord and Merrimack Rivers, with the text of the First Draft*" (Ph.D. diss., Princeton, 1975).

MAINE WOODS ..... Henry D. Thoreau, *The Maine Woods*, ed. Joseph J. Moldenhauer (Princeton: Princeton University Press, 1972).

PAUL .... Sherman Paul, *The Shores of America: Thoreau's Inward Exploration* (Urbana: University of Illinois Press, 1958).

POEMS .... *Collected Poems of Henry Thoreau*, ed. Carl Bode, enlarged edition (Baltimore: The Johns Hopkins Press, 1965).

SEYBOLD .... Ethel Seybold, *Thoreau: The Quest and the Classics* (New Haven: Yale University Press, 1951).

SHANLEY .... J. Lyndon Shanley, *The Making of Walden, with the Text of the First Version* (Chicago: University of Chicago Press, 1957).

STOWELL .... Robert F. Stowell, *A Thoreau Gazetteer*, ed. William L. Howarth (Princeton: Princeton University Press, 1970).

TRANS AP .... *Transcendental Apprenticeship; Notes on Young Henry Thoreau's Reading*, ed. K. W. Cameron (Hartford: Transcendental Books, 1976).

WALDEN .... Henry D. Thoreau, *Walden*, ed. J. Lyndon Shanley (Princeton: Princeton University Press, 1971).

WEEK .... Henry D. Thoreau, *A Week on the Concord and Merrimack Rivers*, ed. Carl F. Hovde (Princeton: Princeton University Press, 1980).

WORKS RWE ...... *The Complete Works of Ralph Waldo Emerson*, centenary edition (Boston: Houghton Mifflin, 1903).

WRITINGS .... *The Writings of Henry D. Thoreau*, Walden edition (Boston: Houghton Mifflin, 1906).

Notes

1. Fall 1837: Commencement

1. See the physical description of T in William Ellery Channing, *Thoreau the Poet-Naturalist*, ed. F. B. Sanborn (Boston: Goodspeed, 1902), p. 33; Edward Waldo Emerson, *Henry Thoreau as Remembered by a Young Friend* (Boston: Houghton Mifflin, 1917), pp. 1–2; and Moncure Conway, "Thoreau," *Eclectic Magazine*, 67 (1866): 191–192, reprinted in *Thoreau, Man of Concord*, ed. Walter Harding (New York: Holt, Rinehart and Winston, 1960), pp. 38–40. For the portraits of T, see Thomas Blanding and Walter Harding, "A Thoreau Iconography" (Geneseo, 1980), Thoreau Society Booklet 30.

2. *Days*, pp. 52–53.   3. *PJ*, 1:8–9.

4. Ralph Waldo Emerson, "Thoreau," *Atlantic Monthly*, 10 (1862):239.

5. *PJ*, 1:14.

2. Harvard under Quincy

1. Samuel Eliot Morison, *Three Centuries of Harvard* (Cambridge: Harvard University Press, 1936), p. 235; Arthur S. Pier, *The Story of Harvard* (Boston: Little, Brown, 1913), pp. 139–140.

2. On the budget, see Samuel Eliot Morison, *The Development of Harvard University* (Cambridge: Harvard University Press, 1930), Seymour E. Harriss, *The Economics of Harvard* (New York: McGraw-Hill, 1970), and Josiah Quincy, *A History of Harvard University* (Cambridge: J. Owen, 1840).

3. Morison, *Three Centuries*, p. 235; Pier, pp. 140–141; letter of June 25, 1837, from Quincy to RWE, in F. B. Sanborn, *Henry David Thoreau* (Boston: Houghton Mifflin, 1887), pp. 53–54.

4. Pier, pp. 138–139.

3. Thoreau at Harvard

1. For T's coursework, see Kenneth W. Cameron, *Thoreau's Harvard Years* (Hartford: Transcendental Books, 1966), pp. 13–19, and *Days*, pp. 32–51.

2. J. Albee, *Remembrances of Emerson* (New York, 1903), p. 33; for T's reading in college see "Books Thoreau Borrowed from the Harvard College Library," in Kenneth W. Cameron, *Emerson the Essayist* (Hartford: Transcendental Books, 1945), 2:191–208; Cameron's *Thoreau's Harvard Years*, and his *Emerson and Thoreau as Readers* (Hartford: Transcendental Books, 1959; rev. ed., 1972).

3. Laurance Thompson, *Young Longfellow* (New York: Macmillan, 1938), p. 242.

4. Concord

1. Lemuel Shattuck, *A History of the Town of Concord* (Boston: Russell, Odiorne, and Co., 1835; rept., 1971); Townsend Scudder, *Concord, American Town* (Boston: Little, Brown, 1947).

2. See Ruth Wheeler, *Concord, Climate for Freedom* (Concord: Concord Antiquarian Society, 1967), and Mary S. Clarke, *The Old Middlesex Canal* (Melrose: The Hilltop Press, 1974).

3. For a succinct account of the changing New England landscape see John Brinkerhoff Jackson, *American Space* (New York: Norton, 1972), chap. 4; for more details see John R. Stilgoe, *Common Landscape of America 1580 to 1845* (New Haven: Yale University Press, 1982); Shattuck reports (p. 213) that of Concord's 12,942 acres in 1831, only 2,048 were in woodland.

4. See 1838 parish expenses, Concord Archives, microfilm roll 004, Concord Free Public Library.

5. Shattuck, chap. 14, "Statistical History."

5. Emerson

1. *LRWE*, 1:394; *JMN*, 4:219; *EC*, pp. 14–15. For an account of Emerson's move to Concord, see Gay Wilson Allen, *Waldo Emerson* (New York: Viking, 1981), chap. 12.

2. Quoted in *The Writer's Quotation Book*, ed. James Charlton (New York: The Pushcart Press, 1980), p. 14.

3. Thomas Paine, *The Age of Reason*, in *Thomas Paine*, ed. H. H. Clark (New York: Hill and Wang, 1944), p. 262.

4. Ralph L. Rusk, *The Life of Ralph Waldo Emerson* (New York: Columbia University Press, 1949), p. 250.

5. *JMN*, 5:379; Emerson's interest in J. G. Herder's *Outlines of a Philosophy of the History of Man* begins with his borrowing this book from the Harvard College library in 1829, and from the Boston Athenaeum in 1831. See Kenneth W. Cameron, *Ralph Waldo Emerson's Reading* (New York: Haskell House, 1966, 1st pub. 1941). For Herder's impact on Emerson, see the 1836 "Philosophy of History" lectures printed in *The Early Lectures of Ralph Waldo Emerson*, ed. Stephen E. Whicher, Robert E. Spiller, and Wallace E. Williams (Cambridge: Harvard University Press, 1964), vol. 2.

6. Moncure D. Conway, *Autobiography* (Boston: Houghton Mifflin, 1904), p. 143, quoted in *Man of Concord*, ed. Walter Harding, p. 111; *JMN*, 5:453–454.

6. The Classics

1. Supplementing Ethel Seybold's *Thoreau, the Quest and the Classics* (New Haven: Yale University Press, 1951) is Kenneth W. Cameron, *Young Thoreau and the Classics* (Hartford: Transcendental Books, 1975), esp. for information on T's school years, and Kenneth W. Cameron, *Thoreau's Harvard Years* (Hartford: Transcendental Books, 1966); Pier, *The Story of Harvard*, pp. 140–141; Morison, *Three Centuries*, p. 260. A useful list of sources about T's reading is given on pp. 132–133 of Cameron's *Emerson and Thoreau as Readers*; *Walden*, p. 100.

2. *PJ*, 1:14, 26, 31.   3. *Works*, 5:214.

4. William James, *The Varieties of Religious Experience* (New York: Longmans, Green and Co., 1902), p. 96; *Walden*, p. 99; *PJ*, p. 29.

7. Germany

1. For the German context of American Transcendentalism, the well-known views of Rene Wellek ("Emerson and German Philosophy," *NEQ*, 16 [1943]: 41–62 and "The Minor Transcendentalists and German Philosophy," *NEQ*, 15 [1942]: 652–680) must be supplemented with Henry A. Pochmann, *German Culture in America* (Madison: University of Wisconsin

Press, 1957); Octavius Brooks Frothingham, *Transcendentalism in New England* (New York: Putnam's, 1876); and J. W. Brown, *The Rise of Biblical Criticism in America 1800–1870* (Middletown: Wesleyan University Press, 1969).

2. *Corr*, p. 19. For T's interest in Schlegel, see *Trans Ap*, p. 22.

3. Thompson, *Young Longfellow*, p. 399.

4. *PJ*, 1:16.

5. Johann Wolfgang von Goethe, *Italian Journey: 1786–1788*, trans. W. H. Auden and Elizabeth Mayer (New York: Random House, 1962; rept. Berkeley: North Point Press, 1982), p. 343.

6. Goethe, *Italian Journey*, p. 363.

7. "Goethe," in *Representative Men*, in *Works RWE*, 4:275; *PJ*, 1:15.

8. Mme. de Stael, *Germany* (Boston: Houghton Mifflin, 1817), 2:360–376. For T on de Stael and on enthusiasm, see *PJ*, 1:32, 181.

8. "Society"

1. Walter Harding, "A Checklist of Thoreau's Lectures," *Bulletin of the New York Public Library* (1948), p. 79. What remains of the lecture "Society" appears in *PJ*, 1:35–39.

2. Thoreau's college essays are in *EEM*; *EEM*, p. 106.

3. *PJ*, 1:7, 23, 32.

4. "Self-Reliance," in *H Works RWE*, 2:31; Mann's view of *Bildung* is discussed in William H. Bruford, *The German Tradition of Self-Cultivation* (Cambridge: Cambridge University Press, 1975).

5. *PJ*, 1:25, 37.   6. *PJ*, 1:38, 117.   7. *PJ*, 1:25.

9. Concord Schoolmaster

1. For parish salaries in 1838 see Town of Concord Records and Archives, Box 13, Roll 004, Item 55. Teachers' salaries for 1837–38 were published in *The Yeoman's Gazette*, April 14, 1838. See also *Days*, pp. 52–54.

2. See "Report of Expenditures for year ending March 5 1838" in *The Yeoman's Gazette*. Numbers of students are given in the April 14 number.

3. Ruth Wheeler, *Concord, Climate for Freedom*, p. 148 discusses violence in the schools.

4. See the "Annual Report of the School Committee of Concord for the year ending Apr. 1, 1846."

5. *Corr*, p. 20.   6. *Corr*, p. 24.   7. *PJ*, 1:44–46.

8. *Corr*, p. 27.

10. Poetry

1. *PJ*, 1:32, 34.

2. See *Trans Ap*, pp. 11–17 for T's extracts from *Outre-Mer*, pp. 31–41 for poetic phrase worksheets.

3. Longfellow's manuscript records of Harvard classes and extensive manuscript lecture materials on Goethe, The History of the Anglo-Saxon Languages, the History of the English Language, and English medieval literature are in the Houghton Library at Harvard, call no *54M.8/ms Am 1340/items 4, 15, 16, 49.

4. *Poems*, pp. 192, 384–385.

5. Ibid., pp. 213–214, 374. For the poem's source in Bosworth, in addition to Turner, see *Trans Ap*, pp. 74, 87–89, 104.

6. From "I love a careless Streamlet," *Poems*, p. 87.

7. *Poems*, pp. 89–91; *PJ*, 1:28.

8. *Works RWE*, 3:9; *Poems*, p. 92.

9. *Poems*, pp. 93, 97.

10. *JMN*, 7:231; *Works RWE*, 9:279, 280; *Poems*, p. 30; *PJ*, 1:104.

11. Summer and Fall 1838

1. *Poems*, p. 105; *PJ*, 1:65.   2. *PJ*, 1:60–64.

3. *PJ*, 1:63–64; *RWE*, "Thoreau," *Atlantic Monthly* 10 (1862): 247.

4. *PJ*, 1:49.   5. *PJ*, 1:50–51.   6. *PJ*, 1:55, 56.

7. *PJ*, 1:56.

12. The Eye of Henry Thoreau

1. Quoted in Herbert Gleason, *Thoreau Country* (San Francisco: Sierra Club Books, 1975), p. xii; *H Works RWE*, 1:20.

2. For T and luminism, see John I. H. Baur, "American Luminism," *Perspectives* (Autumn 1954), pp. 90–98; *The Natural Paradise*, ed. Kynaston McShine (New York: The Museum of Modern Art, 1976); Barbara Novak, *American Painting of the Nineteenth Century*, 2d ed. (New York: Harper and Row, 1979); Barbara Novak, *Nature and Culture* (New York: Oxford University Press, 1980); John Conron, "'Bright American Rivers': The Luminist Landscapes of Thoreau's *A Week on the Concord and Merrimack Rivers*," *American Quarterly*, 32 (1980): 144–166; and esp. Barton L. St. Armand, "Luminism in the Work of Henry David Thoreau: The Dark and the Light," *Canadian Review of American Studies*, 11 (1980): 13–30.

3. Mabel M. Swan, *The Athenaeum Gallery: 1827–1873* (Boston: The Boston Athenaeum, 1940).

4. *The Concord Saunterer*, 15, 2 (Summer 1980): 29. Emerson's Italian acquisitions still hang on the walls of his Concord home.

5. *HCL*, p. 194; *PJ*, 1:155; Henry W. Longfellow, MS lecture of June 15, 1837, on Goethe, in the Houghton Library at Harvard.

6. *PJ*, 1:9, 14, 53, 130; Julian Hawthorne, *Memoirs* (New York: Macmillan, 1938), p. 115.

7. *PJ*, 1:109; *Week*, p. 48; John Ruskin, *Modern Painters* (New York: John Wiley and Sons, 1884), Vol. II, sec. 1, p. 51.

8. *Writings*, 5:247.

13. Self-Culture

1. W. H. Bruford, *The German Tradition of Self-Cultivation* (Cambridge: Cambridge University Press, 1975), pp. 1–2, 232.

2. Ibid., p. vii.

3. Henry W. Longfellow, MS lecture of June 13, 1838, on Goethe, in the Houghton Library at Harvard.

4. Margaret Fuller, "Menzel's View of Goethe," *The Dial*, 1 (1841): 340–347; Frederick H. Hedge, "The Art of Life,—The Scholar's Calling," *The Dial*, 1 (1840): 175–182; Horace Greeley, "Self-Trust," *The Little Corporal*, April 1867. See also Amos Bronson Alcott, *The Doctrine and Discipline of Human Culture* (Boston: James Munroe, 1836), and the excellent discussions by Leo Stoller, "Thoreau's Doctrine of Simplicity," *NEQ*, 29 (1956): 443–461, and David Robinson, "Margaret Fuller and the Transcendental Ethos,"

PMLA, 97 (1982): 83–98; William Ellery Channing, "Self-Culture," in *Works*, new ed. (Boston: American Unitarian Association, 1886), p. 15.

5. See *Young Emerson Speaks*, ed. A. C. McGiffert, Jr. (Boston: Houghton Mifflin, 1938), pp. 261–271.

6. *The Early Lectures of Ralph Waldo Emerson*, ed. Stephen E. Whicher, Robert E. Spiller, and Wallace E. Williams (Cambridge: Harvard University Press, 1964), 2:211–212.

7. Philip Slater, *The Pursuit of Loneliness* (Boston: Beacon, 1970); Quentin Anderson, *The Imperial Self* (New York: Knopf, 1971), p. 4; "Ethics," in *The Early Lectures of Ralph Waldo Emerson*, 2:151.

8. *PJ*, 1:52, 73.   9. *Walden*, p. 158.

14. Ellen

1. *Days*, pp. 94–104; Louise O. Koopman, "The Thoreau Romance," in *Thoreau in our Season*, ed. John H. Hicks (Amherst: University of Massachusetts Press, 1962).

2. *PJ*, 1:74; *Poems*, pp. 64–65.   3. *PJ*, 1:81.

4. Ellen Sewall, letter to her father, Reverend Edmund Quincy Sewall, July 31, MS George L. Davenport, Jr.; "Statement prepared in October 1917 by Elizabeth Osgood Davenport and Louise Osgood Koopman, regarding the youthful romances . . . ," MS George L. Davenport, Jr.

5. Ellen Sewall, letter to Prudence Ward, December 26, 1839, MS George L. Davenport, Jr.; *PJ*, 1:105, 110.

6. *PJ*, 1:132, 158.

7. Part of a draft of T's letter to Ellen survives in T's journal. See *PJ*, 1:193.

8. Ellen Sewall, letter to Prudence Ward, December 26, 1839, MS George L. Davenport, Jr.

9. Ibid., December 26, 1839; November 23, 1839; September 29, 1839, MSS George L. Davenport, Jr.

10. Ibid., November 18, 1840, MS George L. Davenport, Jr.

11. See n. 4, item 2; Ellen Sewall, letter to Prudence Ward, October 26, 1840, MS George L. Davenport, Jr.; Ellen Sewall, diary, July 25, 1841, MS Mrs. Gilbert Tower.

12. Koopman, "Thoreau Romance," p. 102.

15. The Rivers

1. On the relation between mountains and rivers in *A Week*, see Frederick Garber, "A Space for Saddleback . . . ," *Centennial Review*, 24 (1980): 322–337.

2. *Days*, pp. 87, 88.

3. J. Spooner, letter of Sept. 29, 1854, in *The Concord Saunterer*, 12, 2 (Summer 1977): 9; *JMN*, 7:454; Lemuel Shattuck, *A History of the Town of Concord* (Boston: Russell, Odiorne, and Co., 1835; rept., 1971), p. 201.

4. *PJ*, 1:125, 134, 135.

5. Mary S. Clarke, *The Old Middlesex Canal* (Melrose: The Hilltop Press, 1974), p. 99.

6. *PJ*, 1:137.

7. *Week*, pp. 23, 43, 113, 114, 116.

8. Ibid., p. 334.

9. Ibid., pp. 339, 348, 351, 353, 360.

10. Ibid., pp. 389, 390, 393.

11. Ibid., pp. 359, 483; Thomas Blanding, "A Last Word from Thoreau," in *The Concord Saunterer*, 11, 4 (Winter 1976): 16–17.

16. Aeschylus, Bravery

1. *PJ*, 1:100.   2. *PJ*, 1:82, 107.   3. *PJ*, 1:85–86, 91–98.

4. *PJ*, 1:86; *H Works RWE*, 1:239.

5. *PJ*, 1:91, 92.   6. *PJ*, 1:94, 124, 146.

7. Baudelaire, *Intimate Journals*, quoted in *Prose Keys to Modern Poetry*, ed. Karl Shapiro (Evanston: Row, Peterson, 1962), p. 36.

8. Albert Salomon, *In Praise of Enlightenment* (New York: World, 1963), p. 19; *LCR*, II: 361; *PJ*, 1:87, 124.

9. *JMN*, 13:47. For a study of the figure of the soldier, see John Ferling, "A New England Soldier . . ." *American Quarterly*, 33 (1981): 26–45.

10. *Walden*, p. 326.

17. Transcendentalism

1. Doreen Hunter, " 'Frederic Henry Hedge, What Say You?' " *American Quarterly*, 32 (1980): 189. See also Joel Myerson, *The New England Transcen-*

dentalists and The Dial (Rutherford, N.J.: Fairleigh Dickinson University Press, 1980), pp. 156–162.

2. J. A. Saxon, "Prophecy,—Transcendentalism,—Progress," *The Dial*, 2 (1841): 90; Henry A. Pochmann, *German Culture in America* (Madison: University of Wisconsin Press, 1957); O. B. Frothingham, *Transcendentalism in New England* (New York: Putnam's, 1876; rept., 1972), p. 1; *H Works RWE*, 1:206–207. See Raymond P. Tripp's valuable *With Pen of Truth* (Shropshire: Onny, 1972).

3. For T's interest in language theory see Philip F. Gura, *The Wisdom of Words* (Middletown: Wesleyan University Press, 1981).

4. *H Works RWE*, 1:37.

5. *LRWE*, 2:234, 242–243, 271, 281–282, 287.

6. *LRWE*, 2:291, 292.

7. *Week*, p. 437; John Dryden, "A Discourse Concerning the Original and Progress of Satire," in *Essays of John Dryden*, ed. W. P. Ker (Oxford: Clarendon, 1926), 2:75; *EEM*, pp. 122, 123.

8. *EEM*, pp. 123, 124, 125, 126.

18. Summer 1840

1. *PJ*, 1:128, 132. 2. *PJ*, 1:118, 119.

3. *PJ*, 1:171, 196. 4. *PJ*, 1:121, 140–141.

5. Henry Hallam, *Introduction to the Literature of Europe in the Fifteenth, Sixteenth, and Seventeenth Centuries* (Paris: Galignani, 1839), 4:109. For T's knowledge of Hallam see *J*, 1:396. For T's knowledge of Cudworth, see *Trans Ap*, pp. 164–169. For T's version of the hymn to Zeus, see *Trans Ap*, pp. 167–168.

6. *Week*, pp. 64–65. On T's Orphism, see Barbara H. Carson, "An Orphic Hymn in *Walden*,*"* *ESQ*, 20 (1974): 125–130.

7. *LRWE*, 2:327. Though she was baptized Lydia, Emerson called his second wife Lidian, possibly to avoid the New Englander's pronunciation Lydier Emerson.

8. *LRWE*, 2:311, 316, 323

9. *PJ*, 1:167.

19. Fall 1840

1. For T and Fenelon, see *PJ*, 1:156n; for Degerando, see *PJ*, 1:180.

2. *HCL*, p. 192; *Trans Ap*, p. 114: *PJ*, 1:52, 177n (but see *Trans Ap*,

where T's extracts from Murray are given an 1837 date), 173, 175, 177, 186n.

3. *PJ*, 1:173, 177.

4. *PJ*, 1:187n, 188, 196 ff.

5. *PJ*, 1:116; *Poems*, pp. 78, 301; *PJ*, 1:170; *Poems*, pp. vi, 81–82, 387; *PJ*, 1:141, 181, 182, 196.

6. *PJ*, 1:175; *RP*, pp. 3–17; *PJ*, 1:91–98.

7. *RP*, p. 3.

8. *PJ*, 1:193; Ellen Sewall, letter to Prudence Ward, Nov. 18, 1840, MS George L. Davenport, Jr.; *PJ*, 1:196, 197; *Corr*, pp. 41–42. On "The Service," see *Paul*, pp. 83–89.

20. December 1840

1. *PJ*, 1:199, 205.   2. *PJ*, 1:200, 204, 205.

3. *PJ*, 1:207.   4. *Seybold*, pp. 121–122.   5. *PJ*, 1:212.

6. *LRWE*, 2:369; Robert D. Richardson, Jr., "Margaret Fuller and Myth," *Prospects 1978*, ed. Jack Salzman (New York: Burt Franklin, 1978), pp. 169–184; *PJ*, 1:199, 210.

21. Writing

1. Now called *Thoreau's Literary Notebook in the Library of Congress*, published in facsimile by K. W. Cameron (Hartford: Transcendental Books, 1964).

2. *PJ*, 1:237; *TLN*, pp. 2, 22; *PJ*, 1:219, 596.

3. *PJ*, 1:243, 274; *JMN*, 5:221; *PJ*, 1:231; *H Works RWE*, 1:17.

4. For T's books, see Walter Harding, *Thoreau's Library* (Charlottesville: University of Virginia Press, 1957). The revised version in *SAR 1983*, pp. 151–186, is more complete, but not cross-indexed; *PJ*, 1:204, 207, 217, 221, 233.

5. *PJ*, 1:222, 246.

6. See, for example, F. O. Matthiessen, *American Renaissance* (New York: Oxford University Press, 1941), p. 57; *PJ*, 1:273, 276, 287.

22. Thoreau and Emerson

1. *EC*, p. 298.
2. *LRWE*, 2:371, 372, 382, 389.
3. On Jonson, see *PJ*, 1:256, 257, 278; on Coleridge, see *PJ*, 1:220, 330.
4. *LRWE*, 2:377. Margaret Fuller was also reading Goethe's *Theory of Colors* in Feb. 1841; see *The Letters of Margaret Fuller*, ed. Robert N. Hudspeth (Ithaca: Cornell University Press, 1983), 2:204 (the Eastlake translation had come out in 1840); *PJ*, 1:235, 244, 257.
5. *The Concord Freeman*, Mar. 5, 1841; *LRWE*, 2:378; *PJ*, 2:269, 270, 275, 278.
6. *PJ*, 2:276.

23. Brook Farm

1. John Humphrey Noyes, *The History of American Socialisms* (Philadelphia: Lippincott, 1870; rept. in 1966 as *Strange Cults and Utopias of Nineteenth Century America*), p. 24.
2. O. B. Frothingham, *George Ripley* (Boston: Houghton Mifflin, 1888), pp. 307–308; *The Early Lectures of Ralph Waldo Emerson*, ed. Stephen E. Whicher, Robert E. Spiller, and Wallace E. Williams (Cambridge: Harvard University Press, 1964), 2:151; *H Works RWE*, 2:31; Ripley's three letters defending Emersonian liberalism were gathered together in *Letters on the Latest Form of Infidelity, Including a View of the Opinions of Spinoza, Schleiermacher, and De Wette* (Boston, 1840).
3. *PJ*, 1:277–278.
4. *PJ*, 1:301; see the discussion of "Manure is the capital of the farmer" in *The Concord Freeman*, February 12, 1841; *PJ*, 1:291.
5. *PJ*, 1:103, 105, 135, 222, 301.
6. *EC*, p. 300.

24. Self-Reformation

1. *PJ*, 1:219, 234.
2. Noyes, *History of American Socialisms*, pp. 24–25, 26, 103.

3. *PJ*, 1:225, 230.

4. R. W. Emerson, "Thoreau," *Atlantic Monthly*, 58 (1862): 240; *PJ*, 1:234.

5. *PJ*, 1:296, 299.   6. *PJ*, 1:304.

25. The Orient

1. For the Indic context, see Arthur Christy, *The Orient in American Transcendentalism* (New York: Columbia University Press, 1932); F. I. Carpenter, *Emerson and Asia* (Cambridge: Harvard University Press, 1930); and Raymond Schwab, *The Oriental Renaissance*, tr. G. Patterson-Black and V. Reinking (New York: Columbia University Press, 1984). Also useful is Ellen M. Raghavan and Barry Wood, "Thoreau's Hindu Quotations in *A Week*," *American Literature*, 51 (1979): 94–98; *The Works of Sir William Jones* (London: John Stockdale, 1807), 7:86; *PJ*, 1:317.

2. *PJ*, 1:311, 324.

3. *PJ*, 1:313. An important modern statement of this contradiction is Claude Lévi-Strauss, *Tristes Tropiques* (New York: Athenaeum, 1974), chaps. 37 and 38.

4. *PJ*, 1:325.

5. Swami Paramananda, *Emerson and Vedanta* (Boston: The Vedanta Centre, 1918); *PJ*, 1:327; *The Works of Sir William Jones*, 7:99; *The Dial*, 3 (1843): 338, 339.

6. *PJ*, 1:313, 327.

26. Fall 1841

1. *Corr*, p. 53.

2. *Corr*, p. 48; A. B. Alcott, "The Doctrine and Discipline of Human Culture," in *Records of Conversations with Children on the Gospels* (Boston: James Monroe, 1836), pp. xxix, xxx, xxxi, xxxii.

3. "Mr. Park's German" (*Corr*, p. 48) is B. B. Edwards and E. A. Park, *Selections from German Literature* (Andover: Gould, Newman and Saxton, 1839); George Ripley, *A Letter to Mr. Andrews Norton* (Boston: James Monroe,

1839), p. 17; George Ripley, "Schleiermacher as a Theologian," *The Christian Examiner* 73 (March 1836): 5; Ripley, *A Letter . . .* , p. 18.

4. *Corr*, p. 52.

5. Robert Sattelmeyer, "Thoreau's Projected Work on the English Poets," *SAR 1980*. The commonplace books in which Thoreau's work on this project can be examined are those listed in *Howarth* as F5, F6d, F7, and F8. F7 has been published as *TLN*; *PJ*, 1:337, 338, 339.

6. *PJ*, 1:300, 301, 306, 308, 310, 321, 330; *Corr*, p. 45; *PJ*, 1:347.

27. Tragedy

1. *Days*, p. 134.   2. *Corr*, p. 64; *LRWE*, 3:4, 6–10.

3. *Corr*, pp. 62, 63, 64, 66.   4. *Corr*, pp. 64, 67.

5. See *PJ*, 1:364, 365, 368, 369, 372, 376, 382.

6. *PJ*, 1:395; *LRWE*, 3:47, 54.

7. See *PJ*, 1:353–354. For detailed psychological studies of the relation between John and Henry see Raymond D. Gozzi, "Tropes and Figures: A Psychological Study of Henry David Thoreau" (Ph.D. diss., New York University, 1957), chap. 9, "The Brother"; and Richard Lebeaux, *Young Man Thoreau* (Amherst: University of Massachusetts Press, 1977), chap. 6, "The Death of a Brother."

28. Excursions

1. Nathaniel Hawthorne, *The American Notebooks*, ed. Claude M. Simpson (Columbus: Ohio State University Press, 1972), p. 355.

2. The Indic material is in *Howarth* F3, published in *Transcendental Climate*, ed. K. W. Cameron (Hartford: Transcendental Books, 1963). For Thoreau's Indic interests at this time, see also *Howarth* F6b, F6c, F7, F8. For the earliest appearance of *Week* material in the "Long Book," which was T's compositional notebook for his first book, see *Howarth* D1a, the description in *Johnson*, p. 326 ff., and the text in *PJ*, vol. 2.

3. For the books T reviewed for "The Natural History . . ." see *LRWE*, 3:47; *Writings*, 5:127, 128. On Schelling's *Naturphilosophie*, see *Encounter*, September 1981, pp. 74–75.

4. The best discussion of T's characteristic form is *Buell*, chap. 7, "Thoreau and the Literary Excursion."

29. January and February 1843

1. *LRWE*, 3:124; *PJ*, 1:447; *Corr*, pp. 79, 80.
2. *Corr*, pp. 85, 86.
3. See Kevin P. Van Anglen, "The Sources for Thoreau's Greek Translations," *SAR 1980*, pp. 291–299.
4. *Corr*, p. 145; Parker's pioneering edition and commentary on De Wette's *Introduction to the Old Testament* was published in Boston by Little, Brown in 1843, while Parker's long essay-review of "Strauss's Life of Jesus" was republished the same year in *The Critical and Miscellaneous Writings of Theodore Parker* (Boston: Monroe, 1843).
5. *EEM*, p. 211.   6. *Corr*, p. 125.

30. Staten Island

1. *Corr*, p. 78.   2. *Corr*, p. 94.   3. *Corr*, p. 99.
4. *Corr*, pp. 107, 113.   5. *Walden*, p. 259.
6. *PJ*, 1:465, 467.   7. *Corr*, pp. 87, 103, 119.
8. *Corr*, p. 107; see also Max Cosman, "Thoreau and Staten Island," *The Staten Island Historian*, 6, 1 (January-March 1943).

31. New York Literary Scene

1. *Corr*, p. 139.
2. *Corr*, p. 111; *LRWE*, 3:19; *Corr*, p. 128.
3. *Corr*, p. 110.
4. *PJ*, 1: 455, 481; *Corr*, p. 125.
5. *RP*, pp. 19, 20, 31, 42, 43. In addition to the book under review, J. A. Etzler's *The Paradise Within the Reach of all Men . . .* (London, 1842, 1st ed.; Pittsburg, 1833), pt. 2, p. 1; see the same author's *The New World;*

or *Mechanical System* (Philadelphia: Stollmeyer, 1841). On Etzler and T, see *Paul*, pp. 151–155.

6. *RP*, p. 20.

32. "A Winter Walk"

1. *Corr*, p. 112; *Writings*, 5:163. For an excellent discussion of T's movement from fact to myth, see *Buell*, p. 209.

2. *Writings*, 5:163, 169, 172, 178, 182.

3. *Corr*, pp. 137, 138. See T's reply to Emerson, *Corr*, p. 139; *Writings*, 5:167–168. See Gordon E. Bigelow, "Summer under Snow: Thoreau's 'A Winter Walk,'" *ESQ*, 56 OS (1969): 13–16.

4. *Writings*, 5:167.

5. *Corr*, p. 132; *PJ*, 1:480. Thoreau's manuscript reads "not not attain to it." The double negative seems to have been a slip.

33. The Railroad Comes to Concord

1. Henry Adams, *The Education of Henry Adams* (Boston: The Massachusetts Historical Society, 1918), p. 5. John R. Stilgoe says that in America "around 1845 the stability that characterized the synthesis of agricultural and artificial spaces and structures called *landscape* began to erode." *The Common Landscape of America, 1580 to 1845* (New Haven: Yale University Press, 1982), p. 341.

2. *Historical Statistics of the United States* (Washington, D.C.: Government Printing Office, 1975).

3. *Corr*, p. 95; Mary S. Clarke, *The Old Middlesex Canal* (Melrose, 1974), pp. 123–126; *Corr*, p. 117; Ruth Wheeler, *Concord: Climate for Freedom* (Concord: Concord Antiquarian Society, 1967), p. 178; *Corr*, p. 137.

4. *Corr*, p. 137; F. T. McGill, Jr., *Channing of Concord* (New Brunswick, N.J.: Rutgers University Press, 1967), pp. 72–73.

34. Inside the Civilized Man

1. *PJ*, 1:469.   2. *PJ*, 1:469.

3. *PJ*, 1:475, 476; *PJ*, 2:80.

4. See *Howarth*, C6a, C6b, C6c, C6d.

5. *Corr*, pp. 143–144; *PJ*, 1:457, 460, 461, 466; *Corr*, p. 145; *EEM*, pp. 155, 156.

6. *EEM*, p. 159.

7. *EEM*, pp. 163, 166, 169.

35. Spring and Summer 1844

1. *JMN*, 9:70, 71.   2. *JMN*, 9:71, 77.

3. *J*, 2:21–25; *Maine Woods*, p. 62.

4. *Corr*, p. 156. An excellent treatment of this trip is William Howarth, *Thoreau in the Mountains* (New York: Farrar, Straus and Giroux, 1982), pp. 54–80.

5. *Corr*, pp. 154, 156.

36. Fall 1844

1. *Works RWE*, 11:109.

2. See G. W. Allen's account of the emancipation speech in *Waldo Emerson* (New York: Viking, 1981), pp. 426–430.

3. *Days*, p. 175.   4. *PJ*, 2:102–116.

5. *LRWE*, 3:262–263; *EC*, p. 369.

6. See *The Concord Freeman*, October 18 and 25, 1844.

37. Spring 1845

1. *Walden*, pp. 40–41; George H. F. Walling's 1852 map in *Stowell*, p. 10, shows clearly what parts of Concord were wooded and what parts swampy at that time.

2. *EC*, p. 369.

3. *LRWE*, 3:262; *Walden*, p. 155.

4. *Corr*, p. 161.

5. Benjamin H. Hibbard, *A History of the Public Land Policies* (Madison: University of Wisconsin Press, 1925; new ed., 1965), p. 364. T was not

uniformly warm toward agricultural reform. Robert Gross's "The Great Bean Field Hoax" shows how T made fun of the reports by Henry Colman on Massachusetts agriculture.

6. *RP*, pp. 60–61.

38. I Went to the Woods to Live Deliberately

1. *Walden*, p. 162.   2. *PJ*, 2:156.   3. *Corr*, p. 116.
4. *PJ*, 2:161.   5. *Walden*, p. 90; *PJ*, 2:155, 156.

39. Epic of the Leaf

1. *Shanley*, p. 129.

2. See *Johnson*, pp. 326–341; and *Week*, pp. 433–543 for accounts of the composition of *Week*; and *PJ*, 2:102–116 and *Johnson*, pp. 1–165 for early versions.

3. See *Christie*, pp. 250–257 for an account of some of the travel books T drew on for *Week*. See also Jamie Hutchinson, "The Lapse of the Current: Thoreau's Historical Vision in *A Week on the Concord and Merrimack Rivers*" *ESQ*, 25 (1979): 211–223.

4. H. W. Longfellow, *Works*, Standard Library Edition (Boston: Houghton Mifflin, 1886), 7:13.

5. The best account of the relation between Goethe and Thoreau is James McIntosh, *Thoreau as Romantic Naturalist* (Ithaca: Cornell University Press, 1974), pp. 69–80.

40. New Typology of the Leaf

1. J. W. von Goethe, *Italian Journey*, trans. W. H. Auden and E. Mayer (New York: Random House, 1962; rept., Berkeley, North Point Press, 1982), p. 40.

2. Goethe, pp. 306, 363.

3. *Johnson*, pp. 71–72.

4. Ibid., p. 22.

5. Ibid., pp. 62, 63, 71. The best treatment of this aspect of Thoreau's thought is Frederick Garber, *Thoreau's Redemptive Imagination* (New York: New York University Press, 1977). A more traditional view of redemption is stressed in Paul D. Johnson, "Thoreau's Redemptive Week," *American Literature*, 49 (1977): 22–23.

6. *Johnson*, pp. 136, 137. For T's later work on "The Dispersion of Seeds," see William Howarth, *The Book of Concord: Thoreau's Life as a Writer* (New York: Viking, 1982), and John Hildebidle, *Thoreau: A Naturalist's Liberty* (Cambridge: Harvard University Press, 1983).

7. *Johnson*, pp. 147, 155.

41. Winter 1846

1. Thomas Carlyle, *Oliver Cromwell's Letters and Speeches* (Boston: Dana Estes and Co., 1885), 1:3, 7, 14.

2. *EC*, p. 389; *EEM*, p. 223.

3. *EEM*, pp. 224, 229, 232, 246.

4. Thomas Carlyle, *On Heroes, Hero-Worship, and the Heroic in History* (Boston: Dana Estes and Co., 1885), pp. 235, 249; *EEM*, pp. 234, 246, 248.

5. Carlyle, *On Heroes*, p. 244.

6. Ibid., pp. 239, 245; *EEM*, p. 251.

7. *EEM*, p. 251.   8. *EEM*, p. 264.   9. *EC*, p. 381.

42. The New Adam

1. *Historical Statistics of the United States* (Washington, D.C.: Government Printing Office, 1975), 1:163, 164.

2. Adam Smith, *An Inquiry into the Nature and Causes of the Wealth of Nations* (Oxford: Clarendon, 1869; 1st ed., 1776), p. 1; *Walden*, p. 31; *Wealth of Nations*, p. 31; *Walden*, p. 7; *Wealth of Nations*, pp. 34, 40.

3. *Wealth of Nations*, p. 30; *Walden*, p. 82; *Wealth of Nations*, pp. 7, 30.

4. *Wealth of Nations*, pp. 6–7; *Walden*, p. 20.

5. *Walden*, p. 91. In Say's *Catechism of Political Economy*, trans. J. Richter (London: Sherwood, Neeley and Jones, 1816) occur these provocative exchanges: "What do you understand by consumption? Consumption is the

opposite of production: it is a destruction of values produced. We cannot destroy matter any more than we can create it, but we can destroy the utility which has been given to it; and in destroying its utility, we destroy its value" (p. 19); "What is the value of consumption? To procure to the consumer either an enjoyment or a new value, in general superior to the value consumed" (p. 47); "What must be the result of a system, the tendency of which is, to consume for the sole purpose of favoring production? That which must be thought of a system which should propose to burn down a city, for the purpose of benefitting the builders, by employing them to restore it" (p. 47). See the excellent treatment of Say and T by Richard H. Dillman, "Thoreau's Humane Economics: A Reflection of Jean-Baptiste Say's Economic Philosophy," *ESQ*, 25 (1979): 20–25. On the development of T's economic ideas, beginning with the idea that "each man should receive the whole product of his labor," see Leo Stoller, "Thoreau's Doctrine of Simplicity," *NEQ*, 29 (1956): 443–461, and his *After Walden* (Stanford: Stanford University Press, 1957).

43. Spring 1846

1. *PJ*, 2:137, 145.

2. *PJ*, 2:136, 147, 168, 169.

3. *PJ*, 2:137, 141, 170. See the excellent discussion of Thoreau and Wordsworth in Frederick Garber's *Thoreau's Redemptive Imagination* (New York: New York University Press, 1977), and those on Emerson, Thoreau, and Wordsworth in Garber's *The Anatomy of the Self from Richardson to Huysmans* (Princeton: Princeton University Press, 1982), pp. 100–103. See also the useful study by L. R. Fergenson, "Wordsworth and Thoreau: A Study of the Relationship between Man and Nature" (Ph.D. diss., Columbia University, 1971).

4. *PJ*, 2:161, 177.

5. See, in addition to my *Myth and Literature in the American Renaissance* (Bloomington: Indiana University Press, 1978), chap. 4, Louise C. Kertesz, "A Study of Thoreau as Myth Theorist and Mythmaker" (Ph.D. diss., University of Illinois, 1970); and Richard Fleck, "Henry David Thoreau's Interest in Myth, Fable, and Legend" (Ph.D. diss., University of New Mexico, 1970).

44. The Great Awakening

1. *PJ*, 2:149, 191.
2. *PJ*, 2:233, 234–235.
3. *PJ*, 2:235, 236.
4. *Walden*, pp. 88, 96, 97.

45. Summer 1846

1. *PJ*, 2:247, 249, 252–261; Ralph L. Rusk, *The Life of Ralph Waldo Emerson* (New York: Columbia University Press, 1949), p. 311.
2. *Days*, pp. 199–208.
3. Raymond Adams, "Thoreau's Sources for 'Resistance to Civil Government,'" *SP*, 42 (1945): 640–653.
4. *Selections from the Writings of William Lloyd Garrison* (Boston: R. F. Wallcut, 1852), pp. 72–73.
5. For T's use of the phrase, see *Walden*, p. 171. For T's changed views on force see *J*, 6:315, and *RP*, p. 102.
6. *RP*, pp. 63, 65; Adin Ballou, *Non-Resistance in Relation to Human Governments* (Boston: Non-Resistance Society, 1839), p. 5.
7. *RP*, pp. 67, 68, 72, 73, 76; Michael Meyer's excellent study of T's modern political reputation, *Several More Lives to Live* (Westport: Greenwood, 1977), points out (p. 192) that T's "ideas, especially those in 'Civil Disobedience' seem too critical to be examined critically."
8. On T and the poll tax question, see John C. Broderick, "Thoreau, Alcott, and the Poll Tax," *SP*, 53 (1956) 612–626. On T and abolition, see Wendell Glick, "Thoreau and Radical Abolition" (Ph.D. diss., Northwestern University, 1950). Bernard DeVoto, *The Year of Decision* (Boston: Houghton Mifflin, 1961; 1st ed., 1942), p. 496.

46. North Twin Lake and "Ktaadn"

1. A comparison of, for example, Fitz Hugh Lane's view of "Castine from Hospital Island" (1855) with the present aspect of that town reveals the extent to which the Penobscot Bay area has become rewooded since Thoreau's day.

2. *PJ*, 2:311, 315; J. Parker Huber, *The Wildest Country: A Guide to Thoreau's Maine* (Boston: Appalachian Mt. Club, 1981), p. 130.

3. *PJ*, 2:275.   4. *PJ*, 2:277, 311.

5. George Boas, "Primitivism," *Dictionary of the History of Ideas*, ed. Philip Weiner (New York: Scribner's, 1973), 3:5780; For T on *Typee*, see *PJ*, 2:315–318.

6. The myth passage is *PJ*, 2:278–279.

47. Second Year at Walden

1. The first draft of "Ktaadn" is printed in *PJ*, vol. 2; *Bulletin of the New York Public Library* (1948), p. 80; *Shanley*, p. 207.

2. *Corr*, pp. 175, 187, 190; *PJ*, 2:359, 381; *J*, 1:487.

3. *PJ*, 2:233–234, 247, 248–249, 252–261.

4. *Corr*, pp. 174, 185–186; *LRWE*, 3:377, 384.

5. *Corr*, p. 181.

48. Letters to Blake

1. *Clapper*, p. 263; *J*, 3:293; see Leonard Neufeldt, " 'Extravagance' through Economy: Thoreau's *Walden*," *American Transcendental Quarterly*, no. 11 (Summer 1971), pp. 63–69; *Corr*, p. 186.

2. *Corr*, pp. 187, 191.   3. *Corr*, pp. 188, 199, 200.

4. *Corr*, pp. 188, 213.   5. *Corr*, pp. 214, 215, 216, 220.

49. A Perfect Piece of Stoicism

1. See R. D. Hicks, *Stoic and Epicurean* (New York: Scribner's, 1910), R. M. Wenley, *Stoicism and its Influence* (Boston: Marshall Jones, 1924), and Edward Zeller, *Outlines of the History of Greek Philosophy* (New York: Holt, 1890), pp. 229–255.

2. Zeller, p. 233.

3. Marcus Aurelius, *Meditations* (New York: Penguin, 1964), trans. Maxwell Staniforth, p. 73.

4. Ibid., pp. 78, 85.   5. Ibid., p. 68.

6. Ibid., pp. 90, 161.

7. But see Raymond P. Tripp, Jr., "Thoreau and Marcus Aurelius: A Possible Borrowing," *Thoreau Society Bulletin*, 107 (Spring 1969): 7; the letter from Horace Hosmer to Dr. S. A. Jones of Mar. 30, 1891, in *Remembrances of Concord and the Thoreaus*, ed. George Hendrick (Urbana: University of Illinois Press, 1977), pp. 31–32; my "A Perfect Piece of Stoicism," *TSB* 103 (1980): 1–5; and Mary E. Cochnower, "Thoreau and Stoicism" (Ph.D. diss., State University of Iowa, 1938); *PJ*, 1:26; *Channing*, p. 11.

50. The Apollonian Vision

1. *Corr*, p. 221; Friedrich Nietzsche, *The Birth of Tragedy*, trans. Francis Golffing (New York: Doubleday, 1956), p. 30; *Corr*, pp. 222, 225.

2. Walter Otto, *The Homeric Gods*, trans. Moses Hadas (Boston: Beacon, 1964), pp. 78, 79.

3. *Week*, pp. 101, 102; See C. O. [i.e., K. O.] Müller, *The History and Antiquities of the Doric Race*, 2d ed. (London: John Murray, 1839), vol. 1, book 2, pp. 219–370, esp. pp. 239, 298, 313, 314, 315, 327, 335, 370.

4. *Days*, p. 197; Otto, pp. 10, 178–179.

5. Nietzsche, p. 22; *Week*, p. 140.

51. Spring and Summer 1849

1. *Corr*, p. 191.

2. *Corr*, pp. 217, 223–224; *New York Daily Tribune*, May 25, 1848.

3. Harding, "Check List of Thoreau's Lectures," *Bulletin of the New York Public Library* (1948), p. 81.

4. *Week*, pp. 467–470; *Corr*, p. 237.

5. Ibid., p. 471.

6. *TSB*, 27 (Apr. 1949):1–3 gives the text of the review. See the recent discussion by Michael Meyer in "A Case for Greeley's Tribune Review of *A Week*," *ESQ*, 25 (1979): 92–94.

7. *Days*, p. 258; *Corr*, pp. 247, 249.

52. Shipwreck and Salvation

1. *Writings*, 4:3.
2. Ibid., 4:5, 6–7. On death in *Cape Cod*, see *Paul*, pp. 381–386.
3. *Writings*, 4:11, 12, 13, 62, 71, 186, 187. On the relation of the sublime to Thoreau's main themes in *Cape Cod*, see Emory V. Maiden, Jr., "*Cape Cod*, Thoreau's handling of the Sublime and the Picturesque" (Ph.D. diss., University of Virginia, 1971). On the Melvillean tone of the charity house passage, see Joel Porte, "Henry Thoreau and the Reverend Poluphloisboios Thalassa," in *The Chief Glory of Every People*, ed. Matthew J. Bruccoli (Carbondale: Southern Illinois University Press, 1973), pp. 206–209.
4. *Writings*, 4:50–54. Thoreau picked up the material for his comparison of the Cape ministers with the Yezidis or Devil worshipers from Sir Austen Layard's *Nineveh and its Remains* (New York: Putnam's, 1849), chap. 8 (see the bibliography in *Christie*). See also Richard J. Schneider, "*Cape Cod*: Thoreau's Wilderness of Illusion," *ESQ*, 26 (1980): 184–196, and Linck C. Johnson, "Into History: Thoreau's Earliest Indian Book and his First Trip to Cape Cod," *ESQ*, 28 (1982): 75–88.
5. *Writings*, 4:57, 58, 59, 77–78, 108.

53. Fall 1849, Spring 1850

1. H. H. Wilson, in the preface to his translation of *The Vishnu Purana* (Bombay: 1840; rept., 1972), quotes Colebrook on Hindu Pantheism: "the real doctrine of the Indian Scripture is the unity of the Deity; in whom the universe is comprehended." (p. ii); James E. Cabot, "The Philosophy of the Ancient Hindoos," *Massachusetts Quarterly Review* 4 (1849): 403, 420. This article is reprinted in *Trans Ap*.
2. Thoreau's Indic reading for 1849 and 1850 is itemized in *HCL*, p. 195.
3. *Week*, p. 140.
4. *Howarth*, F8 (Berg), p. 218. Thoreau is quoting from Rammohun Roy, *Translation of Several Principal Books, Passages and Texts of the Vedas . . .*, 2d ed. (London: Parbury Allen and Co., 1832), p. 151. Thoreau's translation from Langlois has been published by Arthur Christy as *The Transmigrations of the Seven Brahmins* (New York: W. E. Rudge, 1932); *Trans Ap*, p. 234.

5. For T's extracts from Cabot, see *Trans Ap*, p. 222; for his extracts from *The Vishnu Purana*, see *Howarth* F8, pp. 187–217.

54. Spring 1850

1. *J*, 2:8, 21 ff., 33. 2. *J*, 2:12, 19, 34.

3. *Howarth*, F 15, which should be dated 1851–1858, and F 16, which is mostly 1858–60, follow and continue some but not all the interests of the *Literary Notebook*; *Howarth*, F7; *J*, 2:13, 14.

4. Alexander Von Humboldt, *Cosmos*, trans. E. C. Otte, 5 vols. (New York: Harper, 1851–1875), 1:ix, 2:table of contents; *TLN*, p. 362.

5. *TLN*, p. 359; *J*, 2:9.

55. July 1850

1. *Corr*, p. 259.

2. For accounts of the wreck, see Margaret Fuller Ossoli, *At Home and Abroad*, ed. A. B. Fuller (Boston: Crosby, Nichols, 1850), pp. 443–455, and *Memoirs of Margaret Fuller Ossoli*, ed. R. W. Emerson, W. H. Channing, and J. F. Clarke (Boston: Phillips, Sampson, 1852).

3. *LRWE*, 4:219; *Corr*, p. 262.

4. *J*, 2:49; *Corr*, p. 263; *J*, 2:80.

5. *Corr*, p. 265.

56. August and September 1850

1. *J*, 2:44; *Corr*, p. 265. 2. *Corr*, pp. 265–266.

3. See Bayard Taylor's account in *At Home and Abroad*, p. 447; *J*, 2:80.

4. *J*, 2:51.

57. Fall 1850

1. T. S. Eliot, *Four Quartets* (New York: Harcourt Brace, 1943), p. 23; *J*, 2:71. On *A Yankee.* . . , see *Paul*, pp. 369–378.

2. *Writings*, 5:1, 3, 7. 3. Ibid., 5:12, 78, 80, 81.
4. Ibid., 5:89, 92, 95.
5. *HCL*, p. 195. See also Lawrence Willson, "Thoreau's Canadian Notebook," *Huntington Library Quarterly*, 22 (1959): 179–200; *Writings*, 4:227, 232.

58. The Red Face of Man I

1. See Robert F. Sayre, *Thoreau and the American Indians* (Princeton: Princeton University Press, 1977). In gauging what T knew about Indians, a useful starting point is an unpublished twenty-page typescript by Arthur Christy, "Bibliography of Thoreau's American Indian Notes," in the Morgan Library. See also Edwin S. Fussell, "The Red Face of Man," in *Thoreau: A Collection of Critical Essays*, ed. Sherman Paul (Englewood Cliffs, N.J.: Prentice-Hall, 1962), pp. 142–160, and Joan Sherako Gimlin, "Henry Thoreau and the American Indian" (Ph.D. diss., George Washington University, 1974).
2. *Corr*, pp. 16–18. 3. *PJ*, 2:313, 317.
4. For T's comments on *Typee*, see *PJ*, 2:315–318, on Chateaubriand, see *PJ*, 2:349–353; Henri Baudet, *Paradise on Earth: Some Thoughts on European Images of Non-European Man* (New Haven: Yale University Press, 1965), p. 65.
5. Philip F. Gura, "Thoreau's Maine Woods Indians: More Representative Men," *American Literature*, 49 (1977): 366–384; *Maine Woods*, p. 79.

59. The Red Face of Man II

1. For T's Canadian reading, see *Howarth* F9, called "Canadian Notebook" or "Extracts Relating to Canada, etc."; *Christie*, pp. 95–103.
2. Albert Keiser, "Thoreau's Manuscripts on the Indians, *Journal of English and Germanic Philology* 27 (1928): 196; *Howarth* F10. For Thoreau's use of the title "Indian Books," see Robert Sayre, *Thoreau and the American Indians* (Princeton: Princeton University Press, 1977), pp. 217–220.
3. For T's reading in Schoolcraft, Squier, Davis, and Morgan, see Christy's "Bibliography of Thoreau's American Indian Notes"; Lewis H. Morgan,

League of the Iroquois (Secaucus: Citadel, 1962; 1st ed., 1851), introduction by William N. Fenton, pp. v, 444. For Morgan's comments on the historical sources he himself made only slight use of, see Fenton's introduction, p. xvi.

4. *J*, 2:112–115.

60. November 1850 to April 1851

1. Channing, p. 71; Edward Waldo Emerson, *Henry Thoreau as Remembered by a Young Friend* (Boston: Houghton Mifflin, 1917; rept., 1968), p. 106.

2. See *Buell*, pp. 188–202 on the literary excursion; *Writings*, 5:218, 224. See also Frederick Garber, "Unity and Diversity in 'Walking,'" *ESQ*, 56 OS (1969): 35–39; and *Paul*, pp. 412–416.

3. *Writings*, 5:205, 224–225, 226.

4. Ibid., 5:234, 237, 239, 240.

5. Hayden White, "The Forms of Wildness: Archaeology of an Idea," in *The Wild Man Within*, ed. Edward Dudley and Maximilian Novak (Pittsburgh: University of Pittsburgh Press, 1972), p. 29; Geoffrey Symcox, "The Wild Man's Return: The Enclosed Vision of Rousseau's Discourses," in *The Wild Man Within*, p. 234.

6. White, p. 35; *Writings*, 5:225, 246, 248.

7. *Writings*, 5:247–248. On religious language in "Walking," see Joel Porte, "Henry Thoreau and the Reverend Poluphloisboios Thalassa," in *The Chief Glory of Every People*, ed. Matthew J. Bruccoli (Carbondale: Southern Illinois University Press, 1973), p. 96.

61. Technological Conservative

1. *Walden*, pp. 26, 53.   2. *Days*, pp. 56–57, 157–158.

3. Steve Dunwell, *The Run of the Mill* (Boston: Godine, 1978), pp. 51, 54.

4. *J*, 2:134; Dunwell, p. 33.   5. *J*, 2:135.

6. *Works RWE*, 5:71, 82.

7. Philip E. Slater, *The Pursuit of Loneliness* (Boston: Beacon, 1970), p. 128; *J*, 2:142.

62. Myth and Wildness

1. *J*, 2:140.   2. *Week*, pp. 60, 66.

3. *Maine Woods*, p. 54; a fuller treatment of this is in my *Myth and Literature in the American Renaissance* (Bloomington: Indiana University Press, 1978), ch. 4.

4. *J*, 2:144, 145.

5. See nn. chaps. 53–54; *J*, 2:145.

6. *J*, 2:94–95.

63. Spring 1851

1. Adam Smith, *An Inquiry into the Nature and Causes of the Wealth of Nations* (Oxford: Clarendon, 1869; 1st ed., 1776), p. 10.

2. *J*, 2:194.   3. *J*, 2:196.

4. Michaux's *North American Sylvae* is both well written and beautifully illustrated. It even contains the germ of a remark that later got Thoreau into an editorial tangle with James Russell Lowell. On page 293, Michaux says of the white pine that its "summit is seen at an immense distance aspiring toward heaven." For the excellent discussion of G. B. Emerson's book, see Donald Worster, *Nature's Economy: A History of Ecological Ideas* (Cambridge: Cambridge University Press, 1985; 1st pub. 1977), pp. 68–69; *J*, 2:197–201, 208.

5. *J*, 2:92.

6. Vrest Orton, *The American Cider Book* (New York: Farrar, Straus and Giroux, 1973), pp. 12–14.

7. *J*, 2:209. See also Kevin P. Van Anglen, "A Paradise Regained: Thoreau's Wild Apples and the Myth of the American Adam," *ESQ*, 27 (1981): 28–37.

8. *J*, 2:212; *Writings*, 5:316–317; *J*, 2:222.

64. June 1851

1. I owe the idea for T's concentric worlds to Warner Berthoff's fine book on Melville as a writer, *The Example of Melville* (Princeton: Princeton University Press, 1962).

2. R. W. Emerson, "Thoreau," *Atlantic Monthly*, 10 (1862): 243; *Writings*, 5:211–212.

3. *J*, 2:281.   4. *Walden*, p. 4.

65. *Thoreau, Darwin, and* The Voyage of the Beagle

1. *The Red Notebook of Charles Darwin*, ed. Sandra Herbert (Ithaca: Cornell University Press, 1980), pp. 7, 22.

2. *J*, 2:240, 241, 244.

3. Charles Darwin, *Journal of Researches into the Natural History and Geology of the Countries visited during the Voyage of HMS Beagle Round the World* . . . (New York: Harpers, 1846), p. 44.

4. Ibid., pp. 45, 50; *J*, 2:261–262.

66. *Summer 1851*

1. Kenneth W. Cameron, "Emerson, Thoreau, and the Society of Natural History," *American Literature*, 24 (1952): 21–30; *Christie*, p. 25.

2. *J*, 2:351.   3. *J*, 2:406, 409.

4. *J*, 2:193, 228, 289, 290, 300, 314.

5. *J*, 2:316, 413.   6. *J*, 2:428.

67. *Fall 1851*

1. *J*, 3:113, 118.   2. *J*, 2:467–468.

3. *Seybold*, pp. 70, 71, 99, 103–106; *Cato and Varro: De Re Rustica* (Cambridge: Harvard University Press, 1934), pp. xi–xii, 3, 9, 33; *J*, 2:442–443, 445.

4. *J*, 2:449, 477, 481, 497.

5. *J*, 3:31, 56, 85, 86, 95.

68. *December 1851 to February 1852*

1. *J*, 3:140, 143–144, 147, 170, 189.

2. See *J*, 3:164–166.

69. Lapidae Crescunt

1. In August 1851, T began keeping a notebook for "Extracts mainly concerning Natural History." This is *Howarth* F15, published by K. W. Cameron as *Thoreau's Fact Book . . . in the Harvard College Library* (Hartford: Transcendental Books, 1966). Usually dated from 1853–1858, the notebook begins with extracts from books T was reading in August 1851 (Kalm, Bartram, et al.). The sequel to this, in the Berg collection of the New York Public Library, *Howarth* F16, is a continuation, another book of "Extracts, mostly upon Natural History," and though dated 1853–1860, the contents are mostly after 1858. These two volumes belong together. They are a *set* of extract books, not yet adequately studied, as important for the study of Thoreau as a naturalist as the Indian Notebooks are for his study of the Indians; *J*, 3:117, 164, 165, 175, 181.

2. *Walden*, p. 308; *J*, 3:308, 309.

3. Thoreau quotes p. 1 of Linnaeus on *J*, 3:307; Carl Linnaeus, *Philosophia Botanica* (Vienna: Trattner, 1763), p. 1; *Walden*, pp. 307, 309.

4. *J*, 3:307, 328.

5. See *Howarth* F15 on natural history, F10d on Indian and pre-Columbian history of North America, and F8 on poetry and Indic material. F8 seems to have been last used heavily in the spring of 1850; *J*, 3:239.

70. A Sufficient List of Failures

1. *J*, 3:293; *Shanley*, p. 113; *The Variorum Walden*, ed. Walter Harding (New York: Twayne, 1962), p. 259; R. W. Emerson, "Thoreau," *Atlantic Monthly*, 10 (1862): 244; *Corr*, p. 266.

2. *J*, 2:322, 324; *J*, 3:320.

3. *J*, 2:446, 449; *J*, 2:366–367; *J*, 4:400, 455, 459.

4. *J*, 3:312, 313, 345–346. A recent study of T's pessimism is Richard Bridgeman, *Dark Thoreau* (Lincoln: University of Nebraska Press, 1982). Bridgeman is useful when he asserts the importance of T's darker side, but it is difficult to agree with his claim that T's "most crippling feature was that he dared not be a deeply reflective man." (P. xiv.)

5. *J*, 3:348.

1. *J*, 3:418, 425–426, 432; *J*, 5:135. On T's late critique of Gilpin, see William D. Templeman, "Thoreau, Moralist of the Picturesque," *PMLA*, 47 (1932): 864–889. On T's interest in "roughness," see Gordon V. Boudreau, "Henry David Thoreau, William Gilpin, and the Metaphysical Ground of the Picturesque," *American Literature*, 45 (1973): 357–369. The most thorough and suggestive treatment is Emory V. Maiden, Jr., *"Cape Cod*: Thoreau's Handling of the Sublime and the Picturesque" (Ph.D. diss., University of Virginia, 1971).

2. William Gilpin, *Three Essays on Picturesque Beauty* (London: Cadell and Davis, 1808), pp. 6, 26–27.

3. William Gilpin, *Remarks on Forest Scenery* (Edinburgh: Fraser, 1834; 1st ed., 1791), pp. 50, 145.

4. Gilpin, *Three Essays*, pp. 18, 53. There is an important link between Gilpin and the luminist qualities recent writers have seen in Thoreau. See ch. 12, note 2.

5. Gilpin, *Forest Scenery*, p. 199.

6. Quoted in Elizabeth Barlow, *The Central Park Book* (New York, 1977), p. 12. Further evidence of Olmsted's lifelong interest in Gilpin—he even followed Gilpin's tracks when traveling in Great Britain—is in Laura Wood Roper, *F.L.O.* (Baltimore: Johns Hopkins University Press, 1973). On Gilpin and Cole, see Matthew Baigell, *Thomas Cole* (New York: Watson-Guptill, 1981). On Gilpin and Church, see *Close Observation*, ed. Theodore E. Stebbins, Jr. (Washington: Smithsonian Institution Press, 1978).

1. *J*, 3:17, 332, 336, 366, 369, 370.

2. *J*, 3:439, 452.   3. *J*, 3:372–373; *J*, 6:53.

4. *J*, 3:430, 431, 442.

5. Vincent Scully, *The Earth, the Temple, and the Gods*, rev. ed. (New York: Praeger, 1969), pp. 2, 3.

1. *J*, 3:390; *Corr*, pp. 276, 277, 278, 279.

2. *The Wyeths: The Letters of N. C. Wyeth*, ed. Betsey James Wyeth (Bos-

ton: Gambit, 1971), p. 480; Ann Douglas, *The Feminization of American Culture* (New York: Knopf, 1977), p. 4. Thoreau's notes on *Sacontala* are in *Howarth* F8 pp. 163–166. Thoreau copied out, for example, "My body moves onward, but my restless heart runs back to her, like a light flag borne on a staff against the wind." (P. 164.)

3. *EEM*, p. 271.

4. *EEM*, pp. 268, 269, 270.

5. *Corr*, p. 288; *EEM*, p. 274.

6. *Clapper*, p. 589; *EEM*, pp. 276–277.

7. Mary Douglas, "Purity and Danger Revisited," *Times Literary Supplement*, Sept. 19, 1980, p. 1045.

74. My Year of Observation

1. *J*, 4:198, 227.

2. See, for example, Goethe's remark in a letter to Schiller, Dec. 8, 1798, that "Astrological superstition is based on a vague feeling of the world as a vast totality," *J*, 4:146; *Corr*, p. 283.

3. *Corr*, pp. 283, 284; *J*, 4:223.

4. See William Howarth, *The Book of Concord* (New York: Viking, 1982), pp. 73–79, for T's 1852 journal. Howarth sees the journal as T's main work.

5. *J*, 3:390, 425–426, 438. For T's tables, see Howarth F18-F32; for the little-studied charts, see especially F18d, F19c, F19e, F19f, F20a, F20b, F21a, F22b, F23e, F23f, F27a, F32d (Morgan Library, MS RV 12–C).

6. *J*, 4:312–313, 317, 351.

7. *J*, 4:239; Alfred North Whitehead, *Science and the Modern World* (New York: MacMillan, 1925), pp. 3–4, 5; *J*, 4:163. See the thoughtful discussion of T and Whitehead in Kichung Kim's "Thoreau's Involvement with Nature: Thoreau and the Naturalist Tradition." (Ph.D. diss., University of California, Berkeley, 1969), pp. 27–30, 61, 68. An excellent treatment of T and science is Nina Baym's "Thoreau's View of Science," *Journal of the History of Ideas*, 26 (1965): 221 234.

75. August and September 1852

1. *J*, 4:302, 305, 360. I give the common names from Ray Angelo's indispensable *Botanical Index to the Journal of Henry David Thoreau* (Salt Lake City: Peregrine Smith, 1984), 292–294.

2. *J*, 4:345, 368–375.

3. *The Heart of Thoreau's Journals*, ed. Odell Shepard (Boston: Houghton Mifflin, 1927), p. 71.

4. *J*, 4:381; *J*, 8:192–193.

5. *J*, 5:523; *J*, 8:433.   6. *J*, 9:356.

76. Ante-Columbian History

1. *Clapper*, p. 387.

2. The major manuscripts, in the Berg collection in the New York Public Library, are *Howarth* F30 and F29h. The only part of this to be published so far is an essay, "Huckleberries," ed. Leo Stoller (Iowa City: Windhover Press, University of Iowa, 1970), rept. in *Henry David Thoreau, The Natural History Essays*, ed. Robert Sattelmeyer (Salt Lake City: Peregrine Smith, 1980).

3. *Clapper*, p. 832.

4. Morgan MS MA 596 (*Howarth* F10a), blue sheet tipped in; *Corr*, p. 310.

77. Jesuit Relations

1. Edmund B. O'Callaghan, *Jesuit Relations . . . 1632–1672* (New York: New York Historical Society, 1847), p. 6. There is no record that T read this book. For his reading in other books by O'Callaghan, see A. H. Christy, "Bibliography of Thoreau's American Indian Notes," unpub. MS pamphlet in the Morgan Library. Christy also shows T to have read W. I. Kip, *The Early Jesuit Missions in North America* (New York: Wiley and Putnam, 1846).

2. Lewis Henry Morgan, *League of the Iroquois* (Secaucus: Citadel, 1962; 1st ed. 1851), pp. 23–24.

3. *The Jesuit Relations and Allied Documents*, ed. Ruben G. Thwaites (Cleveland: Burrows Bros., 1897), 5:89, 91, 96, 97.

4. Thwaites, *The Jesuit Relations*, 5:119, 121.

5. *J*, 3:218; *J*, 4:388.

78. Pantheism

1. *J*, 4:419, 453, 470–471, 472, 474, 477, 475.

2. *Corr*, pp. 293, 294.

3. *J*, 5:4, 16.   4. *Corr*, pp. 296–297.

5. *J*, 4:443, 445. Edward Wagenknecht's *Henry David Thoreau: What Manner of Man?* (Amherst: University of Massachusetts Press, 1981) summarizes the long controversy over T's religious beliefs and comes to a different conclusion, finding that T is not a pantheist but "remains fundamentally Christian in refusing to allow the Maker to be swallowed up in what He has made." (P. 171).

6. *J*, 4:460–461.   7. *J*, 4:478.   8. *J*, 5:68, 69.

79. America

1. *RP*, pp. 64, 65, 67.   2. *Writings*, 5:217, 218.
3. Ibid. 5:224.   4. Ibid., 5:222, 223.
5. *J*, 3:237–238.   6. *J*, 3:418; *Corr*, p. 296.

80. Spring 1853

1. *J*, 5:27–28, 51–52, 333–335.

2. *Days*, p. 308. Channing's MS for "Country Walking" is in the Morgan Library; *J*, 5:135, 203.

3. *J*, 13:77.

4. Richard Trench, *On the Study of Words* (New York: W. J. Widdleton, 1876; 1st ed., 1851), pp. 12–15.

5. *J*, 4:466–467. For T's interest in Trench and Kraitsir, see Michael West, "Charles Kraitsir's Influence on Thoreau's Theory of Language," *ESQ*, 20 (1973): 262–274, Gordon V. Boudreau, "Thoreau and Richard C. Trench: Conjectures on the Pickerel Passage of *Walden*," *ESQ*, 21 (1974): 117–124; and esp. Philip F. Gura, *The Wisdom of Words* (Middletown: Wesleyan University Press, 1981), chap. 4. For the effects of this new interest in language on the revision of *Walden* see, for example, *Clapper*, pp. 362, 811.

6. *J*, 4:482.

81. Summer 1853

1. *Days*, p. 316.

2. See *Shanley*, pp. 18–19, *Clapper*, pp. 30–32, and *Walden*, pp. 362–

367, for details of the successive drafts of *Walden*. The Natural History Note-book is *Howarth* F15. See chap. 69, note 1.

 3. *Shanley*, p. 67.   4. *Clapper*, p. 527.

 5. *J*, 5: 197–198; Henry Mayhew, *London Labour and the London Poor* (London: n.p., 1851), pp. iv, 3.

 6. *Clapper*, pp. 707, 708.

82. Fall 1853

 1. *Channing*, p. ix.

 2. F. T. McGill, Jr., *Channing of Concord* (New Brunswick: Rutgers University Press, 1967), p. 134; *Channing*, p. 333; McGill, p. 119.

 3. *J*, 5:459; *Clapper*, p. 707.

 4. *Clapper*, p. 708; Odell Shepard, *Pedlar's Progress, The Life of Bronson Alcott* (Boston: Little, Brown, 1937), p. 402.

 5. *J*, 5:188; *Emerson in his Journals*, ed. Joel Porte (Cambridge: Harvard University Press, 1982), pp. 428, 432. See also the chapter on "Thoreau," in Porte's *Representative Man: Ralph Waldo Emerson in his Time* (New York: Oxford University Press, 1979), in which he gives his most recent version of the subject he first treated in *Emerson and Thoreau: Transcendentalists in Conflict* (Middletown: Wesleyan University Press, 1966).

 6. Ralph L. Rusk, *The Life of Ralph Waldo Emerson* (New York: Columbia University Press, 1949), pp. 455, 456; *J*, 5:515; *Clapper*, p. 713. For the context of Emerson's essay on T, see Gabrielle Fitzgerald, "In Time of War: The Context of Emerson's 'Thoreau,'" *American Transcendental Quarterly* no. 41 (Winter 1979), pp. 5–12. The most detailed, painstaking and persuasive reconstructions of the mature T's emotional life, including his relationship with Emerson, is Richard Lebeaux, *Thoreau's Seasons* (Amherst: University of Massachusetts Press, 1984).

 7. Henry Seidel Canby, *Thoreau* (Boston: Houghton Mifflin, 1939), pp. xii, 248–249.

83. Chesuncook

 1. *Maine Woods*, p. 136; *Corr*, p. 504.

 2. Albert Keiser, "Thoreau's Manuscripts on the Indians," *Journal of English and Germanic Philology* 27 (1928): 199.

3. Aubrey Burl's *Prehistoric Avebury* (New Haven: Yale University Press, 1979) makes extensive use of evidence from Hopewell and Adena cultures in America to illuminate Avebury in England.

4. *Maine Woods*, pp. 101, 119, 151, 152, 155, 156.

5. For Gilpin, see ibid., p. 439. Thoreau made extracts from *Sylva*, *Terra*, and *Pomona* in his Natural History Extract book. See *Thoreau's Fact Book* . . . , 1:92–105, 2:114–133. *Kalendarium Hortense* is mentioned in *J*, 4:87; John Evelyn, *Sylva* . . . , 3d ed. (London: John Martyn, 1679), pp. 1, 2; *J*, 4:85.

6. *Maine Woods*, p. 156.

7. Ibid., pp. 155–156.   8. *Corr*, pp. 311, 313.

84. January 1854

1. For Gilpin, see *HCL*, p. 196, and *J*, 6:55–59. For Price, see *HCL*, p. 196, and *J*, 6:103.

2. *J*, 6:69. The passage is from Cato, *De Agri Cultura*, chap. 3, sec. 1, 2; *J*, 6:82–83; the passages are from Varro, *Rerum Rusticarum*, book 1, chap. 1, secs. 14–15.

3. *J*, 6:68, 86.

4. *Clapper*, pp. 266, 274, 279, 379, 380, 455, 460 ff., 566, 621 ff., 647; *Shanley*, p. 68.

5. Varro, *Rerum Rusticarum*, book 1, chaps. 28–36 describes the four seasons and their subdivisions; chap. 37 introduces the scheme of six. Thoreau had also long known William Howitt's *The Book of the Seasons, or The Calendar of Nature* (Philadelphia: Carey and Lea, 1831). See *EEM*, pp. 26–36; *Trans Ap*, pp. 21–25; *Paul*, pp. 42–45; Hildebidle, *A Naturalist's Liberty*, pp. 67–68.

6. Columella, *Re Rusticae*, book 11, chap. 2, sec. 6; chap. 3, sec. 16.

7. For Evelyn's *Kalendarium Hortense*, see chap. 83, n. 5. For Linnaeus's *Calendarium Florae* (Upsala, 1756), see *Thoreau's Fact Book*, 1:26 27; Gilbert White, *The Natural History of Selborne*, Bohn Library ed. (London: G. Bell and Sons, 1890), p. 302; L. C. Miall, "Introduction" (p. xx) discusses Barrington, whose sixty-two-page blank book *The Naturalist's Journal* was published annually from 1767 on. A list of other eighteenth- and nineteenth-century naturalist's calendars may be found in Benjamin D. Jackson, *Guide*

to the Literature of Botany (New York: Hafner, 1964; 1st ed., 1881), sec. 68, p. 213. On Thoreau and American Phenology, see Victor C. Friesen, *The Spirit of the Huckleberry* (Edmonton: The University of Alberta Press, 1984), p. 98. Phenology in America has also been traced back to J. Bigelow's "Facts Serving to show the Comparative Forwardness of the Spring Season in Different Parts of the U.S.A.," in *Memoirs of the American Academy of Arts & Sciences*, Old Series, vol. 4 (1817).

8. Thoreau's earliest reference to White is Mar. 29, 1853, *J*, 5:65. A copy of the Bohn edition was in T's library.

9. L. C. Miall, "Introduction," to *The Natural History of Selborne* (London: Methuen, 1901), p. xxii.

10. *J*, 6:85, 206, 236–237.

85. *February and March 1854*

1. *J*, 6:91, 109, 112, 152.
2. *J*, 6:99–100; *Clapper*, pp. 806–818. See *Paul*, pp. 348–351.
3. *PJ*, 1:15.   4. *J*, 6:148, 278.   5. *J*, 6:15.
6. *J*, 6:109, 124.   7. *Corr*, p. 321; *J*, 6:185.
8. *J*, 6:168, 176; *Corr*, p. 324.

86. *Spring and Summer 1854*

1. *J*, 6:179, 192, 229, 297–302.   2. *J*, 6:226, 283.
3. *RP*, pp. 96, 101, 102 (compare the passage in *J*, 6:315), 106–107.

87. *July and August 1854*

1. *Hind Swaraj* [Indian Home Rule], in *The Selected Works of Mahatma Gandhi*, ed. Shriman Narayan (Ahmedabad: Navajivan, 1968), 4:174, 201. Thoreau's "Civil Disobedience" and "Life without Principle" are listed in the bibliography appended to this treatise. For T's influence on Gandhi, see George Hendrick, "The Influence of Thoreau's 'Civil Disobedience' on Gandhi's Satyagraha," *NEQ*, 29 (1956): 462–471.

2. *Walden*, p. 323; Lord Charnwood, *Abraham Lincoln* (New York: Holt, 1917), p. 60. Stanley Cavell has shown how T inherits Kant's concern with freedom. The moral motive of *Walden* is, Cavell says, "to answer, by transforming, the problem of the freedom of the will in the midst of a universe of natural laws, by which our conduct, like the rest of nature, is determined." *The Senses of Walden*, exp. ed. (Berkeley: North Point Press, 1981), p. 95.

3. *Walden*, p. 318.

4. Erik H. Erikson, *Childhood and Society*, rev. ed. (New York: Norton, 1963), p. 232.

5. See "The Life Cycle: Epigenesis of Identity," in Erik H. Erikson, *Identity: Youth and Crisis* (New York: Norton, 1968), pp. 91–141. One reason why Richard Lebeaux's *Young Man Thoreau* (Amherst: University of Massachusetts Press, 1975), an Eriksonian study, is so persuasive, is because T shared Erikson's conception of the final phase of the individual life cycle as the phase in which a life is culminated either by integrity or despair; *Walden*, pp. 326, 327. For the most helpful of the many comments on the artist of Kouroo, see *Paul*, pp. 352–353.

6. *J*, 6:402, 403, 426.

88. Night and Moonlight

1. *J*, 6:426, 464, 479.

2. *J*, 6:413, 415.

3. *J*, 6:416, 436; *Corr*, p. 330.

4. *J*, 6:437, 450, 454, 455, 468; *J*, 7:7.

5. Henry D. Thoreau, *The Moon*, ed. F. H. Allen (Boston: Houghton Mifflin, 1927), pp. 25, 43–44; the best treatment of T's moonlight papers is William L. Howarth, "Successor to *Walden*? Thoreau's Moonlight—an Intended Course of Lectures," *Proof*, 2 (1972): 89–115.

6. *The Moon*, pp. 5, 11.

7. "Night and Moonlight," in *Writings*, 5:323, 324, 330; *The Moon*, pp. 8, 25–26, 28–29, 53, 61.

8. *Walden*, p. 333; *The Moon*, pp. 1, 61.

89. New Friends

1. Thomas Blanding and Walter Harding, "A Thoreau Iconography" (Geneseo, 1980), Thoreau Society Booklet 30; on Rowse's tendency to ideal-

ize, see Ralph L. Rusk, *The Life of Ralph Waldo Emerson* (New York: Columbia University Press, 1949), p. 397.

2. Mary Thacher Higginson, *Thomas Wentworth Higginson, the story of his life* (Boston: Houghton Mifflin, 1914), p. 118; "Early Worcester Literary Days" in *The Concord Saunterer* 17, 2 (1984): 6.

3. Henry S. Salt, *Life of Henry David Thoreau* (London: R. Bently and Son, 1890; rept., Haskell House, 1968), pp. 110, 111.

4. *Corr*, pp. 332, 333, 342.

5. Daniel Ricketson, *The Autumn Sheaf* (New Bedford, 1869), p. 15; *Corr*, p. 334; *Daniel Ricketson and his Friends*, ed. Anna and Walter Ricketson (Boston: Houghton Mifflin, 1902), p. 19.

6. Thomas Cholmondeley, *Ultima Thule; or Thoughts Suggested by a Residence in New Zealand* (London: John Chapman, 1854), pp. 1, 189, 196–197, 198.

7. F. B. Sanborn, *Henry D. Thoreau* (Boston: Houghton Mifflin, 1882); see the daguerreotype in the Concord Free Public Library; Horace Traubel, *With Walt Whitman in Camden* (New York: Rowman and Littlefield, 1961; 1st pub. 1912), 1:213, and 3:402; *Corr*, p. 367.

90. Life Without Principle

1. Indispensable for understanding the evolution of this essay is Bradley P. Dean's unpublished M.A. thesis, "The Sound of a Flail—Reconstructions of Thoreau's Early 'Life Without Principle' Lectures," Eastern Washington University, 1984.

2. *RP*, pp. 158, 159, 160, 161, 173, 178, 179.

3. *J*, 3:90, 104, 182; *J*, 7:70. *HCL*, pp. 106–107.

4. *J*, 3, 24; *J*, 7:99, 108, 109.

5. *J*, 7:87, 115, 116, 124; *Corr*, p. 369.

6. *J*, 7:277–278, 416, 417; *LRWE*, 7:512; *Days*, p. 357; *Corr*, pp. 383, 393.

91. Recovery

1. For publication details on *Cape Cod*, see Joseph Moldenhauer's "Historical Introduction" in the forthcoming Princeton edition.

2. *Corr*, pp. 387, 395–396.

3. *Corr*, p. 403. Lévi-Strauss's remark is quoted by Richard Schweder, *New York Times Book Review*, Apr. 14, 1985.

4. R. Spence Hardy, *Eastern Monachism: An Account of the Origin, Laws, Discipline, Sacred Writings, Mysterious Rites, Religions, Ceremonies, and Present Circumstances, of the Order of Mendicants Founded by Gotama Budha* . . . (London: Partridge and Oakey, 1850), p. 42.

5. Christian C. J. Bunsen, *Outlines of the Philosophy of Universal History, Applied to Language and Religion* (London: Longman, Brown, Green, and Longmans, 1854), 2:xv; Christian C. J. Bunsen, *Hippolytus and His Age* (London: Longman, et al., 1854), p. xlvii; Bunsen, *Outlines*, 1:35.

6. Bunsen, *Outlines*, 1:35; see Raymond Schwab, *The Oriental Renaissance*, trans. G. Patterson-Black and V. Reinking (New York: Columbia University Press, 1984), pp. 464–465.

7. *Corr*, p. 654; Virginia Woolf, *Books and Portraits* (New York: Harcourt Brace Jovanovitch, 1981), p. 67; *J*, 3:113.

8. *LRWE*, 4:506; Asher Durand, "Letters on Landscape Painting, Letter II," in *The Crayon*, 1, 3 (1855): 35; *J*, 7:432; Mabel M. Swan, *The Athenaeum Gallery* (Boston, pvt. pr., 1940), p. 101. For Church's oil sketches see Theodore E. Stebbins, Jr., *Close Observation: Selected Oil Sketches by Frederick E. Church* (Washington: Smithsonian Institution Press, 1978); *J*, 7:481–482, 515; *Corr*, p. 389.

9. *J*, 8:3, 26–27, 64.   10. *J*, 8:14, 42, 43, 44.

92. Dispersion of Seeds

1. *Corr*, p. 409; *J*, 8:100, 158.   2. *J*, 8:87, 88, 91, 103.

3. *J*, 8:134; Gay Wilson Allen, *William James; a biography* (New York: Viking Press, 1967), p. 111.

4. *J*, 8:245.   5. *J*, 8:315.   6. *J*, 8:335.

7. *Corr*, pp. 423–424; *Writings*, 5:185; *Corr*, p. 426.

8. *J*, 8:363.   9. *J*, 8:461.   10. *J*, 9:20, 36, 43.

93. Walt Whitman and the Ethics of Intensity

1. *J*, 9:121. Kane's botanical contribution is item 18 in the appendix of Elisha Kent Kane, *Arctic Explorations in the Years 1853, 54, 55* (Philadelphia: Childs and Peterson, 1856).

2. *J*, 11:438.

3. Justin Kaplan, *Walt Whitman: A Life* (New York: Simon and Schuster, 1980), pp. 202–203; H. F. West, "Mr. Emerson Writes a Letter about Walden," Thoreau Society Booklet 9 (Lunenberg, Vt.: The Stinehour Press, 1954).

4. *The Journals of Bronson Alcott*, ed. Odell Shepard (Boston: Little, Brown, 1938), pp. 289–290; *The Letters of A. Bronson Alcott*, ed. Richard L. Herrnstadt (Ames: The Iowa State University Press, 1969), p. 211; *Corr*, p. 445.

5. Horace Traubel, *With Walt Whitman in Camden* (New York: Rowman and Littlefield, 1961), 3:375.

6. *The Journals of Bronson Alcott*, pp. 290–292; *Corr*, pp. 441, 444.

7. *Corr*, pp. 444–445; Kaplan, *Walt Whitman*, p. 203; *LRWE*, 4:520, 521.

8. *Days*, p. 376.   9. *Corr*, p. 446.   10. *J*, 9:169.

11. *HCL*, p. 197; *J*, 9:242, 252, 288; *Corr*, pp. 470, 478.

12. *J*, 9:335–337; Walter Harding, "Thoreau and Kate Brady," *American Literature*, 36 (1964): 347–349.

13. *J*, 9:164, 372.

14. *J*, 9:377–378. For the preliminary sketch of "Crossing Brooklyn Ferry," see Kaplan, *Walt Whitman*, p. 207. The question of intensity has been discussed by Anthony Hilfer in *The Ethics of Intensity in American Fiction* (Austin: University of Texas Press, 1981).

94. *The Indian*

1. *Corr*, pp. 473, 510.   2. *Corr*, p. 488; *Maine Woods*, p. 262.

3. *Corr*, p. 491.

4. Robert F. Sayre, *Thoreau and the American Indian* (Princeton: Princeton University Press, 1977), p. 172; *Maine Woods*, p. 226.

5. *J*, 9:446.   6. *Maine Woods*, p. 219.

7. Ibid., p. 185; *Corr*, p. 491; *Days*, pp. 391–392.

95. *Autumnal Tints*

1. *Corr*, p. 443; *J*, 10:127.

2. *Corr*, p. 497. Ruskin also seems to have led T to George Field's *Chro-*

matography; or a Treatise on Colour and Pigments, and of their Powers in Painting (London: Tilt and Bogue, 1841), a technical book, but one much interested in the literary expression of color.

3. John Ruskin, *Modern Painters, Volume Two* (New York: John Wiley and Sons, 1884; 1st pub. 1846), part 3, sec. 1, chap. 1, p. 5; *LRWE*, 6:239; John Ruskin, *The Two Paths* (Chicago: Belford, Clarke and Co., n.d.), p. 3. For T's interest in *The Elements of Drawing*, see *J*, 10:210.

4. John Ruskin, *The Elements of Drawing* (New York: Dover, 1971; 1st pub. 1857), introduction by Lawrence Campbell, pp. viii, ix–x, 27.

5. Ibid., pp. 148, 156, 158; "Extracts on Natural History," Berg MS, *Howarth* F16, p. 22; *J*, 10:260, 282.

6. *Corr*, pp. 636–637; *Writings*, 9:341, 343.

7. *Writings*, 9:305, 349.   8. Ibid., 9:350, 351.

9. *J*, 10:141, 142. An excellent recent treatment of T's visual sense is Richard J. Schneider, "Thoreau and Nineteenth Century American Landscape Painting," *ESQ*.

96. Louis Agassiz

1. The starting point for understanding T in the context of nineteenth-century science is Donald Worster, *Nature's Economy: A History of Ecological Ideas* (Cambridge: Cambridge University Press, 1985; 1st pub. 1977), especially part 2, "The Subversive Science, Thoreau's Romantic Ecology," and Loren Eiseley's *The Unexpected Universe* (New York: Harcourt Brace, 1969), esp. chap. 6, "The Golden Alphabet." For literary approaches to Thoreau as a naturalist, the most valuable studies are James McIntosh, *Thoreau as Romantic Naturalist* (Ithaca: Cornell University Press, 1974), John Hildebidle, *Thoreau: A Naturalist's Liberty* (Cambridge: Harvard University Press, 1983), and Kichung Kim, "Thoreau's Involvement with Nature: Thoreau and the Naturalist Tradition" (Ph.D. diss., University of California, Berkeley, 1969). The pamphlet announcing T's appointment to the Committee on Examination in Natural History is described in Raymond Borst, "The Henry David Thoreau Collection" in *The Parkman Dexter Howe Library, Part II*, ed. Sidney Ives (Gainesville: University of Florida Press, 1984); *J*, 10:164–165.

2. Edward Lurie's *Louis Agassiz: A Life in Science* (Chicago: University of Chicago Press, 1960) is indispensable. For T's reading in Agassiz and in

others involved in the evolution controversy, such as Hugh Miller, see Robert Sattelmeyer's forthcoming book on T's reading.

3. Lurie, *Louis Agassiz*, pp. 83, 87, 151, 152.

4. Ibid., p. 270; Louis Agassiz, *Contributions to the Natural History of the United States of America* (Boston: Little, Brown, 1857), vol. 1, part 1, "Essay on Classification," pp. 116–117.

5. Lane Cooper, *Louis Agassiz as a Teacher* (Ithaca: Comstock, 1945; 1st ed., 1917), p. 1; Lurie, *Louis Agassiz*, p. 175; J. D. Teller, *Louis Agassiz: Scientist and Teacher* (Columbus: Ohio State University Press, 1947), p. v; Lurie, *Louis Agassiz*, pp. 301, 337, 338.

6. *J*, 9:299; *JMN*, p. 192; *J*, 10:467–468; *JMN*, 14:122–123.

7. Bell's remark is quoted by John Burrow in his excellent 1968 introduction to Darwin's *Origin of Species* (New York: Penguin Books, 1968), p. 15.

97. A Plea for Captain Brown

1. *J*, 11:12, 306, 307–308, 435.

2. *J*, 12:95, 159–160.

3. Bruce Catton, *This Hallowed Ground* (New York: Doubleday, 1956), p. 8; Lawrence Lader, *The Bold Brahmins: New England's War against Slavery* (New York: Dutton, 1961), p. 185.

4. *JMN*, 14:125.   5. *J*, 12:400.

6. T's knowledge of John Brown's part in the Pottawatomie killings is fully discussed in Michael Meyer's "Thoreau's Rescue of John Brown from History," *SAR 1980*, pp. 301–316; *RP*, pp. 115, 138.

7. W. D. Howells, *Literary Friends and Acquaintances* (Bloomington: Indiana University Press, 1968), p. 55; *RP*, pp. 112, 129, 132.

98. Darwin and the Developmental Theory

1. "Extracts on Natural History," *Howarth* F16, pp. 86, 91, 110. Thoreau is translating from the French revolutionist Armand Gaston Camus's *Histoire des animaux d'Aristote* (Paris: chez la veuve Desainte, 1793).

2. Thoreau read Pliny in the Bohn edition translated by John Bostock as *The Natural History of Pliny* (London: Bohn, 1855), then checked it against

his own three-volume Latin edition, the *Historia Mundi* (apud Jacobum Stoer, 1593); "The Dispersion of Seeds" MS, *Howarth* F30, p. 1.

3. *Days*, p. 429. Thoreau's extracts from the *Origin of Species* are in the "Extracts on Natural History" MS, *Howarth* F16, pp. 167–172.

4. John Burrow, "Introduction," *Origin of Species* (New York: Penguin, 1968), p. 11. John B. Wilson's "Darwin and the Transcendentalists," *Journal of the History of Ideas* 26 (1965): 286–290, notes T's endorsement of Darwin's developmental ideas and connects T with the special creation issue. Kichung Kim's 1969 Berkeley dissertation, "Thoreau's Involvement with Nature: Thoreau and the Naturalist Tradition," does not treat T and Darwin. Herbert Uhlig's "Improved Means to an Unimproved End," *TSB*, 128 (1974): 1–3, underestimates T's knowledge of Darwin. William Howarth's *The Book of Concord* (New York: Viking, 1982) first directed attention to the importance of Darwin for T's unfinished and unpublished work on seeds and fruits. John Hildebidle's *Thoreau: A Naturalist's Liberty* (Cambridge: Harvard University Press, 1983) cites T finding in Darwin corroboration for his thoughts about seeds, but underestimates T's grasp of the theoretical issue. Victor Friesen's *The Spirit of the Huckleberry* (Edmonton: University of Alberta Press, 1984) mentions that T was against special creation and for the developmental theory. Robert Sattelmeyer's forthcoming work on T's reading is an informed treatment of the subject. No full-length, fully satisfactory treatment of this important issue yet exists.

5. Burrow, "Introduction," pp. 13, 14, 29.

6. Thomas Malthus, *An Essay on the Principle of Population*, 3d ed. (London: J. Johnson, 1806), pp. 2, 3. Malthus credits Benjamin Franklin with a similar and prior observation; *Charles Darwin's Autobiography*, ed. Sir Francis Darwin (New York: Henry Shuman, 1950), p. 54.

7. Darwin, *Origin of Species*, p. 68.

8. Ibid. pp. 377, 392–393, 414, 437.

9. Darwin, *Origin of Species*, pp. 443, 450; "Extracts on Natural History," *Howarth* F16, pp. 171–172.

99. Beyond Transcendentalism

1. *J*, 13:68, 77.   2. *J*, 13:138, 141, 149.

3. Surviving charts and lists are cataloged in *Howarth* as F18–F32. An illuminating sample is contained in the Morgan Library's MA 610.

4. The "Notes on Fruits" MS, *Howarth* F29h, is in the Berg Collection; "Notes on Fruits," p. 1; *Days*, p. 467.

5. *Corr*, p. 579.

6. *J*, 13:346; Augustine is quoted in H. N. Welhed, *The Mind of the Ancient World* (London: Longmans, 1937), p. 1.

7. *J*, 14:89.

8. See Lurie, *Louis Agassiz*, chap. 7, "Agassiz, Darwin and Transmutation," pp. 252–307; *J*, 14:146, 147.

100. One World at a Time

1. *J*, 14:233, 234, 237, 268; *Walden*, p. 318; Edmund A. Schofield, "The Origin of Thoreau's Fatal Illness," *TSB* 171 (1985): 1–3; *The Journals of Bronson Alcott*, ed. Odell Shepard (Boston: Little, Brown, 1938), p. 334.

2. T's extracts from de Candolle, Blodgett, and Hinds are in "Extracts on Natural History," *Howarth* F16.

3. Walter Harding, "Thoreau's Minnesota Journey: Two Documents" (Geneseo: Thoreau Society, 1962), p. 17.

4. *Days,* p. 446. On Horace Mann, Jr.'s remarkable but brief career, see Louise Hall Tharp, *Until Victory: Horace Mann and Mary Peabody* (Boston: Little, Brown, 1953), pp. 317–318. Cause of death statistics from "Reports of the Selectmen," Concord Free Public Library.

5. *Days*, pp. 455, 456–457; *HM* 954, *Howarth* F25a.

6. *Corr*, p. 641; *Writings*, 9:331.

7. *Days*, pp. 460, 464, 466; Thomas Blanding, "A Last Word from Thoreau," *The Concord Saunterer*, 11, 4 (1976): 16–17.

8. F. B. Sanborn, *The Personality of Thoreau* (Boston, 1901), pp. 68–69.

9. See T's "Leafing" lists and charts, Morgan MS MA 610, *Howarth* F20b.

Index

Freud, Sigmund, 226
Franklin, Benjamin: *The Way to Wealth*, 166; mentioned, 351
Franklin, Sir John, and Arctic, 152, 346
Frost, Rev. Barzillai, 35
Frost, Robert, 259
Fruitlands, 117, 144, 150, 152
Fuller, Arthur, 212
Fuller, Margaret: and Apuleius, 79; and Emerson, 20, 79–80; and feminism, 33; and Goethe, 28, 55; and HDT's "Persius," 74–75; and HDT's "The Service," 85; and Roman Revolution of 1848, 33; shipwrecked, dies, 210–213; *Summer on the Lakes*, 147, 156; *Woman in the Nineteenth Century*, 69; mentioned, 27, 72, 73, 88, 93, 111, 117, 118, 122, 267, 371, 387
Fuller, Richard, 118, 124–125, 327

Galapagos Islands, 242
Gale, Theophilus, 72
Gandhi, Mohandas K. (Mahatma), 316–317
Gardiner, Me., 37
Garrison, William Lloyd, 176, 177, 178, 315
Gerard, John, 361, 382
Gesner, Konrad von, 373
Gibbon, Edward, 82, 351
Gifford, Sanford, 51
Gilpin, William: and Picturesque, 260–265; mentioned, 270, 303, 305, 306, 328, 358
Gleason, Herbert, 51
Gloucester, Mass., 37
Goethe, J. W. von: and *Bildung*, 54; *Conversations*, 20, 28; *Italian Journey*, 8, 25, 28–30, 52, 156–157; and plant morphology, 29–30; on

society, 32; *Theory of Colours*, 97; *Torquato Tasso*, 28, 40; and visual art, 52; *Wilhelm Meister*, 28, 56, 96; mentioned, 7, 27, 119, 192, 245, 254, 311, 318, 350
Goffstown, N.H., 195
Goodwin, Mrs. Marston, 175
Gosse, Philip H., 382
Gould, Augustus A.: *Report on the Invertibrata . . .* , 119; mentioned, 246, 254
Gray, Asa, 344, 376, 387
Gray, Thomas (American novelist), 25
Gray, Thomas (English poet), 40
Greeley, Horace: on HDT's pantheism, 285; and *New York Tribune*, 132; and publication of "Ktaadn," 195; and review of *A Week*, 196; on self-culture, 55; mentioned, 117, 136, 149, 175, 185, 252, 266, 279, 297, 313, 331, 346
Greylock, Mt., 145
Griswold, Rufus, 111
Gura, Philip, 221, 293
Guyot, A., 225

Hadley, Sam (lock-keeper), 65
Hakluyt, Richard, *Voyages*, 155
Hale, Edward Everett, 327
Hall, Lt. Francis, *Travels in Canada*, 13, 241
Hallowell, Me., 37
Hammer-Purgstall, J., 81
Hampsted, N.H., 195
Harding, Walter, 228
Hardy, R. Spence, on Buddhism, 337
Harris, T. W., *A Report on the Insects . .*, 119
Hartshorne, C. H., *Ancient Metrical Tales*, 111
Harvard: marking system of, 10; stu-

449

451

Designer:	Barry Moser
Compositor:	Wilsted & Taylor
Printer:	Maple-Vail Book Mfg. Group
Binder:	Maple-Vail Book Mfg. Group
Text:	11/13 Garamond
Display:	Garamond and Castellar